Frommer's

Buenos Aires

1st Edition

by Michael Luongo

Here's what the critics say about Frommer's:

"Amazingly easy to use. Very portable, very complete."
—*Booklist*

"Detailed, accurate, and easy-to-read information for all price ranges."
—*Glamour Magazine*

"Hotel information is close to encyclopedic."
—*Des Moines Sunday Register*

"Frommer's Guides have a way of giving you a real feel for a place."
—*Knight Ridder Newspapers*

WILEY

Wiley Publishing, Inc.

About the Author

Michael Luongo has written about Argentina for the *New York Times*, the *Chicago Tribune*, *Frommer's Budget Travel*, *National Geographic Traveler*, *Town & Country Travel*, *Advocate*, *Out Traveler*, and numerous other publications. He has visited over 75 countries and all seven continents (and has lived on three of them). Still, Argentina remains one of his favorite places in the entire world, and he cried the first time he left it. He only wishes he could tango better, but after a few more years writing about Buenos Aires, he is sure he'll get that right. You can share in his travel writing and photography adventures at www.michaelluongo.com.

Published by:

Wiley Publishing, Inc.

111 River St.
Hoboken, NJ 07030-5774

ISBN-13: 978-0-7645-8440-4
ISBN-10: 0-7645-8440-5

Editor: Kendra L. Falkenstein
Production Editor: Suzanna R. Thompson
Cartographers: Tim Lohnes and Elizabeth Puhl
Photo Editor: Richard Fox
Production by Wiley Indianapolis Composition Services

Front cover photo: A couple dances the tango on the Plaza Dorrego
Back cover photo: Rooftops in Buenos Aires' scenic city center at dusk

For information on our other products and services or to obtain technical support, please contact our Customer Care Department within the U.S. at 800/762-2974, outside the U.S. at 317/572-3993 or fax 317/572-4002.

Wiley also publishes its books in a variety of electronic formats. Some content that appears in print may not be available in electronic formats.

Manufactured in the United States of America

5 4 3 2

Contents

6 Exploring Buenos Aires   132

7 City Strolls   176

8 Shopping   195

9 Buenos Aires After Dark   216

10 Side Trips from Buenos Aires   238

Index   265

List of Maps

To Mom and Dad, for your 50th anniversary, from the son who is more likely to hop on a plane to South America than on a bus to the suburbs to visit you.

Acknowledgments

I want to give a big thanks to my editor, Kendra Falkenstein, for having the patience to work with me, and to Kathleen Warnock for introducing me to her. Big *abrazos y besos* go to Inés and Debora for their endless help and to Alejandro, Verónica, and everyone else in the Argentine Tourism and Consular Office in New York, and to Eduardo in Miami. A big thanks to Ricardo, Juana, Connie, Claudia, and everyone in the Aerolíneas office. To María and both Carloses and everyone at the National Tourism Office, and to Rubén, Diego, Marcela, and everyone at the Buenos Aires City Tourism office. Thanks to Gabriel of the Museo Evita for sharing his Evita passion and knowledge with me, and to Marta and Alberto for their help in Recoleta Cemetery. To Soledad and Gabriel of the Four Seasons and Cecilia of the Alvear for all their help with Recoleta and more. To Juanita and the Madres, I wish them all love and luck. To Betty, who is like a big sister to me; and to Juan Cruz, Pablito, and Alejandro. To Luis and Lawrence, who were like family when I was living there, and I cannot thank them enough for their support. To María for her help on women's issues, and to Lorena and Fernanda. To Marcos for all his advice and friendship; no one knows Argentina like him. To Mario for his friendship over the years and for being reason enough to love Argentina. To my landlord Juan and everyone at Arce 215 in Las Cañitas, and to Miguel Angel, Mariano, Gabriel, Beba, Christian, and everyone in the Las Cañitas military bases for their historical and ceremonial explanations. Thanks to Caryn for introducing me to tango in Argentina, and to Eduadro, Nora, Suzanna, Michele, Marithe, and Laura for continuing the process. To Carlos and Claudia and Alfredo for all of their help and advice, and to Marta for her special knowledge and insight over the years. To Patricia for all of her gastronomic advice and help. To Clarisa, Francisco, and Martín at GS for answering my constant Argentina questions. To Trisa, Charles, Russel, and everyone on the GS-Bowne team for understanding my travel schedule, and to Ingrid for listening. Thanks also to Bugs in Canada for forwarding that e-mail that told me about the Buenos Aires book to begin with, and to all my editors over the years for whom I have written on this wonderful city. I am sure that I am missing many people who helped me and made living in Argentina special, but please know that you're loved and appreciated!

—Michael Luongo

An Invitation to the Reader

In researching this book, we discovered many wonderful places—hotels, restaurants, shops, and more. We're sure you'll find others. Please tell us about them, so we can share the information with your fellow travelers in upcoming editions. If you were disappointed with a recommendation, we'd love to know that, too. Please write to:

Frommer's Buenos Aires, 1st Edition
Wiley Publishing, Inc. • 111 River St. • Hoboken, NJ 07030-5774

An Additional Note

Please be advised that travel information is subject to change at any time—and this is especially true of prices. We therefore suggest that you write or call ahead for confirmation when making your travel plans. The authors, editors, and publisher cannot be held responsible for the experiences of readers while traveling. Your safety is important to us, however, so we encourage you to stay alert and be aware of your surroundings. Keep a close eye on cameras, purses, and wallets, all favorite targets of thieves and pickpockets.

Other Great Guides for Your Trip:

Frommer's Argentina & Chile
Frommer's South America
Frommer's Peru
Frommer's Adventure Guides: South America

Frommer's Star Ratings, Icons & Abbreviations

Every hotel, restaurant, and attraction listing in this guide has been ranked for quality, value, service, amenities, and special features using a **star-rating system.** In country, state, and regional guides, we also rate towns and regions to help you narrow down your choices and budget your time accordingly. Hotels and restaurants are rated on a scale of zero (recommended) to three stars (exceptional). Attractions, shopping, nightlife, towns, and regions are rated according to the following scale: zero stars (recommended), one star (highly recommended), two stars (very highly recommended), and three stars (must-see).

In addition to the star-rating system, we also use **seven feature icons** that point you to the great deals, in-the-know advice, and unique experiences that separate travelers from tourists. Throughout the book, look for:

Finds	Special finds—those places only insiders know about
Fun Fact	Fun facts—details that make travelers more informed and their trips more fun
Kids	Best bets for kids and advice for the whole family
Moments	Special moments—those experiences that memories are made of
Overrated	Places or experiences not worth your time or money
Tips	Insider tips—great ways to save time and money
Value	Great values—where to get the best deals

The following **abbreviations** are used for credit cards:

AE	American Express	DISC	Discover	V	Visa
DC	Diners Club	MC	MasterCard		

Frommers.com

Now that you have the guidebook to a great trip, visit our website at **www.frommers.com** for travel information on more than 3,000 destinations. With features updated regularly, we give you instant access to the most current trip-planning information available. At Frommers.com, you'll also find the best prices on airfares, accommodations, and car rentals—and you can even book travel online through our travel booking partners. At Frommers.com, you'll also find the following:

- Online updates to our most popular guidebooks
- Vacation sweepstakes and contest giveaways
- Newsletter highlighting the hottest travel trends
- Online travel message boards with featured travel discussions

The Best of Buenos Aires

A country's tragedy has become a tourist's opportunity, and in between the two is hope for an improved economy for all of Buenos Aires, the glamorous capital of Argentina. Up until the peso crisis of December 2001, Buenos Aires was regarded as Latin America's most expensive city, if not one of the world's, with prices for some hotels and restaurants rivaling those of New York and Paris. Many on the South American tourist crawl avoided this sophisticated and beautiful city altogether, staying in the cheaper capitals of the countries that surrounded it. But now that the peso, once on par with the U.S. dollar, has fallen to a third of its former value and stabilized there, tourists from all over the world are flocking to this city, often called the Paris of South America.

Stroll through the neighborhoods of Recoleta or Palermo, full of buildings with marble neoclassical facades on broad tree-lined boulevards, and you know exactly why it got that moniker. European immigrants to Buenos Aires, mostly from Spain and Italy, brought with them the warm ways of Mediterranean culture, wherein friends, family, and conversation were the most important things in life. Whiling away the night over a long meal was the norm, and locals had always packed into cafes, restaurants, and bars until the early morning hours. The peso crisis hit the locals all the harder because of this, making the lifestyle and good times that they cherished almost unattainable for a period of time.

But don't think that the new Buenos Aires is a depressing shell of its former glorious self. Instead, when you get to Buenos Aires, you'll find a city quickly recovering from its former problems, with old cafes and restaurants not only full of patrons but competing with all of the new restaurants and cafes opening up at a breakneck pace all over town.

The crisis also had a remarkable effect on the country's soul. Argentines as a whole are becoming more self-reflective, looking at themselves and the reasons why their country fell into so much trouble and trying to find answers. This has lead, ironically, to an incredible flourishing of all things Porteño, the word Buenos Aires locals use to describe both themselves and the culture of their city. Unable to import expensive foods from overseas anymore, Buenos Aires's restaurants are concentrating instead on cooking with Argentine staples like Pampas grass-fed beef and using locally produced, organic ingredients as seasonings. What has developed is a spectacular array of Argentine-nouvelle cuisine of incredible quality and originality. Chefs can't seem to produce it fast enough in the ever-expanding array of Buenos Aires's restaurants, particularly in the trendy Palermo district on the city's north side.

This new Argentine self-reliance and pride is not just limited to its restaurants. The same thing has happened with the country's fashion. In the go-go 1990s, when the peso was pegged to the U.S. dollar, Argentines loaded up on European labels and made shopping trips to the malls of Miami for their clothing. Now, however, even the middle class cannot afford to do this anymore. Instead, with necessity as the mother of invention, young Argentine designers are opening up their own shops and boutiques in the Palermo Soho neighborhood, putting other Argentines to work sewing, selling, and modeling their designs. Women, especially, will find fantastic and utterly unique fashions in Buenos Aires that you won't find anywhere else in the world, at prices that are unbelievable. And if you're looking for leather goods, say no more. The greatest variety and quality in the world are available all over town.

Importantly, the most Porteño thing of all, the tango, has also witnessed an explosive growth. Up until the peso crisis, Argentines worried that the dance would die out as young people bopped instead to American hip-hop and European techno. But the peso crisis and the self-reflection it created helped bolster the art form's popularity: New varieties of shows for tourists mean you can now see a different form of tango every night of your stay. And, more importantly to residents, the traditional, 1930s-style *milongas* (tango salons), have opened in spaces all over town. These are drawing not only the typical tango dancers but young Argentines, who have rediscovered their grandparents' favorite dance, as well as young ex-pats from all over the world who are making Buenos Aires the world's new hot city, the way Prague was at the end of the Cold War.

The city is also home to an incomparable array of theaters and other traditional venues. Buenos Aires's vast arrays of museums, many in beautiful neoclassical structures along broad tree-lined Avenida Libertador, are as exquisite as the treasures they hold inside.

All of this means there is no time like now to come visit Buenos Aires, a city rich in cultural excitement all at a bargain price unheard of just a few short years ago.

1 Frommer's Favorite Buenos Aires Experiences

- **Best Tango Shows for Tourists:** Tango, a beautiful dance that tells the pained history of its immigrant poor from the beginning of the 20th century, is the ultimate Buenos Aires–defining experience. For an authentic historical look, see the tango show **El Querandí,** Perú 302 (© **11/4345-0331**), which traces the dance's roots from brothel slums, when only men danced it, to its current leggy sexiness. See p. 227. **Señor Tango,** Vieytes 1653 (© **11/4303-0212**), adds Hollywood glamour and Fosse-esque dance moves, as well as horses trampling the stage, in the city's most popular show. See p. 230. You'll find a more gracious experience at **Esquina Carlos Gardel,** Carlos Gardel 3200 (© **11/4876-6363**), in the Abasto neighborhood where Carlos Gardel, the city's most famous tango crooner, actually lived and worked.

A classical symphony accompanies the more traditional instruments in this show. See p. 228.

- **Best Tango Hall for the Experienced or Those Who Want to Watch the Experienced:** If you're an expert tango dancer, or want to at least watch the people who are, head to a *milonga* (tango salon). **El Niño Bien,** Humberto I no. 1462 (© **11/4483-2588**), is like taking a step back in time as you watch patrons dance in an enormous, smoke-filled, Belle Epoque–era hall under ceiling fans. The best dancers come here to show off, though you'll also find instructors looking to mingle with shy potential students who watch from the sidelines. See p. 231. **Salón Canning,** Scalabrini Ortiz 1331 (© **11/4832-6753**), in Palermo Hollywood has what many local dancers call the best tango floor in all of Buenos Aires, a hard, smooth, parquet surface perfect for this dance. The tight space, however, is not big enough for the tango-challenged. See p. 233.

- **Best Architecture Walks:** Buenos Aires abounds in beautiful architecture, especially after its very self-conscious and ambitious rebuilding project before Argentina's 1910 centennial celebration of its independence from Spain. The plan was put into action in the 1880s, and by the turn of the 20th century, entire neighborhoods had been rebuilt. The French Beaux Arts movement was at its worldwide height at that point, meaning much of the city looks more like Paris than any other Latin American city. **Avenida de Mayo,** the city's official processional route linking the Presidential Palace (Casa Rosada) to the National Congress Building, is the longest and best-preserved example of this (see p. 186 for a walking tour of this area). The corner buildings along the wide **Diagonal Norte,** also known as **Avenida Sáenz Peña,** are all topped with fantastic neo-classical domes from the street's beginning at the Plaza de Mayo until it hits the **Obelisco,** Buenos Aires's defining monument, at Avenida 9 de Julio, the world's widest boulevard. Don't miss the neighborhoods of San Telmo and Monserrat either, with their balconied late-19th- and early-20th-century structures, most of which are gracefully decaying as they await gentrification when the economy improves.
- **Best Park Walks:** The Palermo Park system runs along Avenida Libertador and is one of the world's most beautiful. You could spend more than a day here, wandering this tree- and monument-lined part of the city, and still not see it

all. Within the system are numerous small parks such as the Rose Garden and the Japanese Gardens, as well as museums such as the **Museo de Arte Latinoamericano de Buenos Aires (MALBA),** Av. Figueroa Alcorta 3415 (Ⓒ **11/4808-6500;** p. 158), and the **Museo Nacional de Bellas Artes,** Av. del Libertador 1473 (Ⓒ **11/4803-0802;** p. 156). In the Argentine spring—late September and early October—the weather is at its best, and the jacaranda trees here are in their purple-bloomed glory, making this the best time to stroll. In summer months locals who can't escape the city come to jog, suntan, and while away the day in this area. See chapter 6.

- **Best Bird-Watching:** Proof that nature is stronger than whatever humankind throws at it is just a brisk walk away from Buenos Aires's tallest office structures at the **Ecological Reserve** (along the Costanera near Puerto Madero; Ⓒ **11/4893-1588**). In the 1960s and 1970s, demolished buildings and construction debris were dumped into the Río de La Plata. Nature responded by wrapping it with sediment and then grass and small plants, creating a home for a myriad of birds. Wander on your own with caution, as there are still rough areas, or ask a tour company about bird-watching tours. See p. 153.
- **Best (& Most Heartbreaking) Political Experience:** Argentina's political history is a long series of ups and downs, some more tragic than others. Perhaps the worst occurred between 1976 and 1982, when a military government, bent on destroying what it considered political enemies, ruled the country. During that time, up to 30,000 people, mostly college-age, were secretly murdered, their bodies

never found, giving them the name *los desaparecidos,* meaning "the disappeared ones." The **Asociación Madres de Plaza de Mayo** is an organization that aims for justice for their murdered children and marches on the Plaza de Mayo every Thursday at 3:30pm, giving speeches and handing out flyers. They also run a university with a store and library full of books on this painful period of history that has yet to come to an end. See p. 143.

- **Best Evita Experiences:** Visit the Plaza de Mayo, the political heart of Argentina, and look to the facade of the **Casa Rosada (Presidential Palace;** p. 136). The northern balcony, with its three French doors, is where Evita addressed her adoring fans. Just as many people come to see her now at the **Recoleta Cemetery** (p. 146), where she was laid to rest in a tomb belonging to the family of her wealthy father. To understand why it took Argentina more than 50 years to come to terms with this controversial woman, visit the **Museo Evita,** Calle Lafinur 2988 (© **11/4807-9433**), in Palermo, where the story of her life is told through personal objects. See p. 156.

- **Best Museums:** The **MALBA** (Museo de Arte Latinoamericano de Buenos Aires), Av. Figueroa Alcorta 3415 (© **11/4808-6500**), houses an extensive and interesting modern art collection. The building itself, though, is as unique as the art, and nothing is more impressive than the giant sculpture of a man doing pushups suspended over the escalator bay in the central atrium. See p. 158. The **Museo Nacional de Bellas Artes,** Av. del Libertador 1473 (© **11/4803-0802**), was built into a former water-pump station

and houses an impressive art collection, including many Picasso drawings. See p. 156.

- **Best Ethnic Neighborhoods:** With a population that is nearly all white and either of Spanish or Italian descent, Buenos Aires does not on the surface seem to be a very ethnically diverse city despite its cosmopolitan nature. However, head to the neighborhood of **Once,** around Calle Tucumán in particular, for a still-thriving Jewish community. You'll find numerous kosher restaurants, stores, and other businesses owned by or catering to this community. See p. 52. Then head to **Belgrano,** to the city's north, for the very little known Chinatown. Even most people in Buenos Aires know nothing of this community, a flourishing, busy area of restaurants, shops, and other businesses. If you're in town for the Chinese New Year, the area's Dragon Parade is a fun affair to check out. See p. 52.

- **Best Outdoor Markets:** There's no market like the **San Telmo Antiques Fair,** held every Sunday in Plaza Dorrego, the old colonial heart of the San Telmo district. You'll find lots of small antiques and collectibles dealers here along with some kitschy souvenirs, local crafts, and lots of free live tango dancing as good as anything you might pay $50 to see onstage. The **Feria de Plaza Francia,** in front of the Recoleta Cemetery, is another don't-miss market, with great crafts, live music, and a beautiful setting on a grassy hill. See p. 199 and 200, respectively.

- **Best Shopping Experiences:** There's no shortage of **top designer shops** along Calle Alvear, with the same high quality and high style you find throughout North America and Europe, at slightly lower prices befitting the

Argentine economy. **Leather** shops abound on Calle Florida, near Galerías Pacífico, and you can even have items custom-made while you're here. For the best quality high-design items for fashion and home, my favorite shop is **Tienda Puro Diseño Argentino,** Av. Peuyrredón 2501 (℘ **11/5777-6104;** p. 211). For little **boutiques** specializing in the sexy styles Argentine women favor wearing, wander the cobblestone streets of **Palermo Soho.** See chapter 8.

- **Best High-Building Vista Points:** Odd-looking as it might be, the **Palacio Barolo,** Av. de Mayo 1370 (℘ **11/4383-1065**), designed by an architect who took Dante's *Inferno* a little too literally, is finally open to the public for tours so that anyone can see the interesting interior that only office workers were previously privy to. Its tower, which once made it the tallest building in all of South America, provides a sweeping view up and down Avenida de Mayo as well as of the entire city. See p. 143. The **Torre Monumental,** Av. Libertador 49 (℘ **11/4311-0186**), better known by its old name, the British Clock Tower, has a fantastic view to the Río de la Plata and up and down Avenida Libertador. So what if the tower represents a country that Argentina has had some arguments with over the years? It's the view that counts now. See p. 149.

- **Best Oddball Museums:** Two modern-day necessities—taxes and toilets—are honored in two different small museums in Buenos Aires. The **Tax Museum,** Av. de Mayo 1317 (℘ **11/4384-0282**), contains historical items relating to money, coins, and taxes throughout Argentine history. It is one of only three museums in all the world of this type. See p. 154.

The **Museo del Patrimonio,** Av. Córdoba 1750, museum entrance at Riobamba 750 (℘ **11/6319-1882**), in the Aguas Argentinas building, is really about waterworks, but it contains what surely must be the largest toilet collection in the world. Kids will have a blast here. See p. 157.

- **Best Museums for Kids:** Its name is **Museo de los Niños (Children's Museum),** Av. Corrientes 3247 (℘ **11/4861-2325**), and this is certainly a great place to bring the young ones. Full of displays on various careers, presented in a fun way, you'll wish you had such a place when you were young. See p. 154. In the **Museo Participativo de Ciencias,** it's forbidden not to touch. This place (inside the Centro Cultural de Recoleta; ℘ **11/4807-3260**) is full of science and other displays that make learning so fun, kids won't know it's good for them too! See p. 155.

- **Best People-Watching:** Pedestrianized **Calle Florida** is not the elegant shopping street it might have been a generation ago, but all kinds of Porteños find their way here, especially at lunchtime. Day and night, musicians, tango dancers, broken-glass walkers, comedians, and the like entertain the crowds along this street. At night **Avenida Santa Fe** offers another interesting array of people, popping into stores, gossiping at sidewalk cafes, and just checking each other out. See p. 163 and 199, respectively.

- **Best Nightlife Street:** Whether you want to eat at a *parrilla* (an Argentine steakhouse), try some nouvelle cuisine, have some drinks, or do some dancing, **Calle Báez** in Las Cañitas is the place to go. This busy street in Palermo has great restaurants like **Novecento,** Báez 199 (℘ **11/4778-1900**), **El Estanciero,** Báez 202

(© **11/4899-0951**), and numerous other choices. Savor the night afterwards over drinks at trendy **Soul Café,** Báez 352 (© **11/4776-3905**), or dance to hot Latin tunes at **Mambo,** Báez 243 (© **11/**

4778-0115), until the sun comes up over the Río de la Plata. This street has the most intensely packed nightlife on any 3 blocks of Buenos Aires.

2 The Best Hotel Bets

- **Most Luxurious Hotel Choices:** The two hotels I've cited here don't just top my list of hotel choices, they top many travel magazine lists as well. The **Alvear Palace Hotel,** Av. Alvear 1891 (© **11/4808-2100**), is a gilded confection of carved marble and French furniture. It's the ultimate grand hotel experience in Buenos Aires, complete with butler service. See p. 79. The **Four Seasons Hotel,** Posadas 1086–88 (© **800/ 819-5053** in the U.S. and Canada), offers a more subdued form of luxury (elegant without flash), with quiet pampering and a chance to hide away in the hotel's walled garden. See p. 80.

- **Best Historic Hotels:** The **Marriott Plaza Hotel,** Calle Florida 1005 (© **888/236-2427** in the U.S.), is the oldest of the grand hotels still operating in Buenos Aires, and its location on Plaza San Martín can't be beat. See p. 67. The **Hotel Castelar** (© **11/ 4383-5000**) sits on Avenida de Mayo, once the city's most glamorous street. This hotel, adorned with Italian marbles and bronzes, was once the favorite choice of Lorca and other Spanish writers in the 1930s when Buenos Aires was the intellectual and literary capital of the Spanish-speaking world. See p. 76.

- **Best See-and-Be-Seen Hotel:** The brand-new **Faena,** Martha Salotti 445 (© **11/4010-9000**), located in the Puerto Madero district, is my see-and-be-seen choice. The hotel was designed with lots of bars in the lobby and a pool in the front of the hotel so that anyone coming in would know exactly who else was around in the hotel. See p. 63.

- **Best Budget Hotel:** French miracle chain **Hotel Ibis,** Hipólito Yrigoyen 1592 (© **11/5300-5555**), wins in this category hands down. With clean, efficient service, even though these places are the same the world over, its location overlooking Congreso makes an excellent accommodations choice. All the rooms look the same, to be sure, but with the low price here, you can easily ignore that. See p. 85.

- **Best Hotel Gyms:** The **Marriott Plaza Hotel,** Calle Florida 1005 (© **888/236-2427** in the U.S.), has an enormous gym, with more than enough equipment to make sure there's no waiting. See p. 67. The gym in the **Crowne Plaza Pan Americano,** Carlos Pellegrini 551 (© **800/227-6963** in the U.S.), has to be seen to be believed. Sitting in a three-story glass box on the building's roof, being here will make you feel like you are floating over Avenida 9 de Julio when at the pool, or especially on the treadmills. See p. 66.

- **Best Hotel Pools:** In the hot Southern Hemisphere summer months (Dec–Mar), any pool will be a welcome treat in Buenos Aires, but two of them really stand out. The pool at the **Crowne Plaza Pan Americano,** Carlos Pellegrini 551 (© **800/227-6963** in the U.S.), is a combination indoor/outdoor pool, and its location on the roof of the hotel gives the impression of swimming over the city and floating on top of Avenida 9 de Julio. See p. 66. The **Four Seasons,** Posadas 1086–1088 (© **800/819-5053** in the U.S. and Canada), has the only garden swimming pool in all of Recoleta. Lounging poolside here in the walled garden complex gives the feeling of being in a resort, even in the heart of the city. See p. 80.

- **Best Business Hotel:** With its location away from the noise of the city in Puerto Madero, and having one of the largest convention centers in all of Buenos Aires, the **Hilton Buenos Aires,** Av. Macacha Güemes 351 (© **800/ 445-8667** in the U.S.), is a logical business choice. Their business center, complete with translation services, is also one of the largest you'll find anywhere in the city. See p. 66.

3 The Best Dining & Cafe Bets

- **Best** *Parrilla:* You probably heard of this place long before coming to Buenos Aires, and **Cabaña Las Lilas,** Alicia Moreau de Justo 516 (© **11/4313-1336**), deserves every bit of its reputation. It's expensive for sure, running about $35 for a complete meal, but it's worth it: The cuts of beef are so soft, they almost melt in your mouth. In spite of the price, it's casual too, so come in sneakers and shorts if you want. See p. 96.
- **Best Cafe Experiences: Café Tortoni,** Av. de Mayo 825 (© **11/ 4342-4328**), might not have the best service in town, but the incredible history and beauty of this cafe more than make up for that. This was and remains Argentina's intellectual coffee spot of choice, and even the culture-seeking tourists don't overwhelm the space. See p. 104. Sit outside at **La Biela,** Av. Quintana 596 (© **11/4804-0449**), in glamorous Recoleta overlooking the world-famous Recoleta Cemetery. From the view to Iglesia Pilar to the wonderful shade of the gum trees on its sidewalk, this is Buenos Aires at its best. See p. 112.
- **Best Authentic Old Buenos Aires Dining:** Buenos Aires is full of trendy places, but the surefire

bets are where Porteños have eaten for decades. Ham hangs from the rafters and steaks are as thick as the crowds at the Spanish eatery **Plaza Asturias,** Av. de Mayo 1199 (© **11/4382-7334**), but the staff is so busy you can get hurt trying to find the restroom with all the running around they do bringing food from the kitchen to the tables. See p. 113. For more than 40 years, fish lovers have flocked to **Dora,** Leandro N. Alem 1016 (© **11/4311-2891**), an unpretentious but high-quality and high-priced spot on Paseo Colón that's worth every penny. See p. 100.
- **Best Seafood:** Argentina has a long coastline, but it has always been the turf, not the surf, that gave its chefs culinary inspiration. There are two places that defy this trend, including, as above, **Dora,** Leandro N. Alem 1016 (© **11/4311-2891**), the unpretentious seafood spot businesspeople and those in the know have eaten at for 40 years. See p. 100. The other, **Olsen,** in Palermo Viejo at Gorriti 5870 (© **11/4776-7677**), serves up an interesting twist on seafood, Scandinavian-style, with flavors that are very different from anything on the menu elsewhere in Buenos Aires. See p. 120.

- **Best Cigar Bar:** Argentine culture might not be as macho as it's reputed to be, what with female presidential candidates and powerful first ladies, but that ultimate symbol of masculine domination, the cigar, persists at the **Plaza Bar,** Marriott Plaza Hotel, Calle Florida 1005 (© **11/4318-3000**). Here, in a streamlined Art Deco setting reminiscent of Rockefeller Center, men and, more recently, women puff away over business talk. See p. 223.

- **Best Italian Restaurant:** With over half of Buenos Aires from Italian immigrant stock, it's hard to go wrong finding good Italian food in this city: Most *parrillas* offer an excellent array of pasta, usually homemade on the premises. The best formal Italian dining experience in the city, however, is **Piegari,** Posadas 1042 (© **11/4328-4104**), in the Recoleta La Recova area, near the Four Seasons hotel. Their selection of food concentrating on northern Italian cuisine is superb, and they have a stunning array of risottos in particular. See p. 109.

- **Best French Restaurant: La Bourgogne,** Av. Alvear 1891 (© **11/4805-3857**), in the Alvear Palace, is hands down the best French restaurant in Buenos Aires,

and it has been the recipient of numerous awards. Yes, it's very formal and very expensive, but what else would you expect from such a place? See p. 110.

- **Best Restaurant for Kids: Garbis,** Scalabrini Ortiz at Cerviño (© **11/4511-6600**), is an Armenian restaurant chain with what one British ex-pat friend of mine loves to call a "jumpee castle" she can bring her kids to. The best one is in Palermo Soho, and adults can eat in peace while the kids entertain themselves on the indoor playground. See p. 122.

- **Best Value Restaurants:** Little-known family-run **Juana M,** Carlos Pellegrini 1535 (© **11/4326-0462**), a small *parrilla* on the very end of Avenida 9 de Julio in the Recoleta district, wins this distinction for sure, with great meat cuts and an unlimited salad bar, where most meals with drinks hit under the $5 mark. See p. 112. If you're in Puerto Madero, head straight to **La Bisteca,** Av. Alicia Moreau de Justo 1890 (© **11/4514-4999**), a chain restaurant with an all-you-can-eat menu offering high-quality cuts of meat along with a generous salad bar. It's a huge space, but the seating arrangements create a sense of intimacy, and at these prices, it can't be beat. See p. 97.

2

Planning Your Trip to Buenos Aires

A little advance planning can make the difference between a good trip and a great trip. What do you need to know before you go? When should you go? What's the best way to get there? How much should you plan on spending? What safety or health precautions are advised? All the basics are outlined in this chapter—the when, why, and how of traveling to and around Buenos Aires.

1 Visitor Information

IN THE U.S. The Argentina Government Tourist Office has offices at 12 W. 56th St., New York, NY 10019 (© **212/603-0443;** fax 212/315-5545), and 2655 Le Jeune Rd., Penthouse Suite F, Coral Gables, FL 33134 (© **305/442-1366;** fax 305/441-7029). For more details, consult Argentina's Ministry of Tourism website (see "Websites of Note," below).

IN CANADA Basic tourist information can be obtained by the Consulate General of Argentina, 2000 Peel St., Suite 600, Montreal, Quebec H3A 2W5 (© **514/842-6582;** fax 514/842-5797; www.consargenmtl.com); for more details, consult Argentina's Ministry of Tourism website (see "Websites of Note," below).

IN THE U.K. For visitor information, contact the Embassy of Argentina in London (see "Entry Requirements & Customs," below) or consult Argentina's Ministry of Tourism website (see "Websites of Note," below).

IN BUENOS AIRES The central office of the **City Tourism Secretariat,** Calle Balcarce 360 in Monserrat (© 11/4313-0187), is responsible for all visitor information on Buenos Aires but is not open to the general public. Instead, the city uses several kiosks spread throughout various neighborhoods, which have maps and hotel, restaurant, and attraction information. For addresses and hours for these kiosks, see "Buenos Aires City Tourism Kiosks" on p. 44. In addition, individual associations have their own tourist centers providing a wealth of information, such as that for the Calle Florida Business Association in the shopping center Galerías Pacífico and where Calle Florida hits Plaza San Martín.

The **Buenos Aires City Tourism Office** runs a hot line for information (© 11/4313-0187) from 7:30am to 6pm Monday to Saturday, and Sunday 11am to 6pm.

Free tours are also provided by the city (find out more by calling © 11/4114-5791, Mon–Fri 10am–4pm). The majority of the tours are in Spanish, but a few are also in English.

WEBSITES OF NOTE

- **www.embajadaargentinaeeuu.org** Up-to-date travel information from the Argentine embassy in Washington, D.C.
- **www.turismo.gov.ar** This Ministry of Tourism site has travel information for all of Argentina,

Destination Buenos Aires: Red Alert Checklist

- Do any theater, restaurant, or travel reservations need to be booked in advance?
- Did you make sure your favorite attraction is open? Call ahead for opening and closing times.
- If you purchased traveler's checks, have you recorded the check numbers and stored the documentation separately from the checks?
- Did you stop the newspaper and mail delivery, and leave a set of keys with someone reliable?
- Did you pack your camera and an extra set of camera batteries, and purchase enough film?
- Do you have a safe, accessible place to store money?
- Did you bring your ID cards that could entitle you to discounts, such as AAA and AARP cards, student IDs, and the like?
- Did you bring emergency drug prescriptions and extra glasses and/or contact lenses?
- Did you find out your daily ATM withdrawal limit?
- Do you have your credit card PINs? Is there a daily withdrawal limit on credit card cash advances?
- Did you leave a copy of your itinerary with someone at home?
- Do you have the measurements for those people you plan to buy clothes for on your trip?
- Do you have the address and phone number of your country's embassy or consulate with you?

including a virtual tour of the country's tourist regions, shopping tips, links to city tourist sites, and general travel facts.

- **www.buenosaires.gov.ar** A comprehensive government website set up by the city of Buenos Aires with some tourist links and news about the city.
- **www.bue.gov.ar** A comprehensive tourism website set up by the city of Buenos Aires with details on neighborhoods and a calendar of events in English and other languages. The website has lots of extremely detailed and useful information, but it can be cumbersome to work through its windows and pop-ups. Be patient with it.
- **www.palermoviejo.com** Find out what is going on in the city's trendiest neighborhood, full of the newest restaurants and shops.

Palermo Viejo is further divided into Palermo Hollywood and Palermo Soho.

- **www.google.com.ar** If you're good at Spanish, use this Argentina-based division of the popular Google search engine. Clicking on "Páginas de Argentina" will give you the most up-to-date locally produced information.
- **www.subte.com.ar** This website explains in detail the workings of the Buenos Aires subway system and allows you to locate hotels and other sites of interest in relation to subway stops. It also includes downloadable maps and an interactive feature allowing you to figure out travel times between destinations.

You can also e-mail questions or requests for information to sectur usa@turismo.gov.ar.

Argentina

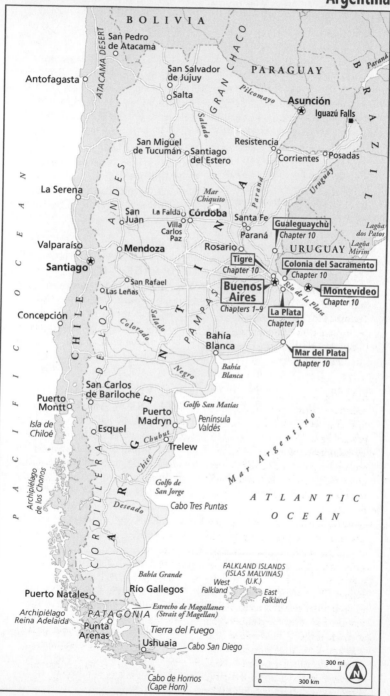

BOLIVIA

San Pedro
de Atacamá

ATACAMA DESERT

Antofagasta

San Salvador
de Jujuy

GRAN CHACO

PARAGUAY

Pilcomayo

B
R
A
Z
I
L

Paraná

Salta

Asunción

Iguazú Falls

Salado

San Miguel
de Tucumán

Santiago
del Estero

Resistencia

Corrientes

Posadas

La Serena

A
N
D
E
S

Mar
Chiquito

Paraná

Uruguay

San
Juan

La Falda

Córdoba

Santa Fe

Villa
Carlos
Paz

Paraná

Gualeguaychú
Chapter 10

Lagôa
dos Patos

Valparaíso

Mendoza

Rosario

URUGUAY

Lagôa
Mirim

Santiago

San Rafael

Tigre
Chapter 10

Colonia del Sacramento
Chapter 10

Las Leñas

**Buenos
Aires**
Chapters 1–9

Río de la Plata

Montevideo
Chapter 10

Concepción

Colorado

Salado

La Plata
Chapter 10

P
A
M
P
A
S

A
R
G
E
N
T
I
N
A

Bahía
Blanca

Mar del Plata
Chapter 10

Negro

Bahía
Blanca

P
A
C
I
F
I
C

O
C
E
A
N

CHILE

San Carlos
de Bariloche

Puerto
Montt

Puerto
Madryn

Golfo San Matías

Península
Valdés

Mar Argentino

Isla de
Chiloé

Esquel

Chubut

Trelew

C
O
R
D
I
L
L
E
R
A

D
E

L
O
S

Archipiélago
de los Chonos

Chico

Golfo de
San Jorge

Deseado

Cabo Tres Puntas

A T L A N T I C

O C E A N

Puerto Natales

Bahía Grande

Río Gallegos

FALKLAND ISLANDS
(ISLAS MALVINAS)
(U.K.)

West
Falkland

East
Falkland

Archipiélago
Reina Adelaida

PATAGONIA

Estrecho de Magallanes
(Strait of Magellan)

Punta
Arenas

Ushuaia

Tierra del Fuego

Cabo San Diego

Cabo de Hornos
(Cape Horn)

0   300 mi
0   300 km

2 Entry Requirements & Customs

ENTRY REQUIREMENTS

Citizens of the United States, Canada, the United Kingdom, Australia, New Zealand, and South Africa require a passport to enter the country. No visa is required for citizens of these countries for tourist stays of up to 90 days. For more information concerning longer stays, employment, or other types of visas, contact the embassies or consulates in your home country. Usually, a hop by boat into neighboring Uruguay or crossing into Brazil during an Iguazu Falls excursion will allow a new 90-day tourist period.

IN THE U.S. Contact the Consular Section of the Argentine Embassy, 1811 Q St. NW, Washington, DC 20009 (© **202/238-6400**). Consulates are also located in Los Angeles, California (© **323/954-9155/6**), Miami, Florida (© **305/580-0530**), Atlanta, Georgia (© **404/880-0805**), Chicago, Illinois (© **312/819-2610**), New York City (© **212/603-0400**), and Houston, Texas (© **713/871-8935**). For more information, try www.embajada argentinaeeuu.org, which has links to the various consulates in the U.S.

IN CANADA Contact the Embassy of the Argentine Republic, Suite 910, Royal Bank Center, 90 Sparks St., Ottawa, Ontario K1P 5B4 (© **613/ 236-2351;** fax 613/235-2659).

IN THE U.K. Contact the Embassy of the Argentine Republic, 65 Brooke St., London W1Y 4AH (© **020/ 7318-1300;** fax 020/7318-1301; seruni@mrecic.gov.ar).

IN NEW ZEALAND Contact the Embassy of the Argentine Republic, Prime Finance Tower, Level 14, 142 Lambton Quay, P.O. Box 5430, Wellington (© **04/472-8330;** fax 04/ 472-8331; enzel@arg.org.nz).

IN AUSTRALIA Contact the Embassy of the Argentine Republic, John McEwen House, Level 2, 7 National Circuit, Barton, ACT 2600 (© **02/6273 9111;** fax 02/6273 0500; info@argentina.org.au).

CUSTOMS

WHAT YOU CAN BRING INTO ARGENTINA

Travelers entering Argentina can bring personal effects—including clothes, jewelry, and professional equipment such as cameras and computers—without paying duty. In addition, they can bring in 21 liters of alcohol, 400 cigarettes, and 50 cigars duty-free.

WHAT YOU CAN TAKE HOME FROM ARGENTINA

Returning **U.S. citizens** who have been away for at least 48 hours are allowed to bring back, once every 30 days, $800 worth of merchandise duty-free. You'll be charged a flat rate of duty on the next $1,000 worth of purchases. Any dollar amount beyond that is dutiable at whatever rates apply.

⸜Tips Passport Savvy

Allow plenty of time before your trip to apply for a passport; processing normally takes 3 weeks but can take longer during busy periods (especially spring). And keep in mind that if you need a passport in a hurry, you'll pay a higher processing fee. When traveling, safeguard your passport in an inconspicuous, inaccessible place like a money belt and keep a copy of the critical pages with your passport number in a separate place. If you lose your passport, visit the nearest consulate or embassy of your native country as soon as possible for a replacement.

On mailed gifts, the duty-free limit is $200. Be sure to have your receipts or purchases handy to expedite the declaration process. *Note:* If you owe duty, you are required to pay on your arrival in the United States, either by cash, personal check, government or traveler's check, or money order, and in some locations, a Visa or MasterCard.

To avoid having to pay duty on foreign-made personal items you owned before you left on your trip, bring along a bill of sale, insurance policy, jeweler's appraisal, or receipts of purchase. Or you can register items that can be readily identified by a permanently affixed serial number or marking—think laptop computers, cameras, and CD players—with Customs before you leave. Take the items to the nearest Customs office or register them with Customs at the airport from which you're departing. You'll receive, at no cost, a Certificate of Registration, which allows duty-free entry for the life of the item.

With some exceptions, you cannot bring fresh fruits and vegetables into the United States. For specifics on what you can bring back, download the invaluable free pamphlet *Know Before You Go* online at **www.cbp.gov**. (Click on "Travel," and then click on "Know Before You Go! Online Brochure.") Or contact the **U.S. Customs & Border Protection (CBP),** 1300 Pennsylvania Ave. NW, Washington, DC 20229 (© **877/287-8667**) and request the pamphlet.

For a clear summary of **Canadian** rules, write for the booklet *I Declare,* issued by the **Canada Border Services Agency** (© **800/461-9999** in Canada or 204/983-3500; www.cbsa-asfc.gc. ca). Canada allows its citizens a C$750 exemption, and you're allowed to bring back duty-free one carton of cigarettes, one can of tobacco, 40 imperial ounces of liquor, and 50 cigars. In addition, you're allowed to mail gifts to Canada valued at less than C$60 a day, provided they're unsolicited and don't contain alcohol or tobacco (write on the package "Unsolicited gift, under $60 value"). All valuables should be declared on the Y-38 form before departure from Canada, including serial numbers of valuables you already own, such as expensive foreign cameras. *Note:* The C$750 exemption can only be used once a year and only after an absence of 7 days.

Citizens of the U.K. who are **returning from a non-E.U. country** have a Customs allowance of: 200 cigarettes; 50 cigars; 250 grams of smoking tobacco; 2 liters of still table wine; 1 liter of spirits or strong liqueurs (over 22% volume); 2 liters of fortified wine, sparkling wine, or other liqueurs; 60 cubic centimeters (ml) of perfume; 250 cubic centimeters (ml) of toilet water; and £145 worth of all other goods, including gifts and souvenirs. People under 17 cannot have the tobacco or alcohol allowance. For more information, contact HM Customs & Excise at © **0845/010-9000** (from outside the U.K., 020/8929-0152), or consult their website at www.hmce.gov.uk.

The duty-free allowance in **Australia** is A$400 or, for those under 18, A$200. Citizens can bring in 250 cigarettes or 250 grams of loose tobacco, and 1,125 milliliters of alcohol. If you're returning with valuables you already own, such as foreign-made cameras, you should file form B263. A helpful brochure available from Australian consulates or Customs offices is *Know Before You Go.* For more information, call the **Australian Customs Service** at © **1300/363-263,** or log on to www.customs.gov.au.

The duty-free allowance for **New Zealand** is NZ$700. Citizens over 17 can bring in 200 cigarettes, 50 cigars, or 250 grams of tobacco (or a mixture of all three if their combined weight doesn't exceed 250g); plus 4.5 liters of wine and beer, or 1.125 liters of liquor.

New Zealand currency does not carry import or export restrictions. Fill out a certificate of export, listing the valuables you are taking out of the country; that way, you can bring them back without paying duty. Most questions are answered in a free pamphlet available at New Zealand consulates and Customs offices: *New Zealand Customs Guide for Travellers, Notice no. 4.* For more information, contact **New Zealand Customs,** The Customhouse, 17–21 Whitmore St., Box 2218, Wellington (© **04/473-6099** or 0800/428-786; www.customs.govt.nz).

3 Money

CASH & CURRENCY

The official Argentine currency is the **peso,** made up of 100 **centavos.** Money is denominated in notes of 2, 5, 10, 20, 50, and 100 pesos and coins of 5, 10, 25, and 50 centavos. Argentina ended its parity with the dollar in January 2002. At the time this book went to press, the exchange rate was slightly under 3 pesos to one U.S. dollar.

Prices have fallen across the board with the peso's devaluation, and the sophisticated city of Buenos Aires has become an unsurpassed bargain for foreign visitors. Often prices are only half what they were before the economic crisis. Prices quoted in this book continue to be quoted in dollars only, but be aware that as tourism increases exponentially in Argentina because of the reduction in prices, hotels have begun trending up in price. Prices in Buenos Aires are typically higher than in the rest of the country.

EXCHANGING MONEY

It's a good idea to exchange at least some money—just enough to cover airport incidentals and transportation to your hotel—before you leave home (though don't expect the exchange rate to be ideal), so you can avoid lines at airport ATMs (automated teller machines). You can exchange money at your local American Express or Thomas Cook office or your bank. If you're far away from a bank with currency-exchange services, American Express offers travelers checks and foreign currency, though with a $15 order fee and additional shipping costs, at www.americanexpress.com or © **800/807-6233.**

U.S. dollars are no longer as widely accepted in Buenos Aires as they were before and immediately after the December 2001 peso crisis. You can, however, still use them to pay in some business-class hotels, tourist-popular restaurants, and businesses catering to large numbers of tourists. Such places will often post their own daily exchange rate at the counter. (In fact, some ATMs in Buenos Aires dispense U.S. dollars as well as pesos.) For the vast majority of your purchases however, you will need pesos. You can convert your currency in hotels, *casas de cambio* (money-exchange houses), some banks, and at the Buenos Aires airport. Exchange American Express traveler's checks for pesos in Buenos Aires at **American Express,** Arenales 707 (© **11/4130-3135**). It is difficult to exchange traveler's checks outside the center of Buenos Aires, so plan ahead to have a sufficient amount of cash in pesos on day trips.

ATMs

The easiest and best way to get cash away from home is from an ATM (automated teller machine). The **Cirrus** (© **800/424-7787;** www.mastercard.com) and **PLUS** (© **800/843-7587;** www.visa.com) networks span the globe; look at the back of your bank card to see which network you're on, then call or check online for ATM locations at your destination. Be sure you know your personal identification number (PIN) before you leave home and be

---

Tips **Small Change**

When you exchange money, ask for some small bills or loose change. Petty cash will come in handy for tipping and public transportation. Consider keeping the change separate from your larger bills, so that it's readily accessible and you'll be less of a target for theft.

---

sure to find out your daily withdrawal limit before you depart. Also keep in mind that many banks impose a fee every time a card is used at a different bank's ATM, and that fee can be higher for international transactions (up to $5 or more) than for domestic ones (where they're rarely more than $1.50). On top of this, the bank from which you withdraw cash may charge its own fee. To compare banks' ATM fees within the U.S., use www.bankrate.com. For international withdrawal fees, ask your bank.

ATMs are easy to access in Buenos Aires and other urban areas, but don't depend on finding them off the beaten path. However, even if your bank allows a certain maximum daily amount to be withdrawn, usually in the range of $500, local ATM limits may be significantly lower (as little as $100), so plan ahead if you know you need large amounts of cash, or test various cash machines before an emergency. It is a good idea to let your bank know ahead of time that you will be using your ATM card overseas so that they do not block transactions in an effort to prevent fraudulent transactions.

TRAVELER'S CHECKS

Traveler's checks are something of an anachronism from the days before the ATM made cash accessible at any time. Traveler's checks used to be the only sound alternative to traveling with dangerously large amounts of cash. They were as reliable as currency, but, unlike cash, could be replaced if lost or stolen.

These days, traveler's checks are less necessary because most cities have 24-hour ATMs that allow you to withdraw small amounts of cash as needed.

However, keep in mind that you will likely be charged an ATM withdrawal fee if the bank is not your own, so if you're withdrawing money every day, you might be better off with traveler's checks—provided that you don't mind showing identification every time you want to cash one.

You can get traveler's checks at almost any bank. **American Express** offers denominations of $20, $50, $100, $500, and (for cardholders only) $1,000. You'll pay a service charge ranging from 1% to 4%. You can also get American Express traveler's checks over the phone by calling © **800/221-7282;** Amex gold and platinum cardholders who use this number are exempt from the 1% fee.

Visa offers traveler's checks at Citibank locations nationwide, as well as at several other banks. The service charge ranges between 1.5% and 2%; checks come in denominations of $20, $50, $100, $500, and $1,000. Call © **800/732-1322** for information. AAA members can obtain Visa checks for a $9.95 fee (for checks up to $1,500) at most AAA offices or by calling © **866/339-3378. MasterCard** also offers traveler's checks. Call © **800/223-9920** for a location near you.

Foreign-currency traveler's checks are useful if you're traveling to one country, or to the euro zone; they're accepted at locations such as bed-and-breakfasts where dollar checks may not be, and they minimize the amount of math you have to do at your destination. **American Express, Thomas Cook, Visa,** and **MasterCard** offer foreign currency traveler's checks.

Tips Dear Visa: I'm Off to Buenos Aires!

Some credit card companies recommend that you notify them of any impending trip abroad so that they don't become suspicious when the card is used numerous times in a foreign destination and block your charges. Even if you don't call your credit card company in advance, you can always call the card's toll-free emergency number if a charge is refused—a good reason to carry the phone number with you. But perhaps the most important lesson here is to carry more than one card with you on your trip; a card might not work for any number of reasons, so having a backup is the smart way to go.

You'll pay the rate of exchange at the time of your purchase (so it's a good idea to monitor the rate before you take the plunge), and most companies charge a transaction fee per order (and a shipping fee if you order online).

If you choose to carry traveler's checks, be sure to keep a record of their serial numbers separate from your checks in the event that they are stolen or lost. You'll get a refund faster if you know the numbers.

CREDIT CARDS

If you choose to use plastic instead of cash, Visa, American Express, Master-Card, and Diners Club are commonly accepted. However, bargain hunters take note: Some establishments— especially smaller businesses—will give you a better price if you pay cash. Credit cards are accepted at most hotels and the more expensive restaurants. But note that you cannot use credit cards in many taxis or at most attractions (museums, trams, and so on). Many new restaurants in Palermo are also not yet accepting credit cards, so ask before eating. I indicate which credit cards, if any,

each restaurant accepts in chapter 5. Like ATM cards, many credit card companies are also now applying fees to international transactions, often as high as 3%. If you have more than one credit card and expect to charge a lot, call the credit card companies before you leave on your trip to find out which charges the lowest, if any, fee. Using the wrong card can make a bargain not such a bargain anymore.

You can get **cash advances** off your credit card at any bank, and you don't even need to go to a teller; you can get a cash advance at the ATM if you know your PIN. If you've forgotten your PIN or didn't even know you had one, call the phone number on the back of your credit card and ask the bank to send it to you. It usually takes 5 to 7 business days, although some banks will do it over the phone.

Another hidden expense to contend with: Interest rates for cash advances are often significantly higher than rates for credit card purchases. More importantly, you start paying interest on the advance *the moment you receive the cash.*

4 When to Go

The seasons in Argentina are the reverse of those in the Northern Hemisphere. Buenos Aires is ideal in fall (Mar–May) and spring (Sept–Nov). The months of October and November in Buenos Aires, when the jacaranda trees have

begun to bloom, are a particularly beautiful time to visit as parks and streets become swathed in purple-flowered splendor. December visitors will still find pleasant weather for the most part. What you won't find in Buenos Aires in

December, in spite of its being overwhelmingly Catholic, are over-the-top Christmas decorations and ritual. January and February can be terribly hot, with humid temperatures soaring to 100°F (38°C). Much of the city is also abandoned at that time by locals who flock to beach resorts in Mar del Plata or Uruguay. January is a time when many tourists do visit, however, resulting in overbooked hotels, yet many restaurants and sites have limited hours during this time period, often closing entirely from January 1 to January 15. You should call ahead to make sure a place is open. While you won't find snow in winter (June–Aug) in Buenos Aires, the weather can be overcast, chilly, and wet, reminiscent of London.

CLIMATE   Except for a small tropical area in northern Argentina, the country lies in the temperate zone, characterized by cool, dry weather in the south, and warmer, humid air in the center. Accordingly, January and February are quite hot—often in the high 90s to more than 100°F (35°C–40°C)—while winter (approximately July–Oct) can be chilly.

HOLIDAYS   Public holidays are January 1 (New Year's Day), Good Friday, May 1 (Labor Day), May 25 (First Argentine Government), June 10 (National Sovereignty Day), June 20 (Flag Day), July 9 (Independence Day), August 17 (Anniversary of the Death of General San Martín), October 12 (Día de la Raza), December 8 (Immaculate Conception Day), and December 25 (Christmas). Most tourist businesses and restaurants will, however, remain open during all but Christmas and New Year's days.

FESTIVALS & SPECIAL EVENTS
A few holidays and festivals are worth planning a trip around. The best place to get information for these events is through your local Argentine tourism office (see "Visitor Information," earlier in this chapter). The Buenos Aires Tourist Office also provides information on all these events through their website www.bue.gov.ar or by calling © **11/4313-0187.**

The Buenos Aires version of Carnaval or Mardi Gras is called **Fiesta de las Murgas,** and though not as colorful as that in Rio de Janeiro, it is celebrated every weekend in February. Various neighborhoods have costumed street band competitions full of loud music, drums, and dancing. Visit www.solomurgas.com for more information.

Chinese Lunar New Year is celebrated generally the first Sunday of the month of February, depending on the actual date of the holiday. Belgrano's Chinatown is small but the dragon-blessing parade is a fun, intimate event kids and adults are certain to enjoy.

The **International Tango Festival** takes place in early March. Its most spectacular night is the last, when Avenida Corrientes is blocked off and thousands of couples dance in the street. Contact the Tourism Office for exact dates.

The **Feria del Libro (Book Festival)** is celebrated from the end of April until the beginning of May. This is one of the world's largest book festivals. Visit www.el-libro.com.ar for dates and the event schedule.

Theater lovers should try to visit Buenos Aires during the **Festival Internacional de Buenos Aires,** a 2-week event of international theater programs, usually held in September. Visit www.festivaldeteatroba.com.ar or call © **11/4374-2829** for more information.

The **World Tango Festival** is celebrated in early to mid-October, with various events, many concentrated in the tango neighborhood of San Telmo. See www.worldtangofestival.com.ar for more information and exact dates.

The world's biggest polo event, the **Argentine Open Polo Championships,** is held in the polo grounds in Palermo, near the Las Cañitas neighborhood, in late November and early December, attracting moneyed crowds from around the world who get to mingle with visiting British royalty. Call the Argentine Polo Association (© 11/4343-0972) for more details.

The **National Gay Pride** parade is held in November, and can switch at the last minute from the first Saturday to the third Saturday of the month, so check Comunidad Homosexual de

Argentina's website at www.cha.org.ar for updated information.

Though Argentina has little in the way of Christmas ritual, **Midnight Mass on Christmas Eve (Noche Buena)** at the Metropolitan Cathedral is a beautiful spectacle. It is usually held at 10pm on December 24. In Argentina, December 24 is a more important day than December 25, and family dinners are held on Christmas Eve rather than on Christmas itself.

5 Travel Insurance

Check your existing insurance policies and credit card coverage before you buy travel insurance. You may already be covered for lost luggage, canceled tickets, or medical expenses.

The cost of travel insurance varies widely, depending on the cost and length of your trip, your age and health, and the type of trip you're taking, but expect to pay between 5% and 8% of the vacation itself.

TRIP-CANCELLATION INSURANCE Trip-cancellation insurance helps you get your money back if you have to back out of a trip, if you have to go home early, or if your travel supplier goes bankrupt. Allowed reasons for cancellation can range from sickness to natural disasters to the State Department declaring your destination unsafe for travel. (Insurers usually won't cover vague fears, though, as many travelers discovered who tried to cancel their trips in Oct 2001 because they were wary of flying.) In this unstable world, trip-cancellation insurance is a good buy if you're getting tickets well in advance—who knows what the state of the world, or of your airline, will be in 9 months? Insurance policy details vary, so read the fine print—and make sure that your airline or cruise line is on the list of carriers covered in case of bankruptcy. A good resource is **"Travel Guard Alerts,"** a list of companies considered high-risk by Travel

Guard International (see website below). Protect yourself further by paying for the insurance with a credit card—by law, consumers can get their money back on goods and services not received if they report the loss within 60 days after the charge is listed on their credit card statement.

For more information, contact one of the following recommended insurers: **Access America** (© 866/807-3982; www.accessamerica.com); **Travel Guard International** (© 800/826-4919; www.travelguard.com); **Travel Insured International** (© 800/243-3174; www.travelinsured.com); and **Travelex Insurance Services** (© 888/457-4602; www.travelex-insurance.com).

MEDICAL INSURANCE For travel overseas, most health plans (including Medicare and Medicaid) do not provide coverage, and the ones that do often require you to pay for services upfront and reimburse you only after you return home. Even if your plan does cover overseas treatment, most out-of-country hospitals make you pay your bills upfront, and send you a refund only after you've returned home and filed the necessary paperwork with your insurance company. As a safety net, you may want to buy travel medical insurance. If you require additional medical insurance, try **MEDEX Assistance** (© 410/453-6300; www.medexassist.com) or **Travel Assistance**

International (© 800/821-2828; www.travelassistance.com; for general information on services, call the company's Worldwide Assistance Services, Inc., at © 800/777-8710).

LOST-LUGGAGE INSURANCE

On domestic flights, checked baggage is covered up to $2,500 per ticketed passenger. On international flights (including U.S. portions of international trips), baggage coverage is limited to approximately $9.07 per pound, up to approximately $635 per checked bag. If you plan to check items more valuable than the standard liability, see if your valuables are covered by your homeowner's policy, get baggage insurance as part of your comprehensive travel-insurance package, or buy Travel Guard's "BagTrak" product. Don't buy insurance at the airport, as it's usually overpriced. Be sure to take any valuables or irreplaceable items with you in your carry-on luggage, as many valuables (including books, money, and electronics) aren't covered by airline policies.

If your luggage is lost, immediately file a lost-luggage claim at the airport, detailing the luggage contents. For most airlines, you must report delayed, damaged, or lost baggage within 4 hours of arrival. The airlines are required to deliver luggage, once found, directly to your house or destination free of charge.

6 Health & Safety

STAYING HEALTHY

Argentina requires no vaccinations to enter the country, except for passengers coming from countries where cholera and yellow fever are endemic.

Some people who have allergies can be affected by the pollution in Buenos Aires's crowded Microcentro, where cars and buses remain mired in traffic jams, belching out pollution. The beautiful spring blossoms also bring with them pollen, and even people not usually affected by plants might be thrown off seasonally and by species of plants different from those in North America and Europe. The smoke in bars and restaurants does not help much either and is an inescapable part of life in the city. It's a good idea to pack a decongestant with you, or asthma medicine if you require it.

Because motor vehicle crashes are a leading cause of injury among travelers, walk and drive defensively. Do not expect buses and taxis to stop for you when crossing the street. Always use a seat belt, which has now become the law in Buenos Aires, even in taxis.

Most visitors find that Argentine food and water are generally easy on the stomach. Water and ice are considered safe to drink in Buenos Aires. However, you should be careful with Argentine steak. Since it is generally served very rare, if not almost raw inside, people with delicate digestive systems or immune deficiency should request it well done (bien cocido). You should also avoid street food and drinks served out of canisters by roving salespeople at the ubiquitous festivals all over the city.

Buenos Aires's streets and sidewalks can be disgustingly unsanitary. While there is a pooper-scooper law on the books, dog owners seem to take delight in letting their pets relieve themselves in the middle of the sidewalk. Even the best neighborhoods are an obstacle course to walk through, and it's a good idea to continually watch where you're stepping. Wash your hands thoroughly after handling your shoes, even if you do not think you have gotten them into anything.

Roaches are also a problem on Buenos Aires's sidewalks. Do not step on them, as that can leave unhatched eggs on the bottom of your shoes to be traipsed home. Never leave a bag or pocketbook directly on the sidewalk either, as you might later find some unexpected passengers stowed away.

DRUGS & PRESCRIPTIONS Be aware that most drugs requiring a prescription in the United States do not necessarily need one in Argentina. Hence, if you lose or run out of a medicine, it might not be necessary to schedule a doctor's appointment to get your prescription. The same goes if you become ill and are sure you know what you need. Many of the pharmacies in the Microcentro have staff who speak English. Not all medicines, however, are a bargain in Argentina.

PLASTIC-SURGERY TOURISM Because of the exchange rate, Argentina is secretly becoming a place for plastic-surgery tourism. If you are planning to be here for a long time, and have been considering cosmetic procedures, Buenos Aires might be a place to have them done. Scanning women on the sidewalks gives you an indication of the popularity of facial and breast augmentation procedures here, and Buenos Aires outpaces Los Angeles in this regard. In fact, it is so common that it is often provided free for locals who have private health insurance.

AUSTRAL SUN The summer sun is hot and strong in Buenos Aires. It's best to bring sunblock, though it is available in stores and pharmacies throughout the city. There are no beaches within the city proper, but many people go tanning in the Palermo and Recoleta parks or in the Ecological Preserve.

MALARIA & OTHER TROPICAL AILMENTS Malaria is not an issue in Buenos Aires. However, the humid summer months of January and February mean you will sometimes find swarms of mosquitoes, particularly along the Río de la Plata and in parks. Bring repellant to avoid bites. To get shots or advice for various illnesses if you are traveling from Buenos Aires to the jungle for long periods of time, contact **Vacunar,** a chain of clinics specializing in vaccinations and preventative illness, with locations all over Buenos Aires (www.vacunar.com.ar). Keep in mind that many shots require a period of time before they become effective. They will also explain country by country what is required if you are traveling to other parts of South America.

WHAT TO DO IF YOU GET SICK AWAY FROM HOME
Any foreign consulate can provide a list of area doctors who speak English. If you get sick, consider asking your hotel concierge to recommend a local doctor—even his or her own. You can also try the emergency room at a local

---

Avoiding "Economy-Class Syndrome"

Deep vein thrombosis, or as it's know in the world of flying, "economy-class syndrome," is a blood clot that develops in a deep vein. It's a potentially deadly condition that can be caused by sitting in cramped conditions—such as an airplane cabin—for too long. During a flight (especially a long-haul flight), get up, walk around, and stretch your legs every 60 to 90 minutes to keep your blood flowing. Other preventative measures include frequent flexing of the legs while sitting, drinking lots of water, and avoiding alcohol and sleeping pills. If you have a history of deep vein thrombosis, heart disease, or another condition that puts you at high risk, some experts recommend wearing compression stockings or taking anticoagulants when you fly; always ask your physician about the best course for you. Symptoms of deep vein thrombosis include leg pain or swelling, or even shortness of breath.

hospital. Many hospitals also have walk-in clinics for emergency cases that are not life-threatening; you may not get immediate attention, but you won't pay the high price of an emergency room visit.

If you suffer from a chronic illness, consult your doctor before your departure. For conditions like epilepsy, diabetes, or heart problems, wear a **MedicAlert identification tag** (© **888/633-4298;** www.medicalert.org), which will immediately alert doctors to your condition and give them access to your records through MedicAlert's 24-hour hot line.

Pack **prescription medications** in your carry-on luggage, and carry prescription medications in their original containers, with pharmacy labels—otherwise they won't make it through airport security. Also bring along copies of your prescriptions in case you lose your pills or run out. Don't forget an extra pair of contact lenses or prescription glasses. Carry the generic name of prescription medicines, in case a local pharmacist is unfamiliar with the brand name.

The medical facilities and personnel in Buenos Aires and the other urban areas in Argentina are very professional. Argentina has a system of socialized medicine, where basic services are free. Private clinics are inexpensive by Western standards. For an English-speaking hospital, call **Clínica Suisso Argentino** (© **11/4304-1081**). The **Hospital Británico** (© **11/4309-6600**), established over 150 years ago during the British empire's heyday also has English-speaking doctors. If you worry about getting sick away from home, you may want to consider **medical travel insurance** (see the section on travel insurance above). In most cases, however, your existing health plan will provide all the coverage you need, but call to make sure. Be sure to carry your identification card in your wallet. You should also ask for receipts or notes from the doctors, which you might need for your claim.

7 Specialized Travel Resources

TRAVELERS WITH DISABILITIES

Buenos Aires is not a very accessible destination for travelers with disabilities. Four- and five-star hotels in Buenos Aires often have a few rooms designed for travelers with disabilities—check with the hotel in advance, and ask specific questions. Some hotels claim to be equipped for those with disabilities but still have one or two stairs leading to their elevator bays, making wheelchair access impossible. American-owned chains tend to be better at accessibility. Hotels with recent renovations sometimes will also have a room with limited capabilities and pull bars in the bathrooms. The tiny crowded streets of the Microcentro can often barely accommodate two people walking together, let alone a wheelchair, and sidewalk cutouts do not exist in all areas.

Fortunately, there are several organizations that can help.

Many travel agencies offer customized tours and itineraries for travelers with disabilities. **Flying Wheels Travel** (© **507/451-5005;** www.flyingwheelstravel.com) offers escorted tours and cruises that emphasize sports and private tours in minivans with lifts. **Access-Able Travel Source** (© **303/232-2979;** www.access-able.com) offers extensive access information and advice for traveling around the world with disabilities. **Accessible Journeys** (© **800/846-4537** or 610/521-0339; www.disabilitytravel.com) caters specifically to slow walkers and wheelchair travelers and their families and friends.

Organizations that offer assistance to travelers with disabilities include **MossRehab** (www.mossresourcenet.org), which provides a library of accessible-travel resources online; **SATH** (Society for Accessible Travel & Hospitality; ✆ **212/447-7284;** www. sath.org; annual membership fees: $45 adults, $30 seniors and students), which offers a wealth of travel resources for all types of disabilities and informed recommendations on destinations, access guides, travel agents, tour operators, vehicle rentals, and companion services; and the **American Foundation for the Blind (AFB;** ✆ **800/232-5463;** www. afb.org), a referral resource for the blind or visually impaired that includes information on traveling with Seeing Eye dogs.

For more information specifically targeted to travelers with disabilities, the community website **iCan** (www.ican online.net/channels/travel/index.cfm) has destination guides and several regular columns on accessible travel. Also check out the quarterly magazine *Emerging Horizons* ($14.95 per year, $19.95 outside the U.S.; www. emerginghorizons.com), and *Open World* magazine, published by SATH (see above; subscription: $13 per year, $21 outside the U.S.).

SENIOR TRAVEL

Argentines treat seniors with great respect, making travel for them easy. The Argentine term for a senior or retired person is *jubilado.* Discounts are usually available; ask when booking a hotel room or before ordering a meal in a restaurant. There are often discounts at theaters and museums too, or even free admission. **Aerolíneas Argentinas** (✆ **800/333-0276** in the U.S.; www. aerolineas.com.ar) offers a 10% discount on fares to Buenos Aires from Miami and New York for passengers 62 and older; companion fares are also discounted.

Members of **AARP** (formerly known as the American Association of Retired Persons), 601 E St. NW, Washington, DC 20049 (✆ **888/687-2277;** www. aarp.org), get discounts on hotels, airfares, and car rentals. AARP offers members a wide range of benefits, including *AARP: The Magazine* and a monthly newsletter. Anyone over 50 can join.

The Alliance for Retired Americans, 8403 Colesville Rd., Suite 1200, Silver Spring, MD 20910 (✆ **301/ 578-8422;** www.retiredamericans.org), offers a newsletter six times a year and discounts on hotel and auto rentals; annual dues are $13 per person or couple. *Note:* Members of the former National Council of Senior Citizens receive automatic membership in the Alliance.

Many reliable agencies and organizations target the 50-plus market. **Elderhostel** (✆ **877/426-8056;** www.elder hostel.org) arranges study programs for those age 55 and over (and a spouse or companion of any age) in the U.S. and in more than 80 countries around the world. Most courses last 5 to 7 days in the U.S. (2–4 weeks abroad), and many include airfare, accommodations in university dormitories or modest inns, meals, and tuition. **ElderTreks** (✆ **800/741-7956;** www.eldertreks. com) offers small-group tours to off-the-beaten-path or adventure-travel locations, restricted to travelers 50 and older. **INTRAV** (✆ **800/456-8100;** www.intrav.com) is a high-end tour operator that caters to the mature, discerning traveler, not specifically seniors, with trips around the world that include guided safaris, polar expeditions, private-jet adventures, and small-boat cruises down jungle rivers.

Recommended publications offering travel resources and discounts for seniors include: the quarterly magazine *Travel 50 & Beyond* (www.travel 50andbeyond.com); *Travel Unlimited: Uncommon Adventures for the Mature Traveler* (Avalon); *101 Tips for Mature Travelers,* available from Grand Circle Travel (✆ **800/221-2610** or 617/350-7500; www.gct.com); and *Unbelievably Good Deals and Great*

Adventures That You Absolutely Can't Get Unless You're Over 50 (McGraw-Hill), by Joann Rattner Heilman.

GAY & LESBIAN TRAVELERS

Argentina remains a very traditional, Catholic society that is fairly closed-minded about homosexuality. Buenos Aires, however, is a more liberal exception to this rule. In particular, the Barrio Norte and San Telmo neighborhoods are gay- and lesbian-friendly, and gays and lesbians are part of the fabric of city life. Gay and lesbian travelers will find numerous clubs, restaurants, and even tango salons catering to them. Buenos Aires has become a major gay-tourism mecca since the peso crisis, almost outshining Rio de Janeiro in popularity for this market. Gay maps are now produced by the Buenos Aires Tourism Office for distribution with standard travel information. Most hotel concierges also easily provide this information, recognizing the importance of the emerging market. The locally produced website www.gayin buenosaires.com.ar also provides more details on many sites of interest.

In 2003 Buenos Aires enacted a Civil Unions law for gay and lesbian couples—the first major Latin American city to do so. While there are visible venues and efforts, for the most part many gays and lesbians remain fairly closeted. Violence is sometimes aimed at the transgendered, even by police.

Be aware of a few rules of thumb in a city where close contact is perfectly normal. Women walk hand in hand on the street, and it does not necessarily mean they are lesbians. It's simply common among women. Men kiss each other hello in public, and again this does not mean they are gay. However, when two men hold hands, it does mean they are gay. It's very rare to see men holding hands, but Buenos Aires is beginning to see surprisingly open expressions of male homosexuality, especially in Barrio Norte along Santa Fe at night.

The International Gay and Lesbian Travel Association (IGLTA; *C* **800/448-8550** or 954/776-2626; www.iglta.org) is the trade association for the gay and lesbian travel industry, and offers an online directory of gay- and lesbian-friendly travel businesses; go to their website and click on "Members." In February 2005 IGLTA hosted an international gay travel conference in Buenos Aires, with official Argentine government recognition of the event.

The **Comunidad Homosexual de Argentina (CHA;** *C* **11/4361-6382;** www.cha.org.ar) is the main gay- and lesbian-rights group in Argentina. They were the main proponents of the Civil Unions law, which they are attempting to expand to the entire country. They also run the annual Gay Pride March, known as Marcha del Orgullo Gay, in November, which proceeds up the traditional Argentine protest route, Avenida de Mayo.

Many agencies offer tours and travel itineraries specifically for gay and lesbian travelers. **Above and Beyond Tours** (*C* **800/397-2681;** www.above beyondtours.com) is the exclusive gay and lesbian tour operator for United Airlines. **Now, Voyager** (*C* **800/255-6951;** www.nowvoyager.com) is a well-known San Francisco–based gay-owned and -operated travel service. **Olivia Cruises & Resorts** (*C* **800/631-6277;** www.olivia.com) charters entire resorts and ships for exclusive lesbian vacations and offers smaller group experiences for both gay and lesbian travelers.

Pride Travel (*C* **11/5218-6556;** www.pride-travel.com) is an Argentina-based company specializing in inbound Buenos Aires travel and other trips throughout South America. They also run the local gay guide publication *La Ronda* and started Argentina's first gay travel magazine, *Pride Travel* in 2005. **Adia Turismo** (*C* **11/4393-0531;** www.adiatur.com) is another Argentina-based company specializing in inbound

Buenos Aires travel. The owner was in charge of the local IGLTA chapter that sponsored the Buenos Aires conference. **BueGay Travel** (© 11/4184-8290; www.buegay.com.ar) handles upscale gay tourism within Buenos Aires and other parts of Argentina. **Calu Travel** (© 11/4372-0510; www.calutravel. com.ar) is a gay travel company that also owns a resort on Mar del Plata's gay beach. **Viajeras Travel** (© 11/4328-1857; www.viajeras.net) is a woman-run travel company, specializing in travel for lesbian visitors to Buenos Aires. The women's scene is harder to tap than the men's scene, so this is a very useful resource.

Since 1992, **Gay.com Travel** and its predecessor **Out and About** (© 800/929-2268; www.outandabout.com) have provided gay and lesbian travelers with objective, timely, and trustworthy coverage of gay-owned and gay-friendly lodging, dining, sightseeing, nightlife, and shopping establishments in every important destination worldwide. The company maintains an office in Buenos Aires for its Spanish-language division, so they also have a large amount of locally produced gay information on Buenos Aires and Argentina. *Out Traveler* (© 800/792-2760; www.outtraveler. com) is a gay travel magazine published by LPI Media, the owners of the U.S. gay news magazine the *Advocate.* Technically, it is the largest-circulation gay magazine in the world and contains an archive of past articles on gay spots around the globe, including many on Buenos Aires and Argentina. *Spartacus International Gay Guide* (Bruno Gmünder Verlag; www.spartacus world.com/gayguide) and *Odysseus* (Odysseus Enterprises Ltd.) are good, annual English-language guidebooks focused on gay men, with some information for lesbians. You can get them from most gay and lesbian bookstores, or order them from **Giovanni's Room** bookstore, 1145 Pine St., Philadelphia,

PA 19107 (© 215/923-2960; www. giovannisroom.com). Within Buenos Aires, the gay monthly magazines *Imperio* and *NX* (www.nexo.org) are available at virtually all central newspaper kiosks and often hang in clear view of passersby. Both list maps and gay guides for Buenos Aires and other Argentine cities. You might also want to check out *Gay Travel A to Z: The World of Gay & Lesbian Travel Options at Your Fingertips,* by Marianne Ferrari (Ferrari International; Box 35575, Phoenix, AZ 85069), a very good gay and lesbian guidebook series.

WOMEN TRAVELERS

In spite of recent female candidates for president like Elisa Carrió and the very visible women-owned and -run businesses in the restaurant and tourism industries, Argentina remains at heart a sexist country. There is a glass ceiling for women in many corporations, and female beauty is highly idealized above all other traits. Men are extremely flirtatious, and leering looks are common and rarely discreet, owing perhaps to the strong Italian influence in the country. While disconcerting, any looks and calls you might get are rarely more than that. Drunk men in clubs can sometimes be physically harassing, however. If you seek to avoid unwanted attention, don't dress skimpily (as many Porteñas do). Women should be cautious when walking alone at night and should take radio-taxis (p. 54) after dark.

In the rare and unlikely event of an assault or sexual attack, contact the police immediately. More help can also be received from the **Centro de Estudios Cultura y Mujer (CECYM),** Guatemala 4294 (© 11/4865-9102; www.cecym.org.ar). It specializes in sexual violence against women, but not all of the staff members speak English. The group also conducts arts programs, intellectual discussions, and other events related to the feminist movement within Argentina.

Single women who want to take advantage of the tango scene or women whose partners refuse to dance can contact **Tanguera Tours** (www.tanguera tours.com), which offers specialized tango tours for groups of women. The tango scene in general, with its strict rules, combining both chauvinism and chivalry, is a safe option for single women to try their hand at dancing. Nothing more than a dance is expected of a woman who accepts an invitation from a strange man to join him on the dance floor. In spite of tango's brothel roots, misbehavior among men is frowned upon in tango settings today. For Latin dancing, try **Mambo** (p. 221) in Las Cañitas, where most people come with groups of friends and the men are not necessarily out on the prowl. **Opera Bay** (p. 221) in Puerto Madero also provides a lower-key dancing environment and is good for mature women.

Those interested in the history of women's rights in Argentina should take note of a few things. As the most powerful woman ever in Argentina, and perhaps all of Latin America, Evita always made equal rights for women part of her agenda. Through her Feminist Peronist Party, women won the right to vote in 1947. Within Congreso, she created a special lounge for female senators to discuss women's issues, called the Salón Rosado, now known as the Salón Eva Perón (p. 142). The current first lady, Cristina Fernández de Kirschner, is an important senator in her own right and was instrumental in border negotiations with Chile over Andean glacier rights, which prevented possible military tensions. Still, as with Evita, beauty, grace, and style are part of her method of influence. Buenos Aires is also perhaps the only major world city to have an entire neighborhood, Puerto Madero, whose streets are named after important female citizens. Pick up the

Women in Buenos Aires pamphlet from the tourism office to learn more about these women and the sites associated with them.

Check out the award-winning website **Journeywoman** (www.journey woman.com), a "real life" women's travel information network where you can sign up for a free e-mail newsletter and get advice on everything from etiquette and dress to safety; or the travel guide *Safety and Security for Women Who Travel,* by Sheila Swan and Peter Laufer (Travelers' Tales, Inc.), offering common-sense tips on safe travel.

JEWISH TRAVELERS

Buenos Aires is one of the world's greatest Jewish centers, with an estimated Jewish population of over 250,000. The historical focus of the community are the neighborhoods of **Once** and **Abasto.** They developed that way in the beginning of the 20th century after immigration of both Ashkenazi Jews from Eastern Europe escaping pogroms and Sephardic Jews who emigrated after the breakup of the Ottoman Empire at the end of World War I. While the communities have generally dispersed to the suburbs, replaced by other immigrants, the area is still home to kosher restaurants, Jewish businesses, and various synagogues. The **Abasto Shopping Center** food court also has the only Kosher McDonald's (p. 127) in the world outside of Israel. With subsequent generations, assimilation and intermarriage have also meant that few Buenos Aires Jews maintain traditions except at holiday times.

In 1992 there was a bomb attack on Buenos Aires's Israeli Embassy, killing 29 people, and in 1994 an attack on the Jewish community group **Asociación Mutual Israelita Argentina (AMIA)** killed 85 people. However, in spite of these attacks engineered by outsiders, most Argentine Jews feel little discrimination. Argentines of all faiths responded to the attacks by massive candlelight vigils. Visit AMIA's website at www.amia.org.ar for more information.

One company that leads Jewish tours of Buenos Aires is **Travel Jewish** (© **949/307-9231** in the U.S. or 11/4106-0541 in Buenos Aires; www.traveljewish.com), a company owned by Deborah Miller, an American who has lived in Buenos Aires. Travel Jewish can plan your trip, including flights and hotels, from beginning to end, or you can take their simple, Jewish-themed day tours once you are in Buenos Aires.

KIDS & TEENS

Argentines love and pamper their children in every way possible. Buenos Aires's kids are also trained from an early age to stay up late in this nocturnal city. Don't be surprised to find yourself passing a playground full of kids and their parents on the swing sets at 2am when you're trying to find your way back to your hotel. There are restaurant chains, such as **Garbis** (p. 122), that have indoor playgrounds, and several museums have been created just for kids, such as the **Museo de los Niños** (p. 154) in Abasto Shopping Center and the **Museo Participativo de Ciencias** (p. 155) in the Centro Cultural Recoleta, where not touching is prohibited. Teens will love the concentration of movie theaters, video arcades, and inexpensive eateries on the pedestrianized **Calle Lavalle** (p. 163). Be aware that with a drinking age of only 18, unsupervised minors who look older than they actually are might have easy access to alcohol.

Having said all that, your children might find it hard to see other children begging on the street and helping their *cartonero* (homeless parent) by looking for discarded paper to sell to recyclers for a very desperate living. The peso crisis has enacted a heavy toll on many Argentine children, creating a young homeless class of beggars. It might be a good idea to explain to your child the inequities within Argentina and the rest of Latin America for that matter if he or she comments on this. In theory, your visiting Argentina will in the long run improve the economy and the plight of these homeless children. It might be tempting to give money to these sad kids, but nutritious wrapped food or school supplies will do them more good in the long run. Trips to Buenos Aires arranged with **Airline Ambassadors** (p. 38), a travel industry nonprofit that allows tourists to vacation and do charity work at the same time, might be ideal for helping children understand the poverty in Argentina in a constructive way.

STUDENT TRAVELERS

Student discounts are very common in Argentina, but usually only if one has appropriate ID. **STA Travel** (© **800/781-4040** in the U.S., 020/7361-6144 in the U.K., or 1300/360-960 in Australia; www.statravel.com) specializes in affordable airfares, bus and rail passes, accommodations, insurance, tours, and packages for students and young travelers, and issues the **International Student Identity Card (ISIC)**. This is the most widely recognized proof that you really are a student. As well as getting you discounts on a huge range of travel, tours, and attractions, it comes with a 24-hour emergency help line and a global voice/fax/e-mail messaging system with discounted international telephone calls. Available to any full-time student over 12, it costs $21.

Buenos Aires is a very fun city for college students on vacation. The legal drinking age in Argentina is 18, but underage drinking is common, although rarely in the excesses found in North America. There are places to drink and socialize all over Buenos Aires. The bars around Plaza Serrano (see chapter 9) in Palermo Soho offer inexpensive beers on tap and pitchers of sangria. This is often served up with inexpensive snacks and live music, meaning having fun won't break a student budget. Students and other young people should pick up the bi-monthly publication **054-The Independent** *Traveler Mag* at the tourist office at the airport. It lists lots of funky and inexpensive places that are perfect for young people.

8 Planning Your Trip Online

SURFING FOR AIRFARES

The "big three" online travel agencies, **Expedia.com, Travelocity.com,** and **Orbitz.com** sell most of the air tickets bought on the Internet. (Canadian travelers should try Expedia.ca and Travelocity.ca; U.K. residents can go to Expedia.co.uk and Opodo.co.uk.). Each has different business deals with the airlines and may offer different fares on the same flights, so it's wise to shop around. Expedia and Travelocity will also send you **e-mail notification** when a cheap fare becomes available to your favorite destination. Of the smaller travel agency websites, **Side-Step** (www.sidestep.com) has gotten the best reviews from Frommer's authors. It's a browser add-on that purports to "search 140 sites at once," but in reality only beats competitors' fares as often as other sites do.

Also remember to check **airline websites,** especially those for low-fare carriers such as Southwest, JetBlue, AirTran, WestJet, or Ryanair, whose fares are often misreported or simply missing from travel agency websites. Even with major airlines, you can often shave a few bucks from a fare by booking directly through the airline and avoiding a travel agency's transaction fee. But you'll get these discounts only by **booking online:** Most airlines now offer online-only fares that even their phone agents know nothing about. For the websites of airlines that fly to and from your destination, see "Getting There," later in this chapter.

Great **last-minute deals** are available through free weekly e-mail services provided directly by the airlines. Most of these are announced on Tuesday or Wednesday and must be purchased online. Most are only valid for travel that weekend, but some (such as Southwest's) can be booked weeks or months in advance. Sign up for weekly e-mail alerts at airline websites or check megasites that compile comprehensive lists of last-minute specials, such as **Smarter Travel.com.** For last-minute trips, **site59.com** and **lastminutetravel.com** in the U.S. and **lastminute.com** in Europe often have better air-and-hotel package deals than the major-label sites. A website listing numerous bargain sites and airlines around the world is **www.itravelnet.com**.

If you're willing to give up some control over your flight details, use what is called an **"opaque" fare service** like **Priceline** (www.priceline.com; www.priceline.co.uk for Europeans) or its smaller competitor **Hotwire** (www.hotwire.com). Both offer rock-bottom prices in exchange for travel on a "mystery airline" at a mysterious time of day, often with a mysterious change of planes en route. The mystery airlines are all major, well-known carriers—and the possibility of being sent from Philadelphia to Chicago via Tampa is remote; the airlines' routing computers have gotten a lot better than they used to be. But your chances of getting a 6am or 11pm flight are pretty high. Hotwire tells you flight prices before you buy; Priceline usually has better deals than Hotwire, but you have to play their "name our price" game. If you're new at this, the helpful folks at **BiddingFor Travel** (www.biddingfortravel.com) do a good job of demystifying Priceline's prices and strategies. Priceline and Hotwire are great for flights within

North America and between the U.S. and Europe. But for flights to other parts of the world, consolidators will almost always beat their fares. *Note:* In 2004 Priceline added nonopaque service to its roster. You now have the option to pick exact flights, times, and airlines from a list of offers—or opt to bid on opaque fares as before.

For much more about airfares and savvy air-travel tips and advice, pick up a copy of *Frommer's Fly Safe, Fly Smart* (Wiley Publishing, Inc.).

SURFING FOR HOTELS

Shopping online for hotels is generally done one of two ways: by booking through the hotel's own website or through an independent booking agency (or a fare-service agency like Priceline; see below). These Internet hotel agencies have multiplied in mind-boggling numbers of late, competing for the business of millions of consumers surfing for accommodations around the world. This competitiveness can be a boon to consumers who have the patience and time to shop and compare the online sites for good deals—but shop they must, for prices can vary considerably from site to site. And keep in mind that hotels at the top of a site's listing may be there for no other reason than that they paid money to get the placement.

Of the "big three" sites, **Expedia** offers a long list of special deals and "virtual tours" or photos of available rooms so you can see what you're paying for (a feature that helps counter the claims that the best rooms are often held back from bargain-booking websites). **Travelocity** posts unvarnished customer reviews and ranks its properties according to the AAA rating system. Also reliable are **Hotels.com** and **Quikbook.com.** An excellent free program, **TravelAxe** (www.travelaxe.net) can help you search multiple hotel sites at once, even ones you may never have heard of—and conveniently lists the total price of the room, including the taxes and service charges. Another booking site, **Travelweb** (www.travel web.com), is partly owned by the hotels it represents (including the Hilton, Hyatt, and Starwood chains) and is therefore plugged directly into the hotels' reservations systems—unlike independent online agencies, which have to fax or e-mail reservation requests to the hotel, a good portion of which get misplaced in the shuffle. More than once, travelers have arrived at the hotel only to be told that they have no reservation. To be fair, many of the major sites are undergoing improvements in service and ease of use, and Expedia will soon be able to plug directly into the reservations systems of many hotel chains—none of which can be bad news for consumers. In the meantime, it's a good idea to **get a confirmation number** and **make a printout** of any online-booking transaction.

In the opaque-website category, **Priceline** (which also now has a nonopaque component to its website) and **Hotwire** are even better for hotels than for airfares; with both, you're allowed to pick the neighborhood and quality level of your hotel before offering up your money. Priceline's hotel product even covers Europe and Asia, though it's much better at getting five-star lodging for three-star prices than at finding anything at the bottom of the scale. On the downside, many hotels stick Priceline guests in their least desirable rooms. Be sure to go to the BiddingForTravel website (see above) before bidding on a hotel room on Priceline; it features a fairly up-to-date list of hotels that Priceline uses in major cities. For both Priceline and Hotwire, you pay upfront and the fee is nonrefundable. *Note:* Some hotels do not provide loyalty program credits or points or other frequent-stay amenities when you book a room through opaque online services.

Frommers.com: The Complete Travel Resource

For an excellent travel-planning resource, we highly recommend **Frommers.com** (www.frommers.com), voted Best Travel Site by *PC Magazine*. We're a little biased, of course, but we guarantee that you'll find the travel tips, reviews, monthly vacation giveaways, bookstore, and online-booking capabilities thoroughly indispensable. Among the special features are our popular **Destinations** section, where you'll get expert travel tips, hotel and dining recommendations, and advice on the sights to see for more than 3,500 destinations around the globe; the **Frommers.com Newsletter,** with the latest deals, travel trends, and money-saving secrets; our **Community** area featuring **Message Boards,** where Frommer's readers post queries and share advice (sometimes even our authors show up to answer questions); and our **Photo Center,** where you can post and share vacation tips. When your research is done, the **Online Reservations System** (www.frommers.com/book_a_trip) takes you to Frommer's preferred online partners for booking your vacation at affordable prices.

SURFING FOR RENTAL CARS

For booking rental cars online, the best deals are usually found at rental-car company websites, although all the major online travel agencies also offer rental-car reservations services. Priceline and Hotwire work well for rental cars too; the only "mystery" is which major rental company you get, and for most travelers the difference between Hertz, Avis, and Budget is negligible.

9 The 21st-Century Traveler

INTERNET ACCESS AWAY FROM HOME

Travelers have any number of ways to check their e-mail and access the Internet on the road. Of course, using your own laptop—or even a PDA (personal digital assistant) or electronic organizer with a modem—gives you the most flexibility. But even if you don't have a computer, you can still access your e-mail and even your office computer from cybercafes.

WITHOUT YOUR OWN COMPUTER

It's hard nowadays to find a city that *doesn't* have a few cybercafes. Although there's no definitive directory for cybercafes—these are independent businesses, after all—two places to start looking are at **www.cybercaptive.com** and **www.cybercafe.com**.

Aside from formal cybercafes, most **youth hostels** nowadays have at least one computer you can get to the Internet on. And most **public libraries** across the world offer Internet access free or for a small charge. Avoid **hotel business centers** unless you're willing to pay exorbitant rates.

Most major airports now have **Internet kiosks** scattered throughout their gates. These kiosks, which you'll also see in shopping malls, hotel lobbies, and tourist information offices around the world, give you basic Web access for a per-minute fee that's usually higher than cybercafe prices. The kiosks' clunkiness and high prices mean they should be avoided whenever possible.

To retrieve your e-mail, ask your **Internet Service Provider (ISP)** if it has a Web-based interface tied to your existing e-mail account. If your ISP doesn't have such an interface, you can use the free **mail2web** service (www.mail2web.com) to view and reply to your home e-mail. For more flexibility, you may want to open a free, Web-based e-mail account with **Yahoo! Mail** (http://mail.yahoo.com). (Microsoft's Hotmail is another popular option, but Hotmail has severe spam problems.) Your home ISP may be able to forward your e-mail to the Web-based account automatically.

If you need to access files on your office computer, look into a service called **GoToMyPC** (www.gotomypc.com). The service provides a Web-based interface for you to access and manipulate a distant PC from anywhere—even a cybercafe—provided your "target" PC is on and has an always-on connection to the Internet (such as with Road Runner cable). The service offers top-quality security, but if you're worried about hackers, use your own laptop rather than a cybercafe computer to access the GoToMyPC system.

WITH YOUR OWN COMPUTER

Wi-Fi (wireless fidelity) is the buzzword in computer access, and more and more hotels, cafes, and retailers are signing on as wireless "hotspots" from where you can get high-speed connection without cable wires, networking hardware, or a phone line (see below). You can get Wi-Fi connection one of several ways. Many laptops sold in the last year have built-in Wi-Fi capability (an 802.11b wireless Ethernet connection). Mac owners have their own networking technology, Apple AirPort. For those with older computers, an 802.11b/**Wi-Fi card** (around $50) can be plugged into your laptop. You sign up for wireless access service much as you do cellphone service, through a plan offered by one of several commercial companies that have made wireless service available in airports, hotel lobbies, and coffee shops, primarily in the U.S. (followed by the U.K. and Japan). **T-Mobile Hotspot** (www.t-mobile.com/hotspot) serves up wireless connections at more than 1,000 Starbucks coffee shops nationwide. **Boingo** (www.boingo.com) and **Wayport** (www.wayport.com) have set up networks in airports and high-class hotel lobbies. IPass providers (see below) also give you access to a few hundred wireless hotel-lobby setups. Best of all, you don't need to be staying at the Four Seasons to use the hotel's network; just set yourself up on a nice couch in the lobby. The companies' pricing policies can be Byzantine, with a variety of monthly, per-connection, and per-minute plans, but in general you pay around $30 a month for limited access—and as more and more companies jump on the wireless bandwagon, prices are likely to get even more competitive.

There are also places that provide **free wireless networks** in cities around the world. To locate these free hotspots, go to **www.personaltelco.net/index.cgi/WirelessCommunities**.

If Wi-Fi is not available at your destination, most business-class hotels throughout the world offer dataports for laptop modems, and a few thousand hotels in the U.S. and Europe now offer free high-speed Internet access using an Ethernet network cable. You can bring your own cables, but most hotels rent them for around $10. **Call your hotel in advance** to see what your options are.

In addition, major Internet Service Providers (ISPs) have **local access numbers** around the world, allowing you to go online by simply placing a local call. Check your ISP's website or call its toll-free number and ask how you can use your current account away from home, and how much it will cost.

If you're traveling outside the reach of your ISP, the **iPass** network has dial-up numbers in most of the world's countries. You'll have to sign up with an iPass provider, who will then tell you how to set up your computer for your destination(s). For a list of iPass providers, go to www.ipass.com and click on "Individuals Buy Now." One solid provider is **i2roam** (© **866/811-6209** or 920/235-0475; www.i2roam.com).

Wherever you go, bring a **connection kit** of the right power and phone adapters, a spare phone cord, and a spare Ethernet network cable—or find out whether your hotel supplies them to guests.

USING A CELLPHONE OUTSIDE THE U.S.

The three letters that define much of the world's **wireless capabilities** are GSM (Global System for Mobiles), a big, seamless network that makes for easy cross-border cellphone use throughout Europe and dozens of other countries worldwide. In the U.S., T-Mobile, AT&T Wireless, and Cingular use this quasi-universal system; in Canada, Microcell and some Rogers customers are GSM, and all Europeans and most Australians use GSM.

If your cellphone is on a GSM system and you have a world-capable multiband phone such as many Sony Ericsson, Motorola, or Samsung models, you can make and receive calls across civilized areas on much of the globe, from Andorra to Uganda. Just call your wireless operator and ask for "international roaming" to be activated on your account. Unfortunately, per-minute charges can be high—usually $1 to $1.50 in western Europe and up to $5 in places like Russia and Indonesia.

That's why it's important to buy an "unlocked" world phone from the get-go. Many cellphone operators sell "locked" phones that restrict you from using any other removable computer memory phone chip (called a **SIM card**) card other than the ones they supply. Having an unlocked phone allows you to install a cheap, prepaid SIM card (found at a local retailer) in your destination country. (Show your phone to the salesperson; not all phones work on all networks.) You'll get a local phone number—and much, much lower calling rates. Getting an already locked phone unlocked can be a complicated process, but it can be done; just call your cellular operator and say you'll be going abroad for several months and

---

Digital Photography on the Road

Many travelers are going digital these days when it comes to taking vacation photographs. Not only are digital cameras left relatively unscathed by airport X-rays, but with digital equipment you don't need to lug armloads of film with you as you travel. In fact, nowadays you don't even need to carry your laptop to download the day's images to make room for more. With a **media storage card,** sold by all major camera dealers, you can store hundreds of images in your camera. These "memory" cards come in different configurations—from memory sticks to flash cards to secure digital cards—and different storage capacities (the more megabytes of memory, the more images a card can hold) and range in price from $30 to over $200. (**Note:** Each camera model works with a specific type of card, so you'll need to determine which storage card is compatible with your camera.) When you get home, you can print the images out on your own color printer or take the storage card to a camera store, drugstore, or chain retailer. Or have the images developed online with a service like **Snapfish** (www.snapfish.com) for something like 25¢ a shot.

Online Traveler's Toolbox

Veteran travelers usually carry some essential items to make their trips easier. Following is a selection of handy online tools to bookmark and use.

- **Airplane Seating & Food.** Find out which seats to reserve and which to avoid (and more) on all major domestic airlines at www.seat guru.com. And check out the type of meal (with photos) you'll likely be served on airlines around the world at www.airlinemeals.net.
- **Foreign Languages for Travelers** (www.travlang.com). Learn basic terms in more than 70 languages and click on any underlined phrase to hear what it sounds like.
- **Intellicast** (www.intellicast.com) and **Weather.com** (www.weather. com). Provide weather forecasts for all 50 states and for cities around the world.
- **Subway Navigator** (www.subwaynavigator.com). Download subway maps and get savvy advice on using subway systems in dozens of major cities around the world.
- **Time & Date** (www.timeanddate.com). See what time (and day) it is anywhere in the world.
- **Travel Warnings** (http://travel.state.gov, www.fco.gov.uk/travel, www.voyage.gc.ca, www.dfat.gov.au/consular/advice). These sites report on places where health concerns or unrest might threaten American, British, Canadian, and Australian travelers. Generally, U.S. warnings are the most paranoid; Australian warnings are the most relaxed.
- **Universal Currency Converter** (www.xe.com/ucc). See what your dollar or pound is worth in more than 100 other countries.
- **Visa ATM Locator** (www.visa.com), for locations of PLUS ATMs worldwide, or **MasterCard ATM Locator** (www.mastercard.com), for locations of Cirrus ATMs worldwide.

want to use the phone with a local provider.

For many, **renting** a phone is a good idea. (Even world-phone owners will have to rent new phones if they're traveling to non-GSM regions, such as Japan or Korea.) While you can rent a phone from any number of overseas sites, including kiosks at airports and at car-rental agencies, I suggest renting the phone before you leave home. That way you can give loved ones and business associates your new number, make sure the phone works, and take the phone wherever you go—especially helpful for overseas trips through several countries,

where local phone-rental agencies often bill in local currency and may not let you take the phone to another country.

Phone rental isn't cheap. You'll usually pay $40 to $50 per week, plus airtime fees of at least a dollar a minute. If you're traveling to Europe, though, local rental companies often offer free incoming calls within their home country, which can save you big bucks. The bottom line: Shop around.

Two good wireless rental companies are **InTouch USA** (© 800/872-7626; www.intouchglobal.com) and **Road-Post** (© 888/290-1606 or 905/272-5665; www.roadpost.com). Give them your itinerary and they'll tell you what wireless products you need. In Touch will also, for free, advise you on whether your existing phone will work overseas; simply call © **703/222-7161** between 9am and 4pm EST, or go to http://intouchglobal.com/travel.htm. For trips of more than a few weeks spent in one country, **buying a phone** becomes economically attractive, as many nations have cheap, no-questions-asked prepaid phone systems. Once you arrive at your destination, stop by a local cellphone shop and get the cheapest package; you'll probably pay less than $100 for a phone and a starter calling card. Local calls may be as low as 10¢ per minute, and in many countries incoming calls are free.

10 Getting There

BY PLANE

Argentina's main international airport is **Ezeiza Ministro Pistarini (EZE;** © **11/4480-9538)**, located 42km (26 miles) to the west of Buenos Aires. Allot at least 45 minutes to an hour for travel between the airport and the city, more in rush hour. You will be assessed a departure tax of approximately $24 upon leaving the country, payable in pesos, dollars, or by Visa credit card. For flights from Buenos Aires to Montevideo (in Uruguay), the departure tax is $5. Passengers in transit and children under 2 are exempt from this tax. However, visitors are advised to verify the departure tax with their airline or travel agent, as the exact amount changes frequently.

Below are the major airlines that fly into Argentina from North America, Europe, and Australia. Argentina's national airline is **Aerolíneas Argentinas** (© **800/333-0276** in the U.S., 0810/222-86527 in Buenos Aires, or 1800/22-22-15 in Australia; www.aerolineas.com.ar). The airline uses New York and Miami as their U.S. hubs. They do not fly daily, but as the country's national airline, Aerolíneas Argentinas is an interesting introduction to the excitement of Argentina and its culture. The female flight attendants tend to be particularly glamorous, and the staff, mostly natives of Argentina, can offer excellent advice for you to use once you are on the ground. Argentine wine is free and liberally served in coach and all classes.

Other operators include **American Airlines** (© **800/433-7300** in the U.S. or 11/4318-1111 in Buenos Aires; www.americanair.com); **United Airlines** (© **800/241-6522** in the U.S. or 0810/777-8648 in Buenos Aires; www.ual.com); **Air Canada** (© **888/247-2262** in Canada or 11/4327-3640 in Buenos Aires; www.aircanada.ca); **British Airways** (© **0845/773-3377** in the U.K. or 11/4320-6600 in Buenos Aires; www.britishairways.com); and **Iberia** (© **0845/601-2854** in the U.K. or 11/4131-1000 in Buenos Aires; www.iberia.com). **LanChile** (© **866/435-9526** in the U.S. and Canada or 11/4378-2222 in Buenos Aires; www.lanchile.com) also provides connections from Miami and New York through Santiago to Buenos Aires. **Qantas Airlines** of Australia (© **13-13-13** in Australia or 11/4514-4730 in Buenos Aires) now has service from Sydney to Santiago with shared service continuing to Buenos Aires on LanChile.

Domestic airlines and flights to Uruguay use **Jorge Newbery Airport** (© **11/4514-1515)**, located only 15 minutes to the north along the river from downtown.

The easiest way to travel Argentina's vast distances is by air. **Aerolíneas Argentinas** (see above) connects most cities and tourist destinations in

Argentina, including Córdoba, Jujuy, Iguazú, Salta, and the beach resorts. Its competitor, **Southern Winds** (© **0810/777-7979;** www.sw.com.ar), serves roughly the same routes. By American standards, domestic flights within Argentina are expensive. Technically, there are different airfares within Argentina for citizens vs. tourists. However, when booking through airline websites or even with travel agencies, tourists can sometimes get the Argentine rate.

If you plan to travel extensively in Argentina from Buenos Aires, consider buying the **Visit Argentina Pass,** issued by Aerolíneas Argentinas. You must purchase the pass in your home country—it cannot be purchased once you are in Argentina. This pass offers discounts for domestic travel in conjunction with your international Aerolíneas Argentinas ticket. Passes are purchasable as one-way coupons for flights within Argentina. Each segment ranges in price from $25 to $260, depending on the destination, not including additional possible fees and taxes. Tickets are exchangeable by date but not by destination and are nonrefundable. For more information, contact the Aerolíneas office in your home country or visit **www.aerolineas.com**.

GETTING INTO TOWN FROM THE AIRPORT

Once at the airport, taxis and remises cost $15 to $20 to the city center. Take officially sanctioned transportation only

and do not accept transportation services from any private individuals. **Manuel Tienda León** (© **11/4314-3636**) is the most reliable transportation company, offering buses and remises to and from the airport. Their buses cost about $6 and use a two-part hub system at their downtown terminal in Plaza San Martín to connect you in smaller buses to your final destination. This can take 1½ hours for connections.

FLYING FOR LESS: TIPS FOR GETTING THE BEST AIRFARE

Passengers sharing the same airplane cabin rarely pay the same fare. Travelers who need to purchase tickets at the last minute, change their itinerary at a moment's notice, or fly one-way often get stuck paying the premium rate. Here are some ways to keep your airfare costs down:

• Passengers who can book their ticket **long in advance,** who can **stay over Saturday night,** or who **fly midweek** or **at less-trafficked hours** may pay a fraction of the full fare. If your schedule is flexible, say so, and ask if you can secure a cheaper fare by changing your flight plans.

• You can also save on airfares by keeping an eye out in local newspapers for **promotional specials** or **fare wars,** when airlines lower prices on their most popular routes. You'll almost never see a sale during peak travel times (Dec–Feb), but if you can travel in the off months, you may snag a bargain.

- Search **the Internet** for cheap fares (see "Planning Your Trip Online," earlier in this chapter).
- Try to book a ticket **in its country of origin.** For instance, if you're planning a one-way flight from Johannesburg to Bombay, a South Africa–based travel agent will probably have the lowest fares. For multileg trips, book in the country of the first leg; for example, book New York–London–Amsterdam–Rome–New York in the U.S.
- **Consolidators,** also known as bucket shops, are great sources for international tickets, although they usually can't beat the Internet on fares within North America. Start by looking in Sunday newspaper travel sections; U.S. travelers should focus on the *New York Times, Los Angeles Times,* and *Miami Herald.* For less-developed destinations, small travel agents who cater to immigrant communities in large cities often have the best deals. *Beware:* Bucket-shop tickets are usually nonrefundable or rigged with stiff cancellation penalties, often as high as 50% to 75% of the ticket price, and some put you on charter airlines, which may leave at inconvenient times and experience delays. Several reliable consolidators are worldwide and available on the Net. **STA Travel** is now the world's leader in student travel, thanks to their purchase of Council Travel. It also offers good fares for travelers of all ages. **ELTExpress (Flights.com; © 800/ TRAV-800;** www.eltexpress.com) started in Europe and has excellent fares worldwide, but particularly to that continent. It also has "local" websites in 12 countries. **FlyCheap (© 800/FLY-CHEAP;** www.1800flycheap.com) is owned

by package-holiday megalith MyTravel and so has especially good access to fares for sunny destinations. **Air Tickets Direct (© 800/778-3447;** www.air ticketsdirect.com) is based in Montreal and leverages the currently weak Canadian dollar for low fares; it'll also book trips to places that U.S. travel agents won't touch, such as Cuba.

- Join **frequent-flier clubs.** Accrue enough miles and you'll be rewarded with free flights and elite status. It's free, and you'll get the best choice of seats, faster response to phone inquiries, and prompter service if your luggage is stolen, your flight is canceled or delayed, or if you want to change your seat. You don't need to fly to build frequent-flier miles—**frequent-flier credit cards** can provide thousands of miles for doing your everyday shopping.
- For many more tips about air travel, including a rundown of the major frequent-flier credit cards, pick up a copy of *Frommer's Fly Safe, Fly Smart* (Wiley Publishing, Inc.).

LONG-HAUL FLIGHTS: HOW TO STAY COMFORTABLE

Long flights can be trying; stuffy air and cramped seats can make you feel as if you're being sent parcel post in a small box. But with a little advance planning, you can make an otherwise unpleasant experience almost bearable.

- Your choice of airline and airplane will definitely affect your legroom. Find more details at www.seat guru.com, which has extensive details about almost every seat on six major U.S. airlines. For international airlines, research firm Skytrax has posted a list of average seat pitches at www.airlinequality.com.
- Emergency-exit seats and bulkhead seats typically have the most

legroom. Emergency-exit seats are usually held back to be assigned the day of a flight (to ensure that the seat is filled by someone able-bodied); it's worth getting to the ticket counter early to snag one of these spots for a long flight. Many passengers find that bulkhead seating (the row facing the wall at the front of the cabin) offers more legroom, but keep in mind that bulkheads are where airlines often put baby bassinets, so you may be sitting next to an infant.

- To have two seats for yourself in a three-seat row, try for an aisle seat in a center section toward the back of coach. If you're traveling with a companion, book an aisle and a window seat. Middle seats are usually booked last, so chances are good you'll end up with three seats to yourselves. And in the event that a third passenger is assigned the middle seat, he or she will probably be more than happy to trade for a window or an aisle.

- Ask about entertainment options. Many airlines offer seatback video systems where you get to choose your movies or play video games—but only on some of their planes. (Boeing 777s are your best bet.)

- To sleep, avoid the last row of any section or a row in front of an emergency exit, as these seats are the least likely to recline. Avoid seats near highly trafficked toilet areas. Avoid seats in the back of many jets—these can be narrower than those in the rest of coach class. You also may want to reserve a window seat so that you can rest your head and avoid being bumped in the aisle.

- Get up, walk around, and stretch every 60 to 90 minutes to keep your blood flowing. This helps avoid **deep vein thrombosis,** or "economy-class syndrome," a

Tips Coping with Jet Lag

Jet lag is a pitfall of traveling across time zones. If you're flying north-south and you feel sluggish when you touch down, your symptoms will be caused by dehydration and the general stress of air travel. When you travel east to west or vice-versa, however, your body becomes thoroughly confused about what time it is, and everything from your digestion to your brain gets knocked for a loop. Traveling east, say, from Chicago to Paris, is more difficult on your internal clock than traveling west, say from Atlanta to Hawaii, as most peoples' bodies find it more acceptable to stay up late than to fall asleep early.

Here are some tips for combating jet lag:

- **Reset your watch** to your destination time before you board the plane.
- **Drink lots of water** before, during, and after your flight. Avoid alcohol.
- **Exercise and sleep well** for a few days before your trip.
- If you have trouble sleeping on planes, **fly eastward on morning flights.**
- **Daylight** is the key to resetting your body clock. At the website for **Outside In** (www.bodyclock.com), you can get a customized plan of when to seek and avoid light.
- If you need help getting to sleep earlier than you usually would, some doctors recommend taking either the hormone **melatonin** or the sleeping pill **Ambien**—but not together. Some recommend that you take 2 to 5 milligrams of melatonin about 2 hours before your planned bedtime—but again, always check with your doctor on the best course of action for you.

potentially deadly condition that can be caused by sitting in cramped conditions for too long. Other preventative measures include drinking lots of water and avoiding alcohol (see next bullet). See "Avoiding 'Economy-Class Syndrome'" on p. 20 for more information.

- Drink water before, during, and after your flight to combat the lack of humidity in airplane cabins—which can be drier than the Sahara. Bring a bottle of water onboard. Avoid alcohol, which will dehydrate you.

- If you're flying with kids, don't forget to carry on toys, books, pacifiers, and chewing gum to help them relieve ear pressure buildup during ascent and descent. Let each child pack his or her own backpack with favorite toys.

BY BUS

The **Estación Terminal de Omnibus,** Av. Ramos Mejía 1680 (© **11/4310-0700**), located near Retiro Station, serves all long-distance buses. You would use this station when connecting to other parts of Argentina, or by long-distance coach from other countries. Due to the high cost of air transport for most South Americans, the continent is served by numerous companies offering comfortable, and at times luxurious, bus services to other capitals, often overnight. This is ideal for student and budget travelers.

Among the major bus companies that operate out of Buenos Aires are **La Veloz del Norte** (© **11/4315-2482**),

serving destinations in the Northwest, including Salta and Jujuy; **Singer** (© **11/4315-2653**), serving Puerto Iguazú as well as Brazilian destinations; and **T.A. Chevallier** (© **11/4313-3297**), serving Bariloche.

The **Estación Terminal de Omnibus,** sometimes referred to as the Retiro Bus Station, is sprawling, enormous and confusing. However, there is a color-coded system that explains in general which destinations of the country are served by which bus lines. Red, for instance, indicates the center of the country, including the province of Buenos Aires, dark blue the south, orange the north, green the northeast, light blue the central Atlantic coast, and gray the international destinations. However, many bus lines indicate names of cities on their destination panels that they no longer serve, so you may have to stand in a line to ask. To help you make sense of it all, use **www.tebasa.com.ar**, the terminal's website. Click on the province where you are traveling and a list of bus companies and phone numbers will come up.

BY CAR

In Buenos Aires travel by *subte* (subway), remise, or radio-taxi (radio-dispatched taxis, as opposed to street taxis) is easier and safer than driving yourself. Rush-hour traffic is chaotic, and parking is difficult. If you have rented a car for whatever reason, park it at your hotel or a nearby garage and leave it there. Most daily parking charges do not exceed $4 or $5. Many recently built hotels have parking on the premises; others use nearby garages.

11 Packages for the Independent Traveler & Escorted General-Interest Tours

These days, so many people plan their trips via websites and e-mail that it's easy to forget that a computer can never replace the knowledge a good travel agent can have of a region and its offerings. Maybe you want to be in a special

hotel for a romantic night or a honeymoon. Buenos Aires's tango history is a major component of its draw, but how do you know the difference from one show to the other or what *milonga* (tango salon) would be the best for a beginner? You might also have time for a few side trips, but is Iguazu Falls better, or should you try a beach destination. And what about the kids? What hotels will make them happiest and how do you keep them interested while you enjoy the shopping and nightlife?

I answer most of these questions with our special tips throughout this book, but nothing can replace the human touch. If you have a special agent you have used for years, ask him or her for advice, or try some of the following specialists who are based in the U.S. and Argentina. See also the above sections for gay and lesbian travelers, women travelers, travelers with disabilities, and senior travelers for even more specially tailored vacation needs when visiting Buenos Aires.

RECOMMENDED U.S.-BASED OPERATORS The following U.S.-based tour companies offer solid, well-organized tours in various price categories, and they are backed by years of experience. All can arrange tours of Buenos Aires, the surroundings, and other parts of Argentina and South America. The charity group Airline Ambassadors is listed here because of its unusual approach to travel, but it only recently included Buenos Aires in its program itinerary.

- **Analie Tours,** 10271 SW 72nd St., Suite 104-B, Miami, FL 33173 (© **800/811-6027;** www.analie tours.com), is a Miami-based tour company that has specialized in Argentina and other parts of South America for years. The company is a *Frommer's Budget Travel* magazine favorite, often featured in its budget blowout pages. Recent specials offered 5-day packages with air included from Miami for $600 per person.
- **Borello Travel,** 7 Park Ave. S., Suite 21, New York, NY 10016 (© **800/811-6027** or 212/686-4911; www.borellotravel.com), is a

New York–based travel firm specializing in upscale travel to Buenos Aires. The owner, Sandra Borello, has run her company for over 17 years and is a native of Buenos Aires. Prices can vary, depending on the season, options, and hotel, but a 1-week package to Buenos Aires can cost about $1,500 per person.

- **Airline Ambassadors International,** 1625 W. Crosby Rd., Suite 132, Carrollton, TX 75006 (© **972/323-2772;** www.airline ambassadors.com), is a nonprofit, Texas-based alliance of airline industry personnel who engage in periodic charitable missions throughout the world. Travelers stay in conventional hotels and see everyday tourist sites but also use some of their time to help the disadvantaged in their destination. The group, which started in 1996, has recently begun operations in Argentina. Participants help out in soup kitchens and in a home for the severely retarded in the Buenos Aires suburbs. This is an ideal learning experience for children to see how disadvantaged children live while engaging with them in a safe and constructive way.

RECOMMENDED BUENOS AIRES–BASED OPERATORS Even if you have arranged things at home, once you're in Buenos Aires, there are always last-minute changes or new things you would like to see. The following companies are all excellent and have English-speaking staff members. All can also provide trips to other cities in Argentina outside of Buenos Aires, as well as South America.

- **Mayer & Mayer and Say Hueque Tourism,** Viamonte 749, Office 601, 1053 Buenos Aires (© **11/ 5199-2517,** -2518, -2519, -2520; www.sayhueque.com), is a highly recommended small company with knowledgeable, friendly service and attention to personalized client care. The company is particularly suited to the young and adventurous but can accommodate anyone's needs. Various tour themes include Literary Buenos Aires, Biking Buenos Aires, and Tango Buenos Aires, among many others. They also offer adventure tours within the vicinity of Buenos Aires such as to the Tigre Delta. Travel agent Marcos Wolff is particularly skilled and offers incomparable attention to his clients' needs. His direct line is $©$ **11/5199-2519.**

- **Euro Tur,** Viamonte 486, 1053 Buenos Aires ($©$ **11/4312-6077;** www.eurotur.com), is one of the largest and oldest travel companies in Argentina, specializing in inbound travel, but they can also help walk-ins to accommodate travelers' needs directly while in Buenos Aires. They can arrange basic city tours to trips of all kinds throughout Argentina and South America.

- **Les Amis,** Maipú 1270, 1005 Buenos Aires ($©$ **11/4314-0500;** www.lesamis.com.ar), is another large Argentine tour company, with offices throughout Buenos Aires and Argentina. They can arrange trips while you are in town for Buenos Aires, Argentina, and many other parts of South America. Within the U.S., they are represented by Gina Heilpern, who maintains an office in New York. She can be reached at $©$ **718-857-5567.**

PRIVATE TOUR GUIDES It's easy to hire guides through your hotel or any travel agency in Buenos Aires. You may also want to contact **AGUITBA** (Asociación de Guías de Turismo de Buenos Aires), Carlos Pellegrini 833, sixth floor C, Buenos Aires ($©$ **11/4322-2557;** aguitba@sion.com), a professional society of tour guides that has tried to promote licensing and other credentials legislation to ensure the quality of guides. Its offices are open Monday to Friday from 1 to 6pm.

12 Tips on Accommodations

SAVING ON YOUR HOTEL ROOM

The **rack rate** is the maximum rate that a hotel charges for a room. Hardly anybody pays this price, however, except in high season or on holidays. To lower the cost of your room:

- **Ask about special rates or other discounts.** Always ask whether a room less expensive than the first one quoted is available, or whether any special rates apply to you. You may qualify for corporate, student, military, senior, or other discounts. Mention membership in AAA, AARP, frequent-flier programs, or trade unions, which may entitle you to special deals as well. Find out the hotel policy on

children—do kids stay free in the room or is there a special rate?

- **Dial direct.** When booking a room in a chain hotel, you'll often get a better deal by calling the individual hotel's reservation desk rather than the chain's main number.

- **Book online.** Many hotels offer Internet-only discounts, or supply rooms to Priceline, Hotwire, or Expedia at rates much lower than the ones you can get through the hotel itself. Shop around. And if you have special needs—a quiet room, a room with a view—call the hotel directly and make your needs known after you've booked online.

- **Remember the law of supply and demand.** Resort hotels are most crowded and therefore most expensive on weekends, so discounts are usually available for midweek stays. Business hotels in downtown locations are busiest during the week, so you can expect big discounts over the weekend. Many hotels have high-season and low-season prices, and booking the day after "high season" ends can mean big discounts.

- **Look into group or long-stay discounts.** If you come as part of a large group, you should be able to negotiate a bargain rate, since the hotel can then guarantee occupancy in a number of rooms. Likewise, if you're planning a long stay (at least 5 days), you might qualify for a discount. As a general rule, expect 1 night free after a 7-night stay.

- **Avoid excess charges and hidden costs.** When you book a room, ask whether the hotel charges for parking. Use your own cellphone, pay phones, or prepaid phone cards instead of dialing direct from hotel phones, which usually have exorbitant rates. And don't be tempted by the room's minibar offerings: Most hotels charge through the nose for water, soda, and snacks. Finally, ask about local taxes and service charges, which can increase the cost of a room by 15% or more. If a hotel insists upon tacking on a surprise "energy surcharge" that wasn't mentioned at check-in or a "resort fee" for amenities you didn't use, you can often make a case for getting it removed.

- **Book an efficiency.** A room with a kitchenette allows you to shop for groceries and cook your own meals. This is a big money saver, especially for families on long stays.

- **Consider enrolling in hotel "frequent-stay" programs,** which reward repeat customers who accumulate enough points or credits to earn free hotel nights, airline miles, complimentary in-room amenities, or even merchandise. These are offered not only by many chain hotels and motels (Hilton HHonors, Marriott Rewards, Wyndham ByRequest, to name a few), but individual inns and B&Bs. Many chain hotels partner with other hotel chains, car-rental firms, airlines, and credit card companies to give consumers additional ways to accumulate points in the program.

LANDING THE BEST ROOM

Somebody has to get the best room in the house—it might as well be you. You can start by joining the hotel's frequent-guest program, which may make you eligible for upgrades. A hotel-branded credit card usually gives it owner "silver" or "gold" status in frequent-guest programs for free. Always ask about a corner room. They're often larger and quieter, with more windows and light, and they often cost the same as standard rooms. When you make your reservation, ask if the hotel is renovating; if it is, request a room away from the construction. Ask about nonsmoking rooms, rooms with views, rooms with twin, queen- or king-size beds. If you're a light sleeper, request a quiet room away from vending machines, elevators, restaurants, bars, and discos. Ask for a room that has been most recently renovated or redecorated.

If you aren't happy with your room when you arrive, ask for another one. Most lodgings will be willing to accommodate you.

13 Recommended Books

A wealth of books have been written on Buenos Aires, both by Argentines and foreigners fascinated by the city.

Collected Fictions (Penguin Books, 1999), the translated short stories of Jorge Luis Borges, is probably a great way to start learning about the city. Borges is Argentina's most important literary figure, and he is immortalized by statues throughout Buenos Aires and a street named after him in Palermo. Many of his most important stories deal with the tumultuous 1920s and 1930s, depicting a dark underworld of gangsters, known as *compadritos,* their battles for women and turf, and betrayal by men they thought were friends. His stories are, in essence, literary tangos, dealing with the same subjects as the famous songs but in prose. Borges can be tedious to get through, but will throw an interesting light on the country's underworld during its golden years of cultural and economic growth.

Santa Evita (Vintage, 1996), by Tomas Eloy Martínez, is a highly controversial book, released around the time of the Madonna movie. Blending fiction and fact, and beautifully so, it tells the ordeal of the preserved corpse of Evita as it made its way around the world. It also sheds an interesting light on the military commanders who, afraid of the Catholic Church, refused to destroy her body, but still went around murdering her followers, all the while with an odd fear and sexual attraction to her lifeless body.

A more biographical account is *Evita: The Real Life of Eva Perón* (W. W. Norton & Company, 1996), by Nicholas Fraser and Marysa Navarro. While there seem to be many truths to Evita, this work remains close to most recognized accounts of her life that appear in other history books and biographies. Still, there is an obvious love behind the work, and the book dismisses the idea of the young Eva's serial sexual relationships with powerful men, simply saying that these men liked her for some unknown reason and helped out her career benignly.

The Story of the Night (Henry Holt, 1997), by Colm Toibin, an Irishman, is a novel whose main character is Richard Garay, an Argentine with an English mother. It offers a wonderful perspective to English speakers of the Islas Malvinas/Falkland Islands War and what it was like to be a potential political enemy during this time. Garay is later hired by the U.S. government as a translator, and essentially a spy. He communicates with members of the U.S. government about the goings on after the war, the beginnings of President Ménem's rise to power, and the privatization of many of Argentina's industries, as well as the thoughts of the country's wealthy ruling class from one regime to another. All this political intrigue also serves as the backdrop to the character's coming out as a gay man, eventually dying of AIDS.

Imagining Argentina, by Lawrence Thornton (Bantam Books, 1988), takes place during Argentina's Dirty War of 1976 to 1982 under the military dictatorship that came into power after Juan Perón's second presidential regime. During this time, perhaps 30,000 Argentines accused of conspiring against the government were tortured and killed. The main character, Carlos Rueda, a theater director, returns home one day to find out that his wife has been taken captive by the government. He never finds her but develops a supernatural power to be able to look at others whose family members have been kidnapped and determine what has happened to them. This is a very graphic novel, detailing the plight of torture victims. While hard to stomach, it throws light on a period of time Argentina is still coming to terms with. The novel was made into a movie in 2003 starring Antonio Banderas and Emma Thompson.

3

Getting to Know Buenos Aires

Most of what a tourist wants to see in Buenos Aires is in a relatively compact area near the old colonial heart of the city, the Plaza de Mayo, established in 1580. From there, the city spread out in a wobbly grid, originally based on the Spanish colonial system. Stretching east to the Río de la Plata is the Puerto Madero neighborhood, a renovated port district now full of restaurants, clubs, and many of the city's newest hotels. The Microcentro, or main business district, sits slightly to the northwest of this area, and is where most hotels and other tourist-related services, such as travel agencies, are located. Directly to the south of Plaza de Mayo is Monserrat, full of government buildings and historical churches. Farther south is the charming San Telmo neighborhood, one of Buenos Aires's oldest districts. This must-see neighborhood's most important attractions are its numerous antiques stores and tango halls. Just beyond this is La Boca, the city's historical Little Italy, where El Caminito, a historical pedestrian zone aimed at tourists, is located. North of the center of the city is the beautiful area of Recoleta, home to Evita's final resting place as well as several upscale hotels. This district, in addition to the neighboring Palermo area, where many of the most important museums, parks, and other sites are located, is best accessed by taxi. Avenidas and calles (streets) are miles and miles long, necessitating knowing the cross street, which I provide in most cases throughout the listings in this book.

1 Orientation

VISITOR INFORMATION

TOURIST CENTERS The central office of the **City Tourism Secretariat,** responsible for all visitor information on Buenos Aires, is located at Calle Balcarce 360 in Monserrat (© **11/4313-0187;** www.bue.gov.ar), but this office is not open to the general public. Instead, you'll find several kiosks (with maps and hotel, restaurant, and attraction information) spread throughout various neighborhoods. These are found at J. M. Ortiz and Quintana in Recoleta, Puerto Madero, the central bus terminal, Calle Florida 100, where it hits Diagonal Norte, and other locations in the city center. Most are open Monday through Friday from 10am to 5pm, and on weekends, though some open and close later (see "Buenos Aires City Tourism Kiosks" on p. 44 for exact hours for each location). In addition, individual associations have their own tourist centers providing a wealth of information, such as that for the Calle Florida Business Association in the shopping center Galerías Pacífico and where the pedestrianized shopping street Calle Florida ends at Plaza San Martín.

INFORMATION BY PHONE The Buenos Aires City Tourism Office also runs an information hot line (© **11/4313-0187**), which is staffed from 7:30am

Buenos Aires at a Glance

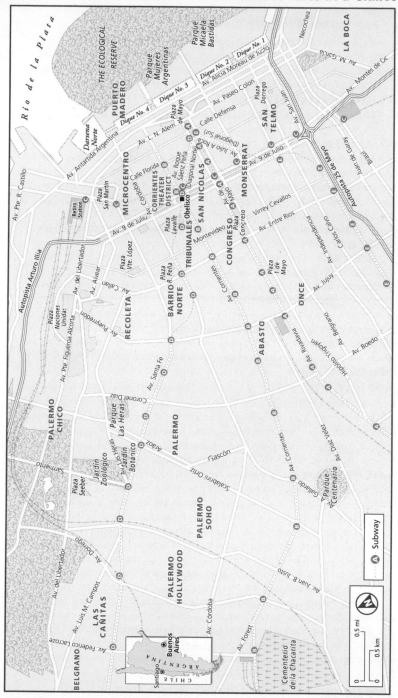

Tips   Buenos Aires City Tourism Kiosks

The city of Buenos Aires has decided to bring information to the people and has closed its old central tourism information office and opened numerous tourism kiosks providing the same information all over the city. In addition to those at the airport, here is a list of those in the city center, including addresses and opening times:

- **Microcentro—Calle Florida:** Calle Florida 100, at Diagonal Norte. Open Monday to Friday from 9am to 6pm, Saturday, Sunday, and holidays 10am to 3pm.
- **San Telmo:** Defensa 1250, at San Juan. Open Monday to Friday from 11am to 5pm, Saturday and Sunday from 11am to 7pm.
- **Puerto Madero:** Alicia Moreau de Justo 200, at Dique 4 (Dock 4). Open Monday to Friday from 11am to 6pm, Saturday and Sunday from 11am to 7pm.
- **Retiro:** Retiro Bus Station, Window 83. Open Monday to Saturday from 7:30am to 1pm.
- **Recoleta:** Av. Quintana 596, at Ortiz. Open Monday to Friday from 10:30am to 6:30pm, Saturday and Sunday from 10am to 7pm.
- **Abasto:** Abasto Shopping Center, main level. Open daily 11am to 9pm.

---

to 6pm Monday to Saturday, and Sunday from 11am to 6pm. The city also provides free tours. Though the majority of these tours are in Spanish, a few are conducted in English. To find out more about the tours, call ℭ **11/4114-5791** (Mon–Fri 10am–4pm).

PUBLICATIONS   The following are publications I recommend picking up once you have hit Buenos Aires. They provide useful information for tourists and have websites you can look at before getting to Buenos Aires. The *Buenos Aires Herald* (www.buenosairesherald.com) is Buenos Aires's English-language daily, and one of the oldest publications on the continent. This newspaper will inform you about what's going on in the news in Argentina and around the world. Plus, they have great event listings of particular interest to English speakers. You'll find the *Herald* on newsstands everywhere for less than a dollar. It can sell out quickly, however, so try to pick it up in the morning. *Ciudad Abierta* (www.buenosaires.gov.ar) is a free weekly newspaper published by the city government telling what is going on culturally all over the city, but it is in Spanish only. Ciudad Abierta is also an interesting cable access channel, which, like the weekly, highlights cultural and tourist interests around the city; it's usually channel 73 on hotel cable systems. *Llegas a Buenos Aires* (www.llegasabuenosaires. com) is another newspaper that has information on culture, arts, tango, and other event listings. It is published weekly and distributed for free at tourist information centers, bars, museums, shops, and other locations throughout the city. *El Tangauta* (www.eltangauta.com) is the tango lover's bible. Published on a monthly basis, it is full of advertising and listings of places to learn tango, dance tango, and buy tango clothes and shoes. It is mostly in Spanish, but select advertising and a few of the articles are in English.

CITY LAYOUT

In order to understand the layout of Buenos Aires, you must gain an understanding of the development of the city in relation to its life-support system, the

Río de la Plata, an enormous silver-brown river that appears to be more like a sea. Buenos Aires began at its historic heart, the Plaza de Mayo, which was laid out in 1580 and is surrounded by the most important national government buildings. During colonial times, the plaza was almost on the edge of the river, and the city's growth snaked along the edges of that river for centuries.

The first port was behind where the Casa Rosada (Presidential Palace) now sits. Landfill over the years pushed the riverbanks farther and farther out. Another port was developed to the south in what is now La Boca, literally "the mouth," which takes its name from a natural harbor formed by a bend in the Río Riachuelo, a tributary that feeds into the Río de la Plata. The San Telmo and La Boca areas grew tremendously in response to increased traffic and immigration through these ports beginning in the middle of the 19th century. The development of Puerto Madero, an expansion of the original colonial port, in the beginning of the 20th century, shifted development to the north of the Plaza de Mayo.

Development along the waterfront eventually triggered people to move farther inland, and areas near new port development sapped wealthier citizens and their money from the older areas. Today the old southern areas of Buenos Aires, historical points of immigration where the fleeing well-to-do are replaced by new and poor immigrants, remain generally poor and working class. La Boca, which was once the city's Little Italy, in particular best exemplifies this by paying homage to its Italian roots in restaurants and displays on gangster history, though the new "immigrants" of today come mostly from the interior of the country. In general, the northern areas of the city, especially Palermo and Recoleta, are full of the well heeled. While these neighborhoods were settled as early as the colonial period, the majority of the structures you'll see today were developed in the beginning of the 20th century.

Buenos Aires fans out from its center, the Plaza de Mayo, in a wobbly grid, as the original streets established by the Spanish were extended farther inland. By the turn of the 20th century, a plan was put into place to essentially rebuild Buenos Aires along the lines of Paris, all in preparation for the celebration of Argentina's centennial in 1910. By creating diagonals and wide boulevards, the plan also hoped to give a sense of order and grandeur to a city that was quickly growing through mass immigration and wealth borne from industry and the exportation of raw materials.

MAIN ARTERIES & STREETS   Two avenidas are defining features of Buenos Aires. The first is **Avenida de Mayo,** a grand boulevard some liken to Paris's Champs-Elysées, others to Madrid's Gran Via. Opened on July 9 (Independence Day) in 1894, it runs east to west, beginning at the Plaza de Mayo and running toward Plaza Congreso, linking the executive and legislative branches of the government. This is the historical government processional route as well as the path that protesters usually take when they have something to complain about. It is lined with some of the city's most beautiful buildings and represents the height of the Beaux Arts architectural movement's expression in Argentina.

Avenida de Mayo intersects with **Avenida 9 de Julio,** the world's widest boulevard, which cuts Buenos Aires in half, running from south to north, beginning near La Boca on the southern end, and ending in the Recoleta and Retiro districts on its northern end at Avenida Libertador. It took decades to complete this boulevard, which was opened on, you guessed it, July 9, 1937. However, they continued working on it up until the 1960s. It terminates on its northern end at the French Embassy. The original plan was to tear the embassy down and continue north, but France refused, and the building makes a nice end to the boulevard. Unfortunately, many other buildings, almost identical to the embassy, were demolished to create Avenida 9 de Julio. One can only imagine the immense architectural heritage that was lost in Buenos Aires's almost insane desire to lay claim to the "title" of city with the widest boulevard in the world.

Two vista-creating diagonal streets leading from the Plaza de Mayo completed the rebuilding process. One is **Diagonal Norte,** also called Avenida Roque Sáenz Peña, which intersects Avenida 9 de Julio at the Obelisco, a monument inaugurated in 1936 to commemorate the 400th anniversary of the unsuccessful original founding of the city by Pedro de Mendoza. This is one of the city's most beautiful stretches, looking like Paris overgrown and on steroids, with each corner of its oversize neoclassical buildings grand and topped by an exquisite dome. The other is **Diagonal Sur,** also called Avenida Julio A. Roca. Unfortunately, it has little of the glamour of its sister diagonal, and save for some government buildings along the beginning of its route near the Plaza de Mayo, has little to write home about.

FINDING AN ADDRESS   Addresses and the numbering of blocks in Buenos Aires follow a completely logical pattern. Building numbers generally jump to the next 100 unit with each block, with the lowest numbers on east-west streets beginning at the points of the street closest to the Río de la Plata. This pattern is broken, however, in Palermo Viejo where some small blocks are numbered at times in units of 50 rather than 100. South-north streets are a little more tricky. While looking at a map would make you think that Avenida de Mayo should be the defining line, it is instead Avenida Rivadavia, since it existed long before the creation of Avenida de Mayo and had always served as this dividing line between the north and south of the city. Street numbering on either side of Rivadavia begins at 1 and progresses from there. No matter how easy you think this may sound, finding addresses becomes far more difficult as the city stretches out and many of the streets begin to bend out. There are dozens of blocks along many of these streets, and it is essential to keep track of cross streets when getting or giving directions. I generally include these in the listings.

FINDING YOUR WAY AROUND   If you can keep track of the information above, you're halfway there. The Río de la Plata lies to the east of the city, along its shore.

Since Avenida 9 de Julio serves as the dividing line between many parts of the city, and essentially ropes off the Microcentro from other neighborhoods, use it as a way of keeping track of where you are. Once on this important thoroughfare, using the Obelisco as a reference point can also be helpful. The only other structures that stand out on Avenida 9 de Julio are the Health Services Building, near the southern termination point by San Telmo (this building predates the boulevard's expansion but was considered too immense to tear down, and so the street was simply extended around it), and the beautiful French neoclassical French Embassy, representing the northern end of the thoroughfare. The most confusing thing about Avenida 9 de Julio is that buildings along it take their addresses from the parallel service roads. Thus, buildings with addresses on calles Carlos Pellegrini, Cerrito, Bernardo de Yrigoyen, and Lima are all actually on Avenida 9 de Julio but might not seem so at first glance just looking at the address on a business card or advertisement.

In general, the five subway lines were constructed under the most important avenidas and calles. For instance, the A-line, the subway's oldest, runs east to west under Avenida de Mayo. The C line runs underneath Avenida 9 de Julio, connecting the two important train stations: Constitución in the south with Retiro in the north. The remaining three lines generally run an east-west route, fanning out from the very center of the city at their beginnings. The E line begins at Plaza de Mayo and runs along Diagonal Sur to Avenida San Juan, though this part of the city has little of interest to the average tourist. The B line runs along Corrientes, skirting the southern edge of Palermo Viejo. Farther out to the north is the D line, which begins at the Plaza de Mayo under Diagonal Norte and runs along Avenida Santa Fe through Barrio Norte on the edge of Recoleta, up through Palermo and Belgrano. If all of this confuses you, the B, C, and D lines converge under the Obelisco, at Obelisco station, close to the intersection of Calle Corrientes and Diagonal Norte. Head here and you can access almost any point of the city served by the subway. This is the city's largest, and most confusing, station.

MAPS   Ask the front desk of your hotel for a copy of *The Golden Map* and *QuickGuide Buenos Aires* to help you navigate the city. Before leaving home, you can also get great maps ahead of time from the Buenos Aires–based company **De Dios,** which has laminated street maps (www.dediosonline.com). Many neighborhoods now also have their own individual maps, tailored to what they offer. Virtually every business in Palermo Viejo has a copy of a series of maps based on shopping, eating, and nightlife in this most trendy part of the city. San Telmo offers a similar map, but with less detail and panache. For most of these maps, you have to head to that neighborhood. Don't hesitate to ask, however, at any of the tourism kiosks for specialized maps—they often have them, but don't have the space to display them. Other specialized maps for Buenos Aires include the *Tango Map,* the *Gay Map,* the *Jewish (Judeo) Map,* and the *Nightlife Map,* among many others, which are available at the tourism kiosks as well as at various businesses in the city. Free metro maps are available at ticket sales counters at every subway station, but they usually don't have enough on hand for demand. Luckily, most other maps either have a small version of the metro map with the rest of their information or have placed metro stops on the street pattern. Almost all metro stations have enormous lighted maps directly at their entrance on street level, so you can tell if you are at the right one. If you miss this, unfortunately, in most cases, you won't see other posted maps within the stations until after you have already entered the turnstiles and headed down to the trains.

THE NEIGHBORHOODS IN BRIEF

Buenos Aires is an enormous metropolis, with nearly 12 million inhabitants in the city and its suburbs. Most of what you'll be interested in, however, is in a compact area, close to the center of the city's historical core, around Plaza de Mayo. Below I list the neighborhoods you're most likely to see as a tourist, including each neighborhood's general boundaries. Keep in mind, though, that even in Buenos Aires, some people and maps call the same areas different names, so keep these descriptions only as a general guide.

Plaza de Mayo Area   This is not so much a district as the historical and political heart of the city, laid out by Don Juan de Garay in 1580 during the second founding of the city. The plaza is surrounded by city and national government buildings and the **Metropolitan Cathedral,** which dates to the late colonial era. The plaza's main defining feature is the **Casa Rosada (Presidential Palace),** home to Evita's famous balcony. It still remains the main point for political demonstrations and also serves as a shelter area for the homeless and the *piqueteros* (demonstrators) who often camp out here at night. The most important ongoing political demonstration that occurs here is that of the **Madres de la Plaza de Mayo.** The demonstrators are made up of the mothers and grandmothers of those who disappeared during the 1976 to 1982 dictatorship in what was known as the **Dirty War.** This demonstration occurs every Thursday beginning at 3:30pm and is a must-see for understanding the country (see p. 143 for more information). Other than the drastically altered **cathedral,** which was remodeled in 1836, the **Cabildo (old city hall)** is the only other remaining colonial building on the plaza. That, too, however, has been severely altered from its original dimensions.

Puerto Madero   This area sits to the east behind the Plaza de Mayo. Once a dilapidated port, the area is now filled with an abundance of restaurants in renovated warehouses. New construction has also placed offices, high-rise residences, and luxury hotels into this neighborhood. The district can feel cold and antiseptic by day because of both its vast expanses and its new construction, so you might want to come at sunset when the water in the port glows a fiery red and the city skyline is silhouetted. This is also perhaps the only neighborhood in a major world city where all its streets are named for women. Puerto Madero's other unique feature is its **Ecological Reserve,** an area of open space created by natural forces revolting against man's abuses. Sediment collected on construction debris dumped into the river here and eventually wild plants and birds settled onto the reclaimed land. There is no convenient subway access to this neighborhood.

Microcentro   No doubt you'll spend plenty of time in this part of Buenos Aires, the city's busy downtown core.

The Microcentro is home to many of the hotels, banks, services, and everything else that makes the city tick. The area's defining feature is the pedestrianized **Calle Florida,** which runs from Avenida de Mayo to Plaza San Martín. It's crowded by day with shoppers and businesspeople. At night sidewalk shows by performance artists thrill tourists and locals alike. The most important shopping center in this district is **Galerías Pacífico,** at the intersection of Calle Córdoba. **Plaza San Martín** on its northern border provides a restful respite from this very compact center. On its edge sits **Retiro Station,** once among the most important points of entry into Buenos Aires from the provinces.

Monserrat   This neighborhood sometimes gets thrown in with many people's descriptions of San Telmo, but it's actually a proper district of its own, though it shares a similar history and a border with San Telmo. Sitting between San Telmo and the Plaza de Mayo, Monserrat is home to some of the city's oldest churches. Additionally, many government buildings have been constructed here. Some are beautiful old Beaux Arts structures; others, built in the mid–20th century, exemplify South American fascist architecture with their smooth massive walls of dark polished marble and granite and heavy, Pharaonic bronze doors that never seem to open. Many unions have headquarters here so that they can more easily speak with government officials (and try to influence their views). Though busy during the day, parts of Monserrat are desolate and possibly dangerous at night. To some Porteños (residents of Buenos Aires), Monserrat extends up the historic **Avenida de Mayo** toward Congreso. Others call this portion of the city **San Cristóbal.**

San Telmo If you think of tango, romance, and a certain unexpressed sensual sadness when you think of Buenos Aires, then you're thinking of San Telmo. This is one of the city's oldest neighborhoods, once the home of the very wealthy until the 1877 outbreak of yellow fever caused many to flee to newly developing areas to the north of the city center. The heart of San Telmo is **Plaza Dorrego,** the city's second-oldest plaza (after the Plaza de Mayo). A few of the buildings on its edges still date from the colonial period. There is a decayed grace here, and travelers who have been to Habana Vieja in Cuba will experience a certain déjà vu. This neighborhood is my favorite, and I like it most during sunset to twilight when the buildings glow gold and their ornamental tops become silhouetted against the sky.

Tango-themed bars make up much of the entertainment in San Telmo, in addition to the restaurants and cafes that have been in operation for almost 150 years. **Calle Defensa,** lined with antiques stores, runs from north to south and is the area's main street. If you have only 1 day to visit this neighborhood, do it on a Sunday when the San Telmo Antiques Fair (p. 199) is in full swing, complete with tango dancers. The event generally runs about 11am to 5pm, and has become so popular that vendors have set up on side streets. Many Porteños still think of the neighborhood as dangerous, based on crime dating back to the 1990s, but rapid gentrification has changed the area completely. Still, take caution at night, just as you should wherever you are.

La Boca Historically, La Boca is Buenos Aires's Little Italy, the main point of entry for Italians at the end of the 19th and beginning of the 20th centuries. Literally, *La Boca* means "the mouth," taking its name from a natural harbor formed by a twist in the Río Riachuelo, a tributary that feeds into the Río de la Plata. Many of the immigrants here settled into haphazardly built boarding houses with metal sheeting called *conventillos.* These were decorated with whatever paint was left over on the docks, creating a mish-mash of colors on each building. The main focal point of La Boca is **El Caminito,** a touristy pedestrianized roadway with plaques and statues explaining neighborhood history surrounded by stores selling T-shirts and souvenirs. Buildings on this street are painted in bold and brilliant colors as a reminder of the area's past. La Boca is my least favorite neighborhood because I feel it overdoes its efforts to draw in tourists to the point where it has nothing authentic to offer. Many will be shocked at this assessment, but if you are short on time, I recommend skipping this neighborhood altogether. That said, the areas of La Boca where tourists do not normally go are more interesting. It's also nice to interact with locals here at night, when there are no tourists around, but I do not recommend you do that, since La Boca (a generally poor neighborhood) is considered dangerous after dark. During the day there are a few art galleries and restaurants here worth a visit, and I have listed in this book what I specifically recommend. There is no convenient subway access to La Boca.

Recoleta The name of this neighborhood comes from an old Spanish word meaning "to remember." Its history dates to the late colonial period and the establishment of a convent here where Recoleta

Cemetery, Evita's final resting place, now sits. Once on the edge of Buenos Aires, Recoleta is now one of its most exclusive shopping and residential neighborhoods. Marble buildings reminiscent of Paris and green leafy streets make up the main impression of this area. The Recoleta Cemetery and the adjacent Iglesia del Pilar are the area's most defining features. **Avenida Alvear,** crowned by the city's most famous hotel, the **Alvear Palace,** is lined with luxurious showrooms (some are in buildings that were once the homes of the city's wealthiest residents) from the most impressive designers. There is no convenient subway access to this neighborhood.

Barrio Norte This neighborhood borders Recoleta, and many consider Barrio Norte to be part of Recoleta. However, while the two are physically similar, Barrio Norte is busier and more commercialized, with shops primarily aimed at a middle- and upper-middle-class clientele. Its main defining feature is Avenida Santa Fe (serviced by the D subway line), where most of these shops are located. This area was also historically home to much of the city's gay population and services, but that is changing over time as these venues spread across the city.

Palermo You might think that half of Buenos Aires is in Palermo, since it's a catchall term for a rather nebulous and large chunk of northern Buenos Aires. The area encompasses **Palermo** proper, with its park system and expensive homes, **Palermo Chico,** which is within Palermo proper, **Palermo Viejo,** which is further divided into **Palermo Soho** and **Palermo Hollywood,** and **Las Cañitas,** which is just to the side of the city's world-famous polo field.

Palermo is a neighborhood of parks filled with magnolias, pines, palms, and willows, where families picnic on weekends and couples stroll at sunset. You might want to think of this part as Palermo Nuevo when compared to Palermo Viejo, described below. Designed by French architect Charles Thays, the parks of Palermo take their inspiration from London's Hyde Park and Paris's Bois de Boulogne. The **Botanical Gardens** and the **Zoological Gardens** are both off of **Plaza Italia.** Stone paths wind their way through the botanical gardens, and flora from throughout South America fills the garden, with over 8,000 plant species from around the world represented. Next door, the city zoo features an impressive diversity of animals. The eclectic and kitschy architecture housing the animals, some designed as exotic temples, is as much of a delight as the animals themselves. Peacocks and some of the other small animals are allowed to roam free, and feeding is allowed with special food for sale at kiosks, making it a great place for entertaining kids.

Palermo Chico, part of Palermo proper, is an exclusive neighborhood of elegant mansions (whose prices were seemingly unaffected by the peso crisis) off of Avenida Alcorta. Other than the beauty of the homes and a few embassy buildings, this small set of streets, tucked behind the **MALBA** museum, has little of interest to the average tourist. Plus, there is no subway access to this neighborhood.

Palermo Viejo, once a run-down neighborhood full of warehouses, factories, and tiny decaying stucco homes few cared to live in as recently as 15 years ago, has been transformed into the city's chicest destination. Once you walk through the area and begin to absorb its charms—cobblestone streets, enormous oak-tree canopies, and low-rise buildings giving a clear view to the open skies on a sunny day—you'll wonder why it had been forsaken for so many years. Palermo Viejo is further divided into **Palermo Soho** to the south and **Palermo Hollywood** to the north, with railroad tracks and Avenida Juan B. Justo serving as the dividing line. The center of Palermo Hollywood is **Plazaleto Jorge Cortazar,** better known by its informal name, **Plaza Serrano,** a small oval park at the intersection of Calle Serrano and Calle Honduras. Young people gather here late at night in impromptu singing and guitar sessions, sometimes fueled by drinks from the myriad of funky bars and restaurants that surround the plaza. The neighborhood was named Palermo Hollywood because many Argentine film studios were initially attracted to its once-cheap rents and easy parking. Palermo Soho is better known for boutiques owned by local designers, with some restaurants mixed in. Both areas were historically where Middle Eastern immigrants originally settled, and this presence is still apparent in the businesses, restaurants, and community centers that remain.

Las Cañitas was once the favored neighborhood of the military powers during the dictatorship period of 1976 to 1982. Because of this remaining military presence, the area remains preeminently safe and is the most secure of all of the central Buenos Aires neighborhoods. A military training base, hospital, high school, and various family housing units still remain and encircle the neighborhood, creating an islandlike sense of safety on the neighborhood's streets. Today, however, the area is far better known among the hip, trendy, and nouveau riche as the place to dine out, have a drink, party, and be seen in the fashionable venues built into converted low-rise former houses on Calle Báez. The polo field where the International Championships take place is also in the neighborhood and is technically part of the military bases. The polo field's presence makes the neighborhood bars and restaurants a great place for enthusiasts to catch polo stars dining out on the town, celebrating their victories in season.

Congreso The western end of the Avenida de Mayo surrounds the massive Congreso building overlooking Plaza Congreso. Though this has been an important area for sightseeing for many years, the whole neighborhood seems to have a run-down feeling to it. Things are beginning to change, however, and numerous hotels have opened in this area, though they are not as well known as those in some of the more glamorous parts of the city. An important feature of this neighborhood, hinting at the area's former glory, is the Café del Molino at the corner of Rivadavia and Callao. An Art Nouveau masterpiece, it was the informal meeting place of politicians and the powerful until shutting its doors in the 1990s. Walking to the north along Callao, you'll also come across blocks of decaying marble and stucco neoclassical buildings that have an almost imperial sense and call to mind Buenos Aires's past wealth and Argentina's desire to rise as a global power.

Corrientes Theater District The Obelisco at the intersection of Corrientes and Avenida 9 de Julio is the defining feature of this part of the city, but while it's nice to look at, this white stone structure won't keep you entertained for long, although the neighborhood surrounding it will. Corrientes was widened in the 1930s, on both sides of Avenida 9 de Julio, and it is lined with the city's most important live theaters and movie palaces. The world-famous Teatro Colón sits a block away from Corrientes in this district, the whole neighborhood acting as Buenos Aires's answer to New York's Broadway. Billboards and big names in bright lights are all over the street here. You should take the time to see a production, even though most are in Spanish only. Though most of the action is at night, some theaters are worth wandering into during the day, as well, in particular the Teatro San Martín, which always has ongoing exhibits. On either side of Corrientes, adjacent streets also have smaller production houses, and there are numerous used-book shops specializing in hard-to-find Spanish-language literature. Starry-eyed hopefuls from the provinces still come into the area hoping for fame, just as Evita once did (her first Buenos Aires apartment was in this district). There are bits of sleaze on Corrientes, because, just as on New York's Broadway, there's a broken heart for every marquee light bulb.

Abasto On first glance, this working- and middle-class neighborhood seems to have little of interest to tourists. However, it is steeped in Buenos Aires history and was where tango crooner Carlos Gardel grew up and lived as an adult. Vestiges of that time period include the **Abasto Shopping Center** on Calle Corrientes, which was once an open-air market, where Gardel sang to the vendors as a child and first became famous. The tango show palace **Esquina Carlos Gardel** was built over a bar he frequented, and his home on Calle Jean Jaures is now a museum.

Once The name of this neighborhood is short for **Once de Septiembre,** and it takes its name from a train station that honors the date when President Sarmiento (president of Argentina 1868–74) died in 1888. Once borders Abasto (see above) and has a similar history and feel. It is most important as a historically Jewish neighborhood. Calle Tucumán, in particular, still retains many Jewish businesses and Kosher restaurants. While the community is no longer as large as it once was, and most Jews have scattered to the suburbs, the importance of this community in Buenos Aires after World War I is evidenced by the variety of Art Deco buildings that Jewish merchants built here. It is a style not as common in other parts of the city and is the best remaining physical evidence of the community's economic impact on the growth of Buenos Aires.

Tribunales The defining feature of this neighborhood is the **Argentine Supreme Court,** from which the area takes its name. This massive building overlooks **Plaza Lavalle,** which is in need of repair even though an ongoing project is trying to put things back together. The court is not generally open to the public, but if you can sneak in, it's worth a look. For tourists, the most important feature of this neighborhood is what sits across the plaza, **Teatro Colón,** the city's supreme cultural center. Other important buildings also overlook the plaza, including **The Roca School,** the Spanish Imperial–style **Teatro Cervantes,** and the synagogue **Templo Libertad,** which contains the **Jewish History Museum.**

Belgrano You'll probably be on a very long trip to Buenos Aires before you venture out to Belgrano, a well-to-do neighborhood in the north of the city, beyond Palermo. It's full of private homes and modern apartments with underground garages and residents who hide behind porter-controlled doors. Its main feature is its Barrancas, a series of hills in the center of the neighborhood and an enormous waterfront park, which is an extension of those in Palermo. While tiny, this is where you'll find Buenos Aires's Chinatown, near the intersection of Arribeños and Mendoza, close to the Belgrano train station. The Chinese Lunar New Year parade is held here on the closest Sunday to the new year in early February.

2 Getting Around

The best way (by far) to get around Buenos Aires is the metro—called the *subte*—the fastest, cheapest way to travel from neighborhood to neighborhood. Buses are also convenient in Buenos Aires, though less commonly used by tourists. The advantage of getting lost on a bus is that you'll be able to see parts of the city obviously not visible from the underground that might help you orientate yourself.

In addition to the maps in this book, you can usually get maps of metro and bus lines from tourist offices and most hotels. (Ask for the *QuickGuide Buenos Aires*.) All metro stations should have maps too, though they're rarely in good supply.

You will also find that Buenos Aires is a great walking city. The beauty of the Buenos Aires streets will pull you further and further along, until you start to realize just how many hours have passed by since you began your stroll.

I've also included information about traveling by taxi and by car below.

BY METRO Five *subte* lines connect commercial, tourist, and residential areas in the city Monday through Saturday from 5am to 11pm and Sunday and holidays from 8am to 10pm. The actual last train at any given station might be earlier, however, as the schedules are more of a guideline than a commitment. The flat fare is 70 centavos (23¢). You can also buy a *subte pass* for 7 pesos ($2.30), valid for 10 *subte* trips. Since the passes are relatively cheap, demagnetize easily, and do not work well in intense humidity, which is most of the summer, you might want to consider buying extra cards as backup. See the inside back cover of this guide for a *subte* map. Although the *subte* is the fastest and cheapest way to travel in Buenos Aires, the system can be crowded during rush hour and unbearably hot in summer. After the subway has closed in the evening, it's best to take a taxi back to your hotel.

You should make sure to ride the A line, itself a tourist site, at least once during your stay in Buenos Aires. The A-line was the first line built, running along Avenida de Mayo, and it still uses the rickety but safe old wooden trains. Perú station in particular retains most of its turn-of-the-20th-century ornamentation, including advertising that mocks the old style from that time period and specially designed kiosks.

Neither the Recoleta nor Puerto Madero neighborhoods have *subte* access, but most of Puerto Madero can be reached via the L. N. Alem *subte* stop on the B line. (It's then a 5- to 20-min. walk, depending on which dock you're going to.) The D runs through Barrio Norte, which borders Recoleta, and depending on where exactly you're going, the area is a 5- to 10-minute walk away. Visit www.subte.com.ar for more information. The interactive site also gives estimated times and transfer information between stations.

Since the peso crisis, wildcat strikes on the subway have been common. However, the workers are usually very polite, often informing passengers ahead of time either by signs posted at the ticket windows or by telling them before passing the turnstiles. And they never leave trains stuck midroute in the tunnels during these stoppages.

BY BUS There are 140 bus lines operating in Buenos Aires 24 hours a day. The minimum fare is 80 centavos (25¢), but this price goes up depending on distance traveled. Pay your fare inside the bus at an electronic ticket machine, which accepts coins only but will give change. Many bus drivers, provided you can communicate with them, will tell you the fare for your destination and help you with where to get off. The *Guia T* is a comprehensive guide to the buses, dividing the city up into various grids. You can buy the guide at bookstores, newspaper kiosks, or on the *subte* from peddlers. Bus lines generally run on the main boulevards. Look for the numbered routes on the poles, which list the main points and neighborhoods the bus will pass through. It's a good idea to take note of main plazas, intersections, and other landmarks that are near your hotel to help with finding your way back. Even hotels on quiet side streets are usually close to a bus route. However, since it can be easy to get lost on the city's buses, I don't recommend them as your main mode of transportation while in Buenos Aires.

ON FOOT You'll probably find yourself walking more than you planned to in this pedestrian-friendly city. Most of the center is small enough to navigate by foot, and you can connect to adjacent neighborhoods by catching a bus or taxi or using the *subte*. Additionally, plazas and parks all over the city supply wonderful places to rest, catch your breath, and watch the locals. Based on the Spanish colonial plan, Buenos Aires is a wobbly grid fanning out from the Plaza de Mayo, which makes it unlikely that you'll get too lost.

BY TAXI The streets of Buenos Aires are crawling with taxis, and fares are inexpensive, with an initial meter reading of 1.60 pesos (55¢) increasing 20 centavos (5¢) every 200m (656 ft.) or each minute. *Remises* and radio-taxis are much safer than street taxis (see "Traveling by Taxi," below). Most of what the average tourist needs to see in the city is accessible for a $2-to-$3 cab ride. Radio-taxis, when hailed on the street, can be recognized by the plastic light boxes on their rooftops. Ordinary taxis, more likely to be run by members of Buenos Aires's infamous taxi mafia, do not have these special lights. A rarely enforced law means taxi drivers can only stop if their passenger side is facing the curb. If you're being ignored by cabs with the red word LIBRE ("Available") flashing on their windshield, cross to the other side of the street and try hailing one from there.

⌒Tips Traveling by Taxi

At the risk of sounding repetitive, I strongly recommend that if you need a taxi, you only take a *remise* or radio-taxi that has been called in advance. If you do take a taxi off the streets, only use those with plastic light boxes on their roofs, indicating that they are radio-taxis. There has been a sharp increase in the number of robberies by street taxi drivers since the economic crisis began. *Remises* are only marginally more expensive than taxis, but far safer. Most hotels have contracts with *remise* companies and will be happy to call one for you. You should also call for a cab from restaurants, museums, and so on (see "By Taxi," above, for phone numbers).

Unlike European cities where taxi drivers go through extensive training to know their way around, Buenos Aires has no such training. Many taxi drivers here are from the provinces and simply do not know their way around Buenos Aires as well as they should. When heading to an off-the-beaten-path destination, or one along the miles-long avenidas, take note of the cross street when telling the driver where to go. Of course, it might be a fun learning venture for the both of you if you get lost. To request a taxi by phone (these drivers tend to be more experienced and safe), consider **Taxi Premium** (© **11/4374-6666**), which is used by the Four Seasons Hotel, or **Radio Taxi Blue** (© **11/4777-8888**), contracted by the Alvear Palace Hotel.

BY CAR   It's definitely not necessary to have a car in Buenos Aires, since public transportation is both cheap and easy. You'd be much better off hiring a *remise* or radio-taxi with the help of your hotel or travel agent. Though it is not recommended, if you must drive, international car-rental companies rent vehicles at both airports. Most hotels can also arrange car rentals.

Most drivers in Buenos Aires only marginally follow driving rules. The one rule that seems to be adhered to, however, is no right turn on red (one more characteristic that makes Buenos Aires the Argentine version of New York City). Argentine law also requires the use of seat belts. Driver's licenses issued by other countries are valid in greater Buenos Aires, but you need an Argentine or international license to drive in most other parts of the country. Fuel is expensive at about $1 per liter ($4 per gal.). A car that uses gasoil (as the name implies, a hybrid fuel of gas and oil) is the cheaper option fuel-wise, about 15% cheaper than regular unleaded gasoline. Many cars in Argentina also operate on natural gas. When refueling cars of this kind, you and all passengers will be required to get out of the car to protect you from the possibility of leaks or explosions.

The **Automóvil Club Argentino (ACA),** Av. del Libertador 1850 (© **11/4802-6061**), has working arrangements with international automobile clubs. The ACA offers numerous services, including roadside assistance, road maps, hotel and camping information, and discounts for various tourist activities.

CAR RENTALS   Many international car-rental companies operate in Argentina with offices at airports and in city centers. Here are the main offices in Buenos Aires for the following agencies: **Hertz,** Paraguay 1122 (© **800/654-3131** in the U.S. or 11/4816-8001 in Buenos Aires); **Avis,** Cerrito 1527 (© **800/230-4898** in the U.S. or 11/4300-8201 in Buenos Aires); **Dollar,** Marcelo T. de Alvear 523 (© **800/800-6000** in the U.S. or 11/4315-8800 in Buenos Aires); and **Thrifty,** Av. Leandro N. Alem 699 (© **800/847-4389** in the U.S. or 11/4315-0777 in Buenos Aires). Car rental is expensive in Argentina, with standard rates beginning at about $90 per day for a subcompact with unlimited mileage (ask for any special promotions, especially on weekly rates). Check to see if your existing automobile insurance policy (or a credit card) covers insurance for car rentals; otherwise, purchasing insurance should run you an extra $15 a day.

FAST FACTS: Buenos Aires

American Express   The enormous American Express building is located next to Plaza San Martín, at Arenales 707 (© **11/4312-1661**). The travel agency is open Monday through Friday from 9am to 6pm; the bank is open Monday through Friday from 9am to 5pm. In addition to card-member services, the bank offers currency exchange (dollars only), money orders, check cashing, and refunds.

Area Code The city area code for Buenos Aires, known locally as a *característica,* is **011**. Drop the 0 when calling from overseas with Argentina's country code, **54**. A **15** in front of a local number indicates a cellular phone. This will need the addition of the **011** when calling from outside of Buenos Aires. Also see "Telephone," below.

Business Hours Banks are open weekdays from 10am to 3pm. Shopping hours are weekdays from 9am to 8pm and Saturday from 9am to 1pm. Shopping centers are open daily from 10am to 10pm. Some small family-owned stores close for lunch, though this is becoming more rare, especially in the Microcentro.

Climate See "When to Go" in chapter 2.

Currency See "Money" in chapter 2. Although U.S. dollars are often accepted in major hotels and businesses catering to tourists, you will need Argentine pesos for ordinary transactions. Credit cards are widely used, although some businesses have suspended accepting credit cards or charge a small additional fee for the convenience. It's easiest to change money at the airport, your hotel, or an independent exchange house rather than at an Argentine bank. Traveler's checks can be difficult to cash: **American Express** (see above) offers the best rates on its traveler's checks and charges no commission. It offers currency exchange for dollars only. ATMs are plentiful in Buenos Aires, but you should only use those in secure, well-lit locations. At some ATMs you can withdraw pesos or dollars. You can also have money wired to **Western Union,** Av. Córdoba 917 (© **0800/800-3030**).

Documents See "Entry Requirements & Customs" in chapter 2.

Driving Rules In cities Argentines drive exceedingly fast and do not always obey traffic lights or lanes. Seat belts are mandatory, although few Argentines actually wear them. When driving outside the city, remember that *autopista* means motorway or highway, and *paso* means mountain pass. Don't drive in rural areas at night, as cattle sometimes overtake the road to keep warm and are nearly impossible to see. See the "Getting Around" section above for more information on getting around by car.

Drugstores Ask your hotel where the nearest pharmacy *(farmacia)* is; they are generally ubiquitous in city centers, and there is always at least one open 24 hours. In Buenos Aires the **Farmacity** chain is open 24 hours, with locations at Lavalle 919 (© **11/4821-3000**) and Av. Santa Fe 2830 (© **11/ 4821-0235**). Farmacity will also deliver to your hotel.

Electricity If you plan to bring a hair dryer, travel iron, or any other small appliance, pack a transformer and adapters because electricity in Argentina runs on 220 volts. Note that most laptops operate on both 110 and 220 volts. Be aware that there are two kinds of outlets in Argentina, the round two-prong European-style, and the Australian-style slanted flat-prong kind. Some hotels will have both throughout a room. It is necessary to have both adapters as you will not know what to expect. These adapters can be cheaply bought throughout Buenos Aires. Luxury hotels usually have transformers and adapters available, as well as American-style plugs at workstations and desks.

Embassies **U.S. Embassy,** Av. Colombia 4300 (🕾 11/4774-5333); **Australian Embassy,** Villanueva 1400 (🕾 11/4777-6580); **Canadian Embassy,** Tagle 2828 (🕾 11/4805-3032); **New Zealand Embassy,** Carlos Pellegrini 1427, fifth floor (🕾 11/4328-0747); **United Kingdom Embassy,** Luis Agote 2412 (🕾 11/4803-6021).

Emergencies The following emergency numbers are valid throughout Argentina. For an **ambulance,** call 🕾 **107;** in case of **fire,** call 🕾 **100;** for **police** assistance, call 🕾 **101.** These numbers are free from any phone. For an English-speaking hospital, call **Clínica Suisso Argentino** (🕾 **11/4304-1081**). The **tourist police** (🕾 **11/4346-5770**) are located at Av. Corrientes 436. They also have a national toll-free number (🕾 **0800/999-0500**).

Information See "Visitor Information" in chapter 2.

Internet Access Cyberspots have begun to pop up on seemingly every corner in Buenos Aires and are found in other cities as well, so it won't be hard to stay connected while in Argentina. Access is reasonably priced (usually averaging under $1 per hour) and connections are reliably good. Internet access is also available in many *telecentros* and *locutorios,* communication stores that have numerous telephones in glass booths and a running meter keeping track of charges for your phone calls where you pay after your call instead of putting in money beforehand. In-room high-speed Internet access is becoming standard in most hotels, but bring a DSL cable with you just in case the hotel runs short of them. Most luxury and even budget hotels now also have Wi-Fi access.

Language Within most shops, hotels, and restaurants in Buenos Aires that cater to tourists, you will almost always find English-speaking staff. However, this is not always the rule in non-touristy places or in budget hotels and restaurants. Argentines speak Spanish, which locally is not called *español* as in other countries, but is instead referred to as *castellano.* Argentine Spanish differs from other countries in its pronunciation of the *ll* and *y* not as a *y* but as English speakers would pronounce a *j.* The word *vos* is substituted for the informal *tú* (both meaning "you" in English), but Argentines happily understand if you do not use *vos* when attempting to speak Spanish with them.

Laundry Nearly all hotels will have both laundry and dry-cleaning services. This service can be very expensive in luxury hotels, as much as $8 a garment. Self-service laundromats are rare in the city, but wash and folds are very common, and are called *lavanderías.* A load of laundry washed, dried, and folded usually runs about $2. Dry cleaners are called *tintorerías.* A suit will run about $3 to $4.

Mail You never have to venture more than a few blocks in Buenos Aires to find a post office, which are open weekdays from 10am to 8pm and Saturday from 10am until 1pm. The main post office (Correo Central) is at Av. Sarmiento 151 (🕾 **11/4311-5040**). In addition, the post office works with some *locutorios* that offer limited mailing services. Airmail postage for a letter 20 grams or less from Argentina to North America or Europe is $1.35. The price for letters trends high after this—for instance, a 30-gram letter is about $3. Parcel rates however, can be inexpensive, as little as $15 for a one-kilogram package. Mail takes on average between 7 and

10 days to get to the U.S. or Europe. The purple-signed and ubiquitous **OCA** is a private postal service with significantly more expensive mailing rates than the government post office.

Maps Reliable driving maps can be purchased at the offices of the **Automóvil Club Argentino,** Av. del Libertador 1850, in Buenos Aires (© **11/4802-6061** or 11/4802-7071). Great laminated city maps of Buenos Aires on various themes are available from the Argentine company **De Dios** (© **11/4816-3514;** www.dediosonline.com). Free maps are available at hotels, tourism kiosks, restaurants, and shops all over Buenos Aires. Within Palermo Viejo, the city's trendiest area, most venues have free themed maps on shopping, sites, and restaurants specifically for that area. Within each area of this book, if there are specialized maps by neighborhood or theme, I generally mention this as well.

Safety Petty crime has increased significantly in Buenos Aires as a result of Argentina's economic crisis. Travelers should be especially alert to pickpockets and purse-snatchers on the streets and on subways, buses, and trains. Tourists should take care not to be overly conspicuous, walking in pairs or groups when possible. Avoid demonstrations, strikes, and other political gatherings if they appear to be violent, though the vast majority are safe and peaceful and an opportunity to talk to locals about politics. In Buenos Aires it's not recommended that you hail taxis off the street. You should call for a radio-taxi instead (see "Traveling by Taxi" on p. 54). Particular areas of the city considered to be unsafe, which I discuss in detail in this guide, are parts of Monserrat, especially at night, and La Boca. Parts of San Telmo have historically been considered dangerous, but in general that is no longer true. However, you should still take precautions. Particular caution should be taken when using the Constitución train station or while in that neighborhood, though I do not discuss it touristically except in terms of a side trip to La Plata (if you insist on getting there by train, see p. 244). In an emergency, call © **100** for police assistance. This is a free call. See the "Women Travelers" section on p. 24 for more information on women traveling in Argentina. With the increase in tourism, Buenos Aires has also engaged in a massive police-hiring program to ensure tourist safety, so you are generally never more than a block or two away from a police officer. In the event of an incident where you cannot find an officer, go to a hotel, restaurant, or shop and ask them to call the police for you. If you feel that you have been ripped off or taken advantage of as a tourist by people offering services, a specific program has been created in Buenos Aires, called the **Tourist Ombudsman.** They can be reached at © **11/4302-7816.** There is also a toll-free national hot line for the **Tourist Police,** specially created to help foreigners with problems. Operators on this line speak English and other languages. They can be reached at © **0800/999-0500.** In spite of all these precautions, remember that most cities in North America are statistically far more violent and crime-ridden than Buenos Aires.

Smoking Smoking is a pervasive aspect of Argentine society, and you will find that most everyone lights up in restaurants and clubs. Most restaurants do, however, provide nonsmoking sections, and if not, there is always the sidewalk seating area outside in good weather. With the increase of tourism from North America, however, many places are becoming less smoky than in the past. *Milongas* (tango salons) aimed at locals are particularly smoke filled, and are best avoided by people with asthma or severe allergies. Tango shows aimed at tourists, though, are relatively smoke-free now.

Taxes Argentina's value added tax (VAT), which is abbreviated locally as IVA, is 21%. You can recover this 21% at the airport if you have purchased local products totaling more than 70 pesos (per invoice) from stores participating in tax-free shopping. Forms are available at the airport. Ask when making purchases or look for the TAX-FREE sign in the store's window. Most shops catering to tourists will gladly explain the procedure to you and provide you with the special receipts you'll need to present to Customs when you leave the country.

Taxis See "Getting Around," earlier in this chapter.

Telephone The country code for Argentina is **54**. The city area code for Buenos Aires, known locally as a *característica,* is **011**. Drop the 0 when calling from overseas with Argentina's country code, **54**. You will however need to use the **011** when calling within Argentina but from outside of Buenos Aires. A **15** in front of a local number indicates a cellular phone. Dialing this from overseas is tricky. You do not use the 15 at all. Instead, dial 54 for the country code, then 9, which indicates to the system you want a cellphone, and then 11 for Buenos Aires, and then the eight-digit Buenos Aires cellphone number. When making domestic long-distance calls in Argentina, place a 0 before the area code. For international calls, add 00 before the country code. Calls to the U.S. and Canada would begin with a 001 and then the city area code and then the normal seven-digit phone number.

Take note that in 2000, Buenos Aires went from a seven-digit-phone-number system to an eight-digit one, with most numbers beginning with a 4. Many people, however, still give out seven-digit phone numbers, and businesses list such numbers on their windows. If someone gives you a seven-digit number, ask if a 4 belongs in front of it for clarification, as with ever-expanding faxes and other communication systems, many numbers are now starting with a 5 or a 6. Phone numbers in the provinces can have anywhere from six to eight digits.

Direct dialing to North America and Europe is available from most phones. International, as well as domestic, calls are expensive in Argentina, especially from hotels (rates fall 10pm–8am). Holders of AT&T credit cards can reach the money-saving **USA Direct** from Argentina by calling toll-free ⓒ **0800/555-4288** from the north of Argentina or 0800/222-1288 from the south. Similar services are offered by **MCI** (ⓒ **0800/555-1002**) and **Sprint** (ⓒ **0800/555-1003** from the north of Argentina, or 0800/222-1003 from the south).

Unless you are calling from your hotel (which will be expensive), the easiest way to place calls in Buenos Aires is by going to a *locutorio* or *telecentro,* found on nearly every city block. Here, private glass booths allow you to place as many calls as you like, dialing directly, after which you pay an attendant. A running meter tells you what you'll owe. Most *locutorios* also have fax machines and broadband Internet computers. Calls to the U.S. or Canada generally run about a peso or less per minute.

There are some coin-operated public phones in Buenos Aires, but most require a calling card, available at kiosks, which are specifically branded for the various communication companies. These cards, which access a system via a toll-free number, are significantly cheaper than even a *locutorio,* sometimes running as little as 10¢ a minute for calls to North America or Europe. Take note that distance does not always bear a relationship to call rates: Calls to other parts of South America and even the provinces within Argentina can cost two to three times that of calls to North America or Europe! Local calls, like all others, are charged by the minute. Dial ⓒ **110** for information, ⓒ **000** to reach an international operator. To dial another number in Argentina from Buenos Aires, dial the area code first, then the local number, the same process for dialing cellular numbers. Be aware that phone numbers in the provinces can have as few as five digits or as many as eight digits, but always ask for clarification when getting a number that seems unusual to you.

Note: If you call someone's cellphone in Argentina, the call is also charged to you, and can cost significantly more than calling a standard land line. It's a good idea to make sure you have either a high-value calling card when trying a cellphone or use a *locutorio* to make sure you are not cut off while calling.

Time   Argentina does not adopt daylight saving time, so the country is 1 hour ahead of Eastern Standard Time in the United States during the Northern Hemisphere summer and 2 hours ahead in the Northern Hemisphere winter. Argentines, being Latinos, do not always run on time. It is rare for events with large numbers of people to start on time, so expect schedule glitches and make allowances accordingly. However, if you are late for an appointment, expect that someone will be taken in your place and you will be even further delayed. Planes are generally on time, but trains and buses can usually be delayed a few minutes. I would not recommend, however, that you head to stations late with this in mind. Argentina also uses military time, the 24-hour clock.

Tipping   A 10% tip is expected at cafes and restaurants, 15% for better service and in fancy places. Give at least $1 to bellboys and porters, 5% to hairdressers, and leftover change to taxi drivers by rounding up to the nearest peso or 50 centavo mark above the charge. Leave about a dollar a day for maid service at hotels, more in fancy places. Bartenders do not expect a tip, and when they get them, it is a happy surprise.

Water   The water is perfectly safe to drink in Buenos Aires.

4

Where to Stay

Hotels in Buenos Aires fall into a range of categories, from the most humble hostels to the newest and most luxurious five-star properties. As tourism continues to flourish throughout the city, new hotels are opening quite rapidly while older ones are being renovated or bought out by international companies hoping to cash in on the volume of people coming to Buenos Aires. Hotels here often fill up in high season, so you should book ahead, even if it is only for your first night or two. Then, if you're not happy with your choice, you can always poke around and try to change your accommodations once you're on the ground.

Immediately after the 2001 peso crisis, many hotel rooms throughout Argentina suddenly were priced at a third of their original cost, which was one factor that attracted so many tourists. However, not all hotel prices are the unbelievable bargains they were at that time: Exponentially increasing amounts of tourists have made available hotel rooms a scarce commodity, and hotels are raising their rates accordingly, and, at times, astonishingly. Additionally, most business hotels (such as the five-stars) never decreased their original rates, since their clientele was comprised mainly of businesspeople on expense accounts. Still, bargains can be had on hotel rooms in Buenos Aires, especially in four-star properties located off the beaten path and in locally owned (rather than international) hotel chains in all categories.

Hotel websites (provided in each hotel's listing) often offer special rates or packages, so it's worth tooling around on their websites before booking. And, no matter what the rack rate is, you should always ask what a hotel's best rate is, as many proprietors are willing to come down in price, especially when they fear a room may be left empty.

Most five- and four-star hotels in Buenos Aires offer in-room safes, 24-hour room service, cable TV, direct-dial phones with voice mail, in-room modem access or Wi-Fi, and many other benefits. The competition between the hotels on this level can be intense, and they often renovate and add amenities to add value. Many—especially the five-stars—also have superb health clubs, pools, and spas, which might be an important factor depending on your interests. Even if you are usually on a budget, I recommend splurging for maybe 1 or 2 nights of your trip if you find a five-star property you really like.

To save money, you will need to compromise, as not all three- or two-star hotels have the above-mentioned amenities (though air-conditioning is now standard in all hotels in Buenos Aires, no matter the category). When dealing with some of the less expensive hotels, your best option is usually to ask to see the available room, or a few of them. This will ensure the room will be up to your standards and can help you choose the best room available, since many recently renovated hotels often have internal variations, with huge rooms and small rooms sometimes offered at exactly the same price.

Local hotels, especially if they are family-run, offer a certain charm that is rarely met by four- and five-star properties. Be aware, however, that while many people in Buenos Aires's travel industry speak English, fewer will at the less expensive or family-run hotels. Also, while a room might not have a particular amenity such as a hair dryer, iron, or coffeemaker, these types of items might still be available upon request at the concierge. The same applies for safes, which might not be in the room but rather only at the front desk. Always ask for a receipt when trying to secure valuable items at the front desk, or at least find out the name of the person who locked them, and if keys for access are only available during certain hours of the day or 24 hours.

Finally, hostels are shared bunk-bed-filled rooms, usually booked by the young and budget-minded adventurous. However, some also have private rooms with attached bathrooms, for one person as well as for groups, so ask before you decide a hostel isn't for you. All the hostels listed in this chapter provide sheets and towels and offer 24-hour access, with no shutout periods.

As for choosing a location, it's a matter of deciding what is best for you and what you want out of your Buenos Aires vacation. In this chapter I have tried to give you a range of hotels based on both location and price. I have also given a brief description of each neighborhood where I've listed hotels. For a more thorough discussion of neighborhoods, however, see "The Neighborhoods in Brief" in chapter 3.

Prices listed below are for rack rates in high season and include the 21% tax levied on hotel rooms. Discounts are almost always available for weekends at business-oriented hotels, low season for all hotels, and may even be available in high season. Web packages and specials can also be found on various hotel sites. Most hotels charge about $4 a night for valet parking, or are close to self-parking facilities they can recommend. You should avoid parking long-term on the street. Few hotels have separate tour desks, but all concierges and front desks can arrange tours and offer advice, and rent cars, bicycles, and other things you might need on your trip.

I give exact prices for hotels below and place them within general price categories by neighborhood. **Very Expensive** refers to hotels costing $300 or more nightly. Keep in mind that some hotels in this category do not offer free breakfasts, which can increase your costs even more. **Expensive** hotels run in the general range of $150 to $299 per night. **Moderate** hotels will run from about $50 to $149 per night. The vast majority of the hotels listed in this chapter are in this range. **Inexpensive** hotels are $49 per night and under, and include hostels, which can run as little as $5 per person for a bed space. Quality and offerings vary most considerably in this price category. All prices listed are rack rates in high season for doubles, but the actual price can be higher or lower depending on a variety of circumstances.

1 Puerto Madero

Puerto Madero is home to some of the newest and most expensive hotels in Buenos Aires. But it's also off the beaten path, necessitating the use of taxis from here. There is a sense of isolation, being cut off from the rest of the city in Puerto Madero, which might be a benefit for people on business trips, or those who like the sense of being whisked away from one scene to another or slipping away peacefully to bed when the day is over. Staying here also puts you near the restaurants of Puerto Madero's historic dock district, meaning you'll never want for places to dine at night. Finally, sunset-viewing from hotel rooms in Puerto Madero is a magnificent sight. The water in the port turns a fiery red, and the city's skyline is magically silhouetted, adding a touch of romance to an area that by day can seem clinical and desolate.

There are no convenient metro stops to this neighborhood. For a map of the hotels listed in this section, see the "Where to Stay in Central Buenos Aires" map on p. 64.

VERY EXPENSIVE

The Faena Hotel and Universe ★★★
The newest of Buenos Aires's five-star hotels, opened in October 2004, the Faena creates a sense of a resort within the confines of the city. The hotel is built into El Porteño, an old grain silo, one of the once-dilapidated historic buildings lining Puerto Madero. Although it's a Philippe Starck–designed hotel, the Faena is different from the barren, all-white environments Starck is normally associated with. Instead, public spaces here might best be described as decayed Edwardian elegance meets country chic, with tin metal sheeting with peeling paint, new ornamental plaster ceiling molding made to look old, and antique Queen Anne–style cabinets. Where possible, original elements of the grain building are maintained. The rooms might best be described as midcentury classical meets modern, based on the white Empire-style furnishings, encased in modern surroundings, with cut-glass mirrors reminiscent of colonial Mexico. White and red are key color elements throughout the oversize rooms, with interesting touches like heavy velvet curtains controlled electronically. There is a home theater in each room. Bathrooms are enormous, completely mirrored, and have oversize tubs. Guests have a choice of different brands of bath products, according to their preferences, which they can pick when making reservations. Some of the rooms facing the city skyline and the port have incredible vistas; others look out over the nearby Ecological Reserve and the Río de la Plata. If you want to work in your room here, you'll have a desk as well as dial-up, high-speed, and Wi-Fi Internet access. The spa is spacious and unique, using the round shapes of the silos to great effect. There are Turkish-style hammam baths and a special stone Incan-style sauna shaped like an igloo. The array of special services is vast, and there are many treatment rooms. You'll also find a huge health-club area with the latest equipment on-premises. Instead of a true concierge, one person, called an "Experience Manager," takes care of you the whole time that you are here. Free private transfers from the airport are provided for each guest. An outdoor pool is at the building's entrance, placed here to make guests feel as if they are in their own home. The hotel also has a residential section, with properties for sale. These vary in size and price, and 20 of them are available for rent on a nonscheduled basis. Several dining, bar, and entertainment areas are in the lobby and elsewhere. The "Universe" in the hotel's name refers to these shared elements, open to guests, residents, and the general public, with a philosophy of mingling and sharing ideas and experiences.

Martha Salotti 445 (at Av. Juana Manso), 1107 Buenos Aires. ℂ **11/4010-9000.** Fax 11/4010-9001. www. faenahotelanduniverse.com. 83 units, including 14 suites; 20 apts of varying size, space, and price also available. From $360 double; from $968 suite. Rates include continental breakfast. AE, MC, V. Parking $12. No nearby metro stations. **Amenities:** 3 restaurants; 3 bars; outdoor heated pool; large health club; spa w/extensive treatments; large sauna w/unique elements; business center w/secretarial services; 24-hr. room service; laundry service, dry cleaning. *In room:* A/C, home theater TV, high-speed Internet and Wi-Fi, minibar, hair dryer, large safe, individualized bath treatments.

Where to Stay in Central Buenos Aires

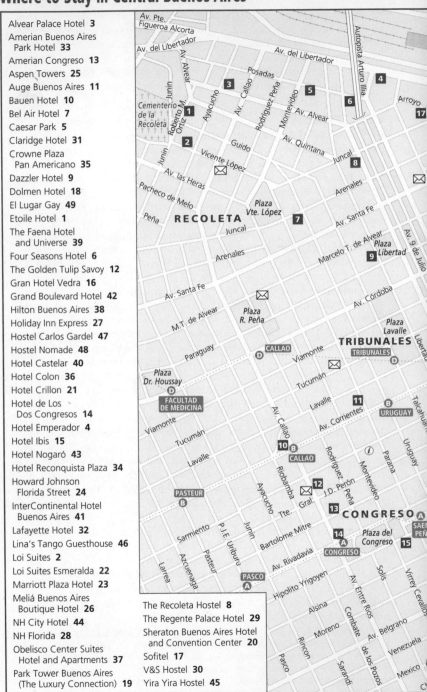

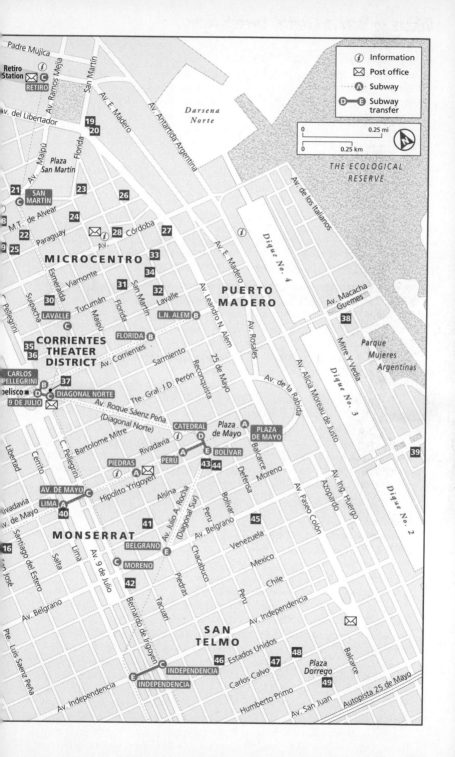

EXPENSIVE

Hilton Buenos Aires ✪✪   The Hilton opened in mid-2000 as the first major hotel and convention center in Puerto Madero. It lies within easy walking distance of some of the best restaurants in Buenos Aires, and is an excellent choice for steak and seafood gourmands. The strikingly contemporary hotel—a sleek silver block hoisted on stilts—features a seven-story atrium with more than 400 well-equipped guest rooms and an additional number of private residences. Spacious guest rooms offer multiple phone lines, walk-in closets, and bathrooms with separate showers and tubs. Those staying on the executive floors receive complimentary breakfast and have access to a private concierge. Next to the lobby, the El Faro restaurant serves California cuisine with a focus on seafood. The hotel has the largest in-hotel convention center in the city.

Av. Macacha Güemes 351 (at Malecón Pierina Dealessi), 1106 Buenos Aires. ✆ **800/445-8667** in the U.S. or 11/4891-0000. Fax 11/4891-0001. www.buenos.hilton.com. 418 units. From $180 double; from $320 suite. AE, DC, MC, V. Parking $8. No nearby metro stations. **Amenities:** Restaurant; bar; modern gym facility w/open-air pool deck and a service of light snacks and beverages; concierge; business center and secretarial services; 24-hr. room service; babysitting; laundry service; dry cleaning. *In room:* TV, minibar, hair dryer, safe.

2 Microcentro

Most of the best and most convenient hotels are found in Recoleta and the Microcentro. The Microcentro is an ideal place to stay if you want to be close to Buenos Aires's shopping and all of the *subte* lines that converge in this region. Theater buffs will also appreciate this location, since most performance venues, including Teatro Colón, are within walking distance of the hotels here. The Microcentro will also give you easy access to the majority of local travel agencies that seem to cluster in this area, which can be convenient for last-minute changes of plan or adding a few day trips outside of the city to your itinerary. Low-cost Internet and telephone centers are everywhere too, so from the standpoint of service, the Microcentro is ideal. If you arrive in Buenos Aires without any reservations, come to this area, since the density of hotels alone will probably mean you won't have to walk around for long before you find something.

For a map of the hotels listed in the section, see the "Where to Stay in Central Buenos Aires" map on p. 64.

VERY EXPENSIVE

Crowne Plaza Pan Americano ✪✪✪   The Crowne Plaza is an enormous hotel, built in two separate stages with its original South Tower dating from 1982, and the more luxurious North Tower from 2000. It faces both the Obelisco and the Teatro Colón, offering convenient access to tourist sites as well as virtually all of the *subte* lines that converge in this part of the city. The South Tower's rooms are of a good size, but many still need renovation, which is ongoing. The North Tower rooms are larger and better appointed and for the small difference in price, they are worth asking for. Decor varies in the North Tower: Some rooms are fully carpeted while others offer elegant hardwood floors, but all of the North Tower's bathrooms are larger, with whirlpool tubs and separate shower units plus marble counters and floors. Valet presses are also standard in the North Tower rooms. All rooms in both towers come with desks, extra side chairs, and ample closet space. The hotel's combination health club, spa, and sauna is perhaps the most amazing and magical in the city and must be experienced, if only for the view. It's in a three-level glass box on top of the North Tower. Swimming in its heated pool, which is both indoors and outdoors, as well as working out on its various machines, gives you the feeling of floating above Avenida 9 de Julio. The health club's restaurant, Kasuga, becomes a sushi bar at night. Two other restaurants are located in the gracious and inspiring lobby, which has Greek frescoes and dark wood and marble accents. Luciernaga, where breakfast is served, is enormous, but its niche-filled layout and Jacobean tapestry-upholstered furniture offers an intimate feeling, and it also serves as the main lobby bar. Tomo I has a modern decor. Both offer international, Argentine, and Italian cuisine.

Carlos Pellegrini 551 (at Corrientes), 1009 Buenos Aires. © **800/227-6963** in the U.S. or 11/4348-5115. Fax 11/4348-5250. www.buenosaires.crowneplaza.com. 386 units. $240 double; from $300 suite. Rates include sumptuous buffet breakfast. AE, DC, MC, V. Free valet parking. Metro: Carlos Pellegrini, 9 de Julio, or Diagonal Norte. **Amenities:** 3 restaurants; enormous health club w/indoor-outdoor pool; exercise room; spa; sauna; concierge; business center; salon; 24-hr. room service; massage service; babysitting; laundry service; dry cleaning. *In room:* A/C, TV, minibar, coffeemaker, hair dryer, iron, safe.

Marriott Plaza Hotel ★★   The historic Plaza was the grande dame of Buenos Aires for most of the 20th century, and the Marriott management has maintained much of its original splendor. (The hotel still belongs to descendants of the first owners from 1909.) The intimate lobby, decorated in Italian marble, crystal, and Persian carpets, is a virtual revolving door of Argentine politicians, foreign diplomats, and business executives. The veteran staff offers outstanding service, and the concierge will address needs ranging from executive business services to sightseeing tours. Although the quality of guest rooms is hit-or-miss while renovations continue, all are spacious and well appointed. Twenty-six overlook Plaza San Martín, providing dreamlike views of the green canopy of trees in the spring and summer. The **Plaza Grill** (p. 101) remains a favorite spot for a business lunch and offers a reasonably priced multicourse dinner menu as well. The hotel's health club is one of the best in the city. Uniquely, guests whose rooms are not ready when they check in are provided access to a special lounge area in the health club where they can rest and shower. The value of this service cannot be overstated when arriving very early after overnight flights from North America. Four rooms are available for those with disabilities, but only two offer full access.

Calle Florida 1005 (overlooking Plaza San Martín), 1005 Buenos Aires. © **888/236-2427** in the U.S. or 11/4318-3000. Fax 11/4318-3008. www.marriott.com. 325 units. $210 double; from $260 suite. Rates include buffet breakfast. AE, DC, MC, V. Valet parking $9. Metro: San Martín. **Amenities:** 2 restaurants; cigar bar; excellent health club w/outdoor pool; exercise room; sauna; concierge; business center; salon; 24-hr. room service; massage service; laundry service; dry cleaning. *In room:* A/C, TV, minibar, coffeemaker, hair dryer, iron, safe.

Park Tower Buenos Aires (The Luxury Connection) ★★★   One of the most beautiful, and expensive, hotels in Buenos Aires, the Park Tower is connected to the Sheraton (see below) next door. The hotel combines traditional elegance with technological sophistication and offers impeccable service. Common areas as well as private rooms feature imported marble, Italian linens, lavish furniture, and works of art. The lobby, with its floor-to-ceiling windows, potted palms, and Japanese wall screens, contributes to a sense that this is the Pacific Rim rather than South America. Tastefully designed guest rooms are equipped with 29-inch color TVs, stereo systems with CD players, and cellphones. The rooms have stunning views of the city and the river. Guests also have access to 24-hour private butler service. The hotel boasts three restaurants, including Chrystal Garden, serving refined international cuisine, El Aljibe, cooking Argentine beef from the grill, and Cardinale, offering Italian specialties. The lobby lounge features piano music, a cigar bar, tea, cocktails, and special liquors.

Av. Leandro N. Alem 1193 (at Della Paolera), 1104 Buenos Aires. © **800/325-3589** in the U.S. or 11/4318-9100. Fax 11/4318-9150. www.luxurycollection.com/parktower. 181 units. From $400 double. AE, DC, MC, V. Valet parking $12. Metro: Retiro. **Amenities:** 3 restaurants; snack bar; piano bar; 2 pools; putting green; 2 lighted tennis courts; fitness center w/gym; wet and dry saunas; concierge; business center and secretarial services; limited room service; massage therapy; laundry service; dry cleaning. *In room:* A/C, TV/VCR, minibar, hair dryer, safe.

Sofitel 🐸🐸🐸   This Sofitel opened in late 2002, the first in Argentina. This classy French hotel, near Plaza San Martín, was created by combining two seven-story buildings to a 20-story neoclassical tower dating from 1929. A glass atrium lobby brings all the buildings together and serves as the entrance. The lobby resembles an enormous gazebo, with six ficus trees, a giant iron-and-bronze chandelier, an Art Nouveau clock, and Botticcino and black San Gabriel marble filling the space. Adjacent to the lobby you will find an elegant French restaurant, **Le Sud** (p. 101), and the early-20th-century-style Buenos Aires Café. The cozy library, with its grand fireplace and dark woods, offers guests an enchanting place to read outside their rooms. The rooms here vary in size, mixing modern French decor with traditional Art Deco styles; ask for one of the "deluxe" rooms or suites if you're looking for more space. Rooms are light-filled with beiges, yellows, and blacks; marble bathrooms have separate showers and bathtubs and feature Roger & Gallet amenities. Rooms above the eighth floor enjoy the best views, and the 17th-floor suite, L'Appartement, covers the whole floor. Many of the staff members speak Spanish, English, and French.

Arroyo 841–849 (at Juncal), 1007 Buenos Aires. © **800/793-4835** in the U.S. or 11/4909-1454. Fax 11/ 4909-1452. www.sofitel.com. 144 units. From $240 double; from $340 suite. AE, DC, MC, V. Valet parking $12. Metro: San Martín. **Amenities:** Restaurant; cafe; bar; indoor swimming pool; fitness center; concierge; business center; 24-hr. room service; laundry service; dry cleaning. *In room:* A/C, TV, minibar, hair dryer, safe.

EXPENSIVE

Claridge Hotel 🐸   The Claridge is living testimony to the once-close ties between England and Argentina. The grand entrance, with its imposing Ionic columns, mimics a London terrace apartment, and the lobby was renovated in 2002 in a classical style with colored marbles. Guest rooms are spacious, tastefully decorated, and equipped with all the amenities expected of a five-star hotel. The restaurant's hunting-themed wood-paneled interior is a registered city landmark, and offers a good-value menu with carefully prepared international food for as little as $8 as well as an inviting breakfast buffet, which is included in the room rate. Because it occasionally hosts conventions, the Claridge can become very busy. The rates at this hotel can go down significantly when booking promotions via the website, pushing it into the moderate category, so check the prices before making any decisions.

Tucumán 535 (at San Martín), 1049 Buenos Aires. © **11/4314-7700.** Fax 11/4314-8022. www.claridge. com.ar. 165 units. $235 double; from $355 suite. Rates include buffet breakfast. AE, DC, MC, V. Valet parking $6. Metro: Florida. **Amenities:** Restaurant; bar; health club w/heated outdoor pool; exercise room; sauna; concierge; business center; 24-hr. room service; massage service; laundry service; dry cleaning. *In room:* A/C, TV, minibar, safe.

Meliá Buenos Aires Boutique Hotel 🐸🐸   Within easy walking distance of Plaza San Martín and Calle Florida, the Meliá is among the best of the city's four-star hotels. Spacious guest rooms colored in soft earth tones feature overstuffed chairs, soundproof windows, and marble bathrooms. Large desks, two phone lines, and available cellphones make this a good choice for business travelers. The staff offers friendly, relaxed service. The Meliá has a small Spanish restaurant and bar.

Reconquista 945 (at Paraguay), 1003 Buenos Aires. ☏ **11/4891-3800.** Fax 11/4891-3834. www.solmelia. com. 125 units. $120 double; from $190 suite. Rates include buffet breakfast. AE, DC, MC, V. Parking $4. Metro: San Martín. **Amenities:** Restaurant; bar; exercise room; concierge; business services; 24-hr. room service; laundry service; dry cleaning. *In room:* A/C, TV, minibar, hair dryer, safe.

Sheraton Buenos Aires Hotel and Convention Center ☆

The enormous Sheraton houses one of the main convention centers in Buenos Aires. Situated in the heart of the business, shopping, and theater district, it's an ideal location for business travelers and tourists. Guest rooms are typical for a large American chain—well equipped, but lacking in charm. What the hotel lacks in intimacy, however, it makes up for in the wide range of services offered to guests regardless of whether they're in town for business or tourism. It shares three restaurants with the neighboring Park Tower Buenos Aires (see above), and its "Neptune" pool and fitness center are among the best in the city.

Av. San Martín 1225 (at Libertador), 1104 Buenos Aires. ☏ **11/4318-9000.** Fax 11/4318-9353. www. sheraton.com. 741 units. $260 double; from $360 suite. AE, DC, MC, V. Valet parking $12. Metro: Retiro. **Amenities:** 3 restaurants; snack bar; piano bar; 2 pools; putting green; 2 lighted tennis courts; fitness center w/gym; wet and dry saunas; concierge; activities desk; car-rental desk; business center; shopping arcade; salon; 24-hr. room service; massage therapy; babysitting; laundry service; dry cleaning. *In room:* A/C, TV, high-speed Internet, minibar, hair dryer, safe.

MODERATE

Amerian Buenos Aires Park Hotel ☆☆ *(Finds)*

This hotel is sometimes simply referred to as the Amerian Reconquista, since this Argentine chain now has several locations in Buenos Aires. One of the best four-star hotels in the city, the modern Amerian is a good bet for tourists as well as business travelers, and it has become a real bargain during the peso crisis, dropping to about half its original price. The warm atrium lobby looks more like California than Argentina, and the highly qualified staff offers personalized service. Soundproof rooms are elegantly appointed with wood, marble, and granite, and all boast comfortable beds, chairs, and work areas. The suites, located on their own floor, come with whirlpool bathtubs. Many services are not directly provided by the hotel, such as massage and babysitting, but can be handled on request. The hotel is just blocks away from Calle Florida, Plaza San Martín, and the Teatro Colón.

Reconquista 699 (at Viamonte), 1003 Buenos Aires. ☏ **11/4317-5100.** Fax 11/4317-5101. www.amerian. com. 152 units, including 14 suites. $96 double; from $145 suite. Rates include buffet breakfast. AE, DC, MC, V. Parking $4. Metro: Florida. **Amenities:** Restaurant and pub; exercise room; sauna; concierge; business center; limited room service; laundry service; dry cleaning. *In room:* A/C, TV, minibar, coffeemaker (in suites only).

Aspen Towers ☆☆

Built in 1995, the Aspen Towers is one of the city's newer and more refined hotels. Its 13-floor tower is contemporary in design, with a light-filled atrium lobby, elegant restaurant, and inviting rooftop pool. Guest rooms are small but classically decorated, with faux-antique furniture and soft-colored linens. All rooms feature marble bathrooms with whirlpool tubs—something you're unlikely to find anywhere else in the city for this price. The hotel is popular with Brazilians, Chileans, and Americans, and lies within easy walking distance of downtown's attractions.

Paraguay 857 (at Suipacha), 1057 Buenos Aires. ☏ **11/4313-1919.** Fax 11/4313-2662. www.aspentowers. com.ar. 105 units. $135–$175 double. Rates include buffet breakfast. AE, DC, MC, V. Parking $4. Metro: San Martín. **Amenities:** Restaurant; cafe; rooftop pool; exercise room; sauna; concierge; business center; limited room service; laundry service; dry cleaning. *In room:* A/C, TV, minibar.

Dolmen Hotel ☆

This four-star hotel's central location in the Microcentro, 1 block from Plaza San Martín, offers two things you usually do not find in this price category—quiet and a heated indoor swimming pool—and so is known for these two elements. The rooms are not the largest, nor are they the nicest, decorated in bright florals and blonde woods. Still, you'll find desk/vanity combinations and a single control panel over the bed for all lights and the air-conditioning unit. Bathrooms are of a good size, with spacious counters, and are well stocked with supplies. Surrounded by buildings of the same size, you won't get great views of the city from most of the rooms. A few of the rooms are also suitable for those with disabilities. Suites offer considerably more space, and since they cost only a little more than the standard room, they are worth springing for. Head upstairs to the pool and gym area for the best views from this glass-enclosed space. The hotel offers free parking in a building next door and free Internet in its business center, though there is no in-room access. The lobby bar, set back deeply in a space behind the concierge, offers another quiet retreat, with a splashy marble-and-brass decor.

Suipacha 1079 (at Santa Fe), 1003 Buenos Aires. ℂ **11/4315-7117**. Fax 11/4315-6666. www.hoteldolmen. com.ar. 146 units, including 22 suites. From $103 double; from $115 suite. Rates include buffet breakfast. AE, MC, V. Free parking. Metro: San Martín. **Amenities:** Restaurant; bar; small heated indoor swimming pool; small health club; sauna; concierge; business center; 24-hr. room service; laundry service; dry cleaning. *In room:* A/C, TV, minibar, hair dryer, safe.

Holiday Inn Express 𝔾   This hotel enjoys a convenient Microcentro location close to Puerto Madero and its restaurants and nightlife. Although there are no room service, concierge, or bellhops, the hotel is friendly, modern, and inexpensive. Guest rooms have large, firm beds, ample desk space, and 27-inch cable TVs; half of them boast river views. Coffee and tea are served 24 hours a day, and the buffet breakfast is excellent.

Av. Leandro N. Alem 770 (at Viamonte), 1057 Buenos Aires. ℂ **11/4311-5200**. Fax 11/4311-5757. www. holiday-inn.com. 116 units. From $140 double. Children under 18 stay free in parent's room. Rates include buffet breakfast. AE, DC, MC, V. Free parking. Metro: L. N. Alem. **Amenities:** Deli; exercise room; whirlpool; sauna; business center. *In room:* A/C, TV.

Hotel Colón   This hotel is in the heart of the city, on Avenida 9 de Julio overlooking the Obelisco, which gives guests here convenient access to virtually all of the city's metro lines. Corner rooms are more spacious, and many of the very large suites come with terraces. The decor varies throughout, and renovations are ongoing in this property, opened in 1984 in an older building. As such, some rooms are hit-or-miss: Some come with very sleek modern interiors, others traditional, but the color theme throughout is creamy white, giving a luminescence to some of the rooms. Double-glazed windows mean the noise is blocked out in spite of its busy surroundings, but don't worry about oversleeping, as each room comes with an alarm clock. Bathrooms are very large, and some of the suite bathrooms have Jacuzzis. The restaurant offers international cuisine and a wraparound view overlooking the Obelisco. Lifeguards oversee the medium-size heated rooftop pool, but this amenity's location in the back of the building means there is no view from up here. A small business center offers Internet access at roughly $1.35 per half-hour, but rooms have only dial-up service.

Carlos Pellegrini 507 (at Corrientes), 1009 Buenos Aires. ℂ **11/4320-3500**. Fax 11/4320-3507. www.colon-hotel.com.ar. 173 units, including 28 suites. From $90 double; from $130 suite. Rates include buffet breakfast. AE, DC, MC, V. Parking $4. Metro: Carlos Pellegrini or 9 de Julio. **Amenities:** Restaurant; bar; medium-size heated swimming pool; small health club; concierge; business center; 24-hr. room service; laundry service; dry cleaning. *In room:* A/C, TV, minibar, hair dryer, safe.

Hotel Crillon ✦ This over-50-year-old French-style hotel enjoys an outstanding location adjacent to Plaza San Martín, next to some of the city's best sights and shops. After completing a renovation in 2002, the Crillon is more comfortable, its guest rooms refitted with furniture and linens. A business center, racquetball and squash courts, a gym, and a sauna have been added as well. The hotel is popular with European and Brazilian business travelers, and offers high-tech conveniences such as wireless Internet access and cellphones, which can be rented through the concierge. Deluxe rooms enjoy views of calles Santa Fe and Esmeralda; the suites (with Jacuzzis) overlook Plaza San Martín. Stay away from interior rooms, which have no views. The hotel staff is extremely helpful.

Av. Santa Fe 796 (at Plaza San Martín), 1059 Buenos Aires. ✆ **11/4310-2000.** Fax 11/4310-2020. www.hotelcrillon.com.ar. 96 units. $95 double; $150 suite. Rates include buffet breakfast. AE, DC, MC, V. Valet parking $5. Metro: San Martín. **Amenities:** Restaurant; bar; concierge; business services; 24-hr. room service; laundry service; dry cleaning. *In room:* A/C, TV, wireless Internet access, minibar, hair dryer, safe.

Hotel Reconquista Plaza ✦ Near busy Calle Florida, this hotel provides a good location and clean, modern amenities. The decor is harvest gold with dark wooden trims, and all rooms have enormous rounded windows looking out onto the street. In spite of their name, suites are not true suites but oversize rooms partially separated by a large wardrobe unit. A sleeper couch in this area provides extra bed space. Some suites have enormous terraces, with views overlooking the Microcentro. Though the balconies are wonderful amenities, the hotel unfortunately does not provide chairs and tables for enjoying them. All rooms have tub/shower combinations, but the tubs are small in the standard rooms. Suite bathrooms are equipped with whirlpools. Double-glazing on the windows locks out noise, an important consideration in this area. Staff is exceptionally friendly and helpful. High-speed Internet access is available from all rooms for about $3 per day, and desks provide a workspace. For the money, this hotel is a good option for business travelers who do not need full services and want a convenient central location. In-room safes are oversize, providing space for a laptop. A small gym and sauna are also part of the offering, and access to a pool can be arranged, but is not available on-site. Cat lovers who travel with their pets are in luck, but dog owners will have to leave the canine at home.

Reconquista 602 (at Tucumán), 1003 Buenos Aires. ✆ **11/4311-4600.** Fax 11/4311-3302. www.reconquistaplaza.com.ar. 60 units, including 9 suites. From $90 double; from $110 suite. Rates include buffet breakfast. AE, MC, V. Parking $4. Metro: Florida. **Amenities:** Restaurant; bar; small health club; sauna; concierge; business center; 24-hr. room service; laundry service. *In room:* A/C, TV, minibar, coffeemaker, hair dryer, large safe.

Howard Johnson Florida Street ✦✦ *(Value* Having taken over this property from Courtyard by Marriott, this Howard Johnson is an excellent choice for travelers who don't require many special services. It has a great location off Calle Florida near Plaza San Martín, with access through a shopping-and-restaurant gallery in the hotel's ground level. Guest rooms come equipped with sleeper chairs (in addition to bed!), large desks and dressers, and well-appointed bathrooms. Rooms are of an above average size in this category. Each room has two phones, and local calls and Internet use are free—a rarity in Buenos Aires. There's a small, airy cafe and bar in the lobby, with additional food served in the gallery below. There are four small budget-priced function rooms available for business and social events off the lobby. The hotel also advertises extensively as gay-friendly accommodations. There is no pool or health club on premises, but access is offered free of charge to a nearby facility.

Calle Florida 944 (at Alvear), 1005 Buenos Aires. ℂ 11/4891-9200. Fax 11/4891-9208. www.hojoar.com. 77 units. $108 double. Rates include buffet breakfast. AE, DC, MC, V. Metro: San Martín. Small pets accepted for fee (about $35). **Amenities:** Restaurant; bar; conference center; business services; 24-hr. room service; laundry service; dry cleaning. *In room:* A/C, TV, high-speed Internet, minibar, coffeemaker, hair dryer, iron, large safe.

Lafayette Hotel ☆ *Kids* The Lafayette Hotel is a good value for a mid-price-range hotel, and is popular with European and Brazilian travelers. The rooms are spacious (some are even large enough to accommodate an entire family), exceedingly clean, and well maintained. Each has a desk and all rooms have Wi-Fi Internet access. A small combination meeting room and business center has 24-hour Internet access on one computer. Bathrooms are hit-or-miss—some are large, others seem like jammed-together afterthoughts. Street-side rooms are great for people-watching in the Microcentro, though you should expect some noise. Back rooms are quieter but offer no views. The location is ideal for Microcentro's Lavalle and Florida street shopping and is only a few blocks from the subway. The buffet breakfast is generous and varied, offering made-to-order omelets on request. The hotel is built in two parts with two different elevator bays, so if staying with friends or family, request rooms in the same division of the hotel.

Reconquista 546 (at Viamonte), 1003 Buenos Aires. ℂ 11/4393-9081. Fax 11/4322-1611. www.lafayette hotel.com.ar. 82 units, including 6 suites. From $65 double; from $80 suite. Rates include generous buffet breakfast. AE, DC, MC, V. Metro: Florida. **Amenities:** Restaurant; bar; concierge; small business center; limited room service; laundry service; dry cleaning. *In room:* A/C, TV, Wi-Fi, minibar, hair dryer, safe.

Loi Suites Esmeralda ☆ *Kids* Previously a Comfort Inn, this Loi Suites (part of a small local chain) lies 3 blocks from Plaza San Martín and the pedestrian walking street Calle Florida. Spacious rooms can accommodate up to six people, making this a good choice for families traveling with children. Renovated in 2001, rooms are decorated in soft whites with kitchenettes and microwaves, and all come with cellphones. The hotel also offers complimentary access to a gym and swimming pool located off-property. A more upscale (five-star) Loi Suites is in Recoleta (p. 81).

Marcelo T. de Alvear 842 (at Esmeralda), 1058 Buenos Aires. ℂ 11/4131-6800. Fax 11/4131-6888. www.loisuites.com.ar. 103 units. $120 double; $205 suite. Rates include buffet breakfast. AE, DC, MC, V. Parking $4. Metro: San Martín. **Amenities:** Restaurant; bar; room service; laundry service. *In room:* A/C, TV, minibar, safe.

NH Florida This is a simple, well-located, four-star hotel less than a block away from the Galerías Pacífico. It was opened in 2001 in an older apart-hotel, and the old original building was completely gutted as if starting from scratch. Views are not the focus at NH Florida, with buildings of the same size surrounding it, but the rooms are larger than most in this price category. Almost all have wood floors with small carpets, adding a simple elegance to the modern decor. All rooms have free high-speed Internet access and a good workstation. Suites are much larger with large doors to wall off the guest areas from the sitting room. At the time of this writing, this hotel had plans to expand by adding new rooms on the first floor. The hotel offers many good services, but its main disadvantage when compared to other accommodations in this category is its lack of a gym or pool. However, for a fee of about $3 per day, clients can have access to nearby facilities. With 11 rooms for those with disabilities, and with its Microcentro location, this is among the most accessible of the hotels I know in Buenos Aires, but I recommend calling and asking specific questions about your disabilities before staying here.

San Martín 839 (at Córdoba), 1004 Buenos Aires. © **11/4321-9850.** Fax 11/4321-9875. www.nh-hotels. com. 148 units, including 20 suites. $112 double; from $135 suite. Rates include buffet breakfast. AE, DC, MC, V. Valet parking $4. Metro: San Martín. **Amenities:** Restaurant; bar; concierge; business center; limited room service; babysitting; laundry service; dry cleaning. *In room:* A/C, TV, minibar, hair dryer, safe.

Obelisco Center Suites Hotel and Apartments

As its name implies, the location of this Argentine-owned hotel puts you right in the center of the city, close to the Obelisco. However, the property does not directly overlook this monument, and only a few rooms offer views of it. The hotel is in two parts, an older apartment complex and the newer hotel section. Both are accessed through the same lobby. Very big on security issues, the hotel has several fire protection procedures proudly in place. Rooms are large and have a bright, flowery decor. Bathroom countertops come with a lot of surface space and the tubs are unusually deep. Whirlpool tubs are available in the large superior rooms, which also have terraces with views to the Obelisco. Though the hotel is near all the major subway lines and theaters, the area and the rooms facing the street can be noisy. Free high-speed Internet access is available in the small business center, which is open 24 hours a day. A gym, sauna, spa, and pool are available for free in a large shared facility a block away from the hotel. The apartments have small efficiency kitchens and come in various size and bedroom combinations. All are simply decorated, with a bright, open feel.

Av. Roque Sáenz Peña 991 (Diagonal Norte at Av. 9 de Julio), 1035 Buenos Aires. © **11/4326-0909.** Fax 11/ 4326-0269. www.obeliscohotel.com.ar. 50 units, 51 apts. From $79–$170 double; $79 apt. Rates include buffet breakfast. AE, DC, MC, V. Parking $4. Metro: Carlos Pellegrini or Diagonal Norte. **Amenities:** Restaurant; bar; concierge; conference center; limited room service; laundry service; dry cleaning. *In room:* A/C, TV, kitchen (in apts), minibar, hair dryer, safe.

The Regente Palace Hotel

Walking into the four-star Regente is like stepping back into the disco era, with its 1970s-style brass-and-neutral-toned rounded brick decor. Plus, the porthole windows in the building's hallways might make you think you're on the *Love Boat*. This place is funky but fashionable in a nonironic, retro kind of way. Even though many of the furnishings seem outdated, all room carpets were replaced in late 2004. Rooms can be on the small side, but all come with desks/vanities as work surfaces. Suites have been renovated in gray tones, and some have Jacuzzi bathtubs. What sets this hotel apart is the brilliant amount of light that comes through the floor-to-ceiling windows that form a virtual glass wall to the outside. The windows are double glazed, and once shut, they silence the sound of the street. Guests can use the hotel's free Internet access from the lobby business center. A small gym is down in the basement, and there is event space for about 400 people in three rooms. The restaurant area, where breakfast is served, is on a brass mezzanine with catwalks suspended over the lobby area. A cascading waterfall in this area provides a pleasant atmosphere. You'll find a few shops and travel services here also. Free parking is provided. Because of steps throughout the building, including in passages leading to elevators, this is not an ideal location for people with limited mobility.

Suipacha 964 (at Córdoba), 1008 Buenos Aires. © **11/4328-6800.** Fax 11/4328-7460. www.regente.com. 137 units, including 28 suites. From $67 double; from $82 suite. Rates include buffet breakfast. AE, MC, V. Free parking. Metro: Lavalle. **Amenities:** Restaurant; bar; small health club; concierge; business center; shopping gallery; 24-hr. room service; laundry service; dry cleaning. *In room:* A/C, TV, minibar, hair dryer, large safe.

INEXPENSIVE

V&S Hostel ★★ Value

Privately owned but part of an Argentine network of hostels, V&S Hostel provides exceptionally friendly service in a convenient

Microcentro location. The hostel is inside a gorgeous turn-of-the-20th-century apartment building. The inexpensive rooms are accented by lavish touches like molded plaster, curved doorway entries, stained-glass ornamentation, and balconies throughout overlooking the Dorrego monument. The owner, Cristina, is stylish and charming and is always happy to offer advice to her clients on where to go and what not to miss. Five private bedrooms with attached shower-stall bathrooms are also available. A light continental breakfast is served, and a kitchen is available for making meals. A quiet library, a TV sitting room, and a patio dining area are some of the areas where guests can mingle. Several computers are also available for hopping onto the Internet. There are no washing machines, but a space is provided for hand-washing clothes and an iron is available. This place is a great value option for young people and other bargain travelers, especially since unlike other hostels, there is air-conditioning here. The concierge desk is staffed only from 8am to 1am, but guests arriving earlier or later who have reservations can make arrangements outside of these hours. There's 24-hour access for all guests, with no lockout period.

Viamonte 887 (at Esmeralda), 1053 Buenos Aires. © **11/4322-0994**. Fax 11/4327-5131. www.hostel club.com or www.argentinahostels.com. 60 bed spaces including 10 in 5 bedrooms with attached bathroom. From $8 per bed; $23–$27 per private room. Rates include continental breakfast. No credit cards. No parking. Metro: Lavalle. **Amenities:** Concierge; Internet center; lockers; shared kitchen. *In room:* Hair dryer.

3 Monserrat

The neighborhood of Monserrat borders San Telmo and is more easily accessed by subway. There are also more four- and five-star hotels here, so staying in Monserrat might be a compromise for people who want San Telmo's romance but a more convenient location for subways and shopping in the Microcentro. Monserrat is distinguished by old turn-of-the-20th-century buildings similar to those in San Telmo, as well as enormous midcentury fascist-style government buildings where it borders the Plaza de Mayo. It can be desolate and a little dangerous in parts of Monserrat at night, so use caution near your hotel.

For a map of the hotels listed in this section, see the "Where to Stay in Central Buenos Aires" map on p. 64.

EXPENSIVE

InterContinental Hotel Buenos Aires ★★★ The InterContinental opened in 1994, and despite its modernity, this luxurious tower hotel was built in one of the city's oldest districts, Monserrat, and decorated in the Argentine style of the 1930s. The marble lobby is colored in beige and apricot tones, heavy black and brass metal accents, and handsome carved-wood furniture and antiques inlaid with agates and other stones. The lobby's small Café de las Luces sometimes offers evening tango performances. The InterContinental is also the only five-star hotel within walking distance of the San Telmo tango district. The **Restaurante y Bar Mediterráneo** (p. 106) serves healthy, gourmet Mediterranean cuisine on an outdoor patio under a glassed-in trellis. Stop by the Brasco & Duane wine bar for an exclusive selection of Argentine vintages. Guest rooms continue the 1930s theme, with elegant black woodwork, comfortable king-size beds, marble-top nightstands, large desks, and black-and-white photographs of Buenos Aires. Marble bathrooms have separate showers and bathtubs and feature extensive amenities.

Moreno 809 (at Piedras), 1091 Buenos Aires. © **11/4340-7100**. Fax 11/4340-7119. www.buenos-aires. interconti.com. 312 units. $150 double; from $300 suite. AE, DC, MC, V. Parking $10. Metro: Moreno. **Amenities:** Restaurant; wine bar; lobby bar; health club w/indoor pool; exercise room; sauna; concierge;

business center; 24-hr. room service; massage service; laundry service; dry cleaning; executive floors; sun deck. *In room:* A/C, TV, dataport, minibar, hair dryer, safe.

NH City Hotel ⭐⭐   The Spanish-owned NH hotel chain opened this property in June 2001 in the old City Hotel, an Art Deco masterpiece that was once one of Buenos Aires's grandest hotels. In a city with few buildings in this style, its jagged ziggurat exterior calls to mind buildings more associated with Jazz Age New York than Argentina. Its lobby has been meticulously renovated, a combination of Art Deco and Collegiate Gothic popular in that time period, with simple beige and brown furnishings offsetting the burnished woods, stained-glass ceiling, and honey-colored marble floors. Many of the large rooms are on the dark side, with a masculine combination of simple materials in red and black. Others are brighter, with white walls and burnt-sienna offsets. All the bathrooms are spacious and luminous, with large counters and an excellent range of toiletries. The safes are among the biggest in the city, with ample room for laptops. Retreating to the rooftop, with its small outdoor heated pool, is a delight, and attendants make sure you feel comfortable as you take in the fantastic view of the river and Uruguay on a clear day, as well as the nearby Plaza de Mayo and the domes of the buildings lining Diagonal Norte. A small health club, complete with a spa, sauna, and Jacuzzi, is also on this level. You can get a massage here or arrange to have one in your room. If you're lucky enough to be in the executive area, it's on this level, too. Of all the hotels near the political center of the city, this is the best, though views from many of the rooms leave something to be desired, while rooms in the back of the hotel contain no view at all due to the ongoing construction of an adjacent building. You have a choice of high-speed Internet or Wi-Fi connections within the rooms, and the small business center also has free 24-hour access through its two computers. A small conference center of meeting rooms for functions of up to 400 people rounds out the business offerings. There are two restaurants in the building. One is casual, while the other, named Clue, is a large, minimalist space with a touch of 1930s style to it. Its formal rules forbid patrons from dining in shorts.

Bolívar 160 (at Alsina), Buenos Aires 1066. ✆ 11/4121-6464. Fax 11/4121-6450. www.nh-hotels.com. 303 units, including 50 suites. From $140 double; from $194 suite. Generous buffet breakfast included. AE, DC, MC, V. Parking $12. Metro: Bolívar or Plaza de Mayo. **Amenities:** 2 restaurants; bar; small gym facility w/open-air pool deck; spa; sauna; concierge; business center; 24-hr. room service; babysitting; laundry service; dry cleaning; executive floor; conference center. *In room:* TV, high-speed Internet access and Wi-Fi, minibar, hair dryer, large safe.

MODERATE

Grand Boulevard Hotel ⭐ *Value*   The Grand Boulevard offers a location similar to the InterContinental (see above) at a much lower price, while still offering a convenient set of services for both business and leisure travelers. Double-glazed German-made windows lock out noise from Avenida 9 de Julio while offering incredible views of that street and the river from higher floors. The restaurant/bar is open 24 hours, and it offers both international cuisine and a special spa menu of light, nutritious foods, detailing caloric content for health-conscious travelers. All rooms offer desks and vanities of varying sizes, and a single bedside panel that controls all room lights. The Argentine Queen beds are slightly larger than an American full, and are comfortable but not the firmest, and all rooms have large closets. High-speed Internet access is free in all rooms, as well as in the 24-hour business center. Subway access is easy, and with the *autopista* (highway) nearby, this is also the city's closest four-star hotel to the airport. Some of the rooms here have limited wheelchair accessibility. A small, glassed-in meeting-room space sits on the roof of the building.

Bernardo de Irogoyen 432 (at Belgrano), 1072 Buenos Aires. © **11/5222-9000.** Fax 11/5222-9000, ext. 2141. www.grandboulevardhotel.com. 85 units. $80 double; from $135 suite. AE, DC, MC, V. Free parking. Metro: Moreno. **Amenities:** Restaurant; bar; small health club w/personal trainer; sauna; concierge; business center; 24-hr. room service; massage service; babysitting; laundry service; dry cleaning. *In room:* A/C, TV, minibar, hair dryer, safe.

Hotel Castelar ★★ *Moments* Opened in 1929, the Hotel Castelar is considered a historic highlight of Buenos Aires, as it was once an important stopping point for Spanish-language literary stars during Argentina's golden years as an intellectual center in the 1930s. It is most famously associated with Spanish playwright Federico García Lorca, who lived here for several months in 1934, taking refuge during the Spanish Civil War. A plaque at the entrance commemorates his stay. The room he lived in has also been preserved, though with a slight sense of kitsch. The lobby retains much of the brass, marble, and heavy plaster elements from its opening. These details extend into the dining area, which, when it was a *confitería* (cafe), was as culturally important as the Café Tortoni (p. 104) farther down Avenida de Mayo. Mario Palanti, the eccentric architect of the nearby Palacio Barolo (p. 143), designed the Castelar. While the golden years of Avenida de Mayo are long over, the hotel allows you to bask in at least some of the charm that remains. The Castelar's spa in the hotel's basement is free for all guests of the hotel (men and women are separated in this area), with additional fees for various services. Enormous, full of white Carrara marble, and built in the Turkish style, it is worth paying the entrance fee of about $8 just to see the place, even if you are not a guest of the hotel. Renovations in all of the units were completed in early 2005; all now have new color patterns, new mattresses, and comfortable furniture. The old wooden touches, speckled glass, and tiled floors in the bathrooms have been retained through the remodeling. The rooms are not very large, but the setup—a small antechamber with the bedroom to one side, the bathroom to the other—adds a sense of privacy to the spaces, even when shared by a couple. Suites are similar, but with an added living area. There are no true rooms for those with disabilities, but some units have slight accommodations such as wider spaces and a few bars in the bathroom.

Av. de Mayo (at Lima and Av. 9 de Julio), 1152 Buenos Aires. © **11/4383-5000.** Fax 11/4383-8388. www. castelarhotel.com.ar. 151 units, including 70 suites. $59 double; $86 suite. Rates include buffet breakfast. AE, DC, MC, V. Parking $3. Metro: Lima. **Amenities:** Restaurant; bar; extensive spa; small health club; business services; limited room service; laundry service; dry cleaning. *In room:* A/C, TV, minibar.

Hotel Nogaró ★ Hotel Nogaró's grand marble staircase leads to a variety of guest rooms noteworthy for their comfort and quiet. Deluxe rooms boast hardwood floors, high ceilings, and small but modern bathrooms with whirlpool tubs in the suites. Standard rooms, while smaller, are pleasant too, with large closets and a bit of modern art. The hotel is a good bet for people who want to stay slightly outside the city center, although you should be careful in Monserrat at night. The staff will arrange sightseeing tours upon request. In keeping with the increasing pricing trend in Buenos Aires, this hotel is no longer the bargain it was, nearly tripling its former rates.

Av. Julio A. Roca 562 (at Bolívar), 1067 Buenos Aires. © **11/4331-0091.** Fax 11/4331-6791. www. nogarobue.com.ar. 140 units. From $132 double; from $145 suite. Rates include buffet breakfast. AE, DC, MC, V. Parking $4. Metro: Bolivar. **Amenities:** Restaurant; business center; 24-hr. room service; babysitting; laundry service. *In room:* A/C, TV, minibar.

INEXPENSIVE

Yira Yira Hostel ⭐ This place is perfect for young travelers and those seeking a bargain in a great location. Yira Yira takes it name from an old tango song, appropriate enough for a place that, though in Monserrat, puts you only blocks from the tango neighborhood of San Telmo. This is a very clean youth hostel, opened in May 2004, with excellent services, considering the price. A small portion of the price you'll pay here goes to the Asociación Madres de Plaza de Mayo (p. 143), so you can also feel that you're doing something socially beneficial by staying here. There is a main living-room space, complete with a TV, where many young people gather with friends, as well as a self-service bar, which even has champagne on offer. Breakfast is included, and the kitchen is available for public use. A small terrace sits outside of the living-room area, with an *asado* (grill) where barbecues are often held. The staff is very helpful and proud of this new hostel. They arrange tours of Buenos Aires with the young and adventurous in mind, such as city biking trips. One private bedroom with attached bathroom is available for up to four people. The remaining spaces all share bathrooms.

Defensa 377 (at Belgrano), 1066 Buenos Aires. © 11/4311-4600. Fax 11/4311-3302. www.yirayirahostel. com.ar. 53 bed spaces, including 4 in 1 private room. From $7 per bed; $25 for private room. Rates include continental breakfast. AE, MC, V. No parking. Metro: Bolívar. **Amenities:** Bar; small gym; sauna; concierge; laundry service; Internet; shared kitchen. *In room:* A/C, lockers.

4 San Telmo

I find San Telmo both romantic and the most authentic of all the touristic neighborhoods in Buenos Aires. However, there aren't many hotels in this area, and most of what I have listed here are hostels catering to the young, the bohemian, and the absolute tango fanatic. San Telmo is rapidly becoming gentrified, so it's nowhere near as dangerous as it was in the past, but you still need to be more cautious here at night than you do in other parts of the city. If you can live without certain luxuries, focusing more on absorbing the extreme Porteño flavor of the area, I highly recommend a night or two here. The young and adventurous may very well want to spend their entire time in Buenos Aires staying in San Telmo. The area is accessed by stations for Subte C running along Avenida 9 de Julio, and these can be a slightly long walk away from some of San Telmo's accommodations.

For a map of the hotels listed in this section, see the "Where to Stay in Central Buenos Aires" map on p. 64.

INEXPENSIVE

El Lugar Gay ⭐ This is Buenos Aires's first exclusively gay hotel, but it is only open to men. Literally, its name means "the Gay Place." El Lugar Gay is located inside of a historic, turn-of-the-20th-century building less than a block from Plaza Dorrego, the heart of San Telmo. It has a homey feel, with industrial chic well blended into a century-old interior. Nestor and Juan, the gay couple who own the building, operate with a friendly staff, but most do not speak much English. Ask for the rooms in the back with the beautiful views of the Church of San Telmo, which is just to the side of the building. The rooms are small and sparse, and some share bathrooms with adjacent rooms, but one group has a Jacuzzi. If you're staying here, you'll need to supply your own shampoo and hair dryer, as they are not provided in the bathrooms. Rooms do not have phones, but some have small desks or tables for use as workstations. Small in-room safes, TVs, and air-conditioning complete the rooms. There is 24-hour free use of an

Internet station in the hotel's public area. The continental breakfast is served late, beginning at 9am, but they will make accommodations if people have special needs. Several flights of narrow stairs leading to the hotel's lobby and the rooms might be a problem for people with limited mobility. The hotel becomes a de facto gay community center at times, with its small cafe and Sunday evening tango lessons (5–7pm) done by the gay tango group La Marshall. These are open to the public, so even if you don't stay here, you can still visit this hotel when in town.

Defensa 1120 (at Humberto I), 1102 Buenos Aires. ✆ **11/4300-4747**. www.lugargay.org. 7 units, some with shared bathroom. From $35–$50 double. Rates include continental breakfast. No credit cards. No parking. Metro: Independencia. **Amenities:** Restaurant; bar; business center. *In room:* A/C, TV, small safe, no phone.

Hostel Carlos Gardel ✪

If you can't get enough of Argentina's most famous tango singer Carlos Gardel in the tango clubs, then stay here, where a red wall full of his pictures is the first thing to greet you. This hostel is built into a renovated old house, and though it has been severely gutted, a few charming elements, like marble staircases, wall sconces, and colored glass windows remain. The location is also very new, having opened in March 2004. Two rooms with private bathrooms are available in this location, but at $43 are expensive considering the lack of amenities other than a bathroom. The staff is friendly, and a large TV room off of the concierge area allows for chatting with them and other patrons. A shared kitchen and an *asado* on the rooftop terrace provide more spaces for interacting. Towels and sheets are provided for guests, but of all the hostels in Buenos Aires, this seems to have the fewest number of bathrooms for the number of guests.

Carlos Calvo 579 (at Perú), 1102 Buenos Aires. ✆ **11/4307-2606**. www.hostelcarlosgardel.com.ar. 45 bed spaces including 10 in 2 private rooms with bathroom. From $5 per bed; $43 private room. Rates include continental breakfast. No credit cards. No parking. Metro: Independencia. **Amenities:** Self-service drink station; concierge; free Internet; shared kitchen; TV room. *In room:* Lockers.

Hostel Nómade ✪

Painted green on the outside and all over the inside, the clean and basic Hostel Nómade is in a charming little house a few blocks from Plaza Dorrego. There are several rooms with bunk beds scattered about, and three of the rooms can be rented privately, but none come with bathrooms. A TV room, complete with a pool table and self-service drink station, creates an environment for everyone to come back and share stories about their adventures in the city. The majority of the clients in this location are young Europeans, mostly Germans. Like most hostels, there do not seem to be enough bathrooms for all the beds in this place, but if you know hostel living, that's the way it usually is. A narrow staircase from the center of the house leads to the enormous rooftop terrace, complete with an *asado* (grill). Towels and sheets are provided for guests.

Carlos Calvo 430 (at Defensa), 1102 Buenos Aires. ✆ **11/4300-7641**. www.hostelnomade.com. 31 bed spaces, including 12 in 3 private rooms. From $6 per bed; $15 private room. Rates include continental breakfast. No credit cards. No parking. Metro: Independencia. **Amenities:** Self-service drink station; concierge; free Internet; shared kitchen; TV room. *In room:* Lockers.

Lina's Tango Guesthouse ✪✪✪ *(Finds)*

If you really want to expose yourself to the tango scene, this is the place to stay. Owner Lina Acuña, who originally hails from Colombia, opened this charming little spot in 1997. She is herself a tango dancer, and wanted to create a space where the tango community from around the world could come together, enjoy each other's company, and share in Buenos Aires's unique tango history. As an establishment owned by a woman, it's also a great place to stay for women traveling alone. Lina, who lives in the house, often goes with her guests on informal trips to *milongas* (tango halls) of San Telmo and other neighborhoods, offering a unique insider's view. The guesthouse's 1960s exterior hides the fact that the building dates from the turn of the 20th century. In the rooms off the back garden, the original doors and other elements remain. She has painted these in kitschy colors more reminiscent of the La Boca neighborhood, and vines and trees add to the authentic Porteño atmosphere. Guests and Lina's friends gather here for conversation, impromptu help with each other's dance techniques, and *asados* on holidays and weekends. Three of the eight guest rooms share bathrooms, and the rooms come in different sizes but are adequate for sharing if you are coming with a friend and want to double-up. Breakfast is included; there is also a small kitchen guests can use to cook their own meals and a washing machine for cleaning up clothes sweaty from a night of tango. Lina is most proud of the shelves she created in all the rooms for her guests' tango shoes. The downside of the place is that it is not a full-service hotel, so it doesn't have Internet access or in-room phones; the TV is in the shared living room; it can be noisy with people talking and dancing in the courtyard; and there is also the periodic barking of Lina's very friendly dog (but no other pets but hers are allowed). But if you're all about tango, so is Lina's Guesthouse, and this is where you should stay.

Estados Unidos 780 (at Piedras), 1011 Buenos Aires. ℰ 11/4361-6817 or 11/4300-7367. www.tango guesthouse.com.ar. 8 units, 5 with bathroom. $20–$50 double. Rates include continental breakfast. No credit cards. No parking. Metro: Independencia. **Amenities:** Self-service kitchen; self-service laundry; tango tours.

5 Recoleta

Most of the best and most convenient hotels are found in Recoleta and the Microcentro. Recoleta is more scenic and not quite as noisy as the Microcentro, but if you stay here, you'll probably find yourself spending more money on cabs, since the area is not accessible by any of the metro *(subte)* lines, except in areas bordering nearby Barrio Norte. Even though taxis don't cost very much in Buenos Aires, using them several times a day can add up. Of course, if you can afford to stay in Recoleta, then the extra cost of taxis might not be an issue for you! Public transportation aside, Recoleta is exceedingly beautiful, and staying here puts you close to the Recoleta Cemetery and Evita's grave as well as the parks and museums of nearby Palermo, which are best accessed by cab to begin with, no matter where you are coming from in the city.

There are no convenient metro stops to this neighborhood. For a map of the hotels in this section, see the "Where to Stay in Central Buenos Aires" map on p. 64.

VERY EXPENSIVE

Alvear Palace Hotel ⟨ℛℛℛ⟩   Located in the center of the upscale Recoleta district, the Alvear Palace is the most exclusive hotel in Buenos Aires and one of the top hotels in the world, continuously winning award surveys in international travel magazines. A gilded classical confection full of marble and bronze, the Alvear combines Empire- and Louis XV–style furniture with exquisite French decorative arts. After a long process, the historically important facade was restored in 2004 to its original glory. The illustrious guest list has included names like Antonio Banderas, Donatella Versace, the emperor of Japan, and Robert Duvall, to name a few. Guest rooms combine luxurious comforts, such as chandeliers, Egyptian cotton linens, and silk drapes, with modern conveniences such as touchscreen telephones that control all in-room functions. Each room is individually decorated according to color palates selected by the matriarch of the family who owns the hotel. All rooms come with personal butler service, cellphones that can be activated on demand, fresh flowers, and fruit baskets. Large marble bathrooms contain Hermès toiletries, and most have Jacuzzi tubs.

The Alvear Palace provides sharp, professional service, and the excellent concierge staff goes to great lengths to accommodate guest requests. As a hotel for the wealthy, the Alvear also often offers special packages related to events such as the annual polo championships in late November and early December. If it's your dream to stay here while in Buenos Aires but you don't think you can afford it, check the website, which sometimes offers discounts when occupancy is low. The Alvear Palace is home to one of the best restaurants in South America (**La Bourgogne;** p. 110). Kosher catering and dining is also available. Even if you are not staying here, I recommend coming for their afternoon lunch buffet in their palm-court-style lobby restaurant, L'Orangerie, which costs a relatively reasonable $25 for a very impressive spread. In addition to the high quality of the food, the Alvear has also selected an exceptionally attractive waitstaff to attend to those who dine here. All of this, within the confines of gilded columns, creates a very memorable dining experience.

Av. Alvear 1891 (at Ayacucho), 1129 Buenos Aires. ℂ **11/4808-2100.** Fax 11/4804-0034. www. alvearpalace.com. 210 units, including 85 "palace" rooms and 125 suites. From $300 double; from $475 suite. Rates include luxurious buffet breakfast. AE, DC, MC, V. No metro access. **Amenities:** 2 restaurants; bar; small health club; spa; concierge; elaborate business center; shopping arcade; 24-hr. room service; massage service; laundry service; dry cleaning; private butler service. *In room:* A/C, TV, high-speed Internet access and Wi-Fi, minibar, hair dryer, safe.

Four Seasons Hotel ⭐⭐⭐ *Kids*   In 2002 the Four Seasons took over the Park Hyatt, which was already one of the city's most luxurious properties. There are two parts to this landmark hotel—the 12-story "Park" tower housing the majority of the guest rooms, and the turn-of-the-20th-century Louis XIII–style "La Mansión," with seven elegant suites and a handful of private event rooms. A French-style garden and a pool separate the two buildings. This is the only outdoor garden pool in all of Recoleta, creating a resortlike feeling in the middle of the city. There's also a well-equipped health club on-premises offering spa treatments including a wine massage and facial. The spa was renovated in mid-2004, and renovations continue on all the rooms to convert them from Hyatt treatments to Four Seasons style. The rooms are all large and come with simple dark furnishings contrasted with light carpeting and other material. The hotel's restaurant, **Galani** (p. 111), serves excellent Mediterranean cuisine in a casual environment. Spacious guest rooms offer atypical amenities like walk-in closets, wet and dry bars, stereo systems, and cellphones. Large marble bathrooms contain separate showers and water-jet bathtubs. People staying on the club floors enjoy exclusive check-in and checkout, additional in-room amenities including a printer, fax machine, and Argentine wine, and complimentary breakfast and evening cocktails. The attentive staff will assist you in arranging day tours of Buenos Aires, as well as access to golf courses, tennis, boating, and horseback riding. Kids receive bedtime milk and cookies.

Posadas 1086–88 (at Av. 9 de Julio), 1011 Buenos Aires. ℂ **800/819-5053** in the U.S. and Canada or 11/ 4321-1200. Fax 11/4321-1201. www.fourseasons.com. 165 units, including 49 suites (7 suites in La Mansión). $250 double; from $300 suite; $3,500 mansion suites. AE, DC, MC, V. Valet parking $10. No metro access. **Amenities:** Restaurant; lobby bar; heated outdoor pool; exercise room; health club; large spa, sauna; concierge; multilingual business center; 24-hr. room service; massage service; babysitting; laundry service; dry cleaning. *In room:* A/C, TV/VCR, high-speed Internet access and Wi-Fi, minibar, hair dryer, safe.

EXPENSIVE

Caesar Park *(Overrated* This classic hotel sits opposite Patio Bullrich, the city's most exclusive shopping mall. Guest rooms vary in size and amenities, but all have been tastefully appointed with fine furniture and elegant linens, marble bathrooms with separate bathtubs and showers, and entertainment centers with TVs and stereos. Larger rooms come with a fresh-fruit basket on the first night's stay. The art collection in the lobby and on the mezzanine is for sale, and there are a few boutique shops on the ground level. Although the hotel, part of a larger international chain, is a member of the Leading Hotels of the World, service is formal and not particularly warm.

Posadas 1232–46 (at Montevideo), 1014 Buenos Aires. © 800/745-8883 in the U.S. or 11/4819-1100. Fax 11/4819-1121. www.caesar-park.com. 170 units. $180 double; from $400 suite. Buffet breakfast included. AE, DC, MC, V. Free valet parking. No metro access. **Amenities:** Restaurant; 2 bars; small fitness center w/indoor pool and sauna; concierge; business center; 24-hr. room service; laundry service; dry cleaning. *In room:* A/C, TV, minibar, coffeemaker, hair dryer, safe.

Hotel Emperador 👤👤 Located on Avenida Libertador, this hotel is Spanish-owned, with a sister hotel in Madrid. It opened in 2001 a few blocks from the Patio Bullrich shopping center in an area some would call Retiro because it is near the train station complex, others Recoleta. The theme here is "Empire" with a modern update; a bust of Julius Caesar overlooks the concierge desk. The lobby evokes a sense of the Old World. Behind the main restaurant, the lobby opens onto a large overgrown patio that has a gazebo and outdoor seating. The English-hunting-lodge-style lobby bar is a place for ladies who lunch and businesspeople to gather for informal discussions. Rooms are very spacious, continuing the imperial theme. Royal-blue carpets with wreath patterns, and elegant furnishings with rich veneers, brass fittings, and gold velvet upholstery await the visitor. The suites, with their walls, multiple doors and entrances, and extra sinks, are ideal for doing business without an invasion of privacy in the sleeping quarters. All bathrooms are oversize, with cream and green marble, and are well stocked with fine supplies. Suite bathrooms are even larger, with separated tub and shower stalls. Each room comes equipped with a large desk and high-speed Internet and Wi-Fi access, which will cost you about $10 a day. The enormous and very impressive top-floor nuptial suites have kitchens. There are three wheelchair-accessible rooms available. The gym is small, very clean, and well lit, with a wet and dry sauna off to the side and separate areas for men and women. A medium-size heated indoor swimming pool is also here; with the space's modern columns, it tries to give the impression of a Roman bath.

Av. del Libertador 420 (at Suipacha), 1001 Buenos Aires. © 11/4131-4000. Fax 11/4131-3900. www.hotel-emperador.com.ar. 265 units, including 36 suites. $194 double; from $230 suite; $1,000 nuptial suite. Rates include buffet breakfast. AE, DC, MC, V. Valet parking $4. Metro: Retiro. **Amenities:** Restaurant; bar; small fitness center w/medium-size indoor heated pool and sauna; concierge; business center; 24-hr. room service; massage; babysitting; laundry service; dry cleaning; garden patio. *In room:* A/C, TV, high-speed Internet access and Wi-Fi, minibar, coffeemaker, hair dryer, safe.

Loi Suites 👤👤 Part of a small local hotel chain, the new Loi Suites Recoleta is a contemporary hotel with spacious rooms and personalized service. A palm-filled garden atrium and covered pool adjoin the lobby, which is bathed in various shades of white. Breakfast and afternoon tea are served in the "winter garden." Although the management uses the term "suites" rather loosely to describe rooms with microwaves, sinks, and small fridges, the hotel does in fact offer some traditional suites in addition to its more regular studio-style rooms.

Loi Suites lies just around the corner from Recoleta's trendy restaurants and bars, and the staff will provide information on city tours upon request.

Vicente López 1955 (at Ayacucho), 1128 Buenos Aires. ℭ 11/5777-8950. Fax 11/5777-8999. www. loisuites.com.ar. 112 units. From $200 double; from $300 suite. Rates include buffet breakfast. AE, DC, MC, V. Parking $4. No metro access. **Amenities:** Restaurant; indoor pool; exercise room; sauna; small business center; limited room service; laundry service; dry cleaning. *In room:* A/C, TV, minibar, fridge, hair dryer, safe.

MODERATE

Bel Air Hotel   Opened in late 2000, the intimate Bel Air has the ambience of a boutique hotel but is no longer the bargain it once was. Although the lobby and building's exterior are more extravagant than the rooms, guests can look forward to comfortable, quiet accommodations. Superior rooms are bigger than standards and only slightly more expensive, while suites have separate sitting areas. Certain rooms contain showers only (no tubs). Next to the lobby, Bis-a-Bis restaurant and bar features window-side tables, great for people-watching along the fashionable Calle Arenales. The majority of the hotel's guests hail from Peru, Chile, and Colombia.

Arenales 1462 (at Paraná), 1061 Buenos Aires. ℭ 11/4021-4000. Fax 11/4816-0016. www.hotelbelair. com.ar. 76 units. $85 double; from $100 suite. Rates include buffet breakfast. AE, DC, MC, V. No parking. Metro: Callao. **Amenities:** Restaurant; bar; gym; business services; limited room service; laundry service; dry cleaning. *In room:* A/C, TV, minibar.

Etoile Hotel ⋆ *Value*   Located in the heart of Recoleta, steps away from the neighborhood's fashionable restaurants and cafes, the 14-story Etoile is an older hotel with a Turkish flair. It's not as luxurious as the city's other five-star hotels, but it's not as expensive either—making it a good value for Recoleta. The hotel labels itself a five-star but is really a high-quality four-star whose convention facilities allow it to retain a higher rating. Guest rooms are fairly large; executive rooms have separate sitting areas and large, marble-lined bathrooms with whirlpool bathtubs. Rooms facing south offer balconies overlooking Plaza Francia and the Recoleta Cemetery (p. 146).

Roberto M. Ortiz 1835 (at Guido overlooking Recoleta Cemetery), 1113 Buenos Aires. ℭ 11/4805-2626. Fax 11/4805-3613. www.etoile.com.ar. 96 units. $110 double; from $160 suite. Rates include buffet breakfast. AE, DC, MC, V. Free parking. No metro access. **Amenities:** Restaurant; rooftop health club w/indoor pool; exercise room; concierge; executive business services; limited room service; laundry service; dry cleaning. *In room:* A/C, TV, high-speed Internet, minibar, hair dryer.

INEXPENSIVE

The Recoleta Hostel ⋆ *Finds*   This is a great inexpensive choice for young people who want to be close to everything and in a beautiful neighborhood, but can't ordinarily afford the accommodations prices that go along with that. The accommodations here are simple, with 11 rooms filled with bunk bed spaces for 4 to 14 people each. There are also seven double rooms, two of which have private bathrooms, but the beds in the private rooms are bunk beds too, so those who want to cozy up will have to deal with that arrangement. The rooms are simple, with bare floors and walls, beds, and a small wooden desk in the private rooms; overall, the decor is rather reminiscent of a convent. Public areas have high ceilings and there is a public kitchen, TV room, laundry service, lockers, and an outdoor patio for guests' use. Bring the laptop too if you want, since the hostel is a Wi-Fi hot spot.

Libertad 1216 (at Juncal), 1012 Buenos Aires. ℭ 11/4812-4419. Fax 11/4815-6622. www.trhostel.com.ar. 76 bed spaces, including 4 in 2 bedrooms with attached bathroom. From $8 per bed; $18 private room with bathroom. Rates include continental breakfast. No credit cards. No metro access. **Amenities:** Concierge; Internet center; lockers; outdoor patio; shared kitchen; Wi-Fi. *In room:* Hair dryer.

6 Barrio Norte

Barrio Norte borders Recoleta, though some, especially real estate agents, say it is actually a part of it. However, the area is distinctly busier and more commercialized with more of a middle-class feel than in the upscale Recoleta. Its main boulevard is busy Santa Fe, full of shops, restaurants, and cafes. This can make staying in Barrio Norte noisier than Recoleta, but still less so than the Microcentro. You also have easy subway access in this neighborhood.

For a map of the hotels listed in the section, see the "Where to Stay in Central Buenos Aires" map on p. 64.

INEXPENSIVE

Bauen Hotel   I'm not recommending this hotel because you'll be impressed by the service, the upkeep of the rooms, or some of the other things that usually impress people when they stay in a hotel. The number one reason for staying in this hotel is because it gives you the best glimpse a tourist can get into a post-peso-crisis phenomenon in Argentina—the development of the worker "Cooperativas" in which employees take over a failed business abandoned by the owners in order to keep their jobs. The Bauen, a disco-era hotel, never made a lot of money, but it was the peso crisis that drove it under. But instead of letting it close, the workers reacted by taking it over and keeping it open. Virtually everything in the hotel dates from its late-1970s opening, from the lobby signs, the curves of the front desk, avocado-colored Formica furniture, shiny globe-shaped lamps, old televisions, and the *pièce de résistance*—the underground disco lounge you might envision John Travolta dancing in. Various events and fundraisers are held here as well; a theater, art gallery, and convention center are on the first level, often hosting events with a left-wing flavor. Union leaders from the provinces frequent this hotel when in town for political reasons. Upper floors have fantastic views of the surrounding city. The staff is also exceptionally friendly and helpful.

Av. Callao 360 (at Corrientes), 1022 Buenos Aires. © 11/4372-1932. Fax 11/4372-3883. 220 units, including 18 suites. From $35 double; from $50 suite. Rates include continental breakfast. AE, MC, V. Metro: Callao. **Amenities:** Restaurant; bar; small health club; sauna; concierge; business center; limited room service; laundry service; convention center; disco lounge; theater. *In room:* A/C, TV.

7 Congreso

Congreso is a historic district that surrounds the building Congreso, at the western terminus of the Avenida de Mayo. In addition to Congreso, the neighborhood contains other grand and imposing buildings, some almost imperial in scale and design. While there is a lot to see in the area, it can seem desolate and seedy at night, especially in the Congreso Plaza, which serves as a hangout for the homeless. The intense government police presence in the area, however, means that in spite of appearances, it is relatively safe at night. With increased tourism to Buenos Aires, more hotels and other activities are beginning to move into this neighborhood.

For a map of the hotels listed in the section, see the "Where to Stay in Central Buenos Aires" map on p. 64.

MODERATE

Amerian Congreso   This establishment offers a combination of standard hotel rooms (which are very large) and apartments and is part of the Argentine-owned Amerian hotel chain. It opened as a hotel in 2003, after renovating the former office structure it moved into, and it offers all the usual services of a hotel. The decor is simple and none of the rooms have great views, due to the hotel's side-street location and the fact that it's surrounded by buildings of generally the same height. Still, for a location in an office district, it is very quiet. A covered rooftop unheated swimming pool is a nice touch, and there's a small sauna on the premises, too. Parking is in the building and is a mere $2, the cheapest of any hotel I looked at. The main disadvantage here is that Internet access is not available in the rooms, and the business center is small, meaning you might have to rely on *locutorios* (phone centers). Stairs to the elevator bay also make this a bad option for people with limited mobility. However, because the hotel is new and in a renovated structure, the chain is making improvements as they go, so you may find added amenities in the near future. For instance, as of this writing, the restaurant is open for breakfast only but plans to expand its hours and add a bar by early 2006. Room service from morning until 9:30pm makes up for this. This is a good-value hotel in terms of size, price, and amenities, in spite of its few deficiencies.

Bartolomé Mitre 1744 (at Callao), 1037 Buenos Aires. ℂ 11/5032-5200. www.amerian.com. 90 units, including 48 apts. From $57 double; from $100 apt. Rates include buffet breakfast. AE, DC, MC, V. Parking $4. Metro: Congreso. **Amenities:** Restaurant; rooftop pool; sauna; concierge; business center; limited room service; massage service; laundry service; dry cleaning. *In room:* A/C, TV, minibar, hair dryer, large safe.

The Golden Tulip Savoy

Ever since the beautiful Argentine commoner Maxima married Dutch Crown Prince William in 2002, Netherlands natives have been flocking to Argentina in droves. The Dutch-owned Golden Tulip, opened in the faded but historic hotel Savoy, is an attempt by Dutch investors to catch that traffic, and the majority of the hotel's clients are from Europe. The original hotel opened in 1910 and was built in an eclectic style, with largely Art Nouveau elements. It was just one small part of the glamorous rebuilding of Avenida Callao in the aftermath of the opening of the nearby Congreso. The hotel became part of the Golden Tulip chain in 2000, and the company has been upgrading and remodeling the hotel slowly, with an eye toward maintaining as much of the structure as possible. Gorgeous moldings, ornamental metal details, and stained glass are part of the original decoration, though the lobby was severely altered in the 1960s and will only be restored to a shadow of this, as too much of the original is now gone. The rooms are very large, in keeping with the old grandeur, and each is entered through its own antechamber, adding to the sense of space, and sports a color pattern of light grays and blues. Rooms facing the street have tiny French balconies, but half of the hotel faces an interior courtyard and therefore offers no views. All rooms are soundproofed against street noise and have high-speed Internet capabilities. Suite bathrooms include a whirlpool bathtub. A small spa offers facials. The hotel's Madrigales restaurant offers Argentine cuisine with interesting Latin American fusion elements. There is no pool, sauna, or gym here, but the hotel has an agreement with a nearby establishment if you're interested in these amenities. The hotel is not yet fully up to par with competitors in its price range, but considering the room sizes and location, once renovations are complete and new services added, this will become a good value.

Av. Callao 181 (at Juan Perón), 1022 Buenos Aires. ℂ 11/4370-8011. Fax 11/4370-8020. www.gtsavoy hotel.com.ar. 180 units, including 8 suites. From $106 double; $194 suite. Rates include buffet breakfast. AE, DC, MC, V. Parking $4. Metro: Congreso. **Amenities:** Restaurant; bar; spa; concierge; small business center; 24-hr. room service; laundry service; conference center. *In room:* A/C, TV, minibar, hair dryer, safe.

INEXPENSIVE

Gran Hotel Vedra *(Value)*   In terms of value for money, location, and the service of staff, there are few places I can recommend in this category more than this small two-star hotel. The hotel has rooms in two parts, accessed by two different elevator bays: the Classic, or older wing, and the Superior, the newer wing. Classic rooms are undergoing renovations and face the Avenida de Mayo. As such, they can be noisy, but have beautiful views of this historic area. They are small, however, and the furniture is arranged tightly in some of them. Superior rooms are larger, but some have no outside windows as they face an interior airshaft. Classic rooms have only showers, while Superior rooms have tub/shower combinations. When making a decision on which to choose, it depends on what is important to you, a view or the size of the room, but whatever your preferences, you should ask to see the room before checking in, especially as many are undergoing a renovation. The staff is very friendly and most speak English. There is a small 40-person meeting center here, but there's no business center and no on-site access to the Internet. The hotel offers an evening checkout for people with night flights for a 50% additional charge. The small restaurant offers basic Argentine food and snacks.

Av. de Mayo 1350 (at San José), 1085 Buenos Aires. ⓒ 11/4383-0883. www.hotelvedra.com.ar. 35 units. From $18–$30 double. Rates include buffet breakfast. AE, MC, V. No parking. Metro: Sáenz Peña. **Amenities:** Restaurant; bar; concierge; limited room service; laundry service; dry cleaning; conference center. *In room:* A/C, TV, minibar, hair dryer, safe.

Hotel de Los Dos Congresos *(Value)*   Renovations are ongoing in this hotel, opened in 1999 in a historically listed building just across from Congreso. This hotel is definitely a bargain, but it's important to see the room before agreeing to take it, as some come in odd shapes and arrangements. A few rooms are split levels, with the bed in lofts; others have very large bathrooms, others small. Within the bathrooms, some have only showers, while others have tub/shower combinations. Suites come with Jacuzzi tubs. Hair dryers are available at the front desk. Rooms facing Congreso have fantastic views, but the windows are not double-glazed, meaning it can be noisy. There is no price differential for rooms with or without views, so make your decision on the basis of whether a view or quiet is more important to you. In spite of some of the problems with the hotel in such an old structure (such as the odd room arrangements), the staff is exceptionally helpful. Most patrons hail from Europe and South America as part of tour groups and the hotel also heavily advertises itself locally as a gay-friendly place to stay. Pets are not a problem, and they don't charge extra for them. Each room has a safe, but they are very small, holding not much more than a wallet. Additional items can be kept at the front desk.

Rivadavia 1777 (at Callao), 1033 Buenos Aires. ⓒ 11/4372-0466 or 11/4371-0072. Fax 11/4372-0317. www.hoteldoscongresos.com. 50 units, including 2 suites. From $40 double; from $53 suite. Rates include buffet breakfast. AE, DC, MC, V. Metro: Congreso. Pets permitted. **Amenities:** Restaurant; bar; concierge; 24-hr. room service; laundry service; dry cleaning. *In room:* A/C, TV, minibar, coffeemaker, small safe.

Hotel Ibis ⭐⭐ *(Value) (Kids)*   The French budget chain Ibis has done it again, bringing their inexpensive chain to the Argentine capital. The hotel opened ceremoniously on May 25, 2001, and though it looks like every other Ibis the world over, the friendliness and helpfulness of the staff is strictly Argentine. Well located on Plaza Congreso, adjacent to the Madres de Plaza de Mayo office, all rooms here have street views, and many face the plaza directly. High floors offer good views of the surrounding city and Congreso. Double-glazed windows lock out noise in this busy location. The rooms are a good size for this price range, and all of them are identical, with a peach-and-mint color pattern. They are all doubles, but an extra bed can be added at a few pesos more for children. Some rooms also connect, so if coming as a family or a group of friends, make sure to request this specifically. Three rooms are also available for those with disabilities. All rooms have cable TV, dial-up Internet service, and a small desk workspace. High-speed Internet is available in their small business center. Bathrooms are bright and clean, all with shower stalls only (no tubs). The slight disadvantages here are that the beds are not the city's firmest and there is no minibar. In an effort to keep costs down, there are no bellboys to help with luggage, which might be a consideration for the elderly or those with disabilities when visiting. Safes and hair dryers are not in the rooms but are available in the lobby concierge area. The restaurant is Argentine with a basic menu and is an incredible value at about $4 for a prix-fixe dinner offering. Breakfast is not included in the rates but costs only about $2.50 per person. The hotel is naturally popular with French tourists, and most of the staff speaks Spanish, English, and French.

Hipólito Yrigoyen 1592 (at Ceballos), 1089 Buenos Aires. (© **11/5300-5555.** Fax 11/5300-5566. www. ibishotel.com. 147 units. From $30 double. AE, DC, MC, V. Parking $3 in a nearby garage. Metro: Congreso. **Amenities:** Restaurant; bar; concierge; business center; laundry service. *In room:* A/C, TV.

8 Tribunales

Tribunales encompasses the area surrounding the Supreme Court building and Teatro Colón, which borders the Corrientes theater district. It's full of government and other important buildings and is close to the Microcentro's shopping but is far less noisy. Its most important feature is Plaza Lavalle.

For a map of the hotels listed in the section, see the "Where to Stay in Central Buenos Aires" map on p. 64.

MODERATE

Dazzler Hotel ⚘ This basic hotel, built in 1978, is virtually unknown to the North American market, with the majority of its clients coming from South America (even though all staff members speak English). Guests here get to take advantage of the hotel's convenient location, a few blocks from Teatro Colón (p. 147). The hotel is situated overlooking Plaza Libertad, which is set against Avenida 9 de Julio. Front rooms have excellent views, but they can be on the noisy side, as there is no double glazing on the windows. All rooms are on the small side but are exceptionally bright, no matter the location, as the windows are floor to ceiling, which gives a larger sense to the rooms. Corner rooms offer the most space. Ask about connecting rooms if coming in a group or family. Large closets and a combination desk and vanity space round out the rooms. Lights and air-conditioning are controlled by a single panel over the bed. The small smoke-glass mirrored lobby has a staircase leading to the large and bright restaurant. Breakfast is served here, and they offer an excellent value on their prix-fixe lunches and dinners, which run about $3 to $5.

Libertad 902 (at Paraguay), 1012 Buenos Aires. (© **11/4816-5005.** www.dazzlerhotel.com. 88 units. From $85 double. Rates include buffet breakfast. AE, MC, V. Metro: Tribunales. **Amenities:** Restaurant; bar; small health club; sauna; concierge; small business center; limited room service; laundry service; dry cleaning. *In room:* A/C, TV, minibar, hair dryer.

INEXPENSIVE

Auge Buenos Aires ⍟   Alejandro Guiggi opened this private-room pension in a renovated apartment building near the Supreme Court. His idea was to make a *conventillo* (Italian immigrant rooming house) style location for guests to have a better understanding of turn-of-the-20th-century Buenos Aires. Faithfully restored details include wooden sashes on the windows, ceiling moldings, and stained-glass details throughout the rooms and public areas. The color pattern and antique furniture he has chosen call to mind a bordello, adding a bit of kitsch to the complex. Many of the rooms also have balconies and French doors, adding to the old-style atmosphere. Rooms can be rented for the day, week, or month with varying prices, becoming significantly less expensive with more time rented. Bathrooms for five of the rooms are shared and include whimsical sinks made from buckets and stools. Three rooms have private bathrooms and are quieter than the main areas of the pension. Breakfast is included and guests have 24-hour access and full use of the communal kitchen. One drawback is that there is no air-conditioning.

Paraná 473, 3B (at Lavalle), Buenos Aires 1017. ⓒ 11/4361-4535. augebuenosaires@yahoo.com.ar. 8 units, 3 with private bathroom. From $30 with shared bathroom; from $40 with private bathroom. Rates include continental breakfast. No credit cards. Metro: Tribunales. **Amenities:** Laundry service; kitchen.

9 Palermo

Palermo Viejo (where the hostel reviewed below is located) is divided into two sections: Palermo Soho and its boutiques, and Palermo Hollywood, known for its restaurants and bars, with Juan B. Justo as the dividing line. This is the trendiest part of Buenos Aires right now, yet it still retains a small-neighborhood feel with its old low-rise houses, cobblestone streets, and oak-tree-shaded sidewalks. Subway access is not the best in this area, however, and there are few major hotels. However, for the young, this area can be a great place to stay as you are near so many bars and nightlife options.

For a map of the hotels listed in the section, see the "Where to Stay & Dine in Palermo" map on p. 116.

INEXPENSIVE

Casa Jardín ⍟   Owner Nerina Sturgeon wanted to create an "artist hostel" in the heart of Palermo Viejo, and she has succeeded in doing so. Built into an old house, this intimate hostel boasts extremely high ceilings, all the better to have more wall space to show off her own and other people's paintings throughout the space. The artist atmosphere is further highlighted by gallery events held here periodically, complete with rooftop parties on the garden-wrapped terrace overlooking the street. The guest rooms are accessed by old French doors and each has just a few beds. In total there are 10 bed spaces, including one that's a single. As a business owned and run by a woman, Casa Jardín is also an ideal location for young women travelers to feel comfortable, even if alone. The only complaint would be the bathroom ratio, which is not enough. There is also no breakfast, but a 24-hour cafe is across the street. A shared kitchen and an Internet station in the living room complete the picture.

Charcas 4416 (at Scalabrini Ortiz), 1425 Buenos Aires. ⓒ 11/4774-8783. Fax 11/4891-9208. www.casa jardinba.com.ar. 10 bed spaces, including 1 single unit. $9 per bed; $13 for single space. No credit cards. Metro: Scalabrini Ortiz. **Amenities:** Self-service drink station; concierge; free high-speed Internet in main room; shared kitchen; TV room. *In room:* Lockers.

10 Abasto

The Abasto neighborhood lies a little outside of the main center of the city, along Corrientes but beyond the theater district. In general, it's a working- and middle-class area, busy, but not distinct architecturally. Historically, it's associated with singer Carlos Gardel, the country's greatest tango star of the 1920s and 1930s. The area, along with the bordering Once neighborhood, is also the historic home of Buenos Aires's Jewish communities, though most have long since moved to the suburbs. This neighborhood is anchored by the enormous Abasto Shopping Center, which is home to many things of interest to families with kids, such as the Museo de los Niños.

For a map of the hotels listed in the section, see the "Where to Dine in Abasto & Once" map on p. 127.

EXPENSIVE

Abasto Plaza Hotel ⏀   This hotel, opened in 2002, is a little off the beaten path, but it shows how the Buenos Aires tourism boom has been spreading to parts of the city outside of the usual tourist haunts. This location is associated with Buenos Aires's tango history, even if on the surface there seems little that is of tourist value nearby. A block away from the hotel are both the Abasto Shopping Center and Esquina Carlos Gardel—both locations built over sites related to the tango crooner. The hotel takes this to heart, with a unique tango shop for shoes, dresses, and other accessories a tourist might need for a night tangoing on the town. Free tango lessons and shows are also part of the offerings on Thursday evenings at 9pm in the lobby, and every day at 8pm there is a free tango show in the restaurant. The rooms are a good size, with rich dark woods and deep red carpets, giving an overall masculine feel to the decor. The location means few rooms offer great views, but the firm beds will ensure you get a good night's sleep. Superior rooms come with whirlpool bathtubs. The restaurant Volver, named for a Gardel song, is brilliantly sunny and decorated in a funky design, complete with silver hands holding up shelves of liquor behind the bar. The small heated outdoor pool sits on the rooftop with access through a small gym. Wi-Fi access is offered throughout the building, and free 24-hour Internet access is available through three computers in the business center. One wheelchair-accessible room is available. While this hotel does not offer much of interest in itself for Jewish travelers, it is the closest full-service hotel to Once and Abasto's historic Jewish communities and sites.

Av. Corrientes 3190 (at Anchorena), 1193 Buenos Aires. ✆ **11/6311-4465.** Fax 11/6311-4465. www.abasto plaza.com. 126 units. From $160 double; from $260 suite. Rates include buffet breakfast. AE, DC, MC, V. Parking $4. Metro: Carlos Gardel. **Amenities:** Restaurant; bar; heated outdoor pool; small health club; concierge; business center; 24-hr. room service; laundry service; dry cleaning. *In room:* A/C, TV, Wi-Fi Internet service, minibar, coffeemaker, hair dryer, iron, safe.

5

Where to Dine

Buenos Aires offers world-class dining with a variety of Argentine and international restaurants and cuisines. With the collapse of the peso, fine dining in Buenos Aires has also become marvelously inexpensive.

Nothing matches the meat from the Pampas grass-fed Argentine cows, and that meat is the focus of the dining experience throughout the city, from the humblest *parrilla* (grill) to the finest business-class restaurant. Empanadas, dough pockets filled with minced meat and other ingredients, are also an Argentine staple, offered almost everywhere.

In this section I'll go over what you can expect to find in Buenos Aires's varied restaurants and where certain types of food are clustered within the city's various neighborhoods.

Buenos Aires's most fashionable neighborhoods for eating out are all found in Palermo. Las Cañitas provides a row of Argentine and Nouvelle-fusion cuisine concentrated on Calle Báez. Palermo Hollywood is quickly matching this with even more trendy hot spots combining fine dining with a bohemian atmosphere in small, renovated, turn-of-the-20th-century houses. These restaurants are now attracting some of the city's top chefs, many of whom have received their training in France and Spain. Some of the most exquisite and interesting cuisine in the city is available in the venues in Palermo Viejo. Both Palermo Viejo and Las Cañitas are near the D subway line, but the best restaurants are often a long walk from metro stations.

That and the 11pm closing of the subway stations means you are best off with cabs to and from these restaurants. Where possible, I give the cross streets for these restaurants to help give guidance to your taxi drivers.

Puerto Madero's docks are lined with more top restaurants, along with a mix of chains and hit-or-miss spots. The Microcentro and Recoleta offer many outstanding restaurants and cafes, some of which have been on the map for decades. Buenos Aires's cafe life, where friends meet over coffee, is as sacred a ritual to Porteños as it is to Parisians. Excellent places to enjoy this include **La Biela** in Recoleta, across from the world-famous Recoleta Cemetery, and **Café Tortoni,** which is one of the city's most beautiful and traditional cafes, on Avenida de Mayo close to Plaza de Mayo. These are two places you should not miss if you want to see Buenos Aires's cafe life (but note that most cafes are filled with cigarette smoke, something that can be a real turnoff to some).

Porteños eat breakfast until 10am, lunch between noon and 4pm, and dinner late—usually after 9pm, though some restaurants open as early as 7pm. If you are an early-bird diner in the North American and British style, wanting to eat from 5pm on, look for restaurants in our listings that remain open between lunch and dinner. If you can make a reservation, I highly recommend doing so. If you do not want to commit, get to places close to their usually 8pm opening time, when you will almost always arrive to a nearly empty

Tips   Bares y Cafés Notables

If you want to dine in an atmosphere recalling the glory days of Buenos Aires's past, choose one from the list of nearly 40 *bares y cafés notables,* historic restaurants, cafes, and bars that have been specially protected by a law stating that their interiors can not be changed. Known as Law No. 35, this special protection granted by the city of Buenos Aires was passed in 1998 and updated in 2002. I list many of these special establishments in this chapter, including Café Tortoni, La Biela, La Perla, Bar El Federal, and many others. Naturally, based on age, these *notables* cluster in Monserrat, Congreso, La Boca, and San Telmo, the city's oldest areas. Ask the tourism office for the map *Bares y Cafés Notables de Buenos Aires,* which lists them all and has photographs of their interiors. If you really like the atmosphere in these unique spots, you can bring a part of them home with you, since all of them sell a coffee-table book with photos from these wonderful places.

restaurant. However, as the clock hits 9pm, virtually every table at the best restaurants will suddenly become completely filled.

Executive lunch menus (usually fixed-price three-course meals) are offered at many restaurants beginning at noon, but most dinner menus are a la carte. There is sometimes a small "cover" charge for bread and other items placed at the table. In restaurants that serve pasta, the pasta and its sauce are sometimes priced separately. Standard tipping is 10% in Buenos Aires, more for exceptional service. When paying by credit card, you will often be expected to leave the *propina* (tip) in cash, since many credit card receipts don't provide a place to include the tip. Be aware that some new restaurants are not yet accepting credit cards, due to still-resonating fears from the peso collapse. Many restaurants close between lunch and dinner, and some close on Sunday or Monday completely, or only offer dinner. In January and February many restaurants offer very limited hours and service, or close for vacations as this is the traditional time when Porteños flee the city to the beach resorts. It's a good idea to call ahead of time during these months to make sure you don't make a trip out to a place

only to become disappointed by a closed and locked door.

Though Buenos Aires is a very cosmopolitan city, it is surprisingly not a very ethnically diverse place, at least on the surface. However, the influences of Middle Eastern and Jewish immigrants who came to this city in the wake of World War I are reflected in a few areas. Middle Eastern restaurants are clustered in Palermo Viejo near the *subte* station Scalabrini Ortiz and also on Calle Armenia. I list several of them below. Since Once and Abasto were the traditional neighborhoods for Jewish immigrants, you'll find many kosher restaurants (some traditional, others recently opened by young people trying to bring back the cuisine they remember their grandparents cooking) along Calle Tucumán in particular. Because many Buenos Aires Jews are Sephardic or of Middle Eastern descent, you'll also find Arabic influences here.

With a renewed definition of what it means to be Argentine, native Indian and Incan influences are also finding their way into some Argentine restaurants. Again, with the neighborhood's view on experimental dining, the best of these are found in Palermo Viejo. Three to try out are the *parrilla* **Lo De Pueyrredón,** owned by a descendant of one of the country's most important families; **Pampa,** a small charming place owned by a woman from the Pampa Province; and **Bio,** a vegetarian restaurant using the Incan grain quinoa in many dishes.

As there are almost as many Italian last names as Spanish ones, it's hard to call those of Italian descent a specific ethnic group within Argentina as you can in the United States, Canada, or Australia. As such, Buenos Aires's Italian food is Argentine food in essence, and pastas and other Italian dishes are usually folded in with traditional Argentine offerings such as grilled beef. La Boca is Buenos Aires's historic Little Italy, the place where Italian immigrants first settled at the end of the 19th and early 20th centuries. The atmosphere in these restaurants plays on this past and caters to tourists, but this is not where the city's best Italian food is served. Instead, it is usually found in old, simple *parrillas* that have operated for decades and include pastas on their menus. Throughout this chapter, most of these are in the "inexpensive" categories all over the city. Additionally, though it is on the pricey side, check out **Piegari** in Recoleta's La Recova restaurant area, which has some of the best northern Italian cuisine in the city.

Asians only make up a tiny portion of Buenos Aires's population and as a whole have had little effect on cuisine offerings. Still, in keeping with international trends, you'll find sushi bars and other restaurants with Japanese and Chinese influences throughout Buenos Aires. All over the city, you will find various sushi fast-food-chain restaurants as well. For Asian authenticity, I also describe a few restaurants in Belgrano's very tiny and little-known Chinatown district.

If you are looking through these listings and still cannot decide what you want to eat, three areas are so loaded with restaurants of all types, one after another, that you are bound to find something that pleases you. Puerto Madero's historical dock buildings are one such place, and it's a bonus that many of the restaurants here are a bargain. Calle Báez in the Las Cañitas area of Palermo is another such area, and is also one of the most happening restaurant scenes in the whole city. Finally, restaurants and bars offering food surround Plaza Serrano in Palermo Hollywood, with many a good choice for the young, funky, and bargain-minded. All of these areas also have plenty of nearby places for heading out for after-dinner drinks and dancing, so you won't have to move all over the city to spend a night out if you concentrate on these areas.

If you still can't make up your mind and want some second opinions, check out **www.restaurant.com.ar**. It provides information in English and Spanish on restaurants in Buenos Aires and other major cities, and allows you to search by neighborhood as well as cuisine type.

Once in Buenos Aires, look for the **De Dios** map company's excellent restaurant map in bookstores everywhere, or order it ahead of time at www.dediosonline.com. Many Palermo Viejo restaurants are on a special Palermo Viejo dining map available at most of the venues in this neighborhood that are listed. Many other neighborhoods, such as San Telmo, also have similar maps.

I list exact prices for main courses and group restaurants into price categories. However, it's all relative. For instance, I have Expensive and Very Expensive categories, but these meals would not be considered pricey by North American or European standards. And in some cases, Inexpensive and Moderate overlap, or a single menu item, such as lobster, might push an ordinarily Inexpensive restaurant into a Very Expensive category. In short, take a look at our specific prices, which are expressed in a range, rather than solely

(*Tips*) Wine Tasting

Part of what makes a meal in Buenos Aires so good is the fine wine selection available, specially chosen to complement beef, chicken, fish, and other items on the menu. Most Argentine wine comes from the Mendoza district, bordering the Andean mountains. Malbecs make up most of the best, with cabernets, champagnes, and even grappas on the menus in the humblest to the most expensive restaurants. If you know nothing about wine, to make sense of the selections and suggestions offered by the waiter or sommelier, you may want to take a wine-tasting class. They are offered all over the city, but I recommend two of them above all others. On the high end of the scale, go to the **Hotel Alvear's Cave de Vines,** which will run you about $65 per person. My other choice is out of the wine-based restaurant **Club del Vino,** which will only cost about $12 per person. For those prices, you'll get about an hour with a sommelier who will explain to you and a group of other interested people about the winegrowing process, the harvest, and how the wine is actually produced. Like fine diamonds, wine is judged by color and clarity, and you'll learn what to look for in every glass. Other points include discerning taste and scent points as well as how to hold a glass of wine without damaging its contents with your hand's body heat to truly enjoy it. After coming to one of these classes, you'll never be embarrassed again when someone asks you what wine goes with what main course.

at the categories. With the current exchange rates, it is very difficult to overspend on food in Argentina. Inexpensive restaurants have main courses ranging from under $1 to about $4 to $5; Moderate restaurants have prices ranging from around $3 to about $7 or $8. Expensive restaurants have main courses of about $7 to $13; and Very Expensive restaurants range from about $13 up to almost $25. Remember that in all restaurants, lunch is usually cheaper, and that there may also be Executive or Tourist menus, which provide a very reasonably priced three-course meal. Tips, drinks, desserts, other menu items, as well as table service and the unavoidable charge for bread and spreads will add to your costs. Keep in mind also that while English is becoming more and more prevalent in Buenos Aires, less expensive restaurants tend to have fewer English speakers on staff.

1 Restaurants by Cuisine

AMERICAN
Kosher McDonald's ★★ (Abasto, $, p. 127)

ARGENTINE
Barbería (La Boca, $$, p. 129)
Bar El Federal ★★ (San Telmo, $$, p. 106)
B'art ★★ (Palermo, $$$, p. 115)
Cabaña las Lilas ★★ (Puerto Madero, $$$, p. 96)

Café de la Ciudad (Microcentro, $$, p. 101)
Café Literario (Microcentro, $, p. 104)
Café Retiro ★★ (Microcentro, $, p. 104)
Café Tortoni ★★ (Microcentro, $, p. 104)
Campo Bravo ★★ (Palermo, $, p. 124)

Key to Abbreviations: $$$$ = Very Expensive $$$ = Expensive $$ = Moderate $ = Inexpensive

Casa de Esteban de Luca ✦
(San Telmo, $, p. 109)
Clásica y Moderna ✦✦
(Barrio Norte, $$, p. 112)
Club del Vino ✦ (Palermo, $$$,
p. 118)
Cluny ✦✦✦ (Palermo, $$$,
p. 118)
Coanico Bar (Palermo, $, p. 125)
Confitería del Botánico
(Palermo, $, p. 125)
Confitería Exedra ✦✦
(Microcentro, $$, p. 102)
Corsario ✦ (La Boca, $, p. 129)
Dora ✦✦ (Microcentro, $$$,
p. 100)
El Galope ✦ (Once, $$, p. 128)
El Obrero ✦✦✦ (La Boca, $,
p. 129)
Gardel de Buenos Aires ✦
(Abasto, $, p. 126)
Gran Victoria ✦ (Plaza de Mayo
area, $$, p. 96)
Inside Resto-Bar ✦ (Congreso, $$,
p. 113)
La Americana ✦✦ (Congreso, $,
p. 114)
La Chacra ✦ (Microcentro, $$,
p. 102)
La Corte ✦✦ (Palermo, $$$,
p. 119)
La Coruña ✦✦ (San Telmo, $$,
p. 107)
La Farmacia ✦ (San Telmo, $$,
p. 108)
La Perla (La Boca, $$$, p. 129)
Las Nazarenas ✦ (Microcentro, $$,
p. 103)
La Sortija (Microcentro, $, p. 105)
La Vieja Rotisería ✦✦
(San Telmo, $$, p. 108)
Lo De Pueyrredón ✦✦
(Palermo, $$$, p. 119)
Lomo ✦ (Palermo, $$$, p. 120)
Macondo Bar ✦✦ (Palermo, $,
p. 125)
Nanaka Bar (San Telmo, $, p. 109)
Pampa ✦✦ (Palermo, $, p. 125)
Pappa Deus ✦ (San Telmo, $$,
p. 108)
Penal1 ✦✦ (Palermo, $$, p. 122)

Plaza Asturias ✦✦ (Congreso, $$,
p. 113)
Plaza del Carmen (Congreso, $$,
p. 114)
República de Acá ✦✦ (Palermo, $$,
p. 123)
Richmond Cafe ✦✦ (Microcentro,
$$, p. 103)
Utopia Bar (Palermo, $$, p. 123)

ASIAN

Asia de Cuba ✦ (Puerto Madero,
$$, p. 97)
Empire ✦ (Microcentro, $$, p. 102)

CAFE/CONFITERIA

Bar El Federal ✦✦ (San Telmo, $$,
p. 106)
Café de la Ciudad (Microcentro, $$,
p. 101)
Café de Madres de Plaza de Mayo
✦✦ (Congreso, $, p. 114)
Café Literario (Microcentro, $,
p. 104)
Café Retiro ✦✦ (Microcentro, $,
p. 104)
Café Tortoni ✦✦ (Microcentro, $,
p. 104)
Café Victoria ✦ (Recoleta, $,
p. 111)
Confitería del Botánico
(Palermo, $, p. 125)
Confitería Exedra ✦✦
(Microcentro, $$, p. 102)
Gran Victoria ✦ (Plaza de Mayo
area, $$, p. 96)
Il Gran Caffe ✦ (Microcentro, $,
p. 105)
La Biela ✦✦✦ (Recoleta, $,
p. 112)
La Coruña ✦✦ (San Telmo, $$,
p. 107)
La Farmacia ✦ (San Telmo, $$,
p. 108)
La Moncloa ✦ (Congreso, $$,
p. 113)
La Perla (La Boca, $$$, p. 129)
Malouva (Palermo, $, p. 125)
Maru Botana ✦ (Recoleta, $,
p. 112)
Petit Paris Café ✦ (Microcentro, $,
p. 106)

Plaza del Carmen (Congreso, $$, p. 114)

Richmond Cafe ✸✸ (Microcentro, $$, p. 103)

CHILEAN

Los Chilenos ✸ (Microcentro, $$, p. 103)

CHINESE

Buddha BA ✸ (Belgrano, $$$, p. 130)

Todos Contentos (Belgrano, $$, p. 131)

Yoko's ✸ (Palermo, $$, p. 124)

FRENCH

La Bourgogne ✸✸✸ (Recoleta, $$$, p. 110)

Le Sud ✸✸ (Microcentro, $$$, p. 101)

Ligure ✸✸ (Microcentro, $$, p. 103)

Te Mataré Ramírez ✸✸✸ (Palermo, $$$, p. 121)

GREEK

Sarkis ✸ (Recoleta, $$, p. 111)

INTERNATIONAL

B'art ✸✸ (Palermo, $$$, p. 115)

Casa Cruz ✸✸ (Palermo, $$$, p. 115)

Catalinas ✸✸✸ (Microcentro, $$$, p. 100)

Clark's ✸ (Recoleta, $, p. 111)

Cluny ✸✸✸ (Palermo, $$$, p. 118)

Coanico Bar (Palermo, $, p. 125)

Inside Resto-Bar ✸ (Congreso, $$, p. 113)

Katrine ✸✸✸ (Puerto Madero, $$$, p. 96)

La Corte ✸✸ (Palermo, $$$, p. 119)

Lola ✸ (Recoleta, $$$, p. 110)

Macondo Bar ✸✸ (Palermo, $, p. 125)

Mamá Jacinta ✸✸ (Once, $$, p. 128)

Maru Botana ✸ (Recoleta, $, p. 112)

Novecento ✸✸✸ (Palermo, $$, p. 122)

Pappa Deus ✸ (San Telmo, $$, p. 108)

Plaza Grill ✸✸ (Microcentro, $$$, p. 101)

Puerto Cristal ✸ (Puerto Madero, $, p. 100)

República de Acá ✸✸ (Palermo, $$, p. 123)

Shefa Abasto ✸ (Abasto, $, p. 128)

Sullivan's Drink House (Palermo, $$$, p. 121)

Te Mataré Ramírez ✸✸✸ (Palermo, $$$, p. 121)

Utopia Bar (Palermo, $$, p. 123)

IRISH

Sullivan's Drink House (Palermo, $$$, p. 121)

ITALIAN

Barbería (La Boca, $$, p. 129)

Broccolino ✸ (Microcentro, $$, p. 101)

Casa Cruz ✸✸ (Palermo, $$$, p. 115)

Club del Vino ✸ (Palermo, $$$, p. 118)

Corsario ✸ (La Boca, $, p. 129)

El Obrero ✸✸✸ (La Boca, $, p. 129)

Gardel de Buenos Aires ✸ (Abasto, $, p. 126)

Il Gran Caffe ✸ (Microcentro, $, p. 105)

La Americana ✸✸ (Congreso, $, p. 114)

La Farmacia ✸ (San Telmo, $$, p. 108)

La Vieja Rotisería ✸✸ (San Telmo, $$, p. 108)

Mamá Jacinta ✸✸ (Once, $$, p. 128)

Nanaka Bar (San Telmo, $, p. 109)

Piegari ✸✸ (Recoleta, $$$$, p. 109)

Plaza Asturias ✸✸ (Congreso, $$, p. 113)

Shefa Abasto ✸ (Abasto, $, p. 128)

Sorrento del Puerto ✸✸ (Puerto Madero, $$, p. 97)

JAPANESE

Asia de Cuba ✸ (Puerto Madero, $$, p. 97)

Morizono ★ (Microcentro, $,
p. 105)
Sushi Club (Palermo, $$, p. 123)
Yoko's ★ (Palermo, $$, p. 124)

KOSHER

El Galope ★ (Once, $$, p. 128)
Kosher McDonald's ★★ (Abasto,
$, p. 127)
Mamá Jacinta ★★ (Once, $$,
p. 128)
Shefa Abasto ★ (Abasto, $, p. 128)

LATINO

Central ★★★ (Palermo, $$$,
p. 118)

MEDITERRANEAN

Bio ★★ (Palermo, $, p. 124)
Catalinas ★★★ (Microcentro, $$$,
p. 100)
Central ★★★ (Palermo, $$$,
p. 118)
De Olivas i Lustres ★★ (Palermo,
$$, p. 121)
Galani ★★ (Recoleta, $$, p. 111)
Le Sud ★★ (Microcentro, $$$,
p. 101)
Restaurante y Bar Mediterráneo
★★ (Monserrat, $$, p. 106)

MEXICAN

Tazz ★ (Palermo, $, p. 126)

MIDDLE EASTERN

Don Galíndez ★ (Microcentro, $,
p. 105)
El Galope ★ (Once, $$, p. 128)
Garbis ★★ (Palermo, $$, p. 122)
Mamá Jacinta ★★ (Once, $$,
p. 128)
Sarkis ★ (Recoleta, $$, p. 111)
Viejo Agump ★ (Palermo, $,
p. 126)

PARRILLA

Campo Bravo ★★ (Palermo, $,
p. 124)
Desnivel ★ (San Telmo, $$, p. 107)
Don Galíndez ★ (Microcentro, $,
p. 105)
El Estanciero ★ (Palermo, $$,
p. 122)

El Galope ★ (Once, $$, p. 128)
El Mirasol ★★ (Recoleta, $$,
p. 110)
El Obrero ★★★ (La Boca, $,
p. 129)
Juana M ★★ (Recoleta, $, p. 112)
La Bisteca ★★ (Puerto Madero,
$$, p. 97)
La Brigada ★ (San Telmo, $$,
p. 107)
La Sortija (Microcentro, $, p. 105)
La Vieja Rotisería ★★ (San Telmo,
$$, p. 108)
Lo De Pueyrredón ★★ (Palermo,
$$$, p. 119)
Mamá Jacinta ★★ (Once, $$,
p. 128)
Nanaka Bar (San Telmo, $, p. 109)
Penal1 ★★ (Palermo, $$, p. 122)

PIZZA

Filo ★ (Microcentro, $, p. 105)

SCANDINAVIAN

Olsen ★★ (Palermo, $$$, p. 120)

SEAFOOD

Corsario ★ (La Boca, $, p. 129)
Dora ★★ (Microcentro, $$$,
p. 100)
Los Chilenos ★ (Microcentro, $$,
p. 103)
Olsen ★★ (Palermo, $$$, p. 120)
Puerto Cristal ★ (Puerto Madero,
$, p. 100)

SPANISH

B'art ★★ (Palermo, $$$, p. 115)
Club Español ★★ (Monserrat, $$,
p. 106)
Plaza Asturias ★★ (Congreso, $$,
p. 113)

THAI

Empire ★ (Microcentro, $$,
p. 102)

URUGUAYAN

Medio y Medio ★ (San Telmo, $,
p. 109)

VEGETARIAN

Bio ★★ (Palermo, $, p. 124)
Shefa Abasto ★ (Abasto, $, p. 128)

2 Plaza de Mayo Area

For a map of the restaurant listed in this section, see the "Where to Dine in Central Buenos Aires" map on p. 98.

MODERATE

Gran Victoria ⓖ CAFE/ARGENTINE   Watch the political world of Argentina go by outside your window as you eat at this great cafe overlooking Plaza de Mayo. In addition to the good people-watching opportunities, this cafe sits in the middle of one of the country's most important historic areas and has stunning views of the Cabildo, Plaza de Mayo, Casa Rosada, and the Metropolitan Cathedral. Food is basic Argentine, with Italian touches, and they have a great dessert selection. I'd recommend coming here for a break when sightseeing in the area, especially since the waitresses have a pleasant sense of humor.

Hipólito Yrigoyen 500, at Diagonal Sur. ⓒ **11/4345-7703.** Main courses $3–$8. AE, MC, V. Mon–Fri 7am–9pm. Metro: Bolívar.

3 Puerto Madero

Not all of Puerto Madero has convenient metro stops, but all restaurants are at most a 20-minute walk from a metro station.

For a map of the restaurants listed in this section, see the "Where to Dine in Central Buenos Aires" map on p. 64.

EXPENSIVE

Cabaña las Lilas ⓖⓖ ARGENTINE   This is where locals always bring out-of-towners to impress them. Widely considered the best *parrilla* in Buenos Aires, Cabaña las Lilas is always packed. The menu pays homage to Argentine beef, which comes from the restaurant's private *estancia* (ranch). The table "cover"— which includes dried tomatoes, mozzarella, olives, peppers, and delicious garlic bread—nicely whets the appetite, but don't forget that you're here to order steak. The best cuts are the rib-eye, baby beef, and thin skirt steak. Order sautéed vegetables, grilled onions, or Provençal-style fries separately. Chicken and fish are also part of the offerings, and vegetarians don't have to stay at home, since there is a large selection of very fresh and crisp salads. Service is hurried but professional, but you can still ask your waiter to match a fine Argentine wine with your meal. This enormous eatery offers indoor and outdoor seating, and in spite of its high price, it is casual and informal with patrons coming in everything from suits to shorts.

Alicia Moreau de Justo 516, at Villaflor in Dique 3. ⓒ **11/4313-1336.** www.laslilas.com. Reservations recommended. Main courses $11–$20. AE, DC, V. Daily noon–midnight. Metro: L. N. Alem.

Katrine ⓖⓖⓖ INTERNATIONAL   One of the top dining choices in Buenos Aires, Katrine (named after the restaurant's Norwegian chef-owner) serves exquisite cuisine in a surprisingly loud and festive dining room for such an exclusive restaurant. You can't go wrong with any of the menu choices, but a couple of suggestions include marinated salmon Scandinavian-style followed by shrimp with vegetables and saffron or thinly sliced beef tenderloin with portobello mushrooms, onions, and a cabernet sauvignon reduction. All of the pasta dishes are excellent, too. Katrine's modern dining room and outdoor terrace overlook the water, and service is outstanding.

Av. Alicia Moreau de Justo 138, at Thompson on Dique 4. ⓒ **11/4315-6222.** Reservations recommended. Main courses $8–$15. AE, DC, MC, V. Mon–Fri noon–3:30pm and 8pm–midnight; Sat 8pm–12:30am. Metro: L. N. Alem.

MODERATE

Asia de Cuba ✺ ASIAN/JAPANESE   Though not associated with the other Asia de Cuba's around the world, this place offers an exciting environment in which to dine. Opened in 2001, the interior is red and black with disco balls and Chinese lanterns hanging from the ceiling. In the back there's a sushi bar and a VIP lounge. Glamorous hostesses glide you to your dining table. Lunchtime is more casual, and less expensive, than at night. Daytime sushi prices start at about $3 per person, doubling to $6 in the evening. A table sushi menu, with 110 different items, is about $113. Dinner comes with all kinds of exotic entertainment, from Arabian belly dancers to stripteasing women suspended above the crowd. Asia de Cuba is also one of the most important clubs in the Puerto Madero area, ideal for an older crowd because a large portion of its clientele is over the age of 40. Dancing begins at about 1:30am Tuesday to Saturday, and if you do not eat here, there is a separate admission charge ranging from $7 to $9 depending on the day. The dining area overlooks the dance area. In addition to the standard Argentine assortment of red wines, there are many white wines and mixed drinks to choose from as well. Drinks are more expensive by about 10% to 20% if you are not having a meal. The ideal is to come here late in the evening, dine, and stay around for a night of dancing.

P. Dealessi 750, at Guemes on Dique 3. © **11/4894-1328** or 11/4894-1329. www.asiadecuba.com.ar. Reservations recommended. Main courses $3–$10. AE, MC, V. Daily 1pm–5am, often later on weekends. No metro access.

La Bisteca ✺✺ ⟨Value⟩ PARRILLA   Puerto Madero's La Bisteca offers a wide range of meal choices at incredible value for the money. This is an all-you-can-eat establishment, locally called a *Tenedor Libre,* with a three-course lunch for about $9 and dinner ranging from about $12 to $14. If you have come to Argentina to try the country's beef, make this a definite stopping point. The high meat quality surprised me here, especially considering the price, and there really was no limit to the number of times I could fill my plate at the various grills situated in the restaurant. For vegetarians, there is also a diverse salad bar. In spite of the restaurant's large size, the lighting and seating arrangements work to create small intimate spaces. At lunchtime the place is full of businesspeople, while at night you'll find a mix of couples, friends, and families. This is a chain, with other locations both within Buenos Aires and throughout Argentina.

Av. Alicia Moreau de Justo 1890, at Peñaloza on Dique 1. © **11/4514-4999**. Main courses $5–$7. AE, DC, MC, V. Daily noon–4pm and 8pm–1am. No metro access.

Sorrento del Puerto ✺✺ ITALIAN   The only two-story restaurant in Puerto Madero enjoys impressive views of the water from both floors. When the city decided to reinvigorate the port in 1995, this was one of the first five restaurants opened (today, there are more than 50). The sleek modern dining room boasts large windows, modern blue lighting, and tables and booths decorated with white linens and individual roses. The outdoor patio accommodates only 15 tables, but the inside is enormous. People come here for two reasons: great pasta and even better seafood. Choose your pasta and accompanying sauce: seafood, shrimp scampi, pesto, or four cheeses. The best seafood dishes include trout stuffed with crabmeat, sole with a Belle Marnier sauce, Galician-style octopus, paella Valenciana, and assorted grilled seafood for two. A three-course menu with a drink costs $7. Sorrento has a second location in Recoleta at Posadas 1053 (© **11/4326-0532**).

Av. Alicia Moreau de Justo 430, at Guevara on Dique 4. © **11/4319-8731**. Reservations recommended. Main courses $5–$9. AE, DC, MC, V. Mon–Fri noon–4pm and 8pm–1am; Sat 8pm–2am. Metro: L. N. Alem.

Where to Dine in Central Buenos Aires

INEXPENSIVE

Puerto Cristal (★) INTERNATIONAL/SEAFOOD   The menu here has every-thing, but fish is the main reason for coming to this restaurant amidst all the oth-ers in Puerto Madero. This is an enormous restaurant with friendly hostesses and theatrical waiter service not in keeping with its low prices; you'll find a constant flurry of changes of silverware and dishes between courses as you dine. A glassed-in central garden in the middle of the dining area adds tranquillity to the restau-rant's industrial-chic design as do the windows overlooking Puerto Madero. Great lunch specials are part of the draw here; their executive menu runs about $6 and usually includes a glass of champagne. (Though other drinks and the table cover will be additional.) There is a slight surcharge for paying with a credit card here.

Av. Alicia Moreau de Justo 1082, at Viilaflor in Dique 3. (© 11/4331-3669. www.puerto-cristal.com.ar. Main courses $3–$5. AE, MC, V. Sun–Fri 6:30am–midnight; Sat 6:30am–2am. No metro access.

4 Microcentro

For a map of the restaurants listed in this section, see the "Where to Dine in Central Buenos Aires" map on p. 64.

EXPENSIVE

Catalinas (★★★) INTERNATIONAL/MEDITERRANEAN   Since 1979, Galician-born Ramiro Rodríguez Pardo has impressed gourmands from Argentina and abroad in his kitchen here, which is defined by culinary diversity and innova-tion. The colorful yet classic dining room—adjacent to the Lancaster hotel—has three open salons, each painted by the Argentine artists Polesello, Beuedit, and Rovirosa. A Venetian crystal chandelier shines on the center dining room, created by the same artist who arranged the chandeliers in the lobby of New York's Plaza Hotel. Tables are large, decorated with white linens, fresh flower arrangements, and porcelain. A three-course, prix-fixe menu, including two bottles of Argentina's finest wines, is offered at lunch and dinner—an excellent value for such an elegant restaurant. The menu changes seasonally but always includes impeccable lobsters, T-bone steaks, and steaks of Patagonian tooth fish. Don't miss Pardo's grilled lamb chops, famous throughout Argentina.

Reconquista 850, at Paraguay. (© 11/4313-0182. Reservations recommended. Main courses $7–$10; fixed-price menu $15. AE, DC, MC, V. Mon–Fri noon–3pm; Mon–Sat 8pm–1am. Metro: San Martín.

Dora (★★) ARGENTINE/SEAFOOD   This restaurant looks like nothing inside or outside, with its almost invisible exterior on the ground floor of an office build-ing and plain brown wooden interiors, its walls lined with bottles of wine. Dora's has been open since the 1940s (and is still run by the same family—third genera-tion—that opened it), and while there may be more chic places to eat, nobody comes here for the decor: Dora's is all about the food. It's loud, noisy, crazy, and chaotic in here, an odd mix of businesspeople from the surrounding offices and casually dressed older locals who have probably been coming here for decades. The specialty at this expensive restaurant is fish, though a few beef, chicken, and pasta dishes are thrown in too, almost as a second thought. The "Cazuela" Dora is the specialty—a casserole of fish, shellfish, shrimp, and just about everything else the sea offers thrown into one pot. Appetizers alone are expensive, from $4 to $14, but some of the options are made with caviar. After such heavy fish and meat selec-tions, a surprisingly varied choice of light fruits in season is on the dessert menu. Naturally, with so much fish, Dora has one of the largest white-wine selections in all of Buenos Aires.

Leandro N. Alem 1016, at Paraguay. © **11/4311-2891**. Main courses $8–$20. V. U.S. dollars accepted. Mon–Thurs 12:30pm–1am; Fri–Sat noon–2am. Metro: San Martín.

Le Sud ⭐⭐ FRENCH/MEDITERANNEAN   Executive chef Thierry Pszonka earned a gold medal from the National Committee of French Gastronomy and gained experience at La Bourgogne before opening this gourmet restaurant in the new Sofitel Hotel. His simple, elegant cooking style embraces spices and olive oils from Provence to create delicious entrees, such as the stewed rabbit with green pepper and tomatoes, polenta with Parmesan and rosemary, and spinach with lemon ravioli. Le Sud's dining room offers the same sophistication as its cuisine, a contemporary design with chandeliers and black marble floors, tables of Brazilian rosewood, and large windows overlooking Calle Arroyo. Following dinner, consider a drink in the adjacent wine bar.

Arroyo 841–849 (Sofitel Hotel), at Suipacha. © **11/4131-0000**. Reservations recommended. Main courses $10–$20. AE, DC, MC, V. Daily 6:30–11am, 12:30–3pm, and 7:30pm–midnight. Metro: San Martín.

Plaza Grill ⭐⭐ INTERNATIONAL   For nearly a century, the Plaza Grill has dominated the city's power-lunch scene, and it remains the first choice for government officials and business executives. The dining room is decorated with dark oak furniture, a 90-year-old Dutch porcelain collection belonging to the owners, Indian fans from the British Empire, and Villeroy & Boch china place settings. Tables are well spaced, allowing for intimate conversations. Order a la carte from the international menu or off the *parrilla*—the steaks are perfect Argentine cuts. Marinated filet mignon, thinly sliced and served with gratinéed potatoes, is superb. The "po parisky eggs" form another classic dish—two poached eggs in a bread shell topped with a rich mushroom-and-bacon sauce. The restaurant's wine list spans seven countries, with the world's best Malbec coming from Mendoza.

Marriott Plaza Hotel, Calle Florida 1005, overlooking Plaza San Martín. © **11/4318-3070**. Reservations recommended. Main courses $7–$10. AE, DC, MC, V. Daily noon–4pm and 7pm–midnight. Metro: San Martín.

MODERATE

Broccolino ⭐ ITALIAN   Taking its name from New York's Italian immigrant neighborhood—notice the Brooklyn memorabilia filling the walls and the mural of Manhattan's skyline—this casual trattoria near Calle Florida is popular with North Americans (Robert Duvall has shown up three times). Many of the waiters speak English, and the restaurant has a distinctly New York feel. Three small dining rooms are decorated in quintessential red-and-white checkered tablecloths, and the smell of tomatoes, onions, and garlic fills the air. The restaurant is known for its spicy pizzas, fresh pastas, and above all its sauces (*salsas* in Spanish). The restaurant also serves 2,000 pounds per month of baby calamari sautéed in wine, onions, parsley, and garlic.

Esmeralda 776, at Córdoba. © **11/4322-7652**. Reservations recommended. Main courses $3–$5. No credit cards. Daily noon–4pm and 7pm–1am. Metro: Lavalle.

Café de la Ciudad CAFE/ARGENTINE   It's hard to believe that considering it's the center of the city, there's only one restaurant with outdoor dining directly overlooking the Obelisco, but it's true. Café de la Ciudad opened 40 years ago and is situated on one of the six corners at the Obelisco, on Avenida 9 de Julio. Coming here is like sitting down to eat in Buenos Aires's Times Square, where you can watch the myriad of flashing electronic ads for Japanese and American companies. Sure, it's a little noisy, and, sure, you're a target for beggars, but you'll be dining under the symbol of the city. The food here comes in large portions; sandwiches, pizzas, and specially priced executive menus are made in a hurry, so it's a great place if you're short on time. The subway station Carlos Pellegrini is right here too. If you're here on a night when the city is in a good mood, especially if the Boca Juniors win a game, you'll get a free show watching the locals gather with their flags to cheer under the Obelisco as cars and taxis hurtle by, beeping and acknowledging the crowd's joy. It's also a 24-hour place, so you can stop off here after going to a club or the nearby theaters and watch the parade of Porteños pass by.

Corrientes 999, at Carlos Pellegrini (Av. 9 de Julio). ℂ **11/4322-8905** or 11/4322-6174. Main courses $1.50–$7. AE, DC, MC, V. Daily 24 hr. Metro: Carlos Pellegrini.

Confitería Exedra 🎰🎰 CAFE/ARGENTINE   "La Esquina de Buenos Aires" (the corner of Buenos Aires) is the tag name for this place. Like a busy city street corner, every walk of life seems to pass through this exciting cafe. It's graced by a stained-glass-and-blonde-wood wall mural, reminiscent of something out of a 1970s church, and topped off with a glitzy Vegas ceiling. Just like at a church, the old waiter, Victor, with more than 20 years experience here, says, "we serve all." And they do. The crowd here is boisterous, in a mix of formal and informal dress, all enjoying each other's company and checking out whomever is walking on Avenida 9 de Julio through the huge glass windows. Because this place is popular late at night and is surrounded by some of the special men's clubs, you might find some working girls and a few other dubious creatures hanging out. Still, it's definitely a spot to hit on weekends when looking for a bite to eat after going clubbing. There's a huge selection of drinks on offer, and the prices go up slightly late at night. The menu is a combination of snacks, fast food, and more interesting and substantial things too, like chicken with pumpkin sauce. The executive lunch menu is $5 to $7 and dinner is a similar bargain.

Av. Córdoba 999, at Carlos Pellegrini (Av. 9 de Julio). ℂ **11/4322-7807**. Main courses $3–$5. AE, MC, V. Sun–Thurs 7am–5am; Fri–Sat 24 hr. Metro: Lavalle.

Empire 🎰 ASIAN/THAI   This is an interesting restaurant in an odd location— a surprisingly desolate part of the Microcentro. It's steps away from everything in the Microcentro but on a very small street that gets little foot traffic on its own and therefore seems remote. Enter this dark space, with paintings of elephants and mosaic decorations made from broken mirrors on the columns, and you'll feel as though you've gone into some kind of funky club instead of a restaurant. For vegetarians seeking a break from the meat offerings everywhere else, this is an ideal place to check out, with its many all-vegetable or -noodle offerings. Many come for drinks alone, sitting at the large bar with shelves of backlit bottles casting a warm glow. Though this place's advertising symbol is the Empire State Building, there's nothing New York about it. Empire is also one of the city's most popular restaurants among gay locals.

Tres Sargentos 427, at San Martín. ℂ **11/5411-4312** or 11/5411-5706. empire_bar@hotmail.com. Main courses $6–$10. AE, MC, V. Mon–Fri 9am–1am; Sat 10:30am–3am. Metro: San Martín.

La Chacra 🎰 ARGENTINE   Your first impression of this restaurant will either be the stuffed cow begging you to go on in and eat some meat or the open-fire spit grill glowing through the window. Professional waiters clad in black pants and white dinner jackets welcome you into what is otherwise a casual environment, with deer horns and wrought-iron lamps adorning the walls. Dishes from the grill include sirloin steak, T-bone with red peppers, and tenderloin. Barbecued ribs and suckling pig tempt you from the open-pit fire, and there are a number of hearty brochettes on offer. Steaks are thick and juicy. Get a good beer or an Argentine wine to wash it all down.

Av. Córdoba 941, at Carlos Pellegrini (Av. 9 de Julio). ℂ **11/4322-1409**. Main courses $4–$6. AE, DC, MC, V. Daily noon–1:30am. Metro: San Martín.

Las Nazarenas ★ ARGENTINE   This is not a restaurant, an old waiter will warn you—it's an *asador*, a form of Argentine grill. More specifically, it's a steakhouse with meat on the menu, not a pseudo-*parrilla* with vegetable plates or some froufrou international dishes for the faint of heart. You only have two choices here: cuts grilled on the *parrilla* or meat cooked on a spit over the fire. Argentine presidents and foreign ministers have all made their way here. The two-level dining room is handsomely decorated with cases of Argentine wines and abundant plants. The food is excellent, and the service is unhurried, offering you plenty of time for a relaxing meal.

Reconquista 1132, at Leandro N. Alem. ℂ **11/4312-5559**. Reservations recommended. Main courses $4–$6. AE, DC, MC, V. Daily noon–1am. Metro: San Martín.

Ligure ★★ *Finds* FRENCH   Painted mirrors look over the long rectangular dining room here, which since 1933 has drawn ambassadors, artists, and business leaders by day and a more romantic crowd at night. A nautical theme prevails, with fishnets, dock ropes, and masts decorating the room; captain's wheels substitute for chandeliers. Meal portions are huge and meticulously prepared—an unusual combination for French-inspired cuisine. Seafood options include the Patagonian tooth fish sautéed with butter, prawns, and mushrooms or the trout glazed with an almond sauce. If you're in the mood for beef, the chateaubriand is outstanding, and the *bife de lomo* (filet mignon) can be prepared seven different ways (pepper sauce with brandy is delightful and made at your table).

Juncal 855, at Esmeralda. ℂ **11/4393-0644** or 11/4394-8226. Reservations recommended. Main courses $4–$6. AE, DC, MC, V. Daily noon–3pm and 8–11:30pm. Metro: San Martín.

Los Chilenos ★ SEAFOOD/CHILEAN   A taste of the long country next door is what you'll find here, and because of that, this restaurant is popular with Chileans who live here or are visiting. It's a simple place, with a home-style feeling. The dining room has long tables where everyone sits together, and it's decorated with posters of Chilean tourist sites and draped with Chilean flags. Fish is one of the restaurant's fortes, and one of the most popular dishes is abalone in mayonnaise.

Suipacha 1024, at Santa Fe. ℂ **11/4328-3123**. Main courses $1–$7. AE, DC, MC, V. Mon–Sat noon–4pm and 8pm–1am. Metro: San Martín.

Richmond Cafe ★★ CAFE/ARGENTINE   Enter this place and find the pace and atmosphere of an older Buenos Aires. The Richmond Cafe, a *café notable*, is all that is left of the Richmond Hotel, an Argentine-British hybrid that opened in 1917 and once catered to the elite. The cafe sits in the lobby of the former hotel, whose upstairs area has been converted into offices. The menu here is traditionally Argentine, and there is a confitería, or cafe, section in the front, serving as a cafe and fast-food eatery. You'll find a mix of locals of all kinds here, from workers grabbing a quick bite to well-dressed seniors who must recall Calle Florida's more elegant heyday. The decor is that of a gentlemen's club, full of wood, brass, and red leather upholstery. Patrons can still let loose downstairs, in a bar area full of billiard tables. In keeping with its role as a confitería, there is an extensive menu of high-quality pastries on offer. The restaurant offers hearty basics like chicken, fish, and beef. A la carte, the food tends on the expensive side, but three-course Executive menus with a drink included are a good bargain, running between $6 and $10 depending on what you choose.

Calle Florida 468, at Corrientes. ℭ **11/4322-1341** or 11/4322-1653. www.restaurant.com.ar/richmond. Main courses $5–$8. AE, MC, V. Mon–Sat 7am–10pm. Metro: Florida.

INEXPENSIVE

Café Literario CAFE/ARGENTINE   This quiet little cafe takes advantage of its location next door to the place where Argentine literary great Jorge Luis Borges was born. It sort of has a loose affiliation with the Fundacion Internacional Jorge Luis Borges, which works to preserve his memory and work. Literature-themed, the cafe has readings and art events on an irregular basis. A range of publications lie on shelves and racks for patrons to peruse while they eat. The idea according to the owners was to have a place where people could come to read and eat and be more relaxed than in a library. On offer are light items like sandwiches, snacks, desserts, and Argentine steak. The building is modern but opens into the patio of the adjacent YWCA, Tucumán 844 (ℭ **11/4322-1550**), inside a gorgeous early-20th-century building built over the now demolished house where Borges was born. Café Literario serves as the cafeteria for the YWCA. Stop in to find out information on plays, art shows, various other events aimed at the general public, and exercise programs strictly for women.

Tucumán 840, at Suipacha. ℭ **11/4328-0391**. Main courses $2–$5. No credit cards. Mon–Fri 8am–6pm. Metro: Lavalle.

Café Retiro ★★ *(Finds* CAFE/ARGENTINE   This cafe is part of a chain, the Café Café consortium. As such, there is nothing spectacular about the food, but it is high quality, consistent, and inexpensive. The main point of dining here is to enjoy the restored elegance of the original cafe, which was part of Retiro Station when it was built in 1915. The place had been closed for many years but was restored in 2001 with the help of a government program. It is now one of the *cafés notables,* whose interiors are considered historically important to the nation. The marble has been cleaned, the bronze chandeliers polished, and the stained-glass windows have been restored, allowing a luminescent light to flow in. This cafe is ideal if you are taking a train from here to other parts of Argentina and the province, such as Tigre, or if you came to admire the architecture of Retiro and the other classical stations in this enormous transportation complex. It's also worth checking out if you came to see the nearby English Clock Tower, which sits in the plaza just outside. The staff is very friendly and full of advice on things to do in Buenos Aires. An attached art gallery in the hallway outside also has changing exhibitions. Friday at 7pm, cafe patrons can enjoy a tango show.

Ramos Meija 1358, at Libertador (in the Retiro Station Lobby). ℭ **11/4516-0902**. Main courses $1.35–$3. No credit cards. Daily 6:30am–10pm. Metro: Retiro.

Café Tortoni ★★★ *(Moments* CAFE/ARGENTINE   You cannot come to Buenos Aires and not visit this important Porteño institution. This historic cafe has served as the artistic and intellectual capital of Buenos Aires since 1858, hosting notable guests such as Jorge Luis Borges, Julio de Caro, Cátulo Castillo, and José Gobello. Wonderfully appointed in woods, stained glass, yellowing marble, and bronzes, the place tells more about its history by simply existing than any of the photos hanging on its walls could. This is the perfect spot for a coffee or a small snack when wandering along Avenida de Mayo. Twice-nightly tango shows at 7:30 and 9:30pm in a cramped side gallery where the performers often walk through the crowd are worth stopping in for. What makes the Tortoni all the more special is that locals and tourists seem to exist side-by-side here, one never overwhelming the other. Do not, however, expect great service: Sometimes only jumping up and down will get the staff's attention, even when they are just a few feet from you.

Av. de Mayo 825, at Esmeralda. © **11/4342-4328**. Main courses $2–$7. AE, DC, MC, V. Mon–Thurs 8am–2am; Fri–Sat 8am–3am; Sun 8am–1am. Metro: Av. de Mayo.

Don Galíndez ★ *Value* PARRILLA/MIDDLE EASTERN   Watch the world go by from here, at the corner of Lavalle and Esmeralda. Everyday shoppers and weird seedy folks will be part of the show from the seats of this combination restaurant, which comes in two parts—half an ordinary Argentine *parrilla*, half a Syrian fast-food restaurant, serving food like shawarma, falafel, and other items beginning at $1. The staff bounces back and forth between the two places. Daily specials aimed at the lunch crowd include the "Plato del Día," a main course, bread, and a drink for a little over $2. They also do takeout. But the best part about the place is sitting at the lunch counter on this corner watching all of Buenos Aires and laughing with the very chatty chefs at the *parrilla*.

Lavalle 798, at Esmeralda. © **11/4322-6705**. Main courses $1–$4. No credit cards. Daily 10am–1am. Metro: Lavalle.

Filo ★ *Finds* PIZZA   Popular with young professionals, artists, and anyone looking for cause to celebrate, Filo presents its happy clients with mouthwatering pizzas, delicious pastas, and potent cocktails. The crowded bar has occasional live music, and tango lessons are offered downstairs a few evenings per week.

San Martín 975, at Alvear. © **11/4311-0312**. Main courses $2–$5. AE, MC, V. Daily noon–4pm and 8pm–2am. Metro: San Martín.

Il Gran Caffe ★ CAFE/ITALIAN   As the name implies, this is a largely Italian restaurant with an extensive selection of pastries, pastas, paninis, as well as more traditional Argentine fare. Located on a busy corner across the street from Galerías Pacífico, it also offers one of the best places for watching the crowds passing by on Calle Florida. A covered canopy on the Córdoba side also provides outdoor seating rain or shine. Realizing the voyeuristic value of its real estate, the restaurant charges 15% more for outdoor dining than indoors. If that bothers the budget-conscious spy in you, the best compromise is to sit inside on their upper-floor level, with its bird's-eye view of the street and the Naval Academy, one of the city's most beautiful landmarks. If you've just come for mixed drinks, they start at about $3 each.

Calle Florida 700, at Córdoba. © **11/4326-5008**. Main courses $3–$6. AE, MC, V. Daily 7am–2am. Metro: Florida.

La Sortija *Value* PARRILLA/ARGENTINE   This is a very basic, small *parrilla*. The decorations are at a minimum, with the emphasis on the food and courteous service instead. A largely wood interior, appearing older than its 2000 opening, awaits patrons. Shelves full of bottles of wine and soda are the only clutter in the place. Most of the patrons are working-class locals who have jobs in the area, and it's very busy after 5pm when they stop in for a bite before making their way home. La Sortija prides itself on what it calls *cocina casera*, or home cooking, and serves very good and well-prepared cuts of meat, such as *bife de chorizo*. They also have sandwiches for takeout. This place offers tremendous value, especially considering the small amount of money it costs to eat here. Pizza, pasta, and chicken round out the menu.

Lavalle 663, at Maipú. © **11/4328-0824**. Main courses $3–$5. No credit cards. Daily 8am–midnight. Metro: Lavalle.

Morizono ★ *Value* JAPANESE   A casual Japanese restaurant and sushi bar, Morizono offers such treats as dumplings stuffed with pork, shrimp and vegetable tempuras, salmon with ginger sauce, and a variety of sushi and sashimi combination platters. Morizono also has locations in Palermo at Paraguay 3521 (© **11/4823-4250**), and Lacroze 2173, in Belgrano (© **11/4773-0940**).

Reconquista 899, at Paraguay. © **11/4314-0924**. Reservations recommended. Main courses $3–$6. AE, DC, MC, V. Mon–Fri 12:30–3:30pm and 8pm–midnight; Sat 8pm–1am. Metro: San Martín.

Petit Paris Café ☆ CAFE   Marble-top tables with velvet upholstered chairs, crystal chandeliers, and bow-tie-clad waiters give this cafe a European flavor. Its large windows look directly onto Plaza San Martín, placing the cafe within short walking distance of some of the city's best sights. The menu offers a selection of hot and cold sandwiches, pastries, and special coffees and teas. Linger over your coffee as long as you like—happily, nobody will pressure you to move.

Av. Santa Fe 774, at Esmeralda. © **11/4312-5885**. Main courses $2–$4. AE, DC, MC, V. Daily 7am–2am. Metro: San Martín.

5 Monserrat

For a map of the restaurants listed in this section, see the "Where to Dine in Central Buenos Aires" map on p. 98.

MODERATE

Club Español ☆☆ SPANISH   This Art Nouveau Spanish club, with its high, gilded ceiling and grand pillars, bas-relief artwork, and original Spanish paintings, boasts the most magnificent dining room in Buenos Aires. Despite the restaurant's architectural grandeur, the atmosphere is surprisingly relaxed and often celebratory; don't be surprised to find a table of champagne-clinking Argentines next to you. Tables have beautiful silver place settings, and tuxedo-clad waiters offer formal service. Although the menu is a tempting sample of Spanish cuisine—including paella and Spanish omelets—the fish dishes are the best.

Bernardo de Yrigoyen 180, at Alsina. © **11/4334-4876**. Reservations recommended. Main courses $4–$8. AE, DC, MC, V. Daily noon–4pm and 8pm–midnight. Metro: Lima.

Restaurante y Bar Mediterráneo ☆☆ MEDITERRANEAN   The Inter-Continental Hotel's exclusive Mediterranean restaurant and bar were built in a colonial style, resembling the city's famous Café Tortoni (p. 104). The downstairs bar, with its hardwood floor, marble-top tables, and polished Victrola playing a tango, takes you back to Buenos Aires of the 1930s. A spiral staircase leads to the elegant restaurant, where subdued lighting and well-spaced tables create an intimate atmosphere. Mediterranean herbs, olive oil, and sun-dried tomatoes are among the chef's usual ingredients. Carefully prepared dishes might include shellfish bouillabaisse; black hake served with ratatouille; chicken casserole with morels, fava beans, and potatoes; or duck breast with cabbage confit, wild mushrooms, and sautéed apples. Express menus (ready within minutes) are available at lunch.

Moreno 809, at Piedras, in the InterContinental Hotel. © **11/4340-7200**. Reservations recommended. Main courses $6–$9. AE, DC, MC, V. Daily 7–11am, 11:30am–3:30pm, and 7pm–midnight. Metro: Moreno.

6 San Telmo

For a map of the restaurants listed in this section, see the "Where to Dine in Central Buenos Aires" map on p. 98.

MODERATE

Bar El Federal ☆☆ *(Moments* CAFE/ARGENTINE   This bar and restaurant, on a quiet corner in San Telmo, represents a beautiful step back in time. Fortunately, as another *café notable,* it will stay that way forever. The first thing that will strike you here is the massive carved-wood-and-stained-glass ornamental stand over the bar area, though it originally came from an old pastry shop and is being reused here. Local patrons sit at the old tables whiling away their time looking out onto the streets, chatting, or sitting with a book drinking tea or espresso. The original tile floor remains, and old signs, portraits, and small antique machines decorate this space, which has been in business since 1864. Bar El Federal is among the most Porteño of places in San Telmo, a neighborhood that has more of these establishments than any other. Some of the staff has been here for decades on end, and proudly so. Food is a collection of small, simple things, mostly sand-wiches, steaks, *lomos* (sirloin cuts), and a very large salad selection. High-quality pastries are also offered to complement the menu.

Corner of Perú and Carlos Calvo. (*C*) **11/4300-4313.** Main courses $2–$6. AE, MC, V. Sun–Thurs 7am–2am; Fri–Sat 7am–4am. Metro: Independencia.

Desnivel (*★*) PARRILLA   This place brings new meaning to the phrase greasy spoon, since everything in here seems to be greasy—from the slippery floor to the railings, glasses, and dishes. Even the walls and the artwork on them seem to bleed grease. Thankfully, the food more than makes up for the atmosphere. This is one of San Telmo's best *parrillas,* and a flood of locals and tourists, often lined up wait-ing at the door, keeps the place hopping. This is especially true on Sunday or when there's a game on television and everyone comes here to watch and eat under the blaring television suspended over the dining area. The decor in this two-level restaurant is unassuming, home-style, and full of mismatched wooden chairs, tablecloths, and silverware. The food, mostly consisting of thick, well-cooked, and fatty steaks, is great. Though prices here are slightly higher than in other *parrillas,* your meal will be worth the price.

Defensa 858, at Independencia. (*C*) **11/4300-9081.** Main courses $5–$8. No credit cards. Daily noon–4pm and 8pm–1am. Metro: Independencia.

La Brigada (*★*) PARRILLA   This San Telmo *parrilla* is reminiscent of the Pam-pas, with memorabilia of gauchos (Pampas cowboys) filling the restaurant. White linen tablecloths and tango music complement the atmosphere, with an upstairs dining room that faces an excellent walled wine rack. The professional staff here makes sure diners are never disappointed, and service is outstanding. Chef-owner Hugo Echevarrieta, known as *el maestro parrillero,* carefully selects meats. The best choices include the *asado* (short rib roast), *lomo* (sirloin steak, prepared with a mushroom or pepper sauce), baby beef (an enormous 850g/30 oz., served for two), and the *mollejas de chivito al verdero* (young goat sweetbreads in a scallion sauce). The Felipe Rutini merlot goes perfectly with baby beef and chorizo. La Brigada has a second outlet in Recoleta at Peña 2475 ((*C*) **11/4800-1110**).

Estados Unidos 465, at Bolívar. (*C*) **11/4361-5557.** Reservations recommended. Main courses $4–$8. AE, DC, MC, V. Daily noon–3pm and 8pm–midnight. Metro: Independencia.

La Coruña (*★★*) (*Moments*) CAFE/ARGENTINE   This extremely authentic old cafe and restaurant bar, another of the *cafés notables* protected by law, is the kind of place you'd expect your grandfather to have eaten at when he was a teenager. Young and old alike come to this bar, which is a very neighborhoody spot, with people catching soccer games on television or quietly chatting away as they order beer, small snacks, and sandwiches. The TV seems to be the only modern thing in here. Music plays from a wooden table-top radio that must be from the 1950s, and two wooden refrigerators dating from who knows when are still in use for storing food. The old couple that owns the place, José Moreira and Manuela Lopéz, obviously subscribe to the view that if it ain't broke, there's no reason for a new one.

Bolívar 994, at Carlos Calvo. © **11/4362-7637**. Main courses $2–$4. No credit cards. Daily 9am–10pm. Metro: Independencia.

La Farmacia ⚝ CAFE/ITALIAN/ARGENTINE   Food and art is how this place likes to describe itself, and there is artwork by local San Telmo artists hanging up all around the dining area. The restaurant has several levels, including an upstairs lounge with a 1930s Art Deco feel, painted red with mismatched furniture, and an air-conditioned lounge for respite in the hot summer. Windows look out onto the street corner, allowing for great people-watching as slow traffic rumbles soothingly by. Some people prefer to take their drinks onto the rooftop terrace where there's no view to the street but where you will get a wonderful outdoor dining experience. Many patrons come here for small, easy-to-prepare things like sandwiches, pastries, and *fiambres* (cut-up bits of cheese and meat meant to be shared over drinks). Italian-inspired items, however, make up the bulk of the main courses, like spinach crepes, *lomo* medallions, and gnocchi. Aperitifs, wine, mixed drinks, and coffee and tea are the liquid highlights of this gathering spot, which is also considered one of the most gay-friendly restaurants in the neighborhood. A small clothing boutique full of vintage and clubby items shares the main floor, opening onto the cafe/lounge.

Bolívar 898, at Estados Unidos. © **11/4300-6151**. www.lafarmaciarestobar.com.ar. Main courses $2–$6. AE, MC, V. Tues–Sun 9am–3am; much later on weekends, depending on crowds. Metro: Independencia.

La Vieja Rotisería ⚝⚝ *(Value* PARRILLA/ITALIAN/ARGENTINE   The slabs of meat cooking at this *parrilla* are so huge you hope the guy cooking doesn't accidentally drop one on his foot and take himself out of commission. That would be bad for him, of course, but equally bad for you, because you would go without eating at one of the best *parrillas* in San Telmo, especially considering the prices. Following the rule "simple is best," this place concentrates on the food, not the decor. Mismatched vinyl tablecloths and old tacky prints and mirrors in baroque frames are part of the visual disorder here. But your eyes should be on the food. Steaks are thick and well prepared, but they also offer interesting twists on the meat here, like *lomo* in a tasty Roquefort sauce. Pastas, salads, fish, and chicken are offered here too—and the latter is served boneless so you don't have to waste any time chowing down on it. The place gets very crowded at night, so make reservations if you're coming after 9pm to make sure you're not waiting outside the window looking in.

Defensa 963, at Estados Unidos. © **11/4362-5660**. Reservations recommended. Main courses $2–$5. No credit cards. Mon–Thurs noon–4:30pm and 7:30pm–12:30am; Fri–Sat noon–4pm and 7:30pm–1:30am; Sun 11:30am–5:30pm and 7:30pm–12:30am. Metro: Independencia.

Pappa Deus ⚝ INTERNATIONAL/ARGENTINE   An interesting menu every day of the week, live music shows, folkloric dancing, and jazz on Friday and Saturday nights make this place one of the best alternatives to tango venues along Dorrego Plaza. The upstairs loft offers a more romantic setting, especially for couples who want a break from strolling along the streets of San Telmo. Built in 1798, the house in which the restaurant is located is among the oldest still standing in all of Buenos Aires.

Bethlem 423, at Defensa, on Plaza Dorrego. © **11/4361-2110**. www.pappadeus.com.ar. Main courses $5–$8. No credit cards. Sun–Thurs 9am–2am; Fri–Sat 9am–4am, often later. Metro: Independencia.

INEXPENSIVE

Casa de Esteban de Luca ⭐ ARGENTINE   This historic house, once inhabited by Argentina's beloved poet and soldier Esteban de Luca (who wrote the country's first national anthem, the "Marcha Patriótica"), was built in 1786 and declared a National Historic Monument in 1941. Today it's a popular restaurant serving pasta and meat dishes. Come on Thursday, Friday, or Saturday night after 9pm for the fun-spirited piano show.

Calle Defensa 1000, at Bethlem. ℂ **11/4361-4338.** Main courses $4–$6. AE, DC, MC, V. Tues–Sun noon–4pm and 8pm–1am. Metro: Independencia.

Medio y Medio ⭐ URUGUAYAN   This place serves Uruguayan *chivitos,* which are *lomo* sandwiches. *Lomo* takes on a different meaning in Uruguay than in Argentina. Unlike in Argentina, where it is only a cut of beef, it can be beef, pork, or chicken cut flat as a filet in Uruguay. It gets served as a hot sandwich with a slice of ham, cheese, and an egg, along with a garnish of tomatoes and lettuce. This is a crowded, busy place, especially at night when patrons sit outside under a canopy at tables painted with *fileteado,* an Italian art of painted filigree borders that has become quintessentially Argentine. At night, starting at 10pm, as you stuff yourself you'll be entertained by Spanish and folkloric singers and guitar players. They charge a 1.50 peso service for this pleasure, but don't worry: Beer gets cheaper here if you buy it with a meal at that time, so that more than makes up for the charge.

Chile 316, at Defensa. ℂ **11/4300-7007.** Main courses $1.50–$4. No credit cards. Mon–Tues noon–2am; Wed noon–3am; Thurs noon–4am; Fri noon–8am; Sat 8am–8am. Metro: Independencia.

Nanaka Bar PARRILLA/ITALIAN/ARGENTINE   Nanaka takes its name from an Argentine Indian word meaning "we," and the management does make sure that anyone is welcome. Sidewalk seating in good weather and a little nook under the staircase are some of the pleasant places to enjoy a meal here. Offerings include *lomo* cooked in interesting ways, such as with mustard sauce and served with crisp, sautéed vegetables called *verduras tivias.* The culture quotient is upped by art on the walls from local artists and the piano, tango, and jazz music softly playing on the sound system. This is also another of San Telmo's gay-welcome spots.

Humberto I no. 599, at Perú. ℂ **11/4362-7979.** Main courses $2–$3. No credit cards. Daily 8am–5am. Metro: Independencia.

7 Recoleta

There are no convenient metro stops in this neighborhood. For a map of the restaurants listed in this section, see the "Where to Dine in Central Buenos Aires" map on p. 98.

VERY EXPENSIVE

Piegari ⭐⭐ ITALIAN   You would not expect such a fine restaurant to be located where it is: under a highway overpass in a part of Recoleta dubbed "La Recova." Piegari has two restaurants located across the street from each other; the more formal focuses on Italian dishes while the other (Piegari Vitello e Dolce) is mainly a *parrilla.* Both restaurants are excellent, but visit the formal Piegari for outstanding Italian cuisine, with an emphasis on seafood and pastas. Homemade spaghetti, six kinds of risotto, pan pizza, veal scallops, and black salmon ravioli are just a few of the mouthwatering choices. Huge portions are made for sharing, and an excellent eight-page wine list accompanies the menu. If you decide to try Pie-gari Vitello e Dolce instead, the best dishes are the short rib roast and the leg of Patagonian lamb.

Posadas 1042, at Av. 9 de Julio in La Recova, near the Four Seasons Hotel. ℂ **11/4328-4104.** Reservations recommended. Main courses $13–$23. AE, DC, MC, V. Daily noon–3:30pm and 7:30pm–1am. No metro access.

EXPENSIVE

La Bourgogne ⭐⭐⭐ FRENCH   The only Relais Gourmand in Argentina, chef Jean Paul Bondoux serves the finest French and international food in the city here. *Travel & Leisure* magazine rated La Bourgogne the number one restaurant in South America, and *Wine Spectator* gave it the distinction of being one of the "Best Restaurants in the World for Wine Lovers." Decorated in elegant pastel hues, the formal dining room serves the city's top gourmands. To begin your meal, consider a warm foie gras scallop with honey wine sauce or perhaps the succulent *ravioli d'escargots*. Examples of the carefully prepared main courses include *chateaubriand béarnaise*, roasted salmon, veal steak, and lamb with parsley and garlic sauce. The kitchen's fresh vegetables, fruits, herbs, and spices originate from Bondoux's private farm. Downstairs, **La Cave** offers a slightly less formal dining experience, with a different menu, though the food comes from the same kitchen as it does in La Bourgogne. Wine tastings are offered Thursday in the restaurant's wine-cellar area called **Cave de Vines;** contact La Bourgogne directly for details.

Av. Alvear 1891, at Ayacucho (Alvear Palace Hotel). ℂ **11/4805-3857.** www.alvearpalace.com. Reservations required. Jacket and tie required for men. Main courses $7–$12. AE, DC, MC, V. Free valet parking. Mon–Fri noon–3pm; Mon–Sat 8pm–midnight. Closed Jan. No metro access.

Lola ⭐ INTERNATIONAL   Among the best-known international restaurants in Buenos Aires, Lola recently completed a makeover, turning its dining room into one of the city's brightest and most contemporary. Caricatures of major personal-ities adorn the walls, and fresh plants and flowers give Lola's dining room a spring-like atmosphere. A French-trained chef offers creative dishes such as chicken fricassee with leek sauce, grilled trout with lemon-grass butter and zucchini, and beef tenderloin stuffed with Gruyère cheese and mushrooms. The chef will pre-pare dishes for those with special dietary requirements as well.

Roberto M. Ortiz 1805, at Guido. ℂ **11/4804-5959** or 11/4802-3023. Reservations recommended. Main courses $7–$12. AE, DC, MC, V. Daily noon–4pm and 7pm–1am. No metro access.

MODERATE

El Mirasol ⭐⭐ PARRILLA   One of the city's best *parrillas*, this restaurant serves thick cuts of fine Argentine beef. Like Piegari (see above), El Mirasol is also located in La Recova, but in spite of this, its glassed dining area full of plants and trellises gives the impression of outdoor dining. Your waiter will guide you through the selection of cuts, among which the rib-eye, tenderloin, sirloin, and ribs are most popular. A mammoth 2½-pound serving of tenderloin is a specialty, certainly meant for sharing. El Mirasol is part of a chain that first opened in 1967. The best dessert is an enticing combination of meringue, ice cream, whipped cream, *dulce de leche*, walnuts, and hot chocolate sauce. The wine list pays tribute to Argentine Malbec, syrah, merlot, and cabernet sauvignon. El Mirasol, which is frequented by business executives and government officials at lunch and a more relaxed crowd at night, remains open throughout the afternoon (a rarity in a city where most restaurants close between lunch and dinner).

Posadas 1032, at Av. 9 de Julio in La Recova near the Four Seasons Hotel. ℂ **11/4326-7322.** www. el-mirasol.com.ar. Reservations recommended. Main courses $6–$45. AE, DC, MC, V. Daily noon–2am. No metro access.

Galani ★★ MEDITERANNEAN   This elegant but informal bistro inside the spectacular Four Seasons Hotel serves Mediterranean cuisine with Italian and Asian influences. The executive lunch menu includes an antipasto buffet with seafood, cold cuts, cheese, and salads followed by a main course and dessert. From the dinner menu, the aged Angus New York strip makes an excellent choice, and all grilled dishes come with béarnaise sauce or *chimichurri* (a thick herb sauce) and a choice of potatoes or seasonal vegetables. Organic chicken and fresh seafood join the menu, along with a terrific selection of desserts. Live harp music often accompanies meals, and tables are candlelit at night. Enjoy an after-dinner drink in Le Dôme, the split-level bar adjacent to the lobby featuring live piano music and occasional tango shows.

Posadas 1086, at Av. 9 de Julio (in the Four Seasons Hotel). ✆ 11/4321-1234. Reservations recommended. Main courses $5–$8. Fixed-price lunch $10. AE, DC, MC, V. Daily 7–11am, noon–3pm, and 8pm–1am. No metro access.

Sarkis ★ MIDDLE EASTERN/GREEK   Located just to the side of the Four Seasons Hotel in the La Recova restaurant area under the overpass for Avenida 9 de Julio, Sarkis's interior has an elegant modern style, looking more like the seating area of a classy nightclub than a restaurant. The menu has Armenian, Lebanese, and very strong Greek influences. Moussaka, Persian rice, and spicy sausages grilled on the *parrilla* are some of the highlights here. Sarkis combines its Middle Eastern routes with its Argentine location, however, and most of the main items are made with beef: You won't find lamb and goat, typical of Middle Eastern cuisine, here at all. Oversize pieces of baklava are part of the dessert offerings. This location opened in 2001; its original venue is still open at calles Thames and Jufré in the heart of Palermo's Middle Eastern district. Table service (the bread and such that is placed on your table) adds about a dollar per person to the final bill, but prices remain reasonable, even in this chic Recoleta location. Coffee grind readings are held every Wednesday to Saturday beginning at 9:30pm, but call ahead of time to make sure the mystic is working (and speaks English) if you're interested.

Av. 9 de Julio 1465, at Posadas, in the La Recova restaurant area near the Four Seasons Hotel. ✆ 11/4394-4888. Main courses $4–$8. AE, MC, V. Daily noon–3:30pm and 7:30pm–12:30 or 1am, depending on the crowds. No metro access.

INEXPENSIVE

Café Victoria ★ CAFE   Perfect for a relaxing afternoon in Recoleta, this cafe's outdoor patio is surrounded by flowers and shaded by an enormous tree. Sit and have a coffee or enjoy a complete meal. The three-course express lunch menu offers a salad, main dish, and dessert, with a drink included, for about $6. Afternoon tea with pastries and scones is served daily from 4 to 7pm. The cafe remains equally popular in the evening, when live music serenades the patio and there are excellent people-watching opportunities. This is a great value for the area, and it's especially convenient if you're sightseeing, as the Recoleta Cemetery and cultural center are located next door.

Roberto M. Ortiz 1865, at Quintana. ✆ 11/4804-0016. Main courses $3–$5. AE, DC, MC, V. Daily 7:30am–11:30pm. No metro access.

Clark's ★ INTERNATIONAL   The dining room here is an eclectic mix of oak, yellow lamps, live plants, and deer antlers. A slanted ceiling descends over the English-style bar with its fine selection of spirits; in back, a 3m-high (10-ft.) glass case showcases a winter garden. Booths and tables are covered with green-and-white checkered tablecloths and are usually occupied by North Americans. Specialties include tenderloin steak with goat cheese, sautéed shrimp with wild mushrooms, and sole with a sparkling wine, cream, and shrimp sauce. There are a number of pasta and rice dishes as well. A large outside terrace attracts a fashionable crowd in the summer. Clark's is a protected *bar notable.*

Roberto M. Ortiz 1777, at Quintana. © **11/4801-9502.** Reservations recommended. Main courses $4–$8. AE, DC, MC, V. Daily noon–3:30pm and 7:30pm–midnight. No metro access.

Juana M ★★ *Value* PARRILLA   This amazing little *parrilla* is easily overlooked, but you shouldn't miss it. A family-owned affair, it takes its name from its owner and is known almost solely to Porteños who want to keep this place all to themselves. Located in the basement of an orphanage, which was once the city's Catholic University, this neoclassical building is one of the few saved from the highway demolition that created the nearby La Recova area where Avenida 9 de Julio intersects with Libertador. This cavernous industrial-chic space is white and luminous by day, with seating for more than 210 patrons. At night, when the space is lit only by candlelight, trendy young patrons flood in, chattering the night away. The menu is simple, high-quality, and amazingly inexpensive, with a free unlimited salad bar with several healthy options.

Carlos Pellegrini 1535 (basement), at Libertador, across from the La Recova area. © **11/4326-0462.** Main courses $3–$4. AE, MC, V. Daily noon–4pm and 8pm–12:30am. No metro access.

La Biela ★★★ CAFE   Originally a small sidewalk cafe opened in 1850, La Biela earned its distinction in the 1950s as the rendezvous choice of race-car champions. Black-and-white photos of these Argentine racers decorate the huge dining room. Today artists, politicians, and neighborhood executives (as well as a fair number of tourists) all frequent La Biela, which serves breakfast, informal lunch plates, ice cream, and crepes. The outdoor terrace sits beneath an enormous 19th-century gum tree opposite the church of Nuestra Señora del Pinar and the adjoining Recoleta Cemetery. This place ranks among the most important cafes in the city, with some of the best sidewalk viewing anywhere in Recoleta. You might just feel like you're in Paris when you come here. La Biela is a protected *bar notable.*

Av. Quintana 596, at Alvear. © **11/4804-0449.** www.labiela.com. Main courses $3–$5. V. Daily 7am–3am. No metro access.

Maru Botana ★ CAFE/INTERNATIONAL   A pleasant little cafe on a small out-of-the-way street in Recoleta, Maru Botana is owned by an Argentine television cooking-show personality. In spite of her fame, the cafe is unpretentious and quiet, with only a few nods to its celebrity chef owner. You'll find a small inside seating area where you can sip tea and have excellent baked goods or light items like salads and sandwiches. It's also near the Israeli Embassy Monument commemorating the fatal 1992 bombing, so it makes a great place to stop and quietly contemplate what you have just seen.

Suipacha 1371, at Arroyo. © **11/4326-7134.** www.marubotana.com.ar. Main courses $1–$5. AE, MC, V. Mon–Fri 9am–8pm. Metro: San Martín.

8 Barrio Norte

For a map of the restaurants listed in this section, see the "Where to Dine in Central Buenos Aires" map on p. 98.

MODERATE

Clásica y Moderna ★★ *Finds* ARGENTINE   This restaurant represents an interesting way to save an important bookstore from extinction by opening a restaurant inside. The bookstore opened in this location in 1938, though the company dates from 1918. Emilio Robert Diaz was original owner, and now his grandchildren run the place. In 1988 books were relegated to the back to make way for diners, but this is one of the best bookstores for English-speaking tourists in the city. You'll find Buenos Aires photo and history books, as well as Argentine short-story collections, all translated into English. While this is a protected *café notable*, the interior has been completely stripped down to the exposed brick, giving the place a dark, industrial feel. Decorations overhead include old bicycles and signs, but it is a pleasant relaxed space where it's easy to chat with the staff as you dine or sit at the bar. There are many light and healthful choices like salads and soy burgers on the menu, though since all come with fries, it evens out the caloric content. Mixed drinks start at about $4. Events of all kinds are held here too, from literary readings to plays, dance shows, and art exhibitions. Shows are held Wednesday to Saturday around 10pm, and there are sometimes two shows, the second one beginning after midnight. Show prices vary from $5 to $8 and are not included in the price of dining here.

Callao 892, at Córdoba. ℰ **11/4812-8707** or 11/4811-3670. www.clasicaymoderna.com. Reservations recommended for shows. Main courses $3–$10. AE, MC, V. Daily 8am–1am. Bookstore hours: Mon–Sat 9am–1am; Sun 5pm–1am. Metro: Callao.

9 Congreso

For a map of the restaurants listed in this section, see the "Where to Dine in Central Buenos Aires" map on p. 98.

MODERATE

Inside Resto-Bar ⍟ INTERNATIONAL/ARGENTINE   This place is very popular with gay clientele. The waitstaff and the owners provide great, attitude-free service here; in fact, the two co-owners work along with their staff, Diego serving and Matias cooking. There is a low-key red-and-black decor, with dim moody lighting, and a second level of tables they open up when it gets crowded. The food is a mix of French and Italian influences and is very flavorfully prepared. This is also a good place to go just for drinks at their small bar, where many locals gather for conversation. On weekends they have special tango shows and male strippers too, after 12:30am. Reservations are accepted and recommended for weekends. Ask about their return coupons, offering great discounts for people who come back during their slow early weeknights.

Bartolomé Mitre 1571, at Montevideo. ℰ **11/4372-5439**. Main courses $5–$8. No credit cards. Daily 7pm–2am, later on weekends depending on the crowds. Metro: Congreso.

La Moncloa ⍟ *Value* CAFE   The surrounding trees here give a calming sense to sidewalk eating in what is normally a busy area on a street just off Plaza Congreso. La Moncloa takes its name from a famous Spanish palace. Basic Argentine fare like empanadas, steaks, and salads are on offer, along with croissant sandwiches and an extensive dessert menu. Lamb is also a main course, not typical of cafe-style eateries. Healthy eaters will enjoy their diet menu. Whatever you order, I recommend taking the time for a break in this restaurant's parklike setting. Coffee runs about a dollar and mixed drinks start at $3. If you don't have time to eat, stop by and grab a menu, as they'll deliver to local hotels.

Av. de Mayo 1500, at Sáenz Peña. ℰ **11/4381-3357** or 11/4382-7194. Main courses $2–$7. AE, DC, MC, V. Daily 7:30am–2am. Metro: Sáenz Peña.

Plaza Asturias ⍟⍟ *Finds* SPANISH/ITALIAN/ARGENTINE   This decades-old place on Avenida de Mayo is about as authentic as it gets, packed mostly with only Porteños who want to keep this place to themselves. It's all about the food here, with touches of Italian, Argentine, and most importantly, authentic Spanish cuisine. They are so busy and have to keep so much food on hand here that there are legs of cured ham literally hanging from the rafters over the diners' heads. Steaks are as thick as the crowds waiting to get into this place, and among their specialties are Spanish casseroles and lots of food with various sauces. Fish is also a big highlight. Be warned: The staff is so busy yelling out orders to the kitchen and bringing food to the tables that you can get hurt trying to find the bathroom.

Av. de Mayo 1199, at San José. © 11/4382-7334. Main courses $6–$10. No credit cards. Daily noon–3am. Metro: Sáenz Peña.

Plaza del Carmen CAFE/ARGENTINE   This is part of a chain, slightly sterile and clean. However, the best part of this cafe is not inside but the view from this corner overlooking Congreso outside. Generally open 24 hours, no matter what time of day it is you can find people having nothing more than croissants and coffee here. Weekdays, the outdoor seating area is a little overwhelming, since there is a huge amount of traffic flowing by this corner. But inside, protected from the noise and the bus and car fumes, everything is just fine. Wait until the weekends, when the sidewalk is less busy, and the outdoor area becomes more ideal. This restaurant offers standard Argentine cuisine in addition to a healthy choice of salads and diet and other light items on its menu. Pizzas, pastas, and other Italian items round out the menu. The best part of it all, though, is its bakery offering American-style donuts. Perfect for the kids, or for a picnic in Plaza Congreso.

Rivadavia 1795, at Callao. © 11/4374-8477. Main courses $5–$8. AE, MC, V. Wed–Sun 24 hr.; Mon–Tues 6am–2am. Metro: Congreso.

INEXPENSIVE

Café de Madres de Plaza de Mayo 𝄐𝄐 (Moments) CAFE   The official name of this cafe is Café Literario Osvaldo Bayer, named for an Argentine political intellectual. This cafe is located inside the lobby of the headquarters and teaching center of the Madres de Plaza de Mayo, just off of Plaza Congreso. What makes the place so special is its location and its left-wing political atmosphere. In few other places in Buenos Aires will you so easily be able to speak with people who had family members disappear during Argentina's military dictatorship, or with young students who have come to study in this building and continue seeking justice in this cause. The Madres bookstore is just to the side of the cafe, and it's full of books and newspapers on liberal causes from throughout Latin America. It also has one of the largest collections of books on Che Guevara anywhere in the world. An Argentine native, he is a personal hero to many of the Madres, and his image adorns walls throughout the building. The fare here is basic and cheap, offering ice-cream popsicles, pastries, and premade sandwiches.

Hipólito Yrigoyen 1584, at Ceballos. © 11/4382-3261. Main courses $2. No credit cards. Mon–Fri 10am–10pm; Sat 10am–8pm. Metro: Congreso.

La Americana 𝄐𝄐 ARGENTINE/ITALIAN   This place calls itself "La Reina de las Empanadas" (the Queen of Empanadas), and that indeed it is. They offer an enormous range of empanadas, all made with a very light dough, never heavy or greasy, with slightly burnt edges. The place is busy and loud, with the constant din of conversation bouncing off the tile and stone walls and the glass-plate windows looking out over Callao. There are tables here as well as a takeout section and an area for standing and eating—some people just can't be bothered sitting and simply scarf down these delicious creations once they get them. The place looks like many of the fast-food-chain emporiums, but don't confuse it with them; this is the only one of its kind. Tables are divided into smoking and nonsmoking sections, but that distinction mostly gets ignored. Waiters are frantic, scurrying from table to table as people change their minds after one bite and order extra rounds. You'll have to keep reminding them of what you ordered if you feel it's taking too much time, but don't blame them: It's just too busy for normal humans to keep up with the pace of the place. Italian specialties like calzones and pizzas round out the menu choices. Deliveries can be made to nearby hotels.

Callao 83, at Bartolomé Mitre. (11/4371-0202. Main courses 40¢–$5. No credit cards. Sun–Thurs 7am–2am; Fri–Sat 7am–3am. Metro: Congreso.

10 Palermo

For a map of the restaurants listed in this section, see the "Where to Stay & Dine in Palermo" map on p. 116.

EXPENSIVE

B'art *★★ (Finds* ARGENTINE/SPANISH/INTERNATIONAL   B'art's owner Adrián Fuentes might have worked for the McDonald's corporation during his 20 years living in the United States, but nothing about this unique place would seem to show that. He returned to his native Argentina after the terrorist attacks of September 11, 2001, seeking to do something to connect himself back to his culture. So he opened this restaurant serving the best Argentine meats, many of which are used for dishes prepared with both Argentine methods and old-world Spanish traditions. Among the menu items are tapas, casseroles, and *pinchos,* a kind of kabob. In addition to the usual meats, chefs cook up rabbit in various forms. Pastas, salads, and other vegetable dishes complete the eclectic menu. The restaurant sits in an 1885 building near the area of Palermo that the famous Argentine writer Jorge Luis Borges said once marked the edge of Buenos Aires proper. Adrián has beautifully restored the building, and he uses antiques like turn-of-the-20th-century brick pulleys for decorative but functional tasks, like carrying wine. He also invites artists to perform on a periodic basis, but some patrons just simply sit at the piano in the waiting area and play the keys while waiting for a table at this delightful restaurant.

Borges 2180, at Paraguay. (11/4777-1112. Main courses $6–$10. No credit cards. Mon–Thurs 10:30am–1am; Fri–Sat 10:30am–2:30am; Sun noon–1am. Metro: Scalabrini Ortiz.

Casa Cruz *★★ (Finds* ITALIAN/INTERNATIONAL   Opened in December 2004, Casa Cruz is one of the city's chicest restaurants. With its enormous polished-brass doors and lack of a sign on the door, you almost feel like you are entering a nightclub, and inside, the dark modern interior maintains the theme. The impressive round bar, always decorated with fresh flower arrangements, is the first thing you'll see before continuing on into the spacious dining area full of polished woods and red upholstery. The place takes its name from its owner, Juan Santa Cruz. This is his first venture into restaurants, and with the attention this restaurant has received in the national and international press, he has done exceedingly well. The menu here is eclectic and interesting, overseen by Germán Martitegui, the same chef who oversees the kitchen at Olsen. Rabbit, sea bass, Parma ham rolls, and other interesting and exotic ingredients go into the many flavorful dishes.

Uriarte 1658, at Honduras. (11/4833-1112. www.casa-cruz.com. Reservations highly recommended. Main courses $10–$14. AE, MC, V. Mon–Sat 8:30pm–3am, later on weekends. No metro access.

Where to Stay & Dine in Palermo

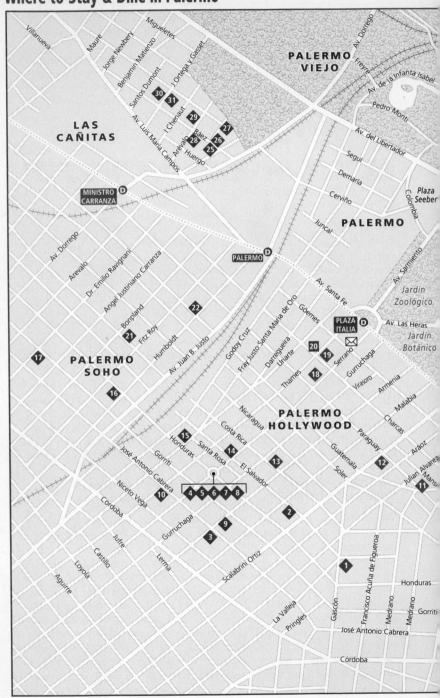

Post office ⊠
Subway ⋯ⓓ

0   0.25 mi
0   0.25 km

PALERMO CHICO

PALERMO

Plaza Alferez Sobral

Parque Las Heras

Plaza República de Chile

ACCOMMODATIONS ■
Casa Jardin **20**

DINING ◆
B'art **18**
Bio **22**
Campo Bravo **28**
Casa Cruz **15**
Central **21**
Club del Vino **10**
Cluny **2**
Coanico Bar **4**
Confitería del Botánico **23**
De Olivas i Lustres **1**
El Estanciero **25**
Garbis **24**
La Corte **29**
Lo De Pueyrredon **9**
Lomo **13**
Macondo Bar **7**
Malouva **19**
Morizono **11**
Novecento **26**
Olsen **17**
Pampa **16**
Penal1 **27**
República de Acá **5**
Sullivan's Drink House **14**
Sushi Club **31**
Tazz **8**
Te Mataré Ramirez **12**
Utopia Bar **6**
Viejo Agump **3**
Yoko's **30**

Central ★★★ *Finds* MEDITERRANEAN/LATINO   If you only have one night to go out for dinner in Palermo Viejo, this is the place you should choose. Federico Olabarrieta opened his restaurant in 2000 and oversees the service and the food here each night from the busy bar. The severe architecture, cold grays, steel elements, and clean white marble slabs belie the warm, wonderful service and food you will receive here. A small patio out back also offers outdoor dining. Lit entirely by candles once darkness sets, the place is transformed and soon fills with a young sophisticated crowd. The building was once the atelier of the daughter of Fernando Botero, the Colombian artist famed for his rounded portraits of people, and Colombian influences in the food celebrate this connection. Federico's Basque heritage is also evident in some of the menu items. The location of the restaurant was previously a fruit market, hence the name "Central" for Central Market, and bins of fresh fruits and vegetables in the vestibule celebrate this previous usage of the space. Food portions are large, and the menu has only eight main selections, which rotate seasonally. All are very good, with complex and contrasting ingredients. Salads are superb, sometimes with bitter flowers thrown in with the greens for colorful, tasty touches. Dinner prices push this into the expensive category, but lunch is a bargain at $4 for a prix-fixe menu. If you've already eaten elsewhere, come for drinks and enjoy them in the lounge area with its low, white leather sofas. Happy hour is from 6:30 to 8:30pm Monday to Friday. The large wine selection offers 25 Malbecs, 12 cabernet sauvignons, 6 merlots, and local champagnes.

Costa Rica 5644, at Fitzroy. ℂ **11/4776-7374** or 11/4776-7370. Reservations recommended. Main courses $8–$10. AE, MC, V. Daily 12:30pm–2 or 3am. Metro: Palermo.

Club del Vino ★ ARGENTINE/ITALIAN   In Palermo Viejo, Club del Vino brings a touch of Italian charm. This restaurant has several pretty dining rooms with a Tuscan rustic feel to them with simple sculptures and tables and chairs draped in red- and wheat-colored cloth. Birds chirp in the overgrown trees and vines in the interior gardens as you eat, giving an outdoor feel even inside. Federico Heinzmann is the executive chef, and before working here, he was at the Marriott Plaza Grill. He received his training throughout Spain, in the Basque region in particular. Because of this, his favorite thing to cook is fish, not a usual item on an Argentine menu, but his meat dishes are very well done too. Naturally, wine tastings are a major part of the offerings, and they are held regularly in an upstairs gallery for $12 a person, lasting about an hour. Make sure to check out the basement, where there is a small museum with old winemaking instruments such as presses and corking machines. The area also holds their extensive wine cellar. Over 350 kinds of wines are stored here; a staff sommelier can help you make your choice. Bottle prices range from $6 to $100, but the majority of them fall in the range of $6 to $12. Twenty percent of the wines are also available in glasses. Club del Vino was established in 1985 and opened in this location in 1994. Music and dancing shows are held Wednesday through Sunday beginning at 7 or 9pm, so make sure to call ahead and make a reservation. As of this writing, a remodel is planned for late 2005 or early 2006.

Cabrera 4737, at Thames. ℂ **11/4833-0048**. Reservations recommended. Main courses $8–$13. AE, MC, V. Daily 7pm–1am, sometimes later on weekends. No metro access.

Cluny ★★★ INTERNATIONAL/ARGENTINE   Opened in May 2004, Cluny has quickly become of the trendiest restaurants in Buenos Aires. The space is casual but elegant, looking more like a modernist living room than a dining room, with neutral color patterns and bursts of burnt orange to brighten things up. A loft space sits above it all and is excellent for hiding away for private conversations or romance. Others choose to dine outside in the patio garden in the restaurant's front space. Sinatra and bossa nova music from the 1960s add to the soft, casual atmosphere. The food, overseen by chef Matias Zuccarino, is the highlight here, and much of it is exotic, with complex offerings like stuffed quail or duck with grilled pumpkin. There are also many salmon dishes and lamb ravioli on offering. Beef, unlike in other Argentine restaurants, seems to be a second thought here, though it is well prepared, with the sirloin grills as a highlight. The extensive wine list runs over eight pages, offering the finest Argentine vintages from Catena Zapata to French imports hitting more than $250 a bottle. In the afternoon they have a fine British tea service, a distinctive feature more associated with the old dowager hotels in the center of the city rather than young and chic Palermo Viejo. While dinner is expensive, budget-priced Executive menus (as low as $5–$6) are on offer in the afternoon, with smaller, less complex versions of the late evening meals.

El Salvador 4618, at Malabia. ⓒ 11/4831-7176. Reservations highly recommended. Main courses $8–$12. AE, MC, V. Mon–Sat 12:30–3:30pm, 4–7:30pm for teatime, and 8:30pm–2am. Metro: Plaza Italia.

La Corte ⨀⨀ ARGENTINE/INTERNATIONAL Located on a quiet side street in the Las Cañitas area of Palermo, away from the chaos of Calle Báez, La Corte has a well-prepared menu and is a romantic choice for a night out. Candlelight and other soft lighting and slow music offer an opportunity for a couple to talk and relax after a day of sightseeing. Still, anyone will enjoy the long white lounges and deep chairs as they sit at the tables. Huge bookshelves with antique clocks and other odds and ends are in the front part of the restaurant, giving a sense of being in a library and adding comfort to the seating arrangements. The tiny bar is beautifully backlit, and many people stop in for drinks from the extensive wine-and-mixed-drink list. The cuts of meat are enormous and tasty, but there is a strong emphasis on the vegetable components of the meal to add texture and flavor. There are starters like sautéed mushrooms and vegetables. Before you begin your meal, the waiters offer a puréed vegetable shot to clean your palate. The very friendly and attentive staff is great at answering questions and attending to your needs. Desserts are very heavy and rich and though well worth it, they're on the expensive side, costing as much as many of the main dishes. The restaurant itself is large, divided up into various levels and spaces, with a few tables on the narrow sidewalk for outdoor dining.

Arévalo 2977, at Báez. ⓒ 11/4775-0999. Reservations recommended. Main courses $7–$9. AE, MC, V. Daily noon–1am, later on weekends. Summer daily 6pm–1am. Metro: Carranza.

Lo De Pueyrredón ⨀⨀ *Finds* PARRILLA/ARGENTINE You may recognize the name of this place from one of the main streets of Buenos Aires. It's owned by Horacio Pueyrredón, a descendant of one of Argentina's most important political families. The place appears humble in spite of Horacio's lineage, and he says very proudly that it is strictly Argentine, serving up the best and most typical food his country can produce. The *parrilla* serves up thick slabs of meat eaten on rustic tables. The building itself is incredible, a restored house that still maintains its ornate floor tiles and stained-glass windows within its doors and patio exit. Exposed brick walls hold changing works by local artists, all of which are for sale. Salads, empanadas, and pastas make up the bulk of the other offerings. They also serve a very traditional and heavy stew called *locro*. It takes over 5 hours to prepare and is a slow-simmered mix of corn, pumpkin, pork, beans, chorizo, blood sausage, and other ingredients. Though this is usually considered a winter dish, they offer it year-round. With the belief that the Indians who once lived in the Pampas are just as Argentine as Horacio is, he also offers items with native influences, such as tamales and *humitas* with *choclo,* an old form of corn. He is also vehemently proud of his long wine list, all of it produced in Argentina. The wide range of unusual, hard-to-find, local cuisine pushes this place into the expensive category, but *parrilla* items begin at a mere $4 a serving. The $25 three-course menú turístico is among the most expensive in this part of the city but is worth it for the high-quality meat and interesting items on the menu. Thursday evenings around 11pm, there is an open mic and guitar playing. Friday and Saturday beginning at 11:30pm, there is a folkloric dance show that lasts about 2 hours.

Armenia 1378, at Cabrera. ✆ 11/4773-7790. Reservations highly recommended. Main courses $4–$25. AE, MC, V. Wed–Sat noon–3pm and 8pm–5am, often later Fri–Sat. No metro access.

Lomo ✪ ARGENTINE   The full name of this restaurant is "Lomo, the Holy Argentine Word," in reference to the worship of meat throughout Argentina. Inside a former cheese factory bankrupted by the peso crisis, this is one of the most interesting reuses of any old building in Palermo Viejo. While the cheese-drying shelves are gone, the joints that held them in the cracking concrete walls remain. The place is lit by a soaring atrium, and stairs lead to the more intimate upper floor with a fireplace and an outdoor section, decorated with indigenous textiles calling to mind the Indians who once roamed the land where cows now graze. Ironically, the restaurant opened on October 17, 2002, the anniversary date of the rise of Peronism, but the high prices and slightly pretentious attitude of the staff are far from the Peronist ideal. A small record shop is on a mezzanine, and patrons can choose music to listen to and buy if they like it. Chef Guillermo González serves up *lomo,* a cut of beef, in interesting ways, including *lomo* ravioli and *lomo* in various crème sauces. Several fish dishes are also on the menu, but the main specialty is wild boar in fennel stock, which takes over 7 hours to prepare. There's also an afternoon *mate* service, which many locals, especially fashionable young mothers with baby strollers, come for. It's like a British tea service, but with *mate* (a South American tea made from a strong herbal grass) and salted toasts instead, bringing an elegant touch to a gaucho tradition. A cover charge of about $1 per person is added to your bill here.

Costa Rica 4661, at Armenia. ✆ 11/4833-3200. Reservations highly recommended. Main courses $6–$14. AE, MC, V. Mon 8:30pm–2am; Tues–Sun 1pm–2am. No metro access.

Olsen ✪✪ SCANDINAVIAN/SEAFOOD   A bit of Scandinavia has landed in Argentina. Olsen is built into what was once a warehouse, and it soars to church-like proportions and has a mezzanine with a few tables overlooking the main dining area. The interior, complete with a central round metal fireplace, has a 1960s mod feel to it with blonde woods, straight lines, and funky dish settings with orange, brown, and black circles on them. The place is set apart from the street by a large wooden fence, which leads into a patio garden overgrown with vines, complete with a metal sculpture fountain on an adjacent wall. It's an extremely tranquil space, with only a few chairs and tables set out here. They sink into the grass, giving the feeling of a living room that has succumbed to nature. Olsen is very popular with tourists and locals alike, and all of the extremely attractive staff speak English. Starters are fun and meant to be shared, like an excellent selection of bagels, tiny pancakes, smoked salmon, smoked herring, caviar, and flavored cheeses and butters. Fish is the main point of this place, and a few of the meat dishes, though flavorful, tend to be on the dry side. Many people come just for the bar, and there is an enormous vodka selection. Absolut rules this part of the restaurant and is available by the shot or the bottle. On Sunday try their brunch, which begins at 10am.

Travel Tip: He who finds the best hotel deal has more to spend on facials involving knobbly vegetables.

Hello, the Roaming Gnome here. I've been nabbed from the garden and taken round the world. The people who took me are so terribly clever. They find the best offerings on Travelocity. For very little cha-ching. And that means I get to be pampered and exfoliated till I'm pink as a bunny's doodah.

** travelocity®

1-888-TRAVELOCITY / travelocity.com / America Online Keyword: Travel

Gorriti 5870, at Carranza. © **11/4776-7677.** restaurantolsen@netizon.com.ar. Reservations recommended. Main courses $7–$12. AE, DC, MC, V. Tues–Thurs noon–1am; Fri–Sat 12:30pm–2:30am, sometimes later if busy; Sun 10am–1am. No metro access.

Sullivan's Drink House *Kids* IRISH/INTERNATIONAL With a decor as green as the Emerald Isle and an international staff full of young people from all over Europe, you'll feel as if you've left Argentina when you step into this place. Traditional Irish food and herb-marinated meat make up the bulk of the offerings here. Cordero Longueville is one of their specialties, based on an old Irish recipe using Patagonian lamb. Sandwiches and a children's meals are also on the menu. Windows to the street give great views, and a VIP lounge, decorated in Old English style, is upstairs, serving as a cigar bar. On the rooftop there's a covered terrace offering even more dining space. No matter what part of the restaurant you choose, Sullivan's has one of the most extensive imported whiskey menus in town, beginning at about $5 per serving. The luck of the Irish is indeed evident in the history of this restaurant: They opened on December 20, 2001, just days before the peso crisis, yet they have survived. If you're in Buenos Aires on St. Patrick's Day, this is definitely the place to be.

El Salvador 4919, at Borges. © **11/4832-6442.** Main courses $7–$12. AE, DC, MC, V. Mon–Thurs 10:30am–1am; Fri–Sat 10:30am–2:30am; Sun noon–1am. Metro: Scalabrini Ortiz.

Te Mataré Ramírez ★★★ *Finds* INTERNATIONAL/FRENCH This is perhaps the most interesting and creative dining experience in Buenos Aires. The name of the restaurant literally means "I am going to kill you, Ramírez." It comes from playful arguments the owner would have with a friend who was a sort of Casanova, and this was a threat the friend often heard from the husbands whose wives he was carrying on affairs with. It's an erotic restaurant, both in its food and decor. Carlos DiCesare, the owner, is himself a devilishly handsome man, looking much younger and fit than his late-40s age. The food he puts out is an interesting mix of flavors and textures. Sensual combinations include garlic and sun-dried tomatoes mixed with sweet elements and poured over sautéed or marinated meats with deeply embedded flavor. This emphasis on contrasts creates some of the most flavorful cooking in town. The ceilings are decorated with paintings of naked men and women with nothing more than high-heeled shoes, mixed in with naughty cherubs. Erotic art hangs on the walls, all of it for sale. The lighting is boudoir red, and wine is consumed out of antique cut crystal glasses that cast red sparkles on the tablecloths. Black-clothed actors perform playfully racy shows on a small stage here, using hand-held puppets who do very naughty things. It's hard to describe this place as romantic, but certainly a dinner here could lead to post-meal hanky-panky when discussing the play's theme. Slow, soft music like jazz and bossa nova plays as you eat, adding to the mood for love. There's another location in the suburbs in San Isidro, at Primera Junta 702 (© **11/4747-8618**).

Paraguay 4062, at Scalabrini Ortiz. © **11/4831-9156.** www.tematareramirez.com. Reservations recommended. Main courses $6–$12. AE, MC, V. Sun–Wed 9pm–midnight; Thurs–Fri 9pm–1am; Sat 9pm–2am. Metro: Scalabrini Ortiz.

MODERATE

De Olivas i Lustres ★★ MEDITERRANEAN Located in Palermo Viejo, this magical restaurant is a Buenos Aires favorite. The small, rustic dining room displays antiques, olive jars, and wine bottles, and each candlelit table is individually decorated—one resembles a writer's desk, another is sprinkled with seashells. The reasonably priced menu celebrates Mediterranean cuisine, with light soups, fresh fish, and sautéed vegetables as its focus. The breast of duck with lemon and honey is mouthwatering; there are also a number of *tapeos*—appetizer-size dishes. For about $9 each, you and your partner can share 15 such dishes brought out individually (a great option provided you have at least a couple of hours). Open only for dinner, this romantic spot offers soft, subtle service.

Gascón 1460, at El Salvador. © **11/4867-3388.** Reservations recommended. Main courses $3–$5; fixed-price menu $8. AE, V. Mon–Sat 7:30pm–1:30am. Metro: Scalabrini Ortiz.

El Estanciero ⋪ *Finds* PARRILLA   In most of the restaurants in the Las Cañitas section of Palermo, it's all about the glamour. Here, however, in the *parrilla* El Estanciero, it's all about the beef, arguably the best in the neighborhood. The portions are not the largest, but the cuts are amazingly flavorful, with just the right mix of fat to add tenderness. If you order the steak rare *(jugoso)*, they also have the sense here not to serve it nearly raw. The restaurant is in two levels, with sidewalk seating at the entrance and a covered open-air terrace above. Both floors have a subtle gaucho accented decor that does not overwhelm the senses with kitsch. Never as crowded as the other restaurants lining the street, this is a great option when the lines are too long at the adjacent "scene"-and-be-seen hot spots.

Báez 202, at Arguibel. © **11/4899-0951.** Main courses $5–$10. AE, MC, V. Daily noon–4pm and 8pm–1am (to 2am weekends). Metro: Ministro Carranza.

Garbis ⋪⋪ *Kids* MIDDLE EASTERN   If you're looking for great Middle Eastern food at reasonable prices or a spot to entertain the kids, Garbis has the answer. Kabobs, falafel, lamb, and other Middle Eastern mainstays are all on the menu, along with great, friendly service. The desert kitsch comes in the form of tiled walls and brilliant colors, making you think you've wound up far away from Argentina. A children's entertainment center is also in the restaurant, so the kids will stay happy while you dine. Tarot card readings on select days add fun for the adults. Call to find out the schedule. This is a chain, with additional restaurants in Belgrano and Villa Crespo.

Scalabrini Ortiz, at Cerviño. © **11/4511-6600.** www.garbis.com.ar. Main courses $3–$8. AE, MC, V. Daily 11am–3pm and 7–11:30pm. Metro: Scalabrini Ortiz.

Novecento ⋪⋪⋪ INTERNATIONAL   With a sister restaurant in Soho, Novecento was one of the pioneer restaurants of Palermo's Las Cañitas neighborhood. Fashionable Porteños pack the New York–style bistro by 11pm, clinking wineglasses under a Canal Street sign or opting for the busy outdoor terrace. Waiters rush to keep their clients happy, with dishes like salmon carpaccio and steak salad. The pastas and risotto are mouthwatering, but you may prefer a steak au poivre or a chicken brochette. Other wonderful choices include filet mignon, grilled Pacific salmon, and penne with wild mushrooms. Top it off with an Argentine wine. At night, with its candle lighting, this makes a romantic choice for couples looking for something special. There is also a large, separated, but slightly sterile, nonsmoking room available.

Báez 199, at Arguibel. © **11/4778-1900.** Reservations recommended. Main courses $4–$7. AE, DC, MC, V. Daily noon–4pm and 8pm–2am; Sun brunch 8am–noon. Metro: Ministro Carranza.

Penal1 ⋪⋪ PARRILLA/ARGENTINE   If you can't get enough of Argentine polo on their world-famous polo grounds, come to this restaurant, just a block from one of the grounds' back entrances. Penal1 takes it name from a play in polo, and has various owners, including Horacio and Bautista Heguy, two brothers who are players for the Indios Chapaleuful team. Every now and then, they come by to check things out. In season during November and early December, you can often find them celebrating here with fellow players. Service is extremely friendly and casual, and other than the owners, you won't find much about polo itself here, except for a mantle with a few trophies and a polo painting that looks more like an ad for Marlboro cigarettes. The food here is simple and inexpensive, consisting mostly of pastas, salads, and meat grilled on the *parrilla*. Lomito Penal1 is their signature sandwich, with *lomo*, lettuce, tomato, cheese, egg, and bacon. There is a large, expensive wine-and-mixed-drink selection, which includes champagne. In fact, drinking here seems to be more of the point than eating. The place is at its height in season when the bar section, graced by an enormous television, plays host to rowdy and happy patrons after polo games. A disco ball hangs from the ceiling, somewhat incongruous with the rest of the building, located in an old house that still retains some of its original elements. The large overgrown garden in front of the restaurant has several tables and is an excellent spot for late-night summer dining.

Arguibel 2851, at Báez. ℂ 11/4776-6030. Main courses $3–$6. No credit cards. Tues–Sun 9pm–2am, much later on weekends depending on crowds. Metro: Carranza.

República de Acá ★★ INTERNATIONAL/ARGENTINE/COMEDY CLUB Charcoal drawings of Hollywood actors and other stars decorate the walls of this place, a fun comedy club and karaoke bar overlooking Plaza Serrano. Drinks are the main event here, but food offerings include pizzas, *picadas*, or small cuts of cheese and meat that you "pick" at, salads, and other easy-to-make small items. Drinks come with free use of the Internet, and the menu will tell you how many minutes of Internet use are included with each drink. About half of this club is taken up by computers. Prices of drinks rise after 11pm by about 10%. At night the shows begin, and there is entertainment of all kinds. On weekends live music shows begin at 10pm, followed by comedy routines at 12:30am, karaoke at 3am, and then dancing until way past the time the sun comes up. There is a $5 entrance fee after 10pm on weekends, which includes one drink. After 2am this drops to a little over $3 to enter and still includes one drink. Many mixed drinks are made with ice cream, very adult interpretations of soda floats. TVs wrap around the whole space, so there is always something to watch. Fine champagnes and a selection of cigars at the bar make this a place to head to when you've got something to celebrate.

Serrano 1549, at Plaza Serrano. ℂ 11/4581-0278. www.republicadeaca.com.ar. Main courses $2–$5. No credit cards. Sun–Thurs 9am–2am; Fri–Sat 9am–7am. Metro: Plaza Italia.

Sushi Club JAPANESE   This restaurant is part of a very popular chain, with many locations throughout the city, but this is one of its nicest outlets. The Sushi Club serves up sushi and other Japanese cuisine in a modern clublike interior, with orange, black, and metallic elements part of the decor. Fish is a big highlight of the menu, along with beef with Japanese seasonings. Their sushi roll selection is enormous and creative, with many taking themes from various countries and using ingredients to match.

J. Ortega y Gasset 1812, at Arce. ℂ 0-810/222-SUSHI (toll-free). Main courses $4–$8. AE, DC, MC, V. Daily noon–5pm and 8pm–3am. Metro: Carranza.

Utopia Bar ARGENTINE/INTERNATIONAL   More cozy and calm than some of the other bars that surround Plaza Serrano, this is an excellent place to grab a drink and a bite to eat in this very trendy and busy area. Yellow walls and soothing rustic wooden tables add a sense of calm, though the live music, scheduled on an irregular basis, can be loud at times. There is an emphasis on the drinks here, and breakfast has a large selection of flavored coffees, some prepared with whiskey, which should really get your day started. At night pizza and sandwiches make up the bulk of the offerings. The upstairs, open-air terrace on the roof of the bar is one of the best spots to sit, but its small size, with just a few tables, makes it hard to claim a spot.

Serrano 1590, at Plaza Serrano. ℂ 11/4831-8572. Main courses $2–$8. AE, MC, V. Daily 24 hr. Metro: Plaza Italia.

Yoko's 𝒢 JAPANESE/CHINESE   This is an elegant, upscale eatery combining elements of Japanese and Chinese cuisines with California accents. The setting is mod, romantic, and chic all at once, with black lacquered tables, red walls, and interesting pieces of black metal sculpture with red accents. The service is friendly, with a large number of waitstaff to attend to the clients. Try their rolls, which are like California wraps, mixing seafood and cheeses. Healthy wok-cooked food and sushi round out the menu.

J. Ortega y Gasset 1813, at Calle Báez. ℂ 11/4776-0018 or 11/4778-0036. Main courses $4–$7. AE, DC, MC, V. Mon–Sat 10am–1am; Sun 6pm–1am. Metro: M. Carranza.

INEXPENSIVE

Bio 𝒢𝒢 𝑓𝑖𝑛𝑑𝑠 VEGETARIAN/MEDITERRANEAN   In a nation where meat reigns supreme, finding an organic vegetarian restaurant is a near impossibility. Bio, opened in 2002, is the exception. Their "meat" is made on the premises from wheat, then marinated to add more flavor. It then becomes an elevated and tasty version of a hamburger. All the ingredients used at Bio are organic, and all are grown or produced strictly in Argentina. Piles of organic cheese line the counters near the chefs, Gaston and Maximo, who are happy to explain the processes by which they work. Quinoa, the ancient Incan grain, is also used in many of the dishes, some of which they describe as Mediterranean-Asian fusion, though with the combinations of so many unusual ingredients, it's really anything goes. But what matters is that everything here is simply delicious and fresh. Chairs and tables are painted a spring green, and on warm days, a few tables are scattered on the sidewalk outside. This is also a great place for veg-heads to go shopping for snacks to bring back to their hotel. They have a small shop inside with organic chips, teas, cheeses, and even organic wine. They also do takeout. As healthful as the place is, smoking is allowed, though the management does try to discourage it.

Humboldt 2199, at Guatemala. ℂ 11/4774-3880. Main courses $4–$6. No credit cards. Tues–Sun noon–3:30pm; daily 8pm–1am, often later on weekends. No metro access.

Campo Bravo 𝒢𝒢 𝒱𝑎𝑙𝑢𝑒 PARRILLA/ARGENTINE   This place serves as the virtual center of the Las Cañitas dining scene. It's relaxed during the day but insane at night. Dining on the sidewalk here, you'll get a great view of the glamorous crowds who get dropped off by taxis to begin their night in this exciting neighborhood. The *parrilla* serves up basic Argentine cuisine, and its enormous slabs of meat are served on wooden boards. A large, efficient waitstaff will take care of you, but they can't do anything about the long wait for an outside table on weekends, sometimes as long as 40 minutes to an hour. There's no way around that since they don't accept reservations. So if you want the priceless location on a Saturday night, do as the locals do and get a glass of champagne and sip it outside on the street and join what looks like a well-dressed and overage frat party. A limited wine selection and imported whiskeys are also part of the drink selection. Can't handle the late nights in Argentina? Well then you're in luck—they don't close between lunch and dinner, so people used to North American dining schedules can still enjoy a great meal here with no wait at all for a table.

Báez 292, at Arévalo. ℂ 11/4514-5820. Main courses $3.50–$5. MC. Mon 6pm–4am; Tues–Sun 11:30am–4am, often later on weekends depending on crowds. Metro: Carranza.

Coanico Bar ARGENTINE/INTERNATIONAL   The movie posters on the outside of this bar are probably the first thing you'll notice. Inside, you'll find a busy place where people eat and drink off tables painted with nude women in the style of Picasso. The bar has overlooked Plaza Serrano for over 20 years, and offers typical bar food like sandwiches and hamburgers but has a larger menu than most of the surrounding bars. Live rock music sometimes entertains the crowd.

Borges 1646, at Plaza Serrano. ✆ **11/4833-0708.** Main courses $1–$3. No credit cards. Daily 10am–4am, sometimes later on weekends. Metro: Plaza Italia.

Confitería del Botánico CAFE/ARGENTINE   Stop here after visiting the nearby zoo or the Botanical Gardens, from which this cafe gets its name. It's on a pleasant corner on busy Santa Fe, but the green spaces of the gardens and Plaza Siria give it a more tranquil sense. The enormous windows seem to bring the park inside. Continental breakfast here is inexpensive; you can also order food from the entire menu at any time of day—the omelets from the dinner menu make any breakfast hearty. Lunch specials run $3 to $4. This is an ideal place for getting takeout to enjoy in the park or zoo.

Av. Santa Fe, at República Siria. ✆ **11/4833-5515.** Main courses $2–$4. AE, MC, V. Sun–Fri 6:30am–midnight; Sat 6:30am–2am. Metro: Plaza Italia.

Macondo Bar 🎭🎭 INTERNATIONAL/ARGENTINE   Macondo Bar is one of the stars of Plaza Serrano, with sidewalk seating and lots of levels overlooking the action. Inside, the restaurant twists around several staircases and low ceilings. It's a loud and busy place for sure, but this kind of setup helps to add a certain sense of intimacy when coming with friends to share conversation over drinks and a meal. Sandwiches, pizzas, salads, and *picadas* (cut-up meat and cheese to pick at over drinks) are on the menu. DJs blast music of all kinds through the bar, from folkloric to techno to electronica. Technically, there's no live music, but sometimes people come around and play on the street in front of the bar.

Borges 1810, at Plaza Serrano. ✆ **11/4831-4174.** Main courses $1–$5. No credit cards. Mon–Thurs 6pm–4am; Fri–Sat 5pm–7am; Sun 5pm–3am. Metro: Plaza Italia.

Malouva CAFE   This is a great location at any time, but it's best late at night when you get the munchies after barhopping in Palermo Viejo. Malouva is open 24 hours and was here long before the neighborhood around it got trendy. As such, you're not here for sophistication but rather for the simple items on the menu and the drink selection. Cheap offerings include salads, pastries, sandwiches, and pizzas. On the downside, service can be slow, and they don't seem to have enough staff for both the indoor and outdoor seating sections. Nevertheless, lots of young local people come here, making weekends especially crowded with kids conversing over large bottles of Quilmes beer. If you're not staying nearby, don't worry about getting a cab from here: It's across the street from a gas station where taxi drivers clean and fuel up, so it's easy to get a car from here to anywhere. In fact, the table next to yours will probably be full of taxi drivers taking a break from their long days.

Charcas 4401, at Thames. ✆ **11/4774-0427.** Main courses $1–$3. No credit cards. Daily 24 hr. Metro: Plaza Italia.

Pampa 🎭🎭 *(Finds* ARGENTINE   This is one of the most interesting new restaurants opened in Palermo Soho, as it celebrates authentic Argentine cuisine while adding Argentine Indian touches. Guadelupe Matteazzi, the friendly owner of the restaurant, moved from the Pampas Province to Buenos Aires, following her children who came here for college. The decor is simple, with rough wooden tables, and everything is the celestial blue and white of the Argentine flag, all the way down to the ashtrays. The restaurant offers food from her region such as *quemú quemú* (rabbit based on an Indian recipe) and other items like Patagonian trout, *lomo* stew, *choripán* (a sausage sandwich), and lamb ravioli. This is country cooking in an urban setting.

Honduras 5143, at Humboldt. ℭ **11/4832-6487.** Main courses $2.50–$5. No credit cards. Daily 10am–12:30am, sometimes later on weekends. Metro: Plaza Italia.

Tazz ℱ MEXICAN   One of the best spots for outdoor seating on all of Plaza Serrano, Tazz has a deceiving exterior. It's in an old house, like so many other restaurants in Palermo Viejo, but step inside and you'll think you've entered the dining hall of a spaceship, with blue glowing lights and walls, mod aluminum panels, and billiard table after billiard table. The booths look like little emergency space capsules that can be released if the mother ship gets attacked. The bulk of the menu here is Mexican (there are hardly any other Mexican restaurants in Buenos Aires), with pitchers of sangria and margaritas adding to the fun (it's really more of a bar than a restaurant). This place is very popular and it has a very young clientele.

Serrano 1556, at Plaza Serrano. ℭ **11/4833-5164.** www.tazzbars.com. Main courses $2–$4. No credit cards. Sun–Thurs noon–3am; Fri–Sat noon–6am. Metro: Plaza Italia.

Viejo Agump ℱ *Finds* MIDDLE EASTERN   Located in the heart of the old Armenian section of Buenos Aires, owner Elizabeth Hounanjian offers authentic Middle Eastern cuisine at Viejo Agump. She wants to make her restaurant a new heart of the community, as it sits in the shadows of both the Armenian church and the Community Center. (*Agump* means "club" or "meeting place" in Armenian.) The exposed brick interior of the old house adds a touch of comfort to the dining area, and mainstays include kabobs and baklava. Sidewalk seating on this tree-lined street is a delight in warm weather. On weekends Arabic belly dancing and coffee-bean readings add to the atmosphere. To arrange a reading, contact the mystic Roxana Banklian and schedule an appointment (ℭ **11/15/4185-2225** cell; roxanabanklin@arnet.com.ar).

Armenia 1382, at José Antonio Cabrera. ℭ **11/4773-5081.** Main courses $2–$5. No credit cards. Mon–Sat 8am–midnight. Metro: Scalabrini Ortiz.

---

11 Abasto & Once

ABASTO

For a map of the restaurants listed in this section, see the "Where to Dine in Abasto & Once" map on p. 127.

INEXPENSIVE

Gardel de Buenos Aires ℱ ARGENTINE/ITALIAN   You won't see any tango-ing here, but this cafe is all Carlos Gardel all the time, celebrating the famous tango singer in many ways. A clock with his face at the 12 o'clock position overlooks the dining area, with its brilliant red tablecloths and rich wood trim. Red walls are adorned in Gardel photos like an iconoclast in a Russian church. A papier-mâché mannequin of him juts out from one of the walls. On top of that, his songs play nonstop from loudspeakers. It's a cute diversion, and in spite of the overwhelming kitsch, the food is good. The menu offers Argentine standards like beef and empanadas, salads, pastas, desserts, sandwiches, pizzas, and other Italian specialties. The house specialty is *fugazzata*—a kind of stuffed pizza. Service is fast and friendly, so this is a great place for grabbing a quick coffee or a sandwich. It's open 24 hours Friday and Saturday, so come by and toast to Gardel after a

Where to Dine in Abasto & Once

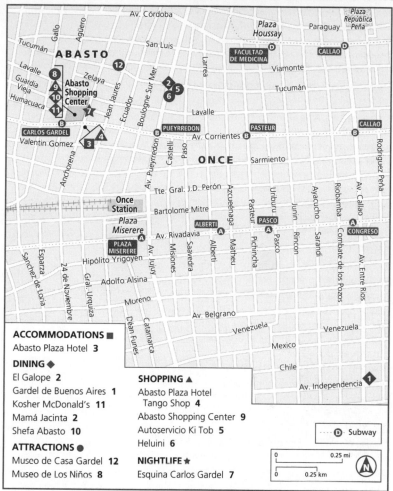

ACCOMMODATIONS ■
Abasto Plaza Hotel **3**

DINING ◆
El Galope **2**
Gardel de Buenos Aires **1**
Kosher McDonald's **11**
Mamá Jacinta **2**
Shefa Abasto **10**

ATTRACTIONS ●
Museo de Casa Gardel **12**
Museo de Los Niños **8**

SHOPPING ▲
Abasto Plaza Hotel
  Tango Shop **4**
Abasto Shopping Center **9**
Autoservicio Ki Tob **5**
Heluini **6**

NIGHTLIFE ★
Esquina Carlos Gardel **7**

- - - - **D** Subway

0   0.25 mi
0   0.25 km

night on the town, picking a drink from their extensive liquor selection. If your hotel is nearby, they also have a takeout menu.

Entre Ríos 796, at Independencia. © **11/4381-4170** or 11/4381-9116. Main courses $2–$6. AE, MC, V. Sun–Thurs 6am–2am; Fri–Sat 24 hr. Metro: Entre Ríos.

Kosher McDonald's 💕💕 *Finds* AMERICAN/KOSHER   Now, I wouldn't ordinarily tell a traveler to eat at McDonald's on vacation, but this one is clearly unique. In keeping with Buenos Aires's reputation as one of the world's greatest Jewish centers, this is the only kosher McDonald's outside of Israel in the world. Rabbi supervision makes sure that kosher rules are strictly followed here. It's your typical McDonald's fare—burgers, fries, salads, fish sandwiches, and the like, but there is nothing dairy here at all. They also sell souvenir mugs and other items to bring home in remembrance of visiting here. Locals of all kinds patronize the place, Jewish or not. And if you only came to gawk and think you can't stand having a Big Mac without cheese, a real kosher no-no, don't worry: Since it's located inside of the Abasto Shopping Center's Food Court, all you have to do is turn around and walk to the regular McDonald's on the other side.

Abasto Shopping Center Food Court, Av. Corrientes 3247, at Agüero. ℂ **11/4959-3709** or 0800/777-6236 for McDonald's Argentina Information Hotline. Main courses $1–$3. No credit cards. Sun–Thurs 10am–midnight; Fri 10am–2pm; Sat 9pm–midnight, but times will vary seasonally depending on sunset. Metro: Carlos Gardel.

Shefa Abasto ✿ *Finds* INTERNATIONAL/ITALIAN/KOSHER/VEGETAR-IAN   Just to the side of the Kosher McDonald's, this is another great option if you are looking for a kosher meal in Buenos Aires. The menu here is varied, offering a large range of pizzas, pastas, and numerous fish dishes. Salads and other light vegetarian menu items mean this is a healthy choice for anyone to stop into, even if they don't care at all about religious food laws. Typical eastern European Jewish items like knishes are unusually light, rather than the heavy fare you might find in New York delis. They also deliver, so pick up a menu if you are staying in the area.

Abasto Shopping Center Food Court, Av. Corrientes 3247, at Agüero. ℂ **11/4959-3708**. Main courses 75¢–$3. No credit cards. Sun–Thurs 10am–midnight; Fri 10am–3:30pm; Sat 9pm–midnight, but times will vary seasonally depending on sunset. Metro: Carlos Gardel.

ONCE

For a map of the restaurants listed in this section, see the "Where to Dine in Abasto & Once" map on p. 127.

MODERATE

El Galope ✿ ARGENTINE/PARRILLA/MIDDLE EASTERN/KOSHER   This place is best described as an Argentine *parrilla,* with Middle Eastern accents and the added twist of being kosher. It's located in what was once the main area of Buenos Aires's Jewish community. The *parrilla* serves up wonderfully juicy and kosher slabs of beef. This is one of Buenos Aires's most popular kosher restaurants. The interior is simple, wood paneled, and home-style, the family that owns the restaurant overseeing its operations. A selection of kosher wines, all made in Argentina, is also on the menu, and you can take a bottle home with you if you'd like. Middle Eastern fare like pitas and hummus as starters or sides and baklava desserts are also on the menu as well as fast food like pastrami sandwiches and salads. Service is low-key, with the waiters phenomenally quiet, seemingly afraid to approach the tables, but the food more than makes up for it.

Tucumán 2633, at Pueyrredón. ℂ **11/4963-6888**. Main courses $2–$8. No credit cards. Sun–Fri noon–3pm; Sun–Thurs 8pm–1am; Sat 9pm–midnight, but times will vary seasonally depending on sunset. Metro: Pueyrredón.

Mamá Jacinta ✿✿ *Finds* INTERNATIONAL/ITALIAN/KOSHER/MIDDLE EASTERN/PARRILLA   Owner José Mizrahi opened this restaurant in 1999 and named it in honor of his Syrian Sephardic grandmother. His idea was to bring to the public the kind of food he remembers eating while growing up, updating it with the international influences that are all the rage in Argentina. He does much of the cooking himself, and chicken dishes are his favorite thing to make. After that, he recommends his fish and rice salad dishes, all served in large enough portions for a table full of patrons to share and enjoy together. French, Japanese, and Italian sausages are grilled on the *parrilla* and can be sampled as starters. Pasta lovers can choose from a wide selection, all custom-made in the restaurant. Try also the *kibbe,* a kind of meat-filled dumpling.

Tucumán 2580, at Pueyrredón. ℂ **11/4962-9149** or 11/4962-7535. mamajacintakosher@hotmail.com. Main courses $2–$8. No credit cards. Mon–Thurs noon–3:30pm and 8–11:30pm; Fri noon–3:30pm; Sat 1 hr. after sunset until midnight; Sun noon–3:30pm. Metro: Pueyrredón.

12 La Boca

For a map of the restaurants listed in this section, see the "Where to Dine in La Boca" map on p. 130.

EXPENSIVE

La Perla *Overrated* CAFE/ARGENTINE   This ancient cafe and bar is one of Buenos Aires's *cafés notables,* cafes with interiors of such historical importance that they are protected by law. It dates from 1899 and has a beautiful interior, loaded with photos of the owners mingling with important visitors from around the world who have come to visit La Boca and this important stop on the tourist circuit. The food is overpriced, however, for what you get. Pizzas, picadas, and a range of coffees and drinks are on offer. If you're in La Boca, it's not a bad place for a drink and to soak up atmosphere on a break, but I would skip this if you want a major meal.

Pedro de Mendoza 1899, at Caminito. ℂ 11/4301-2985. Main courses $6–$10. No credit cards. Daily 7am–9pm. No metro access.

MODERATE

Barbería *Overrated* ARGENTINE/ITALIAN   This is a La Boca institution, with a very colorful interior, old-style banisters, and a waitstaff that prides itself on its Italian La Boca heritage. It's very touristy, though, just steps away from El Caminito's flood of out-of-town visitors and tacky souvenir stands. The owner Nancy, in constantly changing acting and tango costumes, is quite a local character, however, and the walls are full of photos of her with visiting stars. Tango, folkloric, and even drag shows run from noon until 5pm on the sidewalk dining area in front of the cafe, which overlooks the harbor. The food is overpriced for what it is, but the show is included in the price, and that makes up for it. Pastries, such as the Neapolitan *sfogliatella,* a tradition in the area, tend to be on the soggy side, but history is served up with every dish here and the staff is friendly enough.

Pedro de Mendoza 1959, at Caminito. ℂ 11/4303-8256. www.barberia.com.ar. Main courses $2–$7. AE, DC, MC, V. Daily 11am–6pm, later in summer if busy. No metro access.

INEXPENSIVE

Corsario ℜ ARGENTINE/ITALIAN/SEAFOOD   This restaurant takes La Boca's old port heritage to an extreme, adding family-owned charm and warmth to the kitsch. The place was originally a museum, full of old nautical items saved by the family as Boca's connection to the waterfront began to deteriorate. In 1993 they also opened a restaurant serving a mix of Italian, Argentine, and seafood cuisine. Now the purpose of eating outweighs the purpose of seeing the nautical items here, but many of the nautical items are for sale, so wander around and check them out while waiting for your meal. This is the type of place you half-expect Popeye would choose to patronize if he lived here.

Av. Pedro de Mendoza 1981, at Caminito. ℂ 11/4301-6579. Main courses $3–$5. No credit cards. Daily noon–7pm. No metro access.

El Obrero ℜℜℜ *Kids* PARRILLA/ITALIAN/ARGENTINE   Grandfathers are not on the menu in this place, but they come free with every meal. Two old brothers from Barcelona, Spain, who own the place—Marcelino and Francisco Castro—putter around dressed the same as their waiters, making sure everyone is okay. Did you have enough to eat, do you need more bread, are you being taken care of? These are just some of the questions they ask as you dine on thick, juicy, perfectly cooked steaks. Italian food, fish, and chicken are also in the offerings.

Where to Dine in La Boca

DINING ◆
Barberia **2**
Corsario **1**
El Obrero **8**
La Perla **4**

ATTRACTIONS ●
Boca Juniors Stadium
and Museum **7**
Caminito **3**
El Museo Histórico Nacional
(National History Museum) **9**

SHOPPING ▲
Museo Casa—
Taller de Celia
Chevalier **5**

NIGHTLIFE ★
Señor Tango **6**

You can order one-half and one-quarter portions of many items, which is great both because they give you so much and because it means you can bring the kids along without wasting food. Lots of Boca Juniors and other sports memorabilia hanging on the walls remind you that you're in one of the most important soccer/football neighborhoods in the world. This is one of the only places I recommend for serious eating in La Boca, but tables fill up rapidly once 9pm hits, so reserve or come earlier than that. Note that you should arrive here by cab and have the restaurant call a cab for you when you leave. El Obrero is one of the best restaurants in Buenos Aires and should not be missed. However, though I have never personally had a problem in La Boca, it is considered a dangerous neighborhood to wander at night.

Agustín R. Caffarena 64, at Caboto. © **11/4362-9912.** Main courses $3–$4. No credit cards. Mon–Sat noon–5pm and 8pm–2 or 3am, depending on crowds. No metro access.

13 Belgrano

For a map of the restaurants listed in this section, see the "Where to Dine in Belgrano" map on p. 131.

EXPENSIVE

Buddha BA ⊛ CHINESE   This is a very elegant, two-level Chinese teahouse and restaurant in the heart of Belgrano's Chinatown district. It's built into a house, and there is an adjacent garden and art gallery you can check out if you want; the

Where to Dine in Belgrano

DINING ◆
Buddha BA **6**
Garbis **2**
Morizono **1**
Todos Contentos **4**

ATTRACTIONS ●
Cancha de Golf de la
  Ciudad de Buenos Aires **3**

SHOPPING ▲
Buddha Ba Asian Art Gallery **7**
Hua Xia **5**

Ⓓ Subway

gallery sells fine Asian art and antiques. The interesting and creatively named menu has things like Dragon Fire, which is a mix of spicy chicken and curried *lomo;* or Buddha Tears, which is squid in a soy and chicken broth sauce with seasoned vegetables. The atmosphere is very welcoming, and this place makes a great stop if you're exploring this neighborhood in depth.

Arribeños 2288, at Mendoza. ☏ 11/4706-2382. www.buddhaba.com.ar. Main courses $6–$10. MC, V. Wed–Sun 8:30–11:30pm; Sat–Sun 12:30–3:30pm; tea service Wed–Sun 4–7:30pm. Metro: Juramento.

MODERATE

Todos Contentos CHINESE   If you're looking for that busy, authentic China-town feel, come to this place, where you'll find crowded tables full of patrons eating noodle dishes and other Chinese cuisine. Waitresses in embroidered Chinese silk shirts make sure everyone is well taken care of. You'll find a very large selection of standards, such as pork dishes and chow mein, in addition to interesting items like salted tripe on the menu. There is also a very reasonable weekend special running about $3 per person that includes a starter like an egg roll, a noodle meat dish, and a drink. I list this restaurant as moderate, but they also offer lobster on the menu. The prices for this run about $15 per person, which would technically push this into the very expensive category. However, the vast majority of their offerings are very reasonable.

Arribeños 2177, at Mendoza. ☏ 11/4780-3437. Main courses $3–$15. No credit cards. Mon–Fri 11:30am–3:30pm and 7:30–9:30pm; Sat–Sun 9:30am–midnight. Metro: Juramento.

6

Exploring Buenos Aires

The beauty of Buenos Aires is evident the moment you set foot on her streets. You'll find yourself compelled to walk for hours getting to know her, the alluring architecture and atmosphere pulling you along block after block. The city's most impressive historical sites surround Plaza de Mayo, although you will certainly experience Argentine history in other neighborhoods such as La Boca and San Telmo, too. You should also be sure not to miss a walk along the riverfront in Puerto Madero or an afternoon among the plazas and cafes of Recoleta or Palermo. Numerous sidewalk cafes offer respite for weary feet, and there's good public transportation to carry you from neighborhood to neighborhood.

Your first stop should be one of the city tourism centers (see "Visitor Information," in chapter 3) to pick up a guidebook, city map, and advice. You can also ask at your hotel for a copy of *The Golden Map* and *QuickGuide Buenos Aires* to help you navigate the city and locate its major attractions. Various neighborhoods have their own special maps, so ask at the centers or in local businesses.

Buenos Aires might be a bargain destination for travelers now, but when exploring Buenos Aires, it's important to remember that for almost the entire first half of the 20th century, this was one of the wealthiest cities in all of the world. Many of the buildings described in this chapter testify to that extreme wealth, though following revolutions, crisis after crisis, and the fall of the peso, little of that wealth now remains. In particular, buildings and monuments constructed between the 1880s National Unification and the 1910 Independence Centennial celebrations were meant to also represent Argentina's self-conscious hopes of becoming a superpower, and the desire to rival the United States as the preeminent country in the Americas.

Under the Spanish Empire, Buenos Aires was an unimportant backwater, with other Argentine cities, such as Córdoba, more significant and culturally sophisticated. Following the 1880 movement of the capital to Buenos Aires, however, the city sought to overcome its inferiority complex with grand architectural plans. Within the descriptions of these sites, I include, where possible, the philosophy behind their impressive beauty and their role as monuments to what both Argentina and Buenos Aires hoped to achieve. They are not mere baubles; they are the physical remnants of a lost opportunity for glory on the world stage. Maybe you're in Buenos Aires because you've heard about its beauty, or are only curious because the prices here are such a bargain. Regardless of your reason, no matter what areas of the city you explore and how long you stay, you are certain to be impressed by all that Buenos Aires has to offer.

1 Buenos Aires's Most Famous Sights

A Line Subte *ΛΛΛ* *Moments* *Kids* This was the first subway line opened in Buenos Aires, and it still retains its original cars. The line was opened in 1913 and is the 13th-oldest subway system in the world, the oldest in South America, and the 4th-oldest in the Americas as a whole (after New York, Boston, and Philadelphia). This line runs under Avenida de Mayo, beginning at Plaza de Mayo, running through Congreso, which was its original terminus, though it now continues on to Primera Junta thanks to a later extension. Trains are wooden, old, and rickety, and as they proceed along the bends underground, you can watch the whole car shimmy and shake. The car's wooden side panels are made to bend and slip into each other, which is fun or scary depending on how you look at it. Windows are still wooden, with leather pulls to open and close them. Rings, now plastic, are also held by leather straps. Unlike those on the cars of the other four subway lines, the doors on this line do not always open and close automatically, something to be aware of when you reach your station.

The stations between Plaza de Mayo and Congreso still retain most of their ornamentation from the very beginning, but the best station of all is Perú. Here, mock turn-of-the-20th-century ads and ornamental kiosks painted cream and red recall the very beginning of underground transport on this continent. In the summer this line can be even more unbearably hot than the rest of the system, none of which is currently air-conditioned. The Congreso station has a mini-museum inside of glass display cases with revolving exhibitions related to the history of the Congreso building. Well-worn old wooden turnstiles throughout this line remain in use for exiting and still have the old token slots, which are no longer operational. I know of no other place in the world where you can experience firsthand the magic a subway must have been like when it was the highest form of transportation technology at the turn of the 20th century.

The A Line begins at Plaza de Mayo and travels along Av. de Mayo to Congreso and beyond. www.subte.com.ar. Admission 25¢. No metro access.

Cabildo 🍴   This small, white, colonial-style building with a central bell tower was the original seat of city government established by the Spaniards. The building was completed in 1751, but parts of it were demolished to create space for Avenida de Mayo and Diagonal Sur in the late 1800s and early 1900s. The remainder of the building was restored in 1939 and is worth a visit. The small informal museum displays paintings and furniture from the colonial period, and its ledges and windows offer some of the best views of the Plaza de Mayo. The Cabildo is the only remaining public building dating back to colonial times still existing on the Plaza de Mayo. Many people come here just for the changing of the guard in front every hour (which happens at a few other spots around town as well). On Thursday and Friday from 11am to 6pm, the Cabildo's back patio is home to a crafts fair.

Bolívar 65, at Rivadavia. ✆ 11/4334-1782. Admission $1. Tues–Fri 12:30–7pm; Sun 2–6pm. Metro: Bolívar, Catedral, or Plaza de Mayo.

Café Tortoni 🍴🍴🍴 *Moments*   You cannot come to Buenos Aires and not visit this important Porteño institution. I mentioned this cafe in the dining chapter, but at the risk of being repetitive, it is a must-see no matter if you plan to dine there or not. This historic cafe has served as the artistic and intellectual capital of Buenos Aires since 1858, with guests such as Jorge Luis Borges, Julio de Caro, Cátulo Castillo, and José Gobello. Wonderfully appointed in woods, stained glass, yellowing marble, and bronzes, the place tells more about its history by simply existing than any of the photos on its walls. This is the perfect place for a coffee or a small snack when wandering along Avenida de Mayo. Twice-nightly tango shows in a cramped side gallery, where the performers often walk through the crowd, are

Exploring Buenos Aires

Padre Mujica

Retiro Station ⊠ ⓘ ⓒ **RETIRO**

20

Av. Ramos Mejía

San Martín

Av. E. Madero

Av. Antártida Argentina

Dársena Norte

ⓘ Information
⊠ Post office
ⓐ Subway
ⓓ─ⓔ Subway transfer

0   0.25 mi
0   0.25 km

21

v. del Libertador

Av. Maipú

Florida

Plaza San Martín

ECOLOGICAL RESERVE

Av. de los Italianos

29

AN MARTÍN ⓒ **22** **23**

M.T. de Alvear

Esmeralda

Paraguay

⊠ ⓘ Av. Córdoba

24

25

MICROCENTRO

Viamonte

Tucumán

San Martín

Florida

Maipú

Lavalle

Av. Leandro N. Alem

Av. E. Madero

ⓘ

Dique Nº 4

PUERTO MADERO

T. Guevara

Av. Macacha Güemes

C. Pellegrini

Supacha

LAVALLE ⓒ

L.N. ALEM ⓑ

Av. Corrientes

ⓑ **FLORIDA**

Av. Rosales

Av. de la Rábida

Av. Alicia Moreau

Mitre y Vedia

Parque Mujeres Argentinas

CORRIENTES THEATER DISTRICT

Sarmiento

25 de Mayo

Reconquista

Dique Nº 3

de Justo

27 **26**

ⓑ **CARLOS PELLEGRINI**

28

Tte. Gral. J.D. Perón

ⓒ **DIAGONAL NORTE**

9 DE JULIO ⓒ ⊠

Av. Roque Sáenz Peña (Diagonal Norte)

CATEDRAL **32** *Plaza de Mayo*

33

30

31 ⓐ **PLAZA DE MAYO**

Bvd. A. Villaflor

Bartolomé Mitre

Rivadavia

ⓘ

ⓓ

34 ⓐ

ⓔ **BOLÍVAR**

Balcarce

Moreno

Av. Paseo Colón

Azopardo

Av. Ing. Huergo

Dique Nº 2

Libertad

Cerrito

C. Pellegrini

PIEDRAS

35

PERÚ

37

38

39

AV. DE MAYO ⓒ

36 ⓘ ⓐ ⊠

Hipólito Yrigoyen

Alsina

Bolívar

Defensa

41

Rivadavia

Av. de Mayo

LIMA ⓐ

Santiago del Estero

Salta

Lima

MONSERRAT

Av. 9 de Julio

BELGRANO ⓔ

ⓒ **MORENO**

Av. Julio A. Roca (Diagonal Sur)

40

Av. Belgrano

Perú

Venezuela

Chacabuco

México

Perú

42

an José

Av. Belgrano

Bernardo de Irigoyen

Tacuarí

Piedras

Chile

Av. Independencia

⊠

Pte. Luis Sáenz Peña

SAN TELMO

Estados Unidos

43

Balcarce

Av. Independencia

ⓒ **INDEPENDENCIA**

ⓔ **INDEPENDENCIA**

Carlos Calvo

Plaza Dorrego **44**

Primo

Av. Independencia

Humberto

Av. San Juan

Autopista 25 de Mayo

45 *(6 blocks)*

135

worth making time for. What makes the Tortoni all the more special is that locals and tourists seem to exist side-by-side here, one never overwhelming the other. Do not, however, expect great service: Sometimes only jumping up and down will get the staff's attention, even when they are just a few feet from you.

Av. de Mayo 825, at Piedras. (© 11/4342-4328. www.cafetortoni.com.ar. Mon–Thurs 8am–2am; Fri–Sat 8am–3am; Sun 8am–1am. Metro: Av. de Mayo.

Casa de Cultura and Palacio de Gobierno ☆☆ These are two separate buildings, but tours will take you to parts of both. On a street lined with impressive structures meant to give the Champs-Elysées a run for its money, these two buildings are standouts that should not be missed. The Palacio de Gobierno, on the corner of Rivadavia and San Martín, is the new City Hall, the working office of the mayor of Buenos Aires, a white neoclassical building directly fronting the Plaza de Mayo on the block opposite the Cabildo, the old city hall. The original construction was between 1891 and 1902, and it was expanded 10 years later. The adjoining Casa de Cultura, a sumptuous gray granite building with bronze ornamentation and a series of sinuous lanterns protruding along its facade facing the Avenida de Mayo, is the former home of the newspaper *La Prensa,* which was at one time the most important and prestigious paper in Argentina. The paper was started by the Paz family, the former owners of the palace on San Martín now occupied by the Círculo Militar (p. 148). The Casa de Cultura is topped by a statue representing freedom of the press (which was commonly suppressed in Argentina under many regimes). Most of the clientele of the paper were among the wealthy oligarchs, and the beauty of this building reflects this. The dark lobby even has extremely ornate payment-window stands. Etched glass, dark carved woods, and heavy plaster ornamentation make up the bulk of what is seen here. The most impressive room is the Salón Dorado, a French neoclassical masterpiece of gilded columns, painted ceilings, an ornate parquet floor, and a performance stage. Tours take visitors through this room and others throughout the building, but you should also ask for schedules of the various functions hosted here in the evenings, which are usually free. The building is now the headquarters of the city's Office of Culture, and there could be no finer home for them in the city.

Av. de Mayo 575, at San Martín, near Plaza de Mayo. (© 11/4323-9669. Free guided visits Sat 4 and 5pm, Sun every hour 11am–4pm. Metro: Catedral, Bolívar, or Plaza de Mayo.

Casa Rosada and the Presidential Museum ☆☆☆ Perhaps the most photographed building in Buenos Aires, the Casa Rosada is the main presence on the Plaza de Mayo. The Argentine president does not live here, contrary to what many tourists think, but he does work here. (He lives in the suburbs in a mansion in Los Olivos, north of the city.) It is from a balcony of the north wing of this building that Eva Perón addressed adoring crowds of Argentine workers. Hoping for some star-quality glamour for his term of office, former President Carlos Ménem allowed Madonna to actually use it for the 1996 movie, to the shock of many Porteños. Most Argentines, however, associate the balcony with the announcement of military dictator Leopoldo Galtieri's ill-fated declaration of war against the United Kingdom over the Falkland Islands, known here as the Islas Malvinas. Two theories explain why in such a supposedly machismo country the president works in a pink building. One is political—two warring parties, one represented by the color red, the other by white, created a truce by painting the building a color combining both symbols. The other, rather revolting theory is more practical and says that in days past, the building was painted with cow blood that then dried in the sun to a deep pink color.

You can watch the changing of the guard in front of the palace every hour on the hour. To the side of the palace, at the *subte* (subway) entrance, you'll find the Presidential Museum, with information on the history of the building and items owned by various presidents over the centuries. Portions of the museum extend underground into basements of no-longer-existing buildings. Make sure to step outside to look at excavations on the customs house and port area, which existed along the Río de la Plata at this point until landfill projects pushed the shore farther east. You should also ask about the periodic tours of the Casa Rosada itself. These tours are free but must be reserved ahead of time by asking about the schedule of the tours and signing up for them at the museum's front desk. If you're going on one, bring identification and expect to have personal items X-rayed to help ensure the security of the president. The tour will take you through ornate chambers, many overseen by marble busts of past presidents. You won't, however, be allowed to visit the famous balcony no matter how much you cry for Argentina.

Casa Rosada overlooking Plaza de Mayo on Calle Balcarce, at intersection with Yrigoyen. Museum entrance at Yrigoyen 219. ℂ **11/4344-3802.** Free admission. Mon–Fri 10am–6pm. Metro: Plaza de Mayo.

Legislatura de la Ciudad (City Legislature Building) ℛ   A striking neo-classical facade covers this building, which houses exhibitions in several of its halls. Ask about free tours, offered on an informal basis by the guide Alejandra Javier in English or Spanish, Monday through Friday. She will take you into the impressive bell tower, which legend says was made as high as it is so that the city could keep an eye on the nearby president in the Casa Rosada. Portions of the building were also built around an old mansion that once faced the Plaza de Mayo. The view from the corner balcony of this part of the building calls to mind how powerful wealthy families could at one time oversee the entire town from their living room window before the city grew so rapidly. In front of the Legislatura, you'll see a bronze statue of Julio A. Roca. He is considered one of Argentina's greatest generals, but one of his legacies is the slaughtering of tens of thousands of Indians in the name of racial purity within the province of Buenos Aires. He is why, unlike most of Latin America, Argentina is a largely white, rather than mestizo, society.

Calle Perú and Hipólito Yrigoyen. ℂ **11/4338-3167** or 11/4338-3212. www.legislatura.gov.ar. Free admission. Mon–Fri 10am–5pm. Metro: Bolívar.

Manzanas de las Luces (Blocks of Enlightenment) ℛℛ   *Manzana* is an old name for a city block (as well as modern Spanish for an apple), and the name "las Luces" refers to this area being the intellectual center or "light" of the city in the 17th and 18th centuries. This land was granted in 1616 to the Jesuits, who built **San Ignacio**—the city's oldest church—still standing at the corner of calles Bolívar and Alsina. San Ignacio has a beautiful altar carved in wood with baroque details. It is currently under renovation after years of neglect and was also nearly destroyed in the revolution that took Perón out of power in 1955, which also sought to reduce the power of the Catholic Church. Also located here is the **Colegio Nacional de Buenos Aires (National High School of Buenos Aires).** Argentina's best-known intellectuals have gathered and studied here, and the name "block of lights" recognizes the contributions of the National School's graduates, especially in achieving Argentina's independence in the 19th century. Tours in English are usually led on Saturday and Sunday at 3 and 4:30pm and include a visit to the Jesuits' system of underground tunnels, which connected their churches to strategic spots in the city (admission $2). Speculation remains as to whether the tunnels also served a military purpose or funneled pirated goods into the city when it was a smuggling center in the colonial period. The full extent of the tunnels is still unknown and various military dictators, including Perón, added to them in case they needed to escape the nearby Casa Rosada in the event of unexpected coups. *Ratearse,* the Argentine slang for playing hooky, which literally means becoming a rat, comes from the tunnels, as this is where students from the Colegio hid when they did not want to go to class. In addition to weekend tours, the Comisión Nacional de la Manzana de las Luces organizes a variety of cultural activities during the week, including folkloric dance lessons, open-air theater performances, art expositions, and music concerts.

Calle Perú 272, at Moreno. (℃ **11/4342-6973** for tours or 11/4331-9534 for cultural events. Metro: Bolívar.

Metropolitan Cathedral &&   The original structure of the Metropolitan Cathedral was built in 1745; it was given a new facade with carvings telling the story of Jacob and his son Joseph and was designated a cathedral in 1836. The overwhelming look of the cathedral was changed from a traditional Spanish colonial look to a Greek-revival style at that time, with a pediment and colonnade in front, though the sides and back remain similar to the original. Inside lies an ornate mausoleum containing the remains of General José de San Martín, the South American liberator regarded as the "Father of the Nation." (San Martín fought successfully for freedom in Argentina, Peru, and Chile alongside of the better-known Simón Bolívar.) His body was moved here in 1880 to become a rallying symbol of Argentina's unification and rise to greatness when Buenos Aires became the capital of Argentina at the end of a long civil war. The tomb of the unknown soldier of Argentine independence is also here, and an eternal flame burns on the cathedral's facade in his remembrance. Among the chapels of note is the one on the east side of the cathedral with a statue of Jesus with the notation, "Santo Cristo del Gran Amor" or the Holy Christ of Great Love. It was donated

---

Fun Fact   **Men in Uniform—The Changing of the Guard**

Watching the changing of the guard throughout historical sites in Buenos Aires is part of the fun of visiting. Many tourists take particular delight in photographing these men in early-19th-century military clothing parading through Plaza de Mayo on their way to their next station. But did you know there is more than one kind of guard? *Granaderos* guard national monuments such as the San Martín Mausoleum and the Casa Rosada. *Patricios* guard Buenos Aires city-owned buildings, such as the Municipal Palace and the Cabildo. Both are in historical costume dating from the beginning of the 1800s Napoleonic era and independence from Spain. The Patricios represent the oldest branch of the military and were originally formed before independence from Spain in response to British attacks on Buenos Aires. Granaderos were formed after independence. If they're not in front of a building and on their way to a changing of the guard, you can also tell the difference by the pants they wear, white for Patricios, and blue for Granaderos. The Islas Malvinas–Falkland Islands Monument in Plaza San Martín is guarded by the three branches of the military, the Navy, Air Force, and the Army. Wearing a mix of historical and contemporary uniforms, each branch rotates along a 2-week cycle for the honor.

in 1978 by an Argentine soccer player whose family had disappeared. He swore he would donate a statue to the church if they were ever found, and they were. While Argentina is a strongly Catholic nation, it is not very big on ritual. However, the most important midnight Mass in Argentina occurs in this church. Called the "Noche Buena," it is held every December 24, generally at 10pm, but call the cathedral to make sure of the exact time. Unlike most things in Argentina, the processional ceremony starts on time, so get there early if you want to go.

San Martín, at Rivadavia overlooking Plaza de Mayo. © 11/4331-2845. Metro: Bolívar, Catedral, or Plaza de Mayo.

Plaza de Mayo 🀅🀅 *Kids*   Juan de Garay founded the historic core of Buenos Aires, the Plaza de Mayo, upon the city's second founding in 1580. The plaza's prominent buildings create an architectural timeline: the Cabildo, or Old City Hall, and Metropolitan Cathedral are vestiges of the colonial period (18th and early 19th c.), while the Pirámide de Mayo (Pyramid of May) and the buildings of the national and local government reflect the styles of the late 19th and early 20th centuries. In the center of the plaza, you'll find palm trees, fountains, and benches. And though many of these facilities are in need of an upgrade, the plaza is still full of local people at lunchtime, chatting and eating takeout food. The other structures that surround the plaza, government and union offices built in the mid–20th century, are less interesting but typify the severe fascist style popular in South America at the time, with their smooth surfaces and enormous Roman-style metal doors that are forever closed.

Plaza de Mayo remains the political heart of Buenos Aires, serving as a forum for protests, many camping out here overnight. The mothers of the *desaparecidos,* victims of the military dictatorship's campaign against leftists known as the Dirty War, have demonstrated here since 1976. An absolute must-see for understanding Argentina's recent history, you can watch them march, speak, and set up information booths every Thursday afternoon at 3:30pm (see p. 143 for more information).

Mass demonstrations are very common here, and most protests begin in front of the **Casa Rosada** (now separated from the crowds by permanent barricades) and proceed up **Avenida de Mayo** toward **Congreso.** For the most part, these demonstrations are very peaceful, usually led by people who have suffered the economic consequences of the peso crisis, known as *piqueteros*. At times, some protests have been known to break into violence, however, so you must be aware when demonstrations are occurring and should leave immediately if things seem to be getting out of hand.

Plaza de Mayo begins at the eastern terminus of Av. de Mayo and is surrounded by calles Yrigoyen, San Martín, Rivadavia, and Balcarce. Metro: Bolívar, Catedral, or Plaza de Mayo.

MONSERRAT, SAN TELMO & LA BOCA

Centro Nacional de la Música 🀅   This sumptuous building belies its location on a quiet, almost run-down block in San Telmo. Its main exhibition hall boasts an intricate stained-glass ceiling within a cast-iron dome, held up by four oversize and graceful female goddesses and other angel-like figures. The building hosts various lectures, art exhibits, and musical recitals during the day, but often the building itself is the true star. This was the site of the National Library before it was moved to Palermo.

México 564, at Perú. © 11/4300-7374. www.cultura.gov.ar. Admission varies depending on exhibition; free to $1. Metro: Independencia.

Plaza Dorrego ⋆⋆   Originally the site of a Bethlehemite monastery, this plaza, the second-oldest square in the city, is also where Argentines met to reconfirm their declaration of independence from Spain. On Sunday from 10am to 5pm, the city's best **antiques market** ⋆⋆⋆ takes over the square. You can buy leather, silver, handicrafts, and other products here along with antiques, all while tango dancers perform on the square. The tall, darkly handsome dancer nicknamed El Indio is the star of this plaza.

Plaza Dorrego, at the intersection of Defensa and Humberto I. Metro: Independencia.

San Telmo Market ⋆⋆ *Moments*   Though this is definitely a place to shop, the building is also worth seeing on its own. The San Telmo market opened in 1897, and it is a masterpiece not just for its soaring wrought-iron interior, but for the atmosphere of decades ago you still find here. Half of the market is made up of things that locals need—butchers, fresh-fruit-and-vegetable grocers, and little kiosks selling sundries and household items. This part looks like the kind of place your grandmother probably shopped in when she was a child. I recommend chatting with the staff in these places, who seem to have all the time in the world. The other half is more touristy, but never overly so, with various antiques and vintage-clothing shops. There are several entrances to this large market, almost a block in size but squeezed between several other historical buildings.

961 Defensa or Bolívar 998, both at Carlos Calvo. Daily 10am–8pm, but each stand will have individual hours. Metro: Independencia.

The Engineering School—The Eva Perón Foundation   This massive and imposing building, which takes up a whole block, is a site of learning that was once the headquarters for the Eva Perón Foundation, a foundation Evita established in order to distribute funds to needy children and families, as well as, some say, siphon funds for personal use. Today there is little to mark the former use of the building, miraculously saved by the ensuing military regime, which felt it was too important and expensive a building to demolish as had been the case with other sites associated with her. Only a tiny plaque, affixed to a lobby column in 2002, explains the relationship, though someone has vandalized the sign, stealing the image of Evita from it. Nevertheless, this is a grand 1940s classical building, reserved in style, with simple Doric columns on its facade fronting Paseo Colón. It is decorated with sumptuous multicolored marbles on all the floors and walls throughout the structure. As an engineering school, it is brimming with students, but it still maintains a hushed atmosphere of quiet academic pursuits. The dean's office was once Evita's own. As a public building, anyone can enter it, but the school offers no information or tours based on its former use and discourages random wanderers.

Paseo Colón, at México. Metro: Independencia.

Caminito *Overrated*   This is the main attraction in La Boca, Buenos Aires's original Little Italy. A pedestrianized street a few blocks long with a colorful, kitschy collection of painted houses known as *conventillos* (flimsily built houses that immigrants lived in), it's lined with art displays explaining the history of the area. Untold numbers of tacky T-shirt and souvenir vendors and artists set up stalls here and cater strictly to tourists. To be honest, I find this area repulsive and insulting to visitors to Buenos Aires. The history of La Boca is very important to Buenos Aires and the development of the tango. However, what remains here today has little to do with any of that. Even the touristy name of the street "Caminito" has nothing to do with Buenos Aires at all. It's from a song about a flower-filled remote rural village, not an intensely urban neighborhood where Italian-immigrant gangsters, prostitutes, and sailors once roamed the streets committing crimes and other acts of mayhem. To top it all off, in the summertime the stench from the polluted port can also simply be overwhelming.

I am not saying you shouldn't come to La Boca, because that would be a shame, since the neighborhood has real value, but the Caminito does not do it justice. More interesting are the areas a few blocks from here where artists have set up studios such as **Museo Casa—Taller de Celia Chevalier** (see below) or a visit to the **Boca Juniors Stadium and Museum** (see below), which gives you an idea of the psyche of Argentina. It will also be easier to talk with the real residents of La Boca when you wander off the all-too-beaten tourist track rather than those in the tourist industry along the Caminito who attempt to harass you into buying overpriced items or give you flyers with directions to lousy Italian restaurants. Come here to Caminito if you must, and if you're on a tour, you will anyway. However, if you are on a very short stay in Buenos Aires, skip La Boca. For true authenticity and a flavor of old Buenos Aires, choose to see San Telmo instead. I enjoy visiting La Boca at night, when people tell you it is dangerous, because I find that it is easier to talk with locals in a relaxed, non-commercial way at that time. However, I do not recommend that for the average tourist. According to the city government tourism office, a new plan will be created in the near future to redevelop this area and bring back more authenticity. Additionally, in anticipation of Argentina's 2010 bicentennial, the city is planning to redevelop the southern portion of Buenos Aires, which is where La Boca is situated.

Caminito, at Av. Pedro de Mendoza, La Boca. No metro access.

Boca Juniors Stadium and Museum ☆

This stadium overlooks a desolate garbage-strewn lot at the corner of calles Del Valle Iberlucea and Brandsen. But go on game day, when street parties and general debauchery take over the area, and it is another story. This is the home of the *fútbol* (soccer) club Boca Juniors, the team of Argentine legend Diego Maradona, who like his country went from glory to fiery collapse rather quickly. For information on *fútbol* (soccer) games, see the *Buenos Aires Herald* sports section. Wealthy businessman Mauricio Macri, president of the Boca Juniors Fútbol Club, opened the **Museo de la Pasión Boquense** in the stadium, part of his unsuccessful bid to woo Porteños into electing him the city's mayor. This glitzy showstopper is full of awards, TV screens showing important events that happened on the field, and more things related to this legendary team.

Brandsen 805, at Del Valle Iberlucea. ✆ 11/4362-1100. www.museosdeportivos.com. Free admission. Tues–Sun 10am–9pm; holidays 10am–7pm. No metro access.

Museo Casa—Taller de Celia Chevalier ☆☆

I don't get excited about much in La Boca, but I highly recommend this place, a boutique and house museum of an artist located just 2 blocks from El Caminito. Ms. Chevalier grew up in Buenos Aires and creates whimsical paintings based on her childhood memories. She is charming and open, though she only speaks Spanish. She also looks strikingly like Meryl Streep, and has a face with the capability of as many expressions. The house is a restored *conventillo,* the type of houses that Italian immigrants moved into when they came to Buenos Aires before the turn of the 20th century. The house dates from 1885 and was made into her studio museum in 1998. Tours will take you through some of the small rooms, the gardens, and the outhouse. Ms. Chevalier also has blueprints from the city's waterworks on display from 1910, when they put water services into La Boca, many years after other parts of wealthy Buenos Aires got that service.

Irala 1162, at Calle Olavarria. ✆ 11/4302-2337. celia_chevalier@yahoo.com.ar. Admission 65¢. No credit cards for art purchases. Sat–Sun and holidays 2–7pm. Call for appointments on other days. No metro access.

CONGRESO AREA

Congreso 🕀🕀 Opened on May 12, 1906, after nearly 9 years of work, and built in a Greco-Roman style with strong Parisian Beaux Arts influences, Congreso is the most imposing building in all of Buenos Aires. One of the main architects was Victor Meano, who was also involved in designing the Teatro Colón (p. 147), but he was murdered in a love triangle gone wrong before completion of either building. Congreso is constructed of Argentine gray granite, with walls over 1.75m (6 ft.) wide at their base. At night, its copper dome is lit through its tiny windows, creating a dramatic vista point down Avenida de Mayo from the Plaza de Mayo. Congreso is also the best example of the self-conscious Argentine concept of taking architectural elements of the world's most famous buildings and reinterpreting them. For instance, it resembles the U.S. Capitol, with a central dome spreading over the two wings holding the bicameral legislatorial chambers. In addition, the ornamental bronze roofline calls to mind Garnier's opera house and the central pediment is topped by a Quadriga or Triumph carried by four horses, the whole appearance of which directly echoes that over the Brandenburg Gate in Berlin. This sculpture was designed in Venice by artist Victor de Pol, took over 4 years to make, weighs 20 tons, and was cast in Germany.

Tours take visitors through the fantastic chambers, which are adorned with bronzes, statues, German tile floors, Spanish woods, and French marbles and lined with Corinthian columns. The horseshoe-shaped Congressional chamber is the largest, with the Senatorial chamber an almost identical copy but at one-fifth the size. The power of the Catholic Church is also in evident in both chambers—the archbishop has his own seat next to the president of either section of Congress and, though he has no voting power, is allowed to preside over all of the sessions. The old seats for representatives and senators have a form of electronic whoopee cushion—simply by sitting down, attendance is taken based on the pressure of a politician's buttocks against his or her chair. The tour also takes you to the very pink Salón Rosado, now called the Salón Eva Perón. She opened this room once women received the right to vote so that women politicians could sit without men around them to discuss feminist issues. Upon her death, Evita's body was temporarily placed under Congreso's central rotunda so that citizens could view her during the 2-week mourning period in 1952.

The building faces the Plaza Congreso, whose main feature is an enormous fountain called the Dos Congresos. This multilevel confection of statues, horses, lions, condors, cherubs, and other ornaments has stairs leading to a better view for photographing the Congreso. Unfortunately, the park has become quite run-down over the years and the fountain no longer operates and is covered in graffiti.

For more information on Congreso, visit the Congressional Library across the street and request the book *El Congreso de la Nación Argentina* by Manrique Zago, which gives rich detail on the building and its history in English and Spanish. Though both English and Spanish tours of Congreso are available, they are often subject to cancellation depending on functions in the building. Plus, English-speaking tour guides aren't always available in spite of the schedule. Entrance is usually through the Rivadavia side of the building, but can switch to the Yrigoyen doors, so arrive early and also announce to the guards that you are there for a visit.

The tour guide will not be called down unless they know people are waiting. This is an incredible building and worth the confusion. Its beauty also speaks for itself, even if you have to take the Spanish tour and do not know a word of Spanish.

Entre Ríos and Callao, at Rivadavia. ⓒ **11/4370-7100** or 11/6310-7100, ext. 3725. Free guided tours in English on Mon, Tues, Thurs, Fri 11am and 4pm. Spanish tours Mon, Tues, Thurs, Fri 11am, 4pm, and 5pm. Metro: Congreso.

Asociación Madres de Plaza de Mayo ★★★ (Moments)
I have already highly recommended that you visit Plaza de Mayo on Thursday afternoon to see the Madres speak about their missing children in front of the Casa Rosada. Here at their headquarters, on Plaza Congreso, you can learn even more about them. This complex contains the office of the Madres, their teaching institution, the Universidad Popular Madres de Plaza de Mayo, the Librería de las Madres, the Café Literario Osvaldo Bayer, and the Biblioteca Popular Julio Huasi, among other facilities. At this busy center of activity, you will find the Madres themselves, now mostly very old women, surrounded by young people who come to work with them as well as take university classes with a decidedly leftist bent. All levels of the building are open to the public, though one cannot freely enter classroom spaces while teaching is in session. Many lectures, video conferences, and art exhibitions are held throughout the space. The bookstore has perhaps the largest collection of books anywhere in the world on Che Guevara, a Madres personal hero. The large library of reference books on liberal causes is decorated with depictions of events around the world in which people have sought justice from their governments. You should ask for a schedule of events and lectures held in other locations throughout Buenos Aires as well. On Friday, Saturday, and Sunday from 11am to 6pm, there is a market held on Plaza Congreso, in front of the building, which serves as a fundraiser for the Madres. This is also good for children, because it is next to the part of the park with the merry-go-round and other rides. The fair has antiques, crafts, food, and a few interesting book vendors. Sometimes there is also live music.

Hipólito Yrigoyen 1584, at Ceballos. ⓒ **11/4383-0377** or 11/4383-6340. www.madres.org. Various hours, but building is generally open Mon–Fri 10am–10pm; Sat 10am–9pm. Metro: Congreso.

Palacio Barolo ★ (Finds)
Among the most impressive buildings in Buenos Aires, and once the tallest building in South America, this oddly decorated building with a central tower is a showstopper among all the buildings on Avenida de Mayo. Its eclectic design can be called many things, among them Art Nouveau, neo-Gothic, neo-Romantic, and Asian Indian revival. Until recently, the interior was closed to the general public, and few know that tours here began in March 2004. Miqueas Tharigen, the son of the building manager, runs the tours part-time in English and Spanish, using his father's administrative office, preserved from the 1920s, for his work. The design of the building is based on Dante's Inferno. Opened in 1923, it was the work of eccentric Italian architect Mario Palanti, who largely used materials imported from his home country. The entrance is supposed to be Hell, and the patterned medallions on the floor here simulate fire. The interior gallery at this level is decorated with grotesque dragons, and if you look closely, you will notice that those on the east side are female, those on the west are male. Floors 1 through 14 represent Purgatory and 15 to 22 represent Heaven. The interior is significantly less interesting than the exterior and lobby. However, tours take you to the rooftop lighthouse, meant to represent God and Salvation. The view from here, up and down Avenida de Mayo, especially to Congreso, is unparalleled. The building is also designed so that at 7:45pm on July 9, Argentine Independence Day, the Southern Cross directly lines up over the tower. Palanti had hoped that Italy would

The Madres de Plaza de Mayo: A Union of a Mother's Pain

That even the cruelest man should somehow identify with a mother's pain in trying to find her missing child was part of the concept behind the Madres de Plaza de Mayo when it was formed in 1976. The military government that came into power that year, after the fall of Isabel Perón's administration, began what it called a reorganization of society based largely on making up lists of suspected socialist dissidents and making them disappear. An estimated 13,000 to 30,000 *desaparecidos,* (disappeared ones), mostly young people, were kidnapped, tortured, and murdered during this era. Many were thrown naked into the Atlantic rather than buried so that they could never be found or identified. The children of the dead were given out as gifts to childless military families. This era of murdering people for their political beliefs was called the *Guerra Sucia* (Dirty War). It did not end until the collapse of the military government upon defeat in the Islas Malvinas/Falkland Islands War in June 1982.

It is easy to think of the dead as statistics and the mothers as simply a curiosity for tourists and history buffs, but this terrible chapter of Argentina's history is far from closed. Unfortunately, both young Argentines who have no recollection of this period as well as old Argentines involved in the murders wish the mothers would simply go away. Still, though many of the original mothers have died, their work goes on.

Juanita Pargament, one of the about 14 original founding members, is now 90 and treasurer of the Madres. Her son Alberto José Pargament, a 31-year-old psychologist at the time, disappeared on November 20, 1976. To this day, she has no idea what happened to him.

According to Juanita, mothers of the disappeared began individually going to police stations and military buildings asking about their children. "In every place, they said 'No, we didn't take them.'" Juanita explained that the mothers of the missing joined together because "with the voice of one mother" they would never be taken seriously by the military powers but that "the voice of 20 or 30 mothers is harder to ignore, and we waited for a reply."

Their work was extremely dangerous, and the mothers were themselves threatened with punishment. The first gatherings of the Madres in Plaza de Mayo were on Saturdays in April 1977. However, since there weren't many people around the plaza on weekends, they changed their meeting day to Thursday. It was only then that other citizens began becoming aware of what was going on and Juanita said that "many others were staying and talking in the Plaza de Mayo." Realizing the power the Madres began to wield, the government started arresting them that year. Ten mothers were taken to the police station one Thursday, and then 10, 15, and 61 mothers on the successive Thursdays. Juanita explained that "the military began to fear the mothers."

Eventually, to humor the mothers, the government said they could march, as long as they spoke with no one, and this tradition continues today with the silent main march around the Pirámide de Mayo, called "La Marcha de la Resistencia." *Pañuelos* (handkerchiefs) are painted in a circle surrounding the Pirámide, marking the nearly 30-year-old route.

Mothers would write the names of their children, which they were not allowed to say to anyone, on handkerchiefs and wear them on their heads as they marched in the hopes someone would know their child's whereabouts and perhaps contact them later. Yet even this proved too much for the military, which closed the plaza for a year between 1978 and 1979. The mothers then moved on to churches, other demonstrations, and ads in newspapers. Young people who helped the mothers at this stage began to disappear as well.

American involvement in the military regime and approval of torture of dissidents is disputed, but Juanita hypothesizes that many of the methods used were taught to the Argentine military by the U.S. Army School of the Americas, an anti-Communist training school based in Panama and closed under the Clinton administration. There are also accounts of American companies based in Argentina allowing torture of their employees on their premises. However, the Carter administration assigned Tex Harris, an employee at the U.S. embassy at the time, to investigate the atrocities and try to prevent them. Harris took seriously Carter's notion of taking human rights into consideration when dealing with the governments of other countries and said that "human rights became part of the fabric of diplomacy" at the U.S. embassy in Argentina between 1977 and 1979. Harris's intervention for many of the mothers who came to him may have saved thousands of lives. To my friends whose family members were saved because of his intervention, he will always be a hero. Many European embassies also had employees working to save lives by providing passports and smuggling people out of the country.

After the military regime fell out of power in 1982, little was done to bring the murderers to justice. In fact, under Ménem during the 1990s, immunity was granted to many and there were few investigations. Still, the Madres never stopped marching. With Kirschner's winning of the presidency in 2003, the Madres have found new hope, and investigations have been reopened. Kirschner also removed immunity for politicians who tortured and murdered dissidents, many of whom remain in power in Argentina to this day and have never answered to their crimes. As a young leftist, Kirschner personally lost friends during this period and understands the mothers more than any previous president.

There are different schools of thought regarding the mothers, and even they argue about whether economic reparations, monuments, and museums will bring an end to the dispute or whether they should push to continue investigations to ensure that those who murdered their children are arrested and brought to trial. Juanita belongs to the group of mothers seeking answers and justice. "We don't want monuments, we don't want museums, but talking about the struggles of our children. They were patriotic. They gave their lives to change things in their country." Yet no matter each mother's view on closure, Juanita said the fight goes on for all of them. "Our demands are very different. We are very old, but very strong in our actions."

allow Dante's ashes to be brought here, and he had designed a statue of him with a receptacle for his ashes for this purpose. Though Dante's ashes were never brought here, the statue remained in the lobby until 1955 when it was stolen during the revolution that deposed Perón. Palanti designed a similar version of this building in Montevideo, as well as the Hotel Castelar a few blocks down Avenida de Mayo. Tours are scheduled as listed below, but if you contact Miqueas, he will make other arrangements as well as do evening tours. Be aware that elevators and passages are tiny in the building, and groups of more than 10 people will have time delays for a usually 40-minute tour.

Av. de Mayo 1370, at San José, administrative office 9th floor, desks 249–252. ☎ 11/4383-1065, 11/4383-1063, or 11/15-5027-9035 (cell). www.pbarolo.com.ar. Admission $3.35. Tours Mon and Thurs on the hour 2–7pm, or by arrangement. Metro: Sáenz Peña.

RECOLETA

Recoleta Cemetery ⭐⭐⭐ (Moments) (Kids)   Open daily from 8am to 6pm, this is the final resting place of many of the wealthiest and most important Argentine historical figures. Weather permitting, free English-language tours are held every Tuesday and Thursday at 11am, and the administrative office next door also provides cemetery maps. Once the garden of the adjoining church, the cemetery was created in 1822 and is among the oldest in the city. You can spend hours here wandering the grounds that cover 4 city blocks, which represent the most expensive real estate in the city, full of tombs adorned with works by local and international sculptors. More than 6,400 mausoleums form an architectural free-for-all, including Greek temples and pyramids. The most popular site is the tomb of Eva "Evita" Perón, which is always heaped with flowers and letters from adoring fans. To prevent her body from being stolen as it had been many times by the various military governments installed after her husband's fall from grace in 1955, she was finally buried in a concrete vault 8.1m (27 ft.) underground in 1976. Many other rich or famous Argentines are buried here as well, including a number of Argentine presidents whose tomb names you'll recognize match some of the streets of the city.

Most tourists who come here visit only Evita's tomb and leave, but among the many, two are worth singling out and should not be missed while exploring here. One is the tomb of the Paz family, who owned the newspaper *La Prensa*, as well as the palatial building on Plaza San Martín now known as the Círculo Militar (p. 148). It is an enormous black stone structure covered with numerous white marble angels in turn-of-the-20th-century dress. The angels seem almost to soar to the heavens, lifting up the spirit of those inside with their massive wings. The sculptures were all made in Paris and shipped here. Masonic symbols such as anchors and pyramid-like shapes adorn this as well as many other Recoleta tombs.

Another tomb I recommend making sure to see while here is that of Rufina Cambaceres, a young woman who was buried alive. She had perhaps suffered a coma, and a few days after her interment, workers heard screams from the tomb. Once opened, there were scratches on her face and on the coffin from her trying to escape. Her mother then built this Art Nouveau masterpiece, which has become a symbol of the cemetery. Her coffin is a Carrara marble slab, carved with a rose on top, and it sits behind a glass wall, as if her mother wanted to make up for her mistake and sadness in burying her, and make sure that all could keep an eye on her coffin if she were ever to come back again. Adorned by a young girl carved of marble who turns her head to those watching her, she looks as if she is about to break into tears, and her right hand is on the door of her own tomb.

(Kids) Recoleta's Living Residents

The dead are not the only residents in Recoleta Cemetery. About 75 cats also roam among the tombs. The cats are plumper than most strays because a dedicated group of women from the area come to feed and provide them with medical attention at 10am and 4pm. Normally, the cats hide away from visitors, but at these times, they gather in anticipation at the entrance. This is a good time to bring children who might otherwise be bored in the cemetery. The women, who pay for their services on their own, welcome donations of cat food.

Calle Junín 1790, at Plaza Francesa. Administrative office next door at Calle Junín 1760. © 11/4804-7040 or 11/7803-1594. Free admission. Free English-language tours, weather permitting, Tues and Thurs 11am. No metro access.

TRIBUNALES

Teatro Colón (Colón Theater) ⭐⭐⭐ *(Moments)* Buenos Aires's golden age of prosperity gave birth to this luxurious opera house, and it was Argentina's way of announcing to the world that it was on the same level culturally as Paris, London, or New York. The building is one of the crowning visual delights of Avenida 9 de Julio, though its true entrance faces Plaza Libertad on the opposite side of the building. (The Teatro predates the design of Av. 9 de Julio, explaining this unusual entrance issue.) Over the years, the theater has been graced by the likes of Enrico Caruso, Luciano Pavarotti, Julio Bocca, Maria Callas, Plácido Domingo, Arturo Toscanini, and Igor Stravinsky.

Work began on the building in 1880 and took close to 28 years to complete, largely because the first two architects died during the building process. One of the architects, Victor Meano, who also worked on Congreso, was murdered in a love triangle gone wrong in a tragedy as dramatic as any on the stage he helped to create. The majestic building finally opened in 1908 and combines a variety of European styles, from the Ionic and Corinthian capitals and stained-glass pieces in the main entrance to the Portuguese marble staircase and French furniture, chandeliers, and vases in the Golden Hall. In the main theater—which seats 3,000 in orchestra seats, stalls, boxes, and four rises—an enormous chandelier hangs from the domed ceiling painted by Raúl Soldi in 1966 during a previous renovation.

The theater's acoustics are world-renowned. In addition to hosting visiting performers, the Colón has its own philharmonic orchestra, choir, and ballet company. Opera and symphony seasons last from February to late December. **Guided tours,** which let you view the main theater, backstage, and costume and underground stage design workshops, take place hourly between 11am and 3pm weekdays and from 9am to noon on Saturday. Call © **11/4378-7130** for information on tours.

Calle Libertad 621 or Calle Toscanini 1180, overlooking Av. 9 de Julio and Plaza Libertad. © 11/4378-7100. www.teatrocolon.org.ar. Tour admission $2.50. Seating for events $2–$45. Metro: Tribunales.

Escuela Presidente Roca ⭐ Workers in this building say that people often mistake it for the Teatro Colón, which sits nearby. Designed as a Greek temple, it's easy to see why, and it is one of the most impressive buildings on Plaza Libertad. Though not technically open to the public, polite curious visitors will be allowed

Tips Teatro Colón Tickets & Renovation

The shows at the Teatro Colón are more than worth it, but seeing a performance can be frustrating unless you know some things ahead of time. Currently, tickets for events cannot be purchased more than 2 days in advance. (Management claims it will change this policy to 30 days in advance sometime during 2005 and also allow Web sales for tickets, but I wouldn't hold my breath.) Because of this policy, one of the first things you should do when you get to Buenos Aires is to head to the theater to see the schedule and buy tickets. The building is also undergoing an ongoing renovation in preparation for its 100th anniversary in 2008, and as such, will be closed completely in 2006 and 2007. If you are in Buenos Aires while it is open, do not even think about putting off seeing this building for a tour or performance.

into the courtyard with its Doric colonnade and may be able to peek inside. The upstairs areas, which include a theater and activity center for the school's children have beautifully frescoed ceilings with Greek decoration. Opened in 1904, this public school is seeking funding for its restoration, but some worry that after a renovation, the building would likely be taken over by the government for other uses, as it is located in such an important political area of the city.

Libertad and Tucumán, overlooking Plaza Libertad next to Teatro Colón. Metro: Tribunales.

PLAZA SAN MARTIN AREA

Círculo Militar *ARA* You're certain to notice this grand marble building overlooking Plaza San Martín. The Círculo Militar is one of the most beautiful buildings in all of Buenos Aires, and it seems to have been plucked out of France's Loire Valley. It was built as the mansion of the Paz family, the owners of the newspaper *La Prensa*, whose original office was on Avenida de Mayo and is now the Casa de Cultura (p. 136). The Paz family was one of the wealthiest and most powerful families in the whole country, and some will still call this building by its two old names—Palacio Paz or Palacio Retiro. But it is now officially called the Círculo Militar, named for the society of retired military officers that bought the building in 1938. It was built in stages spanning 1902 to 1914, under the direction of the French architect Louis H. M. Sortais. The commissioner of the project, family patriarch José Clemente Paz, died in 1912 and never saw its completion. (If you go to Recoleta Cemetery [p. 146], don't miss his tomb, among the most impressive in the cemetery.) Marble and other materials throughout the building were imported from all over Europe. Most rooms are reminiscent of Versailles, especially the bedrooms and the gold-and-white music hall with an ornate parquet floor and windows overlooking the plaza. Other rooms are in the Tudor style, and the Presidential Room, where only the men would retreat for political conversation, is the most unusual. Very masculine and dark, it is lit by strange chandeliers decorated with naked hermaphrodite characters with beards and breasts, whose faces contort as they are lanced through their private parts. It is unknown why this was the decorative theme of a room for politics. The six elevators are original to the building and the overall height of the building is eight stories, though with their high ceilings, there are only four levels to the building. The most impressive room is the round Hall of Honor, which sits under an interior rotunda and even has a balconied second level overlooking a stage. It was a private mini–opera house, covered in multicolored marble and gilded bronze, used now for conferences. They claim to have tours in English, but usually the guide will only speak Spanish.

Av. Santa Fe 750, at Maipú, overlooking Plaza San Martín. © 11/4311-1071. www.circulomilitar.org. Admission $1.35. Tours Mon–Fri 11am, 3pm, 4pm, and sometimes in English Wed–Thurs 3pm. Metro: San Martín.

Islas Malvinas–Falkland Islands War Memorial 𝒦𝒦   In many English-speaking countries (which most of the readers of this book are likely from), the notion of a country like Argentina challenging a major world power like Great Britain to war is almost ridiculous, and when it actually happened, it was treated by English-language media. This short war lasted from April to June 1982, and it remains an extremely touchy and serious subject among Argentines. Regardless of your personal opinion on the logic of Argentina declaring war on Great Britain, any conversation with locals on the topic must be treated very delicately. The war came during a period of rapid inflation and other troubles when the Argentine military government, under the leadership of General Leopoldo Galtieri, was looking for a way to distract attention from its failed economic policies. Argentina lost the war, suffering over 700 casualties, and this sparked exactly what Galtieri was hoping to avoid, the collapse of his government. Democracy returned to Argentina, and the six-year Dirty War, under which 30,000 political opponents were tortured and murdered, finally ended. The United States had tried to balance itself and serve as a diplomatic channel between the two countries during the war, but it generally sided with Great Britain, in technical violation of the Monroe Doctrine. The legal basis of Argentina's claim to the Falkland Islands, known here as Las Islas Malvinas (and you had better use that term, not the British one, while you're here), is due to their being a portion of Argentina's territory when it was still ruled by Spain. However, as a fledgling nation after independence, Argentina could do little to prevent Great Britain from setting up a fishing colony and base there. To most Argentines, having lost the war does not mean that they have no rights to the islands, and diplomatic maneuvers continue with the ongoing dispute. The argument is over more than mere sovereignty: Oil reserves have been discovered in the area.

This monument contains Vietnam memorial–like stark plaques with lists of names of the Argentines who died. An eternal flame burns over a metallic image of the islands, and the three main branches of the military, the Army, the Navy, and the Air Force, take 2-week rotations guarding the monument. The location of the monument, at the bottom of a gentle hill under Plaza San Martín, is itself a message. It faces the Torre Monumental, previously known as the British Clock Tower, a gift from British citizens who made a fortune developing the nearby Retiro railroad station complex. Like checkmate in a game of chess, the two sides, Argentina and Great Britain, stand facing each other, symbolically representing the dispute that has no end.

Av. Libertador, under Plaza San Martín, across from Retiro Station. Metro: San Martín or Retiro.

Torre Monumental (British Clock Tower) 𝒦   This Elizabethan-style clock tower, which some call the Argentine Big Ben, was a gift from the British community of Buenos Aires after building the nearby Retiro railroad station complex. At the turn of the 20th century, Argentina had vast natural resources like grain and cattle waiting to be exploited, but it was the British Empire that had the

investment capability and technology to create Retiro and connect Buenos Aires to its hinterlands to get products to markets overseas. This, however, was always a sore point, and for years many Argentines felt exploited by Great Britain. Recently the tower was renamed the Torre Monumental, in response to the very common post–Islas Malvinas/Falkland Islands War renaming of anything associated with Great Britain, yet nearly all locals still call it the British Clock Tower (see "British Names Post–Islas Malvinas," below). The monument survived the war unscathed, but a few years later, during an anniversary memorial service, an angry mob attacked it. They destroyed portions of the base and also toppled a statue of George Canning, the first British diplomat to recognize the country's independence from Spain. (It's now safely kept at the British Embassy.) The Islas Malvinas–Falkland Islands War Memorial (p. 149) was purposely placed across the street as a permanent reminder of Britain's battle with Argentina. There is little to see in the monument itself, save for a small museum of photographs. The main attraction here is the view: A free elevator ride will take you to the top floor with its wraparound view of the port, the trains, and the city of Buenos Aires itself. There is also a small Buenos Aires city tourism information center inside.

Av. Libertador 49, across from Plaza San Martín, next to Retiro Station. ℂ 11/4311-0186. www. museos.buenosaires.gov.ar. Free admission. Thurs–Sun 11am–6pm. Metro: Retiro.

MICROCENTRO

Obelisco   The Obelisco is one of the defining monuments of Buenos Aires. It was inaugurated in 1936 to celebrate the 400th anniversary of the first, and unsuccessful, founding of the city by Pedro de Mendoza. (The city was later re-established in 1580.) It sits at the intersection of Corrientes and Avenida 9 de Julio, which is the heart of the city and the Theater District. The Obelisco is the focal point of the vista between Plaza de Mayo and Diagonal Norte, meant to mimic the vistas found in Paris around Place de la Concorde. A church was demolished to create the site, and on both sides, Corrientes bulges into a circle to accommodate it. An oval parklike cutout with a gentle hill along Avenida 9 de

---

⟨Fun Fact   **British Names Post–Islas Malvinas**

British influence was once visible all over Buenos Aires, but following the Islas Malvinas/Falkland Islands War, the city has made an effort to honor Argentines in places once named for British heroes. The person worst affected by this was George Canning, the British foreign secretary who recognized Argentina's independence from Spain. He once had a major Buenos Aires thoroughfare named after him, since changed to Scalabrini Ortiz, the only reminder being Salón Canning, a tango hall on that street. At subway station Malabia, under many layers of paint, you might find the old signs that once announced it as Station Canning. Worst of all, though, was the statue of him that was once part of the Torre Monumental, formerly known as the British Clock Tower. An angry mob tore down this statue during an Islas Malvinas/Falkland Islands War anniversary service. British citizens shouldn't be worried, though; you can still visit Canning at the embassy, where his statue is now well protected. And besides, Argentines speak more English now than they ever did before the war, keeping Canning's memory alive, at least in the language.

Julio surrounds it, along with bronze plaques representing the various Argentine provinces. When Argentines have something to celebrate, the Obelisco is where they head. If you're in town when Argentina wins an international event, you can be sure hundreds of people will gather around the Obelisco with flags in their hands, waving them at the cars who honk in celebration as they head past. Certainly, the Obelisco would have a great vista, but it is not a structure built as a viewing spot.

Av. 9 de Julio, at Corrientes. Metro: Carlos Pellegrini, Diagonal Norte, or 9 de Julio.

Paseo Obelisco   This shopping complex and underground pedestrian causeway (which you may have to pass through at some point on your trip anyway) is worth a short trip in itself. Paris, New York, London, and virtually every major city with a subway once had similar underground complexes, but this area under the Obelisco, where three subway lines meet, seems to have been unchanged since the 1960s. The shops are nothing special—several barber shops, shoe-repair spots, and stores selling cheap clothing and other goods make up the bulk of them. Yet, together, with their cohesive old signs, fixtures, and furnishings, they look like the setting for a movie.

Subway entrances surrounding the Obelisco, along Av. 9 de Julio. Metro: Carlos Pellegrini, Diagonal Norte, or 9 de Julio.

Galería Guemes *Finds*   This is a sumptuous building, though its modern entrance on Calle Florida would make you think otherwise. Its back entrance on San Martín, however, still retains all of its original glory. This is a shopping gallery with a mix of stores without distinction and several kiosks that obscure the views, but look around at the walls and decorations. The architecture is a mix of Art Nouveau, Gothic, and neoclassical all heavily ornamented, and was the creation of the architect who designed the now-closed Café del Molino next door to Congreso. Make sure to look also at the ornate elevator banks, which lead to the offices above. The building also houses the Piazzolla tango show. The Art Nouveau theater in which it sits was closed for nearly 40 years and was only recently restored. Of all of the tango show palaces in Buenos Aires, this is the most beautiful.

Calle Florida 165, at Perón. Metro: Florida.

Centro Cultural de Borges   You can shop all you want in Galerías Pacífico, but if it's culture you're after, you can find it there too. Inside of the shopping mall is this arts center named for Jorge Luis Borges, Argentina's most important literary figure. You'll find art galleries, lecture halls with various events, an art cinema, art bookstore, the **Escuela Argentina de Tango,** which offers a schedule of lessons tourists can take with ease (© 11/4312-4990; www.eatango.org), and the ballet star **Julio Bocca's Ballet Argentino** performance space and training school full of young ballet stars and their not-to-be-missed performances (© 11/5555-5359; www.juliobocca.com).

Enter through Galerías Pacífico or at the corner of Viamonte and San Martín (the back of the Galerías Pacífico Mall). © 11/5555-5359. www.ccborges.com.ar. Various hours and fees. Metro: San Martín.

OTHER SITES

Biblioteca Nacional (National Library)   Opened in 1992, this modern architectural oddity stands on the land of the former Presidential Residence in which Eva Perón died. (The building was demolished by the new government so that it would not become a holy site to Evita's millions of supporters after her death.) With its underground levels, the library's 13 floors can store up to five million volumes. Among its collection, the library stores 21 books printed by one of the earliest printing presses, dating from 1440 to 1500. Visit the reading room—occupying two stories at the top of the building—to enjoy an awe-inspiring view of Buenos Aires. The library also hosts special events in its exhibition hall and auditorium.

Calle Aguero 2502. ✆ 11/4807-0885. Free admission. Weekdays 9am–9pm; weekends noon–8pm. No metro access.

Plaza Serrano 🛦🛦 *Moments* This is the bohemian heart of Palermo Viejo. During the day there is not much going on here, but at night this plaza comes alive with young people gathering to drink, celebrate, sing, dance, play guitar, and just generally enjoy being alive. Many of the kids are dread-headed Rastafarians, and it's easy to join and chat with any of them, and many sell funky jewelry and other crafts while they gather together. The plaza is surrounded by numerous bars and restaurants, which I describe in chapter 5. On Saturday and Sunday from 11am to 6pm, there is an official but not-to-be-missed fair here with even more funky jewelry and arts and crafts. The true name of this plaza is Plazoleta Julio Cortazor, but few people will call it that. The plaza is at the intersection of Calle Serrano and Calle Honduras, but Calle Serrano is also named Calle Borges on some maps.

Plaza Serrano, at the intersection of Serrano/Borges and Honduras. www.palermoviejo.com. No metro access.

Chacarita Cemetery 🛦 Less well known than its far more glamorous sibling Recoleta, Chacarita Cemetery sits in the Chacarita neighborhood, close to Palermo Hollywood. This is a middle-class cemetery, and on weekends, unlike in Recoleta, you are more likely to see real families burying and visiting relatives. It is in two parts, one very similar to Recoleta, with enormous, aboveground tombs, though generally less decorated. After a traffic circle and chapel area dividing the two sections, the cemetery continues on to acres of underground mausoleums, giving the appearance of an open, parklike setting. Within the older section there are also grand tombs for members of workers' unions and other associations and pantheons for members of the arts, which rival anything in Recoleta. A few tombs of note here include that of Carlos Gardel, decorated with his statue and hundreds of plaques of honor. Tradition holds that visitors should put a lighted cigarette into his outstretched hand for good luck. General Juan Domingo Perón is also buried here, and his tomb is often plastered with Peronist posters. He did not have the luck of being in Recoleta as his wife did. Agustín Magaldi, the tango singer historically associated with Evita's move to Buenos Aires, is also buried here. While mocked in the play and movie, he was an honored star of tango in the 1930s, considered one of the country's greatest at the time.

Entrance at Av. Guzman, at the intersection with Corrientes/Triunvirato. ✆ 11/4552-0040. Daily 8am–6pm. Metro: Lacroze.

Plazoleta Carlos Pellegrini 🛦 I think this is one of the most beautiful of all the small plazas in Buenos Aires, not just for the plaza itself, but for what surrounds it. This is the most Parisian-appearing part of Recoleta, and what helps it to be so is that the ornate Belle Epoque French Embassy presides over it. The Brazilian Embassy, another beautiful building in a former mansion, also overlooks the plaza. A large, recently restored statue of Carlos Pellegrini sits in the center of the plaza. It was created in France by Félix Coutan and dedicated in 1914. A small fountain and a bench add to the relaxed environment. Nearby are several other mansions, including the Louis XIII–style "La Mansión," which is part of the Four Seasons. The park is the terminus of the Avenida Alvear, the city's most exclusive shopping street, close to where it hits Avenida 9 de Julio. The collection of intact buildings here will give you an idea as to the beauty that was lost in Buenos Aires with the widening of Avenida 9 de Julio in the 1960s. In fact, demolition of the French Embassy, which France refused, was part of the plan.

Plazoleta Carlos Pellegrini, Av. Alvear at Cerrito (Av. 9 de Julio). No metro access.

Plazoleta Siria   After visiting the adjacent Botanical Gardens and the zoo, or if you've gone after they have closed, head to this pleasant tiny park on the corner of Avenida Santa Fe and República Arabe Siria. It's chess playing central for old men from the neighborhood who gather here by the dozens. Many also play Truco, an Argentine card game. Sometimes they can be very competitive. If you think you're any good, ask for a place and join them.

Corner of Av. Santa Fe and República Arabe Siria, in Palermo. Metro: Plaza Italia.

The Israeli Embassy Memorial ⋇   In 1992 a bomb ripped through the Israeli Embassy in Buenos Aires on a peaceful and seemingly out-of-the-way corner of Recoleta at the intersection of calles Suipacha and Arroyo. Twenty-nine people lost their lives in the tragedy, and—as with the 1994 attack on the Jewish community group, the Asociación Mutual Israelita Argentina, which killed 85 people—the true culprits are unknown but suspected to have been working with overseas groups. Under President Kirschner, investigations related to the bombings have recently been reopened. The site is now a very tranquil place for contemplation, converted into a park graced by 22 trees and seven benches to represent the people who died in the embassy bombing. The outline of the once-elegant building remains, like a ghost speaking for the dead.

Calles Suipacha and Arroyo. www.amia.org.ar. Metro: San Martín.

Ecological Reserve ⋇⋇   The Ecological Reserve is an unusual and unexpected consequence of highway construction throughout Buenos Aires during the mid–20th century. Construction debris and the rubble of demolished buildings were unceremoniously dumped into the Río de la Plata. Over time, sand and sediment began to build up, and then grass and trees began to grow. The birds followed, and now the area is a preserve. Various companies will take people on biking and bird-watching tours of the area. Ask your travel agent about it or see our list of tour companies (p. 38). Since there are few genuine beaches in the Buenos Aires area, some people come here to suntan, sometimes in the nude. Whatever you do, don't go into the water since it is heavily polluted and still full of rough construction debris in some parts. In spite of its being a preserve, development is slowly encroaching on the area as the Puerto Madero area grows. And, though the police do have a patrol station here, some homeless people also camp out here.

Along the Costanera near Puerto Madero. ℭ **11/4893-1588**. No metro access.

2 Museums

Museo de las Armas de la Nación ⋇ (Kids)   This small museum in the impressive Círculo Militar overlooking Plaza San Martín is very helpful for gaining a better understanding of the Argentine side of the Falkland Islands War. In Argentina that war is called the Guerra de las Islas Malvinas, using the name of the island chain from when it was part of the Spanish Empire, which is the basis for Argentina's dispute with Great Britain. In spite of losing the war, Argentina still lays claim to the islands. Calling them by their English name is likely to cause an argument even with the politest Argentine. The curator of the museum is Isidro

Abel Vides, a veteran of the war. Among the items of note related to the war is a display about the sinking of the *General Belgrano,* in which 323 Argentines died, the greatest individual loss of life in a single event of the war. Other displays show uniforms of the time period. Children will like the huge collection of toy soldiers showing the history of military costume in Argentina and other countries up until the 1940s. There are also models of old forts from the Argentine frontier. Gun collections show arms used in Argentina and other parts of the world. Most of these weapons were produced in the United States, demonstrating that by the time of the U.S. Civil War, U.S. companies were the major supplier of arms used throughout the Americas. Other items of note include rifles spanning 5 centuries, cannons, samurai suits, swords, and replica armored suits. The museum also contains a small library of military books and records and is of note for scholars looking for information on Argentina's various military dictatorships and the Islas Malvinas/Falkland Islands War. The Círculo Militar, located in the former mansion of the Paz family (p. 148), is a social club for retired members of the military. Here, there is also a private section of the museum containing more historical military documents and artifacts, which is not open to the general public. However, if you are a current or retired member of the military in your home country, they sometimes make exceptions.

Av. Santa Fe 702, at Maipú overlooking Plaza San Martín. © 11/4311-1071. www.circulomilitar.org. Admission $1. Museum and library Mon–Fri noon–7pm. Metro: San Martín.

Museum of the Federal Administration of Public Revenue (Tax Museum) *Finds*   Numismatists, accountants, and others interested in the history of money and taxes will enjoy this small and unique museum, one of only three of its type in the world. Photographs, tax record books, and other documents here tell the history of Customs and other forms of tax collection in Argentina. One room has also been set up in a re-creation of 1930s tax offices, complete with period machines. The highlight of the museum's collection is a desk used by Manuel Belgrano, the man who designed the Argentine flag. The building itself is an incredible work of art and was formerly the Majestic Hotel. Though decaying, the lobby is a dark and sumptuous orgy of marble and bronze, which opened in time for the 1910 Centennial celebrations. Its most famous guest was the Infanta Isabel, who stayed here to represent Spain for the festivities at the time.

Av. de Mayo 1317, at San José. © 11/4384-0282. www.afip.gov.ar. Free admission. Mon–Fri 11am–5pm. Metro: Sáenz Peña.

Museo de Los Niños *Kids*   I wish I had one of these when I was growing up. This museum, located in the Abasto Shopping Center, is a fun way for your kids to learn about different careers and learn a little about Buenos Aires too, since many of the displays relate to the city. First, for the city, they have miniature versions of the Casa Rosada, Congreso, and a street layout to demonstrate how traffic flows, so it's a great way to orient your kids to Buenos Aires. Various careers can be explored here with a miniature dentist's office, doctor's office, TV station with working cameras, gas station and refinery, working radio station, and a newspaper office to learn about journalism. The bank has interactive computers, too. Some of the things have a corporate feel to them, like a McDonald's where kids can play in the kitchen and serve you for a change. Another is the post office imitating a branch of the private OCA mail service company. Here, kids can write out postcards, which they say get sent to the mayor of Buenos Aires. Even more fun is a giant toilet where kids learn what happens in the sewer system after they use the bathroom. Intellectual kids can also seek some solitude in the library, and budding

dramatists can play dress-up onstage in a little theater, complete with costumes. A patio has small rides for little children too, when the big kids are too rambunctious. Don't worry if the kids wear you out—there are couches for weary parents to rest on, too. If you're here in a group at birthday-party time, have one here. They say kids of all ages up to 16 will enjoy it, but I think that after 12 years old, kids might not think it is as fun a place to be.

Abasto Shopping Center Food Court, Av. Corrientes 3247. Ⓒ 11/4861-2325. AE, DC, MC, V. Admission $2.50, family/group discounts available, free for seniors and kids under 3. Tues–Sun and holidays 1–8pm. Metro: Gardel.

Museo Participativo de Ciencias ⋒⋒ ⟨Kids⟩

Okay, so you came to the Centro Cultural de Recoleta, adjacent to the Recoleta Cemetery, to see art and be sophisticated. Well, here's the place to bring the kids afterward, or let them wander in on their own. In this museum, unlike so many others, it's prohibited not to touch! There are two floors full of science displays where kids can touch, play, and see how electricity, gravity, and many other things work, all designed to be fun. Communications rooms, mechanical rooms, and wave and sound rooms all have various interactive stands that are aimed at kids of all ages. Sure, it's a noisy place, but if you can find a way to make learning fun, it's not a bad side effect.

Inside of the Centro Cultural de Recoleta, adjacent to the Recoleta Cemetery. Ⓒ 11/4807-3260 or 11/4806-3456. www.mpc.org.ar. Admission $2. Daily 3:30–7:30pm. No metro access.

Museo de Casa Gardel ⋒

Carlos Gardel, the preeminent Argentine tango singer whose portraits you see all over the city and who is nicknamed Carlitos, bought this house in 1927 for his mother, with whom he lived when he was not traveling. The house dates from 1917, and in keeping with tango history, it once served as a brothel. It served various functions after his mother's death in 1943, from a tailor shop to a tango parlor, until it reopened as a museum in his honor on June 24, 2003, the 68th anniversary of his death in a plane crash. Visitors will find articles about him from the time, original musical notes, contracts, portraits of his singing partner José Razzano, records and sheet music from the period, as well as some of his clothing including his signature fedora. His kitchen, bathroom, and ironing room remain almost untouched from the time he lived here. Most tours are in Spanish, but there are some in English on a periodic basis. This small, out-of-the-way museum is a must-see not only for tango lovers but also to understand this important man in Argentine history, whose work brought tango to the world. A favorite phrase in Buenos Aires is that Carlos sings better every day, meaning as time passes, his music, the most Porteño thing of all, becomes more and more important to Argentines.

Jean Jaures 735, at Tucumán. Ⓒ 11/4964-2071 and 11/4964-2015. www.museos.buenosaires.gov.ar. Admission $1.35. Mon and Wed–Fri 11am–6pm; Sat–Sun and holidays 10am–7pm. Metro: Carlos Gardel.

Templo Libertad and the Jewish History Museum ⋒

This impressive Byzantine-style temple is the home of the CIRA (Congregación Israelita de la República de Argentina). Sitting a block from the Teatro Colón, it is one of the stars of Plaza Libertad. The small building housing the temple's administrative office also contains the Jewish History Museum, known also as the Museo Kibrick after its founder. You'll find material related to the Jewish community in Buenos Aires, with both Sephardic and Ashkenazi items from their original homelands. Menorahs, altar cloths, spice holders, and various pieces of religious art make up the bulk of the collection. Special exhibits also relate the history of Jewish agricultural colonies in rural parts of Argentina.

Libertad 769, at Córdoba overlooking Plaza Libertad. ℂ 11/4814-3637. www.mpc.org.ar. Admission $1. Tues and Thurs 3:30–6pm. Museum closes entirely Dec 15–Mar 15, but special requests might be honored. Metro: Tribunales.

Museo Evita 🏵🏵🏵   It is almost impossible for non-Argentines to fathom that it took 50 years from the time of her death for Evita, the world's most famous Argentine, to finally get a museum. The Museo Evita opened on July 26, 2002, in a mansion where her charity, the Eva Perón Foundation, once housed single mothers with children.

While the museum treats her history fairly, looking at both the good and the bad, it is quickly obvious to the visitor that each presentation has a little bit of love for Evita behind it, and indeed, members of the family are involved in the museum. Evita's grandniece, Cristina Alvarez Rodríguez, is president of the historical group that runs the museum, and she is often in the building meeting with the staff. Gabriel Miremont, the museum's curator, is Argentina's preeminent expert on Evita history, and he had become personally interested in Evita while a child when he was forbidden from listening to lyrics to the Evita play. It was technically illegal at the time to do so while a military dictatorship ruled the country following the collapse of Perón's second government in 1976. Thus, while historically accurate, the museum has a close personal touch, which makes it different from most museums.

The Museo Evita's displays divide Evita's life into several parts, looking at her childhood, her arrival in Buenos Aires to become an actress, her ascension as Evita, first lady and unofficial saint to millions, and finally her death and legacy. You will be able to view her clothes, remarkably preserved by the military government, which took power after Perón's 1955 fall. Other artifacts of her life include her voting card, as only through Evita did Argentine women gain the right to vote. There are also toys and schoolbooks adorned with her image, given to children to indoctrinate them into the Peronist movement. The most touching artifact of all, though, is a smashed statue of Evita hidden for decades by a farmer in his barn, despite the possibility of being jailed for saving it. Whether you hate, love, or are indifferent to Evita, this is a museum that no visitor to Argentina should miss. Digesting the exhibits here will help you truly understand why she remains such a controversial figure within the Argentine psyche.

Calle Lafinur 2988, at Gutierrez. ℂ 11/4807-9433. www.evitaperon.org. Admission $2. Tues–Sun 2–7:30pm. Metro: Plaza Italia.

Museo Nacional de Arte Decorativo (National Museum of Decorative Arts) 🏵   French architect René Sergent, who designed some of the grandest mansions in Buenos Aires, also designed the mansion housing this museum. The building is itself a work of art, and it will give you an idea of the incredible mansions that once lined this avenue, overlooking the extensive Palermo park system. The building's 18th-century French design provides a classical setting for the diverse decorative styles represented within. Breathtaking sculptures, paintings, and furnishings make up the collection, and themed shows rotate seasonally. The **Museo de Arte Oriental (Museum of Eastern Art)** displays art, pottery, and engravings on the first floor of this building.

Av. del Libertador 1902, at Lucena. ℂ 11/4801-8248. Admission $1. Mon–Fri 2–8pm; Sat–Sun 11am–7pm. No metro access.

Museo Nacional de Bellas Artes (National Museum of Fine Arts) 🏵🏵
This building, which formerly pumped the city's water supply, metamorphosed into Buenos Aires's most important art museum in 1930. The museum contains

the world's largest collection of Argentine sculptures and paintings from the 19th and 20th centuries. It also houses European art dating from the pre-Renaissance period to the present day. The collections include notable pieces by Renoir, Monet, Rodin, Toulouse-Lautrec, and van Gogh, as well as a surprisingly extensive collection of Picasso drawings.

Av. del Libertador 1473, at Agote. ℂ 11/4803-0802. Free admission. Tues–Sun 12:30–7:30pm. No metro access.

The Water Palace and the Museo del Patrimonio 🎖 (Kids)   Many people pass by this massive High Victorian structure on Avenida Córdoba in Barrio Norte and wonder what it is. This is Buenos Aires's Water Palace, a fantastic structure of over 300,000 lustrous, multicolored faience bricks made by Royal Doulton and shipped from Britain. Its original interior engineering components were made in various countries, with Belgium as the largest contributor. Originally, the Water Palace was meant to be a humble building, constructed as a response to the yellow fever epidemic that hit San Telmo and other neighborhoods in Buenos Aires in 1877. In the days before plumbing, drinking water was held in collecting pools in individual homes, which helped to spread the disease. Alarmed, the city began looking for a spot to construct new, sanitary facilities to prevent another outbreak. As this was the highest point in the city, meaning water stored here could use gravity to flow down the pipes into residences, this location was chosen for the water tower.

However, two things happened that changed the plans, creating the 1887 building seen here now. First, Buenos Aires was made the capital of Argentina in 1880, and the city planners felt the building must not only serve a purpose but reflect the glory of a new nation seeking its place in the world. (Still, Argentina did not have the technology, hence the need for foreign help in construction.) In addition, the yellow fever epidemic itself meant that the area surrounding this location was quickly filling up with new mansions for wealthy families fleeing San Telmo. The water purification building needed to not only fit in its surroundings, but to outshine them.

The engineering works have been removed, and the building is now the headquarters of the water company Aguas Argentinas. It also contains one of the most unusual museums in the whole city, one kids will get a kick out of. Explaining the history of water sanitation in Argentina and the world, this museum is home to hundreds of toilets spanning the decades. Some are dissected, showing their interior workings. Others are multifunctional prison toilets with sink and toilet joined together, along with faucets, giant sewer pipes, and anything to do with waterworks. The museum also has an extensive library with plans, books, and other materials related to waterworks around the world, making it a worthwhile stop for students and engineers.

Av. Córdoba 1750, at Riobamba; museum entrance at Riobamba 750, 1st floor. ℂ 11/6319-1882 or 11/6319-1104. www.aguasargentinas.com.ar. Admission $1. Mon–Fri 9am–1pm; guided tours in Spanish Mon, Wed, and Fri at 11am. Metro: Facultad de Medicina.

Museo de la Ciudad   Like one big common attic for Buenos Aires, the Museo de la Ciudad is a kitschy collection of everything and anything related to the history of this city. It's built into an old pharmacy in Monserrat dating from 1894. Whether it's tango, Little Italy, bicycles, or a doll collection, this museum gives you a glimpse into the pride Porteños have for even the everyday aspects of their lives, no matter how disorganized the place feels.

Alsina 412, at Bolívar. ℂ 11/4331-9855. Admission $1. Mon–Fri 11am–7pm; Sat–Sun 3–7pm. Metro: Bolívar.

El Museo Histórico Nacional (National History Museum) 🏛🏛   Argentine history from the 16th through the 19th centuries comes to life in the former Lezama family home. The expansive Italian-style mansion houses 30 rooms with items saved from Jesuit missions, paintings illustrating clashes between the Spaniards and Indians, and relics from the War of Independence against Spain. The focal point of the museum's collection is artist Cándido López's series of captivating scenes of the war against Paraguay in the 1870s.

Calle Defensa 1600, in Parque Lezama. © 11/4307-1182. Free admission. Tues–Sun noon–6pm. Closed Jan. Metro: Constitución.

MALBA-Colección Constantini 🏛🏛🏛   The airy and luminescent Museo de Arte Latinoamericano de Buenos Aires (MALBA) houses the private art collection of art collector Eduardo Constantini. One of the most impressive collections of Latin American art anywhere, temporary and permanent exhibitions showcase names like Antonio Berni, Pedro Figari, Frida Kahlo, Cândido Portinari, Diego Rivera, and Antonio Siguí. Many of the works confront social issues and explore questions of national identity. Even the benches are modern pieces of art. The atrium offers access to the various floors under an enormous metal sculpture of a man doing pushups over the escalator bay. In addition to the art exhibitions, Latin films are shown Tuesday through Sunday at 2 and 10pm. This wonderful museum, which opened in late 2001, is located in Palermo Chico.

Av. Figueroa Alcorta 3415, at San Martín. © 11/4808-6500. www.malba.org.ar. Admission $1.75. Free admission on Wed. Wed–Mon noon–8pm. No metro access.

3 Neighborhoods Worth a Visit

LA BOCA

La Boca, on the banks of the Río Riachuelo, originally developed as a trading center and shipyard. This was the city's first Little Italy, giving the neighborhood the distinct flavor it maintains today. La Boca is most famous for giving birth to the tango in the numerous bordellos, known as *quilombos,* which once served this largely male population.

The focus of La Boca is the **Caminito** (p. 140), a pedestrian walkway, named ironically after a tango song about a rural village. The walkway is lined with humorously sculpted statues and murals explaining its history. Surrounding the cobblestone street are corrugated metal houses painted in a hodgepodge of colors, recalling a time when the poor locals decorated with whatever paint was left over from ship maintenance in the harbor. Today many artists live or set up their studios in these houses. Along the Caminito, art and souvenir vendors work side by side with tango performers. This Caminito "Fine Arts Fair" is open daily from 10am to 6pm. La Boca is, however, a victim of its own success, and it has become an obscene tourist trap. While the area is historically important, most of what you will find along the Caminito are overpriced souvenir and T-shirt shops and constant harassment from people trying to hand you flyers for mediocre restaurants. In the summer the smell from the heavily polluted river becomes almost overbearing. Come to this area because you have to, but if you are short on time, don't let the visit take up too much of your day. What remains authentic in the area is off the beaten path, whether art galleries or theaters catering both to locals and to tourists, or the world-famous **Estadio de Boca Juniors** (**Boca Juniors Stadium and Museum;** p. 141).

Use caution in straying too far from the Caminito, however, as the less patrolled surrounding areas can be unsafe. The police are here not for protecting the locals but for the tourists. Once the shopkeepers go home, so do they. Still, at dusk and away from the Caminito is where you will have the most interesting interactions with the neighborhood residents who quietly reclaim the streets and stroll along the waterfront. Most come not from Italy now, but from the poor interior provinces of the country. *Caution:* It's best to avoid La Boca at night.

SAN TELMO

Buenos Aires's oldest neighborhood, San Telmo originally housed the city's elite. But when yellow fever struck in the 1870s—aggravated by substandard conditions in the area—the aristocrats moved north. Poor immigrants soon filled this neighborhood, and the houses were converted to tenements, called *conventillos.* In 1970 the city passed regulations to restore some of San Telmo's architectural landmarks. Still, gentrification has been a slow process, and the neighborhood maintains a gently decayed, very authentic atmosphere, reminiscent of Cuba's old Havana. It's a bohemian enclave, attracting tourists, locals, and performers 7 days a week on its streets. The collapse of the peso has also meant that a glut of antiques, sold for ready cash, are available for purchase. The best shops and markets in San Telmo line **Calle Defensa.** After Plaza de Mayo, **Plaza Dorrego** is the second-oldest square in the city. For a description of the square, see p. 140.

San Telmo is full of tango clubs; one of the most notable is **El Viejo Almacén** ☆, at Independencia and Balcarce. An example of colonial architecture, it was built in 1798 and was a general store and hospital before its reincarnation as the quintessential Argentine tango club. Make sure to make it here at night for a show (p. 228). If you get the urge for a beginner or refresher tango course while you're in San Telmo, look for signs advertising lessons in the windows of clubs.

PALERMO

Palermo ☆☆☆ is a catchall term for a rather nebulous and large chunk of northern Buenos Aires. It encompasses **Palermo** proper with its park system, **Palermo Chico, Palermo Viejo,** which is further divided into **Palermo Soho** and **Palermo Hollywood,** and **Las Cañitas,** which is just to the side of the city's world-famous polo field.

PALERMO NEIGHBORHOODS

Palermo Chico is an exclusive neighborhood of elegant mansions off of Avenida Libertador, whose prices were seemingly unaffected by the peso crisis. Other than the beauty of the homes and a few embassy buildings, this small set of streets tucked behind the MALBA museum has little of interest to the tourist.

Palermo proper is a neighborhood of parks filled with magnolias, pines, palms, and willows, where families picnic on weekends and couples stroll at sunset. Designed by French architect Charles Thays, the parks take their inspiration from London's Hyde Park and Paris's Bois de Boulogne. Take the metro to Plaza Italia, which lets you out next to the **Botanical Gardens** ☆ (© 11/4831-2951; p. 164) and **Zoological Gardens** ☆ (© 11/4806-7412; p. 164), open dawn to dusk, both good spots for kids. Stone paths wind their way through the botanical gardens. Flora from throughout South America fills the garden, with over 8,000 plant species from around the world represented. Next door, the city zoo features an impressive diversity of animals.

Parque Tres de Febrero ☆☆, a 1,000-acre paradise of trees, lakes, and walking trails, begins just past the Rose Garden off Avenida Sarmiento. In summer paddleboats are rented by the hour. The **Jardín Botánico,** located off Plaza Italia, is another paradise, with many South American plants specially labeled. It is famous for its population of abandoned cats, tended by little old ladies from the

Evita Perón: Woman, Wife, Icon

Maria Eva Duarte de Perón, known the world over as Evita, captured the imagination of millions of Argentines because of her social and economic programs for the working classes. An illegitimate child of a wealthy businessman, she was born in Los Toldos, deep in the province of Buenos Aires. At 15, she moved to the capital to pursue her dreams of becoming an actress. She achieved moderate success, but was known more for her striking beauty than for her talent. In 1944 she met Colonel Juan Perón, a rising figure in the Argentine government during a volatile period in the country's history. They married in 1945 and Evita became an important part of his presidential campaign.

Once Perón took office, she created the Eva Perón Foundation, which redirected funds traditionally controlled by Argentina's elite to programs benefiting hospitals, schools, elderly homes, and various charities. In addition, she raised wages for union workers, leading to the eventual growth of the Argentine middle class, and she succeeded in gaining women the right to vote in 1947. When Evita died of cancer on July 26, 1952, the working classes tried (unsuccessfully) to have her canonized. She is buried in the Recoleta Cemetery, in her father's family's tomb. She is one of the only non-aristocratic figures in this most elite of final resting places.

You will find that even today there is considerable disagreement among Argentines over Evita's legacy. Members of the middle and lower classes tend to see her as a national hero, while many of the country's upper classes believe she stole money from the wealthy and used it to embellish her own popularity. Since the 50th anniversary of her death, the establishment of the Museo Evita (p. 156), and the return of the Peronist party to power, her role in the country's history has been revisited far less emotionally.

neighborhood, another delight for kids to watch. Nearby, small streams and lakes meander through the **Japanese Gardens** ★★ (© **11/4804-4922;** daily 10am–6pm; admission $1; p. 165), where children can feed the fish (*alimento para peces* means "fish food") and watch the ducks. Small wood bridges connect classical Japanese gardens surrounding the artificial lake. A simple restaurant offers tea, pastries, sandwiches, and a few Japanese dishes such as sushi and teriyaki chicken. You'll also find notes posted here for various Asian events throughout the city.

Palermo Viejo, once a run-down neighborhood of warehouses, factories, and tiny decaying stucco homes few cared to live in as recently as 15 years ago, has been transformed into the city's chicest destination. Palermo Viejo is further divided into **Palermo Soho** to the south and **Palermo Hollywood** to the north, with railroad tracks and Avenida Juan B. Justo serving as the dividing line. The center of Palermo Hollywood is Plazaleto Jorge Cortazar, better known by its informal name, Plaza Serrano, a small oval park at the intersection of calles

Serrano and Honduras. Young people gather here late at night in impromptu singing and guitar sessions, sometimes fueled by drinks from the myriad of funky bars and restaurants that surround the plaza. On weekends there is a crafts festival, but you'll always find someone selling bohemian jewelry and leather goods no matter the day. The neighborhood gained its name because many Argentine film studios were initially attracted to its once cheap rents and easy parking. Palermo Soho is better known for boutiques owned by local designers, with some restaurants mixed in.

Las Cañitas was once the favored neighborhood of the military powers during the dictatorship period of 1976 to 1982, and the area remains the preeminently safe and secure neighborhood of all of the central Buenos Aires neighborhoods. A military training base, hospital, high school, and various family housing units still remain and encircle the neighborhood, creating an island-like sense of safety on the area's streets. Today, however, the area is far better known among the hip, trendy, and nouveau-riche as the place to dine out, have a drink, party, and be seen in the fashionable venues built into converted low-rise former houses on Calle Báez. The polo field where the International Championships take place is also in the neighborhood and is technically part of the military bases. The polo field's presence makes the neighborhood bars and restaurants great places for enthusiasts to catch polo stars in season dining out on the town, celebrating their victories.

RECOLETA

The city's most exclusive neighborhood, La Recoleta has a distinctly European feel, which locals say is a piece of Paris transplanted. Here, tree-lined avenues lead past fashionable restaurants, cafes, boutiques, and galleries. Much of the activity takes place along the pedestrian walkway Roberto M. Ortiz and in front of the Cultural Center and Recoleta Cemetery. This is a neighborhood of plazas and parks, a place where tourists and wealthy Argentines spend their leisure time outside. Weekends bring street performances, art exhibits, fairs, and sports.

The **Recoleta Cemetery** ✿✿✿ (p. 146), open daily from 8am to 6pm, pays tribute to some of Argentina's historical figures and is a place where the elite can show off its wealth. Weather permitting, free English guided tours take place every Tuesday and Thursday at 11am from the cemetery's Doric-columned entrance at Calle Junín 1790.

Adjacent to the cemetery, the **Centro Cultural Recoleta** ✿ (p. 174) holds art exhibits, theatrical and musical performances, and the **Museo Participativo de Ciencias** (p. 155). Next door, the **Buenos Aires Design Recoleta** (p. 201) features shops specializing in home decor. Among the best is **Tienda Puro Diseño Argentino** (p. 211), which features high-quality items designed and manufactured strictly in Argentina.

PLAZA DE MAYO

Juan de Garay founded the historic core of Buenos Aires, the **Plaza de Mayo** (p. 139), in 1580. The plaza is the political heart of the city, serving as a forum for protests.

The Argentine president goes to work at the **Casa Rosada** ✿✿✿ (p. 136). It was from a balcony of this mansion that Eva Perón addressed adoring crowds of Argentine workers. You can watch the changing of the guard in front of the palace every hour on the hour, and around back is the **Presidential Museum** (p. 136) with information on the history of the building and items owned by various presidents over the centuries.

The original structure of the **Metropolitan Cathedral** 🟊🟊 (p. 138) was built in 1745 and given a new facade and designated a cathedral in 1836. The **Cabildo** 🟊 (p. 133), the original seat of city government established by the Spaniards was completed in 1751 and restored in 1939. A striking neoclassical facade covers the **Legislatura de la Ciudad (City Legislature Building;** p. 137), which houses exhibitions in several of its halls; ask about tours. Farther down Calle Perú are the **Manzanas de las Luces (Blocks of Enlightenment)** 🟊🟊 (p. 137), which served as the intellectual center of the city in the 17th and 18th centuries. **San Ignacio**, the city's oldest church, still standing at the corner of calles Bolívar and Alsina, has a beautiful altar currently under renovation. Also located here is the **Colegio Nacional de Buenos Aires (National High School of Buenos Aires)**, where Argentina's best-known intellectuals have gathered and studied (p. 137). In addition to weekend tours, the Comisión Nacional de la Manzanas de las Luces (🕾 **11/4331-9534**) organizes a variety of cultural activities during the week.

PUERTO MADERO

Puerto Madero became Buenos Aires's second major gateway to trade with Europe when it was built in 1880, replacing in importance the port at La Boca. But by 1910 the city had already outgrown it. The Puerto Nuevo (New Port) was established to the north to accommodate growing commercial activity, and Madero was abandoned for almost a century. Urban renewal saved the original port in the 1990s with the construction of a riverfront promenade, apartments, and offices. Bustling and businesslike during the day, the area attracts a fashionable, wealthy crowd at night. It's lined with elegant restaurants serving Argentine steaks and fresh seafood specialties, and there is a popular cinema showing Argentine and Hollywood films, as well as several dance clubs such as **Opera Bay** and **Asia de Cuba.** The entire area is rapidly expanding, with high-rise luxury residences making this a newly fashionable, if somewhat isolated and artificial, neighborhood to live in. Of note is that all of the streets in Puerto Madero are named for important women in Argentine history. Look for the Buenos Aires City Tourism brochure *Women of Buenos Aires* to learn more about some of them. At sunset take a walk along the eastern, modern part of the renovated area, and watch the water shimmer in brilliant reds as the city forms a backdrop.

As you walk out from the port, you'll also come across the **Ecological Reserve** 🟊🟊 (p. 153). This area is an anomaly for a modern city, and exists as proof that nature can regenerate from an ecological disaster. In the 1960s and 1970s, demolished buildings and debris were dumped into the Río de la Plata after the construction of the *autopista* (highway system). Over time, sand and sediment began to build up, plants and grasses grew, and birds now use this space as a breeding ground. If you're interested, you can ask travel agents about bird-watching tours. In the summer adventurous Porteños use it as a beach, but the water is too polluted to swim in and you must be careful of jagged debris and the homeless who set up camp here. In spite of limited protection, Puerto Madero development is slowly creeping onto the preserve.

PLAZA SAN MARTIN & THE SURROUNDING MICROCENTRO AREA

Plaza San Martín 🟊🟊🟊, a beautiful park at the base of Calle Florida in the Retiro neighborhood, acts as the nucleus of what's considered the city's Microcentro. In summer months Argentine businesspeople flock to the park on their lunch hours, loosening their ties, taking off some layers, and sunning for a while amidst the plaza's flowering jacaranda trees. A monument to General José de San Martín towers over the scene. The park is busy at all hours, and even the playground will be teeming with kids and their parents out for a post-midnight stroll. Plaza San Martín was once the location of choice for the most elite Porteño families at the beginning of the 20th century. The San Martín Palace, now used by the Argentine Ministry of Foreign Affairs; the Círculo Militar, once the home of the Paz family who own the *La Prensa* newspaper; and the elegant Plaza Hotel testify to this former grandeur. The construction of the modern American Express building unfortunately destroyed this once completely classical area.

Plaza San Martín cascades gently down a hill, at the base of which sits the **Islas Malvinas–Falkland Islands War Memorial** (p. 149), a stark circular wall engraved with the names of the nearly 750 killed in the war and an eternal flame, overseen by guards from the various branches of the military. The memorial directly faces the Elizabethan-style **British Clock Tower,** recently renamed the **Torre Monumental** (p. 149), though most locals still use the old name. It was a gift from the British who built and ran the nearby Retiro train station complex. Oddly, it remained unscathed during the war but was attacked by a mob years later who also toppled an accompanying statue of George Canning, the British foreign secretary who recognized Argentina's independence from Spain. The tower is open to the public and provides a good view of the city and the river.

Calle Florida ★★★, the main pedestrian thoroughfare of Buenos Aires, is teeming with stores. The busiest section, extending south from Plaza San Martín to Avenida Corrientes, is lined with boutiques, restaurants, and record stores. It extends all the way through Avenida de Mayo to the south, turning into **Calle Perú,** where many international banks have retail branches. Day and night here, street performers walk on glass, tango, and offer comedy acts. You'll find the upscale **Galerías Pacífico** (p. 201) fashion center on Calle Florida, where it intersects Calle Viamonte. Most of the shopping on the street itself, however, is middle of the road. Leather stores abound, so compare prices and bargain by stopping into a few before finalizing your purchase. Calle Florida intersects with **Calle Lavalle,** a smaller version of itself, which has even more stores, most of lesser quality, and some inexpensive *parrillas* worth visiting. The street is also home to numerous video- and electronic-game arcades, so it's a good place for teenagers to hang out in while you shop around, though it might be easy for them to get into trouble as seedy characters do hang around this area.

Avenida Corrientes ★ is a living diary of Buenos Aires's cultural development. Until the 1930s, Avenida Corrientes was the favored hangout of tango legends. When the avenue was widened in the mid-1930s, it made its debut as the Argentine Broadway, and Evita's first apartment was here so she could more easily search for work after arriving in the city. Today Corrientes, lined with Art Deco cinemas and theaters, pulses with cultural and commercial activity day and night. It is also home to many bookstores, from the chains that sell bestsellers and offer English-language guidebooks, to independent bargain outlets and rare-book sellers. The **Obelisco,** Buenos Aires's defining monument (p. 150), marks the intersection of Corrientes with **Avenida 9 de Julio.** Whenever locals have something to celebrate, this is where they gather, and it's exciting to watch flag-carrying crowds shouting and cheering after Argentina wins an international event.

4 The Palermo Gardens Complex & Zoo

More than a neighborhood with a park in it, Palermo has the feel of a park where some people happen to live. This wide, miles-long expanse of green open space along the waterfront exists within the city because it was once an enormous estate until the middle of the 1800s. While you'd need a long time to really see the entire complex fully, I have listed some must-see highlights below.

The park contains the Rose Gardens, the Planetarium, the Patio, several museums, jogging trails, and far too many monuments to count. The area expands out beyond Jorge Newberry, the domestic airport, into the neighboring district of Belgrano. Easy to get lost in, you'll never need to worry, as cabs cruise the boulevards that cut through the park.

Botanical Gardens 🌟🌟 *(Kids)*   The Botanical Gardens are a true delight, with a few acres of open space and a myriad of tree-lined walkways. A central greenhouse is often the location of rotating art shows, with young artists standing and sweating next to their artwork. Plants from all over the world are here, including many from Argentina and other parts of South America. They're signed with their local and Latin names, making for a fun lesson for kids as you walk along. Not all the paths are well maintained, however, so watch your step. If you're here without the kids, the gardens are also a romantic spot. Bring a picnic basket and share some quality time, as you'll easily see many of the locals doing.

Like the Recoleta Cemetery, this is another cat lover's paradise, and you'll find plenty of women from the neighborhood coming to take care of these strays. The cats are also more playful and friendly here, and like to come up to visitors to be pet. Sit on a bench and you'll very likely find one cuddling up next to you.

Av. Las Heras, at Plaza Italia, across from the subway entrance. ℂ 11/4831-2951. Free admission. Daily 8am–6pm. Metro: Plaza Italia.

Zoological Gardens 🌟🌟🌟 *(Kids)*   The Buenos Aires city zoo features an impressive diversity of animals, including indigenous birds and monkeys, giant turtles, llamas, elephants, and a polar bear and brown bear habitat. The eclectic and kitschy architecture housing the animals, some designed as exotic temples, is as much of a delight as the inhabitants. A giant lake is close to the entrance of the zoo and is teeming with pink flamingos hanging out near mock Byzantine ruins in the center of the lake. Overlooking the water is a building, which looks like a Russian church, that contains monkey cages. Camels are surrounded by Moroccan-style architecture, and the kangaroo holding pens are painted with aboriginal designs. The lions, the kings of the jungle, are in a castle complex with its own moat. The most stunning building, however, is the Elephant House. Built to look like an Indian Temple, it is overgrown with vines to make you feel as if you are a jungle explorer and have come across an elephant sanctuary. They have three elephants, two of which are African, and one of which is Asian.

The Asian elephant, named Mara, was rescued by the zoo after years of abuse as a circus animal. Having been caged too tightly, she suffers from an emotional illness, standing in one place while she shakes her head back and forth. The other elephants, named Pupy and Kuki, seem to take care of her, and will try to prod her along at feeding time and massage their heads against her. It is sad and yet interesting to watch the social behavior of these magnificent and enormous creatures. I recommend making sure to save time to see them.

Make sure to also see the polar bears, whose habitat comes with an underwater viewing area. All the caretakers are great with kids throughout the zoo, but here they especially take their time to explain, at least in Spanish, the bears and also feed them so kids can watch them retrieve food from the water. In the back of the zoo is an enclosed jungle habitat full of various plant species that even has a waterfall and a rope bridge that a caretaker will lead you through. Giant bugs are also in display cases here. It's hot and steamy inside, just like the real jungle, and the interior is a labyrinth surrounded by plants, so keep an eye on kids because they can easily get lost.

Peacocks and some of the small animals are allowed to roam free, and feeding is allowed with special food for sale for $1 to $2 at kiosks. Animals on the loose will flock to your kids, and many of the cages have special feeding chutes where the animals will line up to greet them. Boats can also be rented on the lake in the front of the zoo, but as of the time of this writing, they were making repairs. The zoo is a must for anyone, but especially families with kids. I recommend at least half a day to explore here, and a full day if you have kids.

Av. Las Heras, at Plaza Italia across from the subway entrance. ℂ 11/4806-7412. Admission $2, additional charges for boats, jungle habitat, and other extras; multi-amenity and family passes also available for purchase. V. Hours change throughout the year, but are generally Tues–Sun 10am–6pm; closed Mon except Jan–Feb. Metro: Plaza Italia.

Japanese Gardens and Cultural Center ⟨⟩ (Finds (Kids   Tucked in the midst of

all the other Palermo gardens is this tiny gem opened in 1969 in honor of an official visit by one of the Japanese princes. Special landscaping, rock islands, and small red bowed bridges give the feeling of being in the Orient as soon as you step through the gates here. Carp swim in the large central lake, a delight for children as well as adults. Beyond the lake lies the Cultural Center, with a small museum and various art exhibitions. Kids can also learn origami folding and many other Asian crafts. There are numerous Asian fairs held throughout the year here within both the center and the park, so pick up one of their calendars while visiting or check out the website below for more details.

Av. Figueroa Alcorta, at Av. Casares. ℂ 11/4807-7843. www.jardinjapones.com. Admission $1.50 for gardens, $1 for Cultural Center. Daily 10am–6pm, though hours vary with exhibitions and fairs. Metro: Plaza Italia.

La Rural and Opera Pampa ⟨⟩   The grand Belle Époque stadium known as La

Rural was built at the turn-of-the-20th century overlooking Plaza Italia. It served as the parade grounds for the Sociedad Rural Argentina, an association of wealthy landowners from all over the country founded in 1866. During their annual meetings in Buenos Aires, they would parade their most prized animals, along with their gaucho workers, and compete for awards. By promoting Argentina's agricultural resources, it was through this association that Argentina was able to become an important world economic force by the end of the 1800s. Their headquarters remain in Buenos Aires on the 400 block of Calle Florida. A modern exhibition hall has been added and is often the site of international expos, conferences, and other exhibitions.

To get an idea of what the experience was like in the society's heyday, tourists should book a night with **Opera Pampa,** an event held in the old stadium. The show covers the at times very violent history of Argentina, beginning with the Spanish conquest of the Indians, the 1810 Independence, Roca's slaughter of thousands of Indians in the province of Buenos Aires through European immigration to Buenos Aires at the beginning of the 20th century. (Which is why Buenos Aires is largely a white society, differentiating it from other Latin American capitals.) The scenes related to Indian history are exceedingly violent and sad, and include the song "Fuera Fuera" ("Away, Away") as the Indians are forced to leave and one

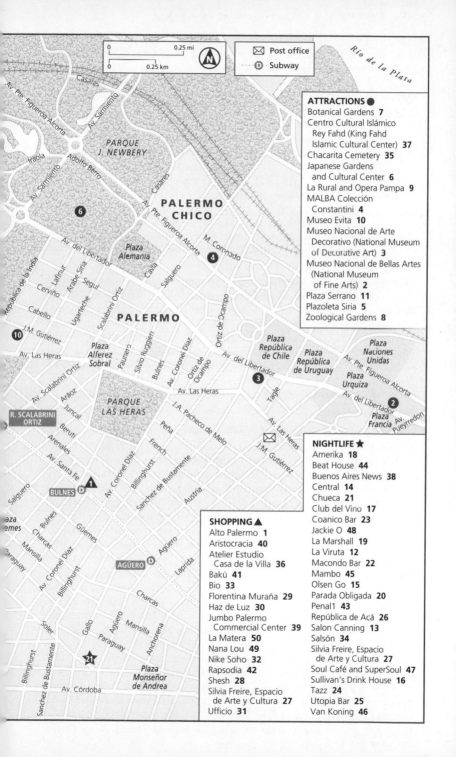

Post office ⊠
Subway ·· Ⓓ

Río de la Plata

ATTRACTIONS ●
Botanical Gardens **7**
Centro Cultural Islámico
  Rey Fahd (King Fahd
  Islamic Cultural Center) **37**
Chacarita Cemetery **35**
Japanese Gardens
  and Cultural Center **6**
La Rural and Opera Pampa **9**
MALBA Colección
  Constantini **4**
Museo Evita **10**
Museo Nacional de Arte
  Decorativo (National Museum
  of Decorative Art) **3**
Museo Nacional de Bellas Artes
  (National Museum
  of Fine Arts) **2**
Plaza Serrano **11**
Plazoleta Siria **5**
Zoological Gardens **8**

PARQUE
J. NEWBERY

PALERMO
CHICO

PALERMO

Plaza
Alemania

Plaza
Alferez
Sobral

PARQUE
LAS HERAS

Plaza
República
de Chile

Plaza
República
de Uruguay

Plaza
Naciones
Unidas

Plaza
Urquiza

Plaza
Francia

R. SCALABRINI
ORTIZ

BULNES Ⓓ

AGÜERO Ⓓ

Plaza
Monseñor
de Andrea

NIGHTLIFE ★
Amerika **18**
Beat House **44**
Buenos Aires News **38**
Central **14**
Chueca **21**
Club del Vino **17**
Coanico Bar **23**
Jackie O **48**
La Marshall **19**
La Viruta **12**
Macondo Bar **22**
Mambo **45**
Olsen Go **15**
Parada Obligada **20**
Penal1 **43**
República de Acá **26**
Salon Canning **13**
Salsón **34**
Silvia Freire, Espacio
  de Arte y Cultura **27**
Soul Café and SuperSoul **47**
Sullivan's Drink House **16**
Tazz **24**
Utopia Bar **25**
Van Koning **46**

SHOPPING ▲
Alto Palermo **1**
Aristocracia **40**
Atelier Estudio
  Casa de la Villa **36**
Bakú **41**
Bio **33**
Florentina Muraña **29**
Haz de Luz **30**
Jumbo Palermo
  Commercial Center **39**
La Matera **50**
Nana Lou **49**
Nike Soho **32**
Rapsodia **42**
Shesh **28**
Silvia Freire, Espacio
  de Arte y Cultura **27**
Ufficio **31**

Indian remains behind begging a soldier to let him stay on his land. The most dramatic scenes are those relating to San Martín and the revolution, full of charging horses and simulated cannon fights. More cheery portions include gaucho gatherings in *pulperías,* which were country bars where they would sing and dance after working on the *estancias* (farms). The national dance, the *Zamba,* which is performed with white handkerchiefs, is featured in these scenes. (The tango, in spite of its fame and association with Argentina, is not the national dance.) The show is excellently choreographed and exciting to watch. Afterward, patrons are treated to an enormous all-you-can-eat *asado* (Argentine barbecue), in the stadium's dining hall. An evening here will give you a far better understanding of Argentina's history. I would recommend it for children in that it is historically educational, but parents have to make a decision on balancing that with the violence.

La Rural Stadium and Exhibition Hall on Av. Las Heras, at the intersection of Av. Santa Fe overlooking Plaza Italia. Opera Pampa office and information is at Av. Sarmiento, at Calle Paso. (C) **11/4777-5557**. www.opera pampa.com.ar. Sociedad Rural Argentina www.sra.org.ar. Tickets are $40 show only, $60 show and dinner. Showtimes Fri–Sat 8pm, dinner following. Metro: Plaza Italia for La Rural Stadium, and Puerreydon for Opera Pampa office.

5 Religious Buildings Worth Checking Out

Iglesia San Nicolás de Bari ✶✶ *Kids*   This is an exceedingly beautiful and impressive church built for a local Italian Roman Catholic community. Its interior is reminiscent of a mini–Saint Peter's with its interior of Corinthian columns and white marble with colored accents. The block that surrounds it also has an array of exceptionally interesting buildings of various styles from the beginning of the 20th century, with a beauty not usually seen on most of Avenida Santa Fe. Take note of the Art Deco Casa de Teatro in particular.

Santa Fe 1364, at Uruguay. (C) **11/4813-3028**. Metro: Callao.

Centro Cultural Islámico Rey Fahd (King Fahd Islamic Cultural Center) ✶
With its broad expanses, well-tended lawn, minarets, and palm trees, the Centro Cultural Islámico brings a little bit of the Middle East to Buenos Aires. Overlooking the polo grounds, this enormous structure, with its severely modern architecture that becomes simply radiant in strong sunlight, is the largest Islamic center and mosque in all of Latin America. At night the two minarets are lit and cast a striking contrast with the surrounding apartment complexes behind it. The project began under the influence of President Ménem, who though Catholic at the time of his presidency, is of Syrian Muslim descent. Construction began in 1998, and it was opened in 2000. The center is open to the general public for free tours twice a week in Spanish and sometimes in English, Tuesday and Thursday at noon. Lasting 45 minutes, you will see the gardens, interior courtyard, library, and other spaces. Institutions can make special requests for tours at other times. The Centro offers classes of Koran and Arabic language and it has a library open to the public daily from 10am to 5pm. Though the Centro is closed to the public on Muslim holidays, Muslim visitors to Buenos Aires are welcome to visit for activities. Estimates of the Islamic and Arabic community in Argentina run at about 750,000. Many Argentines call anyone of Arabic or Muslim descent "Turcos," or Turks, regardless of their country of origin, based on the fact that the majority came here from places such as Syria, Armenia, and Lebanon, areas once controlled by the Ottoman Empire, the capital of which is now in modern-day Turkey.

Av. Bullrich 55, at Libertador. (C) **11/4899-0201**. www.ccislamicoreyfahd.org. Free tours Tues and Thurs at noon. Metro: Palermo.

Claustros del Pilar (Basílica Nuestra Señora del Pilar) ☞☞ This impos-ing white Spanish colonial church overlooks Recoleta Cemetery. While many visit inside to see the worshipping area, few take the time to discover the reli-gious art museum within the former convent area, full of gorgeous pieces from Buenos Aires's early years. A step back in time, the convent retains the original flooring, stairs, walls, and other components from its 1732 construction. Most interesting are the windows with panes made from agate so that light could come into the structure but no one would be able to see the nuns. Other high-lights include the ornate ecclesiastical wardrobes on display.

Junín 1904, next to Recoleta Cemetery. ✆ 11/4803-6793. Admission $1. Tues–Sat 10:30am–6:15pm; Sun 2:30–6:15pm. No metro access.

Basílica y Convento de San Francisco (San Francis's Church and Convent) ☞ The San Roque parish of which this church belongs is one of the oldest in the city. A Jesuit architect designed the building in 1730, but a final reconstruction in the early 20th century added a German baroque facade, along with statues of Saint Francis of Assisi, Dante, and Christopher Columbus. Inside, you'll find a tapestry by Argentine artist Horacio Butler along with an extensive library.

Calle Defensa and Alsina. ✆ 11/4331-0625. Free admission. Hours vary. Metro: Plaza de Mayo.

6 Architectural Highlights

MUST-SEES FOR ARCHITECTURE BUFFS

Buenos Aires is full of architectural highlights, since it purposely put on an architectural show at the turn of the 20th century, part of its desire to present itself as a sophisticated city with which to be reckoned. I have discussed many of the most important buildings throughout this chapter and in the walking tours listed in chapter 7. Here, however, are some particularly impressive stand-outs, not all of which are open to the public.

Centro Naval ☞☞ Inaugurated in 1914 and designed by the Swiss architect Jacques Dunant, this building is an incredible combination of Italian rococo ele-ments and rustication all executed in a high Beaux Arts style. The building is made of cast stone and is extremely well maintained. The ornate bronze doors feature shields, arrows, and other symbols of war, overseen by a nude bronze sea god in a Spanish galleon announcing triumph through a conch shell. Other bronze boats line the balustrades on the upper floors. The building is not open to the public, but at times they will allow people in the small lobby. There are also various events and functions held here, including weddings, so if you hear of any, find a way to get yourself invited.

Calle Florida 801, at Córdoba, across from the Galerías Pacífico. Not usually open to the public. Metro: San Martín.

Confitería del Molino ☞☞ Unfortunately, not only will you not be able to enter this incredible masterpiece, it is also rapidly crumbling away. Across the street from Congreso, this was once among the city's most important cafes, where politicians would mingle with well-to-do citizens and dignitaries from around the world. The cafe closed in 1997, and the building is now only rarely open to the public for events designed to raise consciousness of the need to restore the build-ing before it disappears forever. (So bad is its condition, plants and moss are grow-ing on the facade.) Primarily Art Nouveau, stained glass and ornate tile work were

Kids   **Especially for Kids**

The following Buenos Aires attractions have major appeal to kids of all ages:

- Museo de Los Niños (p. 154)
- Museo Participativo de Ciencias (p. 155)
- Zoological Gardens (p. 164)
- The Water Palace and the Museo del Patrimonio (p. 157)
- Museo de las Armas de la Nación (p. 153)

In addition to the sights listed above, a number of playgrounds are of particular interest to kids. One of them, where you'll often see parents and their kids even after midnight, is in **Plaza San Martín.** A merry-go-round and swing sets are in **Plaza Congreso,** across from the headquarters of the Madres de Plaza de Mayo. You'll also find playgrounds in the **Botanical Gardens** (p. 164). Take note that the Middle Eastern restaurant **Garbis** (p. 122) also has an indoor playground.

once part of the ornamentation here, and its main feature is its tower imitating a windmill. The architect was Francesco Gianotti, an Italian who also designed Galería Guemes and its theater housing the Piazzolla tango show. These are open to the public if you want to get an idea of Molino's fabulous interior (p. 151).

Callao 10, at Rivadavia, next to Congreso. Not open to the public. Metro: Congreso.

Teatro Nacional Cervantes 🎭🎭   One of the country's most important theaters, the architecture here puts on a show all its own. Built in Spanish Habsburg Imperial style, it overlooks Plaza Lavalle only 2 blocks from the more famous Teatro Colón. The building was a gift from two Spanish actors who opened the theater in 1921. However, within a few years, it went bankrupt and was taken over by the Argentine government. The ornate interior is decorated with materials from Spain including tapestries from Madrid and tiles from Valencia and Tarragona. The theater is open to the public for tours and has productions throughout the year, so ask when visiting about upcoming shows.

Libertad 815, at Córdoba, overlooking Plaza Lavalle. ☎ 11/4816-7212. Guided tours Tues 2pm. Metro: Tribunales.

7 Self-Guided & Organized Tours

FREE BUENOS AIRES CITY TOURISM OFFICE TOURS

The Buenos Aires City Tourism Office offers an excellent array of free city tours. Participants are taken through various zones of the city on buses or meet at a designated point and walk through a neighborhood as a guide explains the highlights. Most of the tours are conducted in Spanish; however, a few are in Spanish and English. Sometimes whether an English-speaking guide will be on hand can change at the last minute, based on the schedules of the available guides, so it makes sense to sign up for a tour anyway and see what happens. You can always leave if you do not understand, or someone will more than likely be able to translate.

Ask for information about the tours at the many Buenos Aires **Visitor Information Kiosks** (listed on p. 44). You can also call the hot line for information

(© **11/4313-0187**). It's staffed from 7:30am to 6pm Monday to Saturday, and Sunday from 11am to 6pm. Or call the organization directly about the free tours (© **11/4114-5791;** Mon–Fri 10am–4pm; ask to speak with Rubén Forace, who is in charge of them). The tours are on a space-available basis, so you'll have to register for them.

The tours cover the most important neighborhoods: Palermo, San Telmo, La Boca, Recoleta, the Plaza de Mayo, Belgrano, and many others but are not offered every day. Ask for the brochure *Free Guided Tours,* which tells you when they are scheduled while you are in town, at the **Visitor Information Kiosks.**

They also offer four specialized free tours that relate to historic Buenos Aires figures. Called *Itinerarios Evocativos,* these include Eva Perón, Carlos Gardel, Jorge Luis Borges, and Federico García Lorca. These will also be listed in the *Free Guided Tours* brochure, but each tour is not held every month. However, each of the Itinerarios Evocativos does have its own pamphlet that lists the places, addresses, and a description of each of the sites that would be visited on the tour. You can therefore do these tours on your own on a self-guided basis if they are not offered while you are in town.

Another interesting free self-guided city tour service offered by the Buenos Aires City Tourism Office is the Cellular Telephone Tours. Ask for the brochure, currently only in Spanish, called *Conocé la historia de Buenos Aires desde tu celular.* The brochure has instructions for each itinerary, where you call a number and punch codes to hear speeches and other information (in either English or Spanish) when near historical sites. When I tried this system, I didn't think it worked very well. However, it was very new at the time of this writing, so the problems might have been worked out by the time you arrive in Buenos Aires. While, in theory, this information service is free, don't forget that you will be charged for the airtime itself, making the cost of using this service possibly significant. Still, the system's complete flexibility and ability to allow you to hear recordings from the past certainly makes this different from any other tour option out there.

BOAT TOURS

Buenos Aires seems to ignore its riverfront location in many ways, and it seems to have no real connection to the water other than a view from its tall buildings. The two tours listed below, however, allow you to see the city from the water.

Navegando Buenos Aires, Puerto Madero at Alicia Moreau de Justo 872, next to the Frigate Sarmiento dock (© **11/4342-4849;** www.navegandobuenos aires.com), are low-rising boats that look like greenhouses skimming the Puerto Madero waterfront. They pass under the numerous low bridges in the Puerto Madero area and then head to La Boca. They operate twice a day Monday through Friday, and the trips last about an hour and a half. Adults ride for about $5 and children are about $3. Only cash is accepted.

Buenos Aires Boats, La Boca Docks, at base of Caminito (© **11/4303-1616;** www.bueboats.com), leave four times a day daily from the port in La Boca near where Caminito hits the waterfront. Trips last about an hour and a half and go from La Boca to the Río de la Plata. Tours cost about $5 for adults, $3.50 for seniors and children, and are free for those under 3. Group discounts are available. Only cash is accepted.

In addition, La Boca also has small **ferry boats** at the base of the no-longer-functioning Puente N. Avellaneda (that big metal rusty thing overlooking La Boca that has actually been declared a UNESCO heritage site). These are the boats locals use to cross the river to come back and forth to Buenos Aires from the very poor suburbs in Avellaneda. Costing only 50 centavos, they are fun to ride, but I suggest crossing and coming directly back instead of exploring the other side of the river, because Avellaneda is considered dangerous if you do not know where you are going. Few tourists take these boats, so you will be especially welcomed onboard by locals who rarely meet foreigners. Though it seems so far-fetched considering the setting, some locals half-jokingly call these boats the La Boca Gondolas, considering the Italian heritage of the area. Whatever you do, do not touch the heavily polluted water full of industrial waste and sewage. Only cash is accepted.

BIKE TOURS

Buenos Aires Urban Biking (© 11/4855-5103 or 11/15-5175-6388 [cell]; www.urbanbiking.com) offers four different themes for biking throughout Buenos Aires: northern areas of the city, southern areas including the Ecological Reserve, Buenos Aires at Night, and the Tigre Delta outside of the city. Equipment is provided by the company and prices and trip lengths vary by itinerary, from a half day to a full 8-hour day. They also operate in La Plata, the capital of the province of Buenos Aires. Guides speak English, Spanish, French, and Portuguese.

Lan and Kramer Bike Tours (© 11/4311-5199) leads groups, which generally meet and start their trips in Plaza San Martín. There are several tour routes, some of which pass through the Ecological Reserve along the Puerto Madero waterfront. Rates begin at about $25 per person and tours last from 3 to 6 hours, depending on the itinerary.

BUS TOURS

Travel Line (© 11/5555-5373; www.travelline.com.ar) offers more than 20 tours with various themes within Buenos Aires and into the surrounding suburbs. Participants are picked up at their hotel and tours can last anywhere from 4 hours up to a full day; some include meals. Themes include Eva Perón, tango tours, Fiesta Gaucho (which visits an *estancia,* or farm), City by Night, and the Tigre Delta among many others. Prices vary but range from $10 to $90. American Express, Discover, MasterCard, and Visa are accepted.

JEWISH-THEMED TOURS

Travel Jewish (© 949/307-9231 in the U.S. or 11/4106-0541 in Buenos Aires; www.traveljewish.com), is owned by Deborah Miller, an American who has lived in Buenos Aires, and offers Jewish tours of Buenos Aires. It can plan your trip from beginning to end, including flights and hotels, or simply conduct Jewish-themed day tours for you to enjoy once you are in Buenos Aires. Prices depend on the season; a 10-day tour of Buenos Aires, Patagonia, and Iguazu Falls costs around $2,240 per person (based on double occupancy). Half-day Jewish Buenos Aires tours begin at $80 per person. MasterCard and Visa are accepted.

TANGO TOURS

There are literally hundreds of tours for people interested in tango here in Buenos Aires, the city where it all began. Below, I've listed just a sample. For more information, you should also see *"Milongas* (Tango Salons & Dance Halls)" in chapter 9.

- **ABC Tango Tours**   Gabriel Aspe, who is one of the co-owners of this company, also manages one of the tango shows at the Café Tortoni and is a native of Argentina. The company offers several tango-show-palace event tours as well as tours to traditional tango houses. Call © 11/15-5697-2551 (cell) or go to www.abctango.com.

- **Amantes del Tango** Eduardo and Nora run this association and offer individual tours and private lessons. Both are well-established tango performers and Nora's work has been featured in *National Geographic* magazine. Call ✆ **11/4703-4104** or 11/15-5753-9131 (cell) or go to www.amantesdel tango.com.
- **Buenos Aires Tango Off** This company offers several tango-themed tours, including its unusual "Dos Pasiones Argentinas," which takes the "Land of Evita and Tango" phrase to heart by combining tango lessons with a visit to the Museo Evita (though she was known to hate the dance, ironically). Call ✆ **11/4829-1416** or 11/4829-1417.
- **Tango with Judy** Judy, an American tango dancer who moved to Buenos Aires with her husband and knows the scene well, offers highly specialized and individual tango tours, some of which can be combined with lessons. Call ✆ **11/4863-5889** or go to www.tangowithjudy.com.
- **Tanguera Tours** Single women who want to take advantage of the tango scene or women whose partners refuse to dance can contact Tanguera Tours, which offers specialized tango tours for groups of women. The company owner, Laura Chummers, is a perky American who really knows the scene and makes it accessible for women of any skill level, but she won't let you be a wall-flower at any of the places she takes you. Call ✆ **11/4953-2775** or go to www.tangueratours.com.

SPORTS TOURS

Go Football Tours (✆ **11/4816-2681** or 15/4405-9526 [cell]; www.gofoot ball.com.ar) brings you to the game. Sports lovers will enjoy having all the thinking done for them, from knowing which team is playing when to getting tickets and getting to the game itself. The company picks you up at the door of your hotel and takes you to the stadium and then back to the hotel again. Visit their website to plan what games fit into your travel schedule. They also have tours to tennis, polo, and many other sports events. Visa and cash are accepted. Most events run about $40, including tickets and transportation.

Golf Day (✆ **11/4824-8531** and 11/4826-8531) is perfect for busy executives who don't have the time to plan a day of golf but want to try to squeeze a few holes in before leaving Buenos Aires. This company will pick you up, take you to a local golf course, provide lunch, and then bring you back to your hotel. They prefer more than a day's notice, if possible, when making a reservation. Prices range from about $60 and up.

WALKING TOURS

See chapter 7 for five walking tours I've created. See "Free Buenos Aires City Tourism Office Tours," above, for a description of available free Buenos Aires walking tours provided by the Buenos Aires Tourist Office.

In addition to the above, **Los Santos Tours** (✆ **11/4325-8100;** turismo xbuenosaires@netafull.com.ar) has several themed walking itineraries through different Buenos Aires neighborhoods. Price and duration will vary by itinerary, but the full-city tour can last up to 7 hours. Prices range from $16 to $24, and some itineraries include a snack or lunch.

IN VIP Visit BA (✆ **15/5063-6602;** www.invisitba.4t.com) offers highly customized tours, some of which are strictly walking while others are bus and walking combinations. Prices vary by itinerary but can range from $15 to $25 per person and up depending on the group size and itinerary complexity.

8 Cultural Centers & Language Courses

There's no shortage of culture in Buenos Aires, and the centers I've listed below offer cultural events during the day and in the evenings. You should also be sure to look in the various headings within this chapter, since various museums and religious centers also have their own cultural centers.

Asociación Argentina de Cultura Inglesa ✯ This multifunctional facility was established over 77 years ago by a British ambassador who wanted to do more to promote British culture within Argentina. He was highly successful in his efforts, and today the AACI teaches English to over 25,000 students a year, has several film, theater, culture, and art programs, and generally provides a very welcoming environment for any English speaker who is homesick. Events can range from being completely upper-crust (celebrating Shakespeare) to raunchy (*Absolutely Fabulous* TV program showings). Pick up their various brochures and event listings at the center itself, or look up listings in the English-language *Buenos Aires Herald.*

Suipacha 1333, at Arroyo. ✆ 11/4393-2004. www.aaci.org.ar. Various hours, generally Mon–Fri 9am–9pm. Metro: San Martín.

Buenos Aires Escuela de Español This school offers immersion programs, classes for tango fanatics, Spanish for children, as well as other Spanish-language programs.

Av. Rivadavia 1559, 2C, at Montevideo, near Plaza Congreso. ✆ 11/4381-2076. www.baesp.com. Metro: Congreso.

Centro Cultural Recoleta ✯✯✯ *Kids* Adjacent to the cemetery, this arts center holds permanent and touring art exhibits along with theatrical and musical performances. Designed in the mid–18th century as a Franciscan convent, it was reincarnated as a poorhouse in 1858, serving that function until it became a cultural center in 1979. The first floor houses the interactive and very kid-friendly children's science museum, the **Museo Participativo de Ciencias,** where it is "forbidden not to touch" (p. 155). One of the city's best art and culture bookstores, Asunto Impresa: Libreria de la Imagen, is also located in the lobby of the center and should definitely be looked at while you're here. The Centro Cultural has so many things going on, you should pick up copies of their calendar listing everything so you don't miss a thing while you're in town.

Junín 1930, next to Recoleta Cemetery. ✆ 11/4807-6340. www.centroculturalrecoleta.org. Tues–Fri 2–9pm; Sat–Sun and holidays 10am–9pm. Various hours for theater productions and special events. No metro access.

IBL Spanish School If you want to learn Spanish while you're traveling, try a class at this school, which offers group classes in addition to one-on-one lessons.

Calle Florida 165, 8th floor, at Bartolomé Mitre. ✆ 11/4331-4250. www.ibl.com.ar. Metro: Catedral.

9 Sports

There's no shortage of sporting events in Buenos Aires, from the highbrow International Polo championships where locals hobnob with European royalty, to soccer events where the crowds are as rowdy as the players. Check the papers for events and times when in town, especially the English-language *Buenos Aires Herald.* If you want to have your experience planned for you (ticket choice, ticket purchase, and being escorted to and from the game), check out the two companies I mention in "Sports Tours" in "Self-Guided & Organized Tours," above.

SPECTATOR SPORTS

HORSE RACING   Over much of the 20th century, Argentina was famous for its thoroughbreds. It continues to send prize horses to competitions around the world, although you can watch some of the best right here in Buenos Aires. In the center of the city, you can see races at **Hipódromo Argentino de Palermo,** Av. del Libertador 4205, at Dorrego (℗ **11/4778-2839**), in Palermo, a track made in a classical design with several modern additions. The Hipódromo is open all year. Entry is free and race times run from late afternoon until past midnight. In the suburbs, a few miles from Buenos Aires, is also the **Hipódromo de San Isidro,** Av. Márquez 504, at Fleming in San Isidro (℗ **11/4743-4010**). This modern location is open year-round. Most races begin in the early afternoon through the early evening, and entry prices range from 35¢ to $2, depending on your seating area. Check the *Buenos Aires Herald* for more exact race schedule information for both arenas.

POLO   Argentina has won more international polo tournaments than any other country, and the **Argentine Open Championship,** held late November through early December, is the world's most important polo event. There are two seasons for polo: March through May and September through December, held at the **Campo Argentino de Polo,** Avenida del Libertador and Avenida Dorrego (℗ **11/4576-5600**). Tickets can be purchased at the gate for about $25 per person. This is one of the most important polo stadiums in the world, and visits by European royalty are not uncommon in season. Contact the **Asociación Argentina de Polo,** Hipólito Yrigoyen 636 (℗ **11/4331-4646** or 11/4342-8321), for information on polo schools and events. **La Martina Polo Ranch** (℗ **11/4576-7997**), located 60km (37 miles) from Buenos Aires near the town of Vicente Casares, houses more than 80 polo horses, as well as a guesthouse with a swimming pool and tennis courts.

SOCCER   One cannot discuss soccer (called *fútbol* here) in Argentina without paying homage to Diego Armando Maradona, Argentina's most revered player and one of the sport's great (if fallen) players. Any sense of national unity dissolves when Argentines watch their favorite clubs—River Plate, Boca Juniors, Racing Club, Independiente, and San Lorenzo—battle on Sunday in season, which runs from February until November. There is also a summer season when teams travel, so essentially soccer never really stops here in Buenos Aires. Passion for soccer here could not run hotter. Try to catch a game at the **Estadio Boca Juniors,** Brandsen 805 (℗ **11/4309-4700**), in San Telmo, followed by raucous street parties. Ticket prices start at $3 and can be purchased in advance or at the gate.

OUTDOOR ACTIVITIES

GOLF   Argentina has more than 200 golf courses. Closest to downtown Buenos Aires is **Cancha de Golf de la Ciudad de Buenos Aires,** Av. Torquist 1426, at Olleros (℗ **11/4772-7261**), which is 10 minutes from downtown and boasts great scenery and a 71-par course. Prices here range from $7 to play during the week to $10 on weekends, with additional fees for caddies and other services. **Jockey Club Argentino,** Av. Márquez 1700 (℗ **11/4743-1001**), is in San Isidro about 30 minutes from downtown. It offers two courses (71- and 72-par) designed by Allister McKenzie. Prices here begin at about $40 to $60 to enter the course, but additional fees must be paid to caddies and for other services.

7

City Strolls

Buenos Aires is a great walking city. No matter where you start out, the beautiful architecture and tree-lined streets are likely to pull you along as you explore various areas. If you get lost, friendly Porteños will help you out along the way, as well as offer advice on their favorite things to check out. Here, I've figured out a few itineraries for you, but I'm sure you'll find plenty of your own along the way.

WALKING TOUR 1	HISTORICAL CALLE FLORIDA: NOT JUST A SHOPPING DESTINATION
Start:	Corner of calles Córdoba and Florida.
Public Transportation:	Metro: San Martín.
Finish:	Calle Florida at Diagonal Norte.
Time:	2 hours, not including eating or shopping stops.
Best Times:	Daylight hours in the midafternoon, when you can see the buildings most clearly and mostly all are open.
Worst Times:	Can be done anytime, but after 8pm a few interiors might not be visible.
Walking Level:	Easy and also wheelchair accessible in most cases.

Pedestrianized Calle Florida mostly has a reputation as a shop-till-you-drop destination. However, there is superb architecture and history here as well. I highlight the most beautiful features of the street below, but I also recommend that you try as hard as possible to keep your head up as you walk along. While at

---

Finds **More Do-It-Yourself Excursions**

The Buenos Aires City Government Kiosks scattered throughout the city have maps that can be used for self-guided tours, and *The Golden Map* (p. 47) available at almost all hotels also has some self-guided walks for various neighborhoods in the city. One pamphlet that the city provides contains information about a special cellphone tour, where participants punch in codes at various destinations and hear explanations in English, Spanish, and other languages, including recordings of historical events at the various locations. Ask for this specific brochure, but know that the phone system does not always work well. Other themed tours include Women of Buenos Aires or focus on important historical figures like Evita, Lorca, Borges, Gardel, and others with addresses and descriptions of the places you will see, though some of these cover large distances not suitable for being covered solely by walking.

Walking Tour 1: Historical Calle Florida

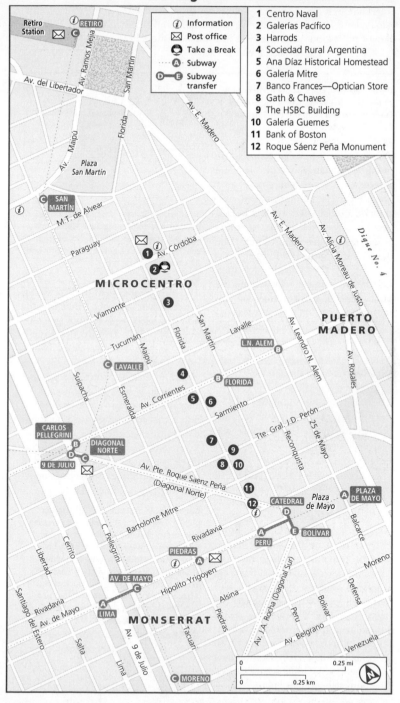

Legend:
- (i) Information
- ✉ Post office
- 😊 Take a Break
- ···Ⓐ··· Subway
- Ⓓ—Ⓔ Subway transfer

1 Centro Naval
2 Galerías Pacífico
3 Harrods
4 Sociedad Rural Argentina
5 Ana Díaz Historical Homestead
6 Galería Mitre
7 Banco Frances—Optician Store
8 Gath & Chaves
9 The HSBC Building
10 Galería Guemes
11 Bank of Boston
12 Roque Sáenz Peña Monument

storefront level many of the buildings on this street have been modernized, the remainder of the facades often remain exquisite. The last portion of this trip along Calle Florida also takes you into Buenos Aires's bank district nicknamed "La City" after London's financial district.

To start the tour, begin at the northeastern corner of Calle Florida, where it hits Calle Córdoba. You will be in front of Córdoba 810, which is the:

❶ Centro Naval

This is one of the city's most exquisite buildings, a masterpiece of cast stone architecture. A nude sea god in a Spanish galleon, announcing triumph through a conch shell, oversees its corner doorway. Naval themes continue along the upper balustrades. The building was opened in 1914 and was designed by Swiss architect Jacques Dunant. It's not generally open to the public, but sometimes they let you into the circular lobby. If you ever get invited to an event here, make sure to go.

Cross Calle Córdoba heading south and stop just after crossing the street, at the:

❷ Galerías Pacífico

The most famous shopping mall in Buenos Aires, Galerías Pacífico was opened in 1891. The building was designed to recall the Galleria Vittorio Emanuele II in Milan, with its long halls, glass cupola, and several tiers of shops. An economic crisis shortly after its opening, however, meant that it was converted into office space for the Pacífico Railroad Company. Enter into the building and see the central staircase, where all the halls meet. In 1945, while still an office building, paintings about the history of mankind were installed under the main dome, and the shopping center has daily information sessions explaining the history of the paintings. In 1992 everything old became new again, and the building was converted back into a shopping center.

TAKE A BREAK If you're hungry, make a pit stop in the **food court** at the Galerías Pacífico. Try a fast-food *asado* (Argentine grill), and finish your meal with a Patagonian chocolate treat—you won't be sorry!

When you're finished shopping here, head back out the door facing Calle Florida and turn left, staying on Calle Florida and proceeding to the block between Viamonte and Tucumán to:

❸ Harrods

The British once had such a strong presence here that they brought not only railroads and technology with them but their favorite department stores as well. Harrods closed in the early 1990s, was revived, and then closed for a second time. For now, all you can do is stare inside through the enormous plate glass windows. You will notice that for a long-closed building, the interior is rather well maintained. Every so often, there are art exhibitions inside, so if you hear of one, come to see it and the inside of this once-important shopping landmark.

Continue walking south on Calle Florida until you get to Lavalle, another pedestrianized street. No need to look out for cars here, as there are only people at this busy intersection, which is sometimes full of street performers. (Take a break here and watch them if they catch your attention.) After crossing Lavalle, stop midblock and face the building at Calle Florida 460 on your right, or west, side. It's the:

❹ Sociedad Rural Argentina

Surrounded by modern shop fronts, this small, ornate French rococo building seems out of place among its ordinary neighbors. The people working inside almost undoubtedly feel the same way, for this is the headquarters of the Sociedad Rural Argentina, an organization created in the mid-1800s by the country's wealthiest oligarchs. This society was integral to the creation of Argentina's great agricultural wealth. The door to this important institution is almost always closed, but if you find it open, take a chance and wander in to see the Belle Epoque interior. There are, however, no official visits to the building.

Continue walking south on Calle Florida until you get to Avenida Corrientes. Cross the street and stop in front of Burger King, which was once the site of the:

❺ Ana Díaz Historical Homestead

Women's-history buffs take note: While men usually get all the credit for founding cities, Spanish explorer Juan de Garay's 1580 expedition, which permanently founded Buenos Aires, was not without a lady's touch. Ana Díaz, whose house was located on the property where Burger King now sits, came along with him. The first time that the Spanish tried to settle the city of Buenos Aires in 1536, it was an all-male group of explorers and the settlement failed. Who knows how many times it might have taken to settle Buenos Aires if a woman hadn't been around to take care of things the second time around. Ana Díaz's original home is long gone, but was located on this corner. A stunning turn-of-the-20th-century home was later built here and was intact until Burger King got its hands on it. Still, enter the hamburger joint and take a walk up the staircase to your left. Try not to gasp in awe as you head upstairs to the colonnaded rotunda, stained-glass ceilings, and various rooms with their ornamental plaster ceilings. Imagine what the ground floor looked like before ground meat took over. This is one of the most stunning hidden gems of Calle Florida. On the Corrientes side of the building, you can read plaques that explain more about Ana Díaz and her unfortunately

often-overlooked importance to the founding of Buenos Aires.

Upon leaving Burger King, turn to the right and continue up Calle Florida. Don't stop until midblock between Corrientes and Sarmiento. Then face the east side of the street to see the:

❻ Galería Mitre

This is one of the most visually impressive and unusual buildings on Calle Florida. It was designed in a robust Spanish colonial style, imitating the Argentine missions along the Paraguayan border. The most unique feature is the ornamentation around the doorway and the frieze above it, with men in 16th-century Spanish clothing, executed in a rustic manner. This crude but ornate ornamentation mimics art created by Indian slaves for their Spanish masters in that region of Argentina during the early colonial period in the late 1500s and early 1600s. The building had been closed for a few years but is now undergoing a renovation for use as office space.

Continue in the same direction on Calle Florida, crossing Sarmiento. Stop midblock before Perón, this time facing the west side of the street, so that you're looking at the:

❼ Banco Francés—Optician Store

At street level you'll wonder why you've stopped here (no, I don't want you to use the ATM). But look up and you'll see a beautiful 1920s-era building that was once an optician's headquarters. Notice the bronze eyeglasses ornamenting the windows and the beautiful maidens surrounding them.

Continue up Florida in the same direction, stopping just as you hit Calle Perón, and look to the corner opposite, on the west side, to see:

❽ Gath & Chaves

You'll notice the BANCO MERIDIEN sign under a glass-and-wrought-iron doorway simulating old Parisian subway entrances. Look above and you will still see the old name of this one-time British department store on the corner tower—Gath & Chaves. Like Harrods, it shows the former importance of British culture on Argentina. Inside, only hints of the former beauty remain in the bank lobby.

Continue up Florida to Perón, but do not cross it yet. Instead, face your left, or east, side for a glimpse of the:

❾ HSBC Building

This ornate Spanish Gothic building, one of my favorites, is faced with travertine marble and the corner entrance is covered with heavy bronze doors.

Cross Perón and walk half a block on Florida, stopping on the east side in front of Florida 165, the:

❿ Galería Guemes

The Calle Florida entrance of this turn-of-the-20th-century shopping gallery is nothing special, and the most interesting thing is the sign for Piazzolla Tango, held in the basement theater. However, step through the threshold and you'll find one of the city's most exquisite buildings. It was designed by Francesco Gianotti, an Italian architect who also designed the now-closed Confitería del Molino. At night the gallery is not open to the public except for those seeing the tango show. However, you can still wander in, as the entranceway is not locked. No matter what time you go, don't miss the ornamental elevator bays with their bronze details while inside.

Continue south on Florida and cross Calle Bartolomé Mitre. Stop immediately, facing the wedge-shaped building on your left, or east, side at Calle Florida 99. This is the:

⓫ Bank of Boston

This is another ornate Spanish colonial building, even more exquisite than the HSBC bank, full of exquisite details on its facade and within the interior. Much of the limestone and

structural steel necessary to make this building came from the United States. The 4-ton bronze doors were made in England. Since the peso crisis, the building has often been a flashpoint for anti-American sentiments and is at times covered with YANKEE GO HOME graffiti. If the building is open, enter its spacious lobby, with its slender columns supporting an ornate gilded and coffered ceiling. The building is topped by an enormous and ornate cupola, part of the row of them on Diagonal Norte, marking each intersection with the connecting streets. (This pattern begins at Plaza de Mayo and continues up Diagonal Norte, where it intersects with Av. 9 de Julio, forming the vista point for the Obelisco.)

When leaving the building, face the plaza and look at the:

⓬ Roque Sáenz Peña Monument

Inaugurated in 1936, this Art Deco monument is to Roque Sáenz Peña, president of Argentina in the early 1910s, who died while in office. It overlooks Diagonal Norte, which is also sometimes known as Avenida Roque Sáenz Peña. The construction of Diagonal Norte was part of a plan to rebuild Buenos Aires with vista points along the lines of Haussmann's redesign of Paris. Diagonal Norte was completed in the mid-1930s.

This statue marks the end of this walking tour. During the daytime you can head across the street to the Buenos Aires City Tourism Kiosk, the modern metal structure with a winged cover, if you need any kind of information or help. Behind it, if you need travel assistance, you'll find the main customer service center for Aerolíneas Argentinas. If you just want to head home after the tour, the D line Catedral subway station is here, or walk a little toward Plaza de Mayo for more subway line access (lines A and E).

Walking Tour 2: Plaza San Martín & Retiro

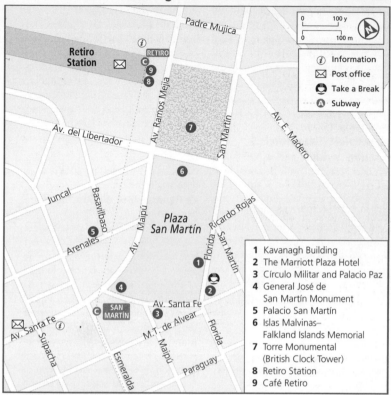

1 Kavanagh Building
2 The Marriott Plaza Hotel
3 Círculo Militar and Palacio Paz
4 General José de San Martín Monument
5 Palacio San Martín
6 Islas Malvinas–Falkland Islands Memorial
7 Torre Monumental (British Clock Tower)
8 Retiro Station
9 Café Retiro

WALKING TOUR 2	GETTING TO KNOW PLAZA SAN MARTIN & RETIRO
Start:	The east side of Plaza San Martín, facing the Kavanagh Building.
Public Transportation:	Metro: San Martin.
Finish:	Retiro Station.
Time:	1½ hours if you're just walking; 3 to 4 hours if you go inside all buildings mentioned.
Best Times:	Monday through Saturday between 11am and 4pm.
Worst Times:	At night when things are closed.
Walking Level:	Moderate, but steps and hill overlooking San Martín as well as an expanse of Retiro can be a slight challenge.

At the turn of the 20th century, some of Buenos Aires's most fabulous mansions were built overlooking Plaza San Martín, and quite a few remain. The enormous plaza, with its overgrown trees and lazy atmosphere, will call to mind the squares of Savannah, Georgia. The Retiro area spreads down a gentle hill from the plaza and encompasses the train station complex built by the British, once the main entrance to this grand city.

Start in the plaza itself, looking toward the east at the:

❶ Kavanagh Building

At the time of its construction in 1936, this was the tallest building in South

America, standing at about 120m (400 ft.) with over 30 stories. Designed as a residential structure, it took more than 16 years to sell the apartments in this Art Deco building. Now it is only the third-tallest building in the city.

Turn to your right and walk a few meters up the park (you'll be making a circle around the plaza) until you see the:

❷ Marriott Plaza Hotel

The grande dame of Buenos Aires's hotels, the Marriott Plaza Hotel (p. 67), opened in 1908, is among the city's most traditional hotels. At the time it opened, the hotel was considered so far from the main hotel district (along Av. de Mayo) that many assumed the hotel, now approaching its 100-year anniversary, would fail. Numerous famous guests and royalty have stayed here. The facade of the hotel will soon undergo a much-needed cleaning and face-lift.

Continue to walk toward your right around the plaza, with Calle Florida to your left shoulder. Stop when you get to where Calle Santa Fe hits the park and look at the:

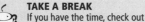
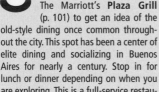

TAKE A BREAK

If you have the time, check out The Marriott's **Plaza Grill** (p. 101) to get an idea of the old-style dining once common throughout the city. This spot has been a center of elite dining and socializing in Buenos Aires for nearly a century. Stop in for lunch or dinner depending on when you are exploring. This is a full-service restaurant, so expect the meal to take longer than running in for just a snack. If you're here in the middle of the day, check out the cigars in the adjacent Plaza Bar, where local businesspeople often puff away over business strategy meetings.

❸ Círculo Militar & Palacio Paz

Perhaps the most beautiful of the Beaux Arts mansions in Buenos Aires, the Círculo Militar looks plucked from the Loire Valley. It was the home of the

Paz family and took almost 12 years to build; the patriarch who commissioned it died waiting. The family owned the *La Prensa* newspaper. The Palacio Paz is now home to the Círculo Militar, an elite organization for retired military officers that bought the building in 1938. The Museo de las Armas, which sheds light on the Islas Malvinas/Falkland Islands conflict, is also in the building.

Continue walking around the plaza to your right. Stop at the:

❹ General José de San Martín Monument

This fantastic monument celebrates General José de San Martín, who battled against Spain in the wars of independence and is known as the founder of the Argentine nation. Though the statue was originally designed in 1862, it was expanded in 1900 into the over-the-top spectacle you see here, with San Martín atop his horse in the middle on a raised platform, surrounded by soldiers and their women seeing them off before battle. The statue is a favorite hangout spot for the young, and it's where visiting dignitaries from other countries usually leave a ceremonial wreath. The best time to see this statue is in October and November, when the jacaranda trees are in full bloom.

Turn around so that the statue of San Martín is to your back and cross the very wide Calle Maipú, being careful of traffic in this chaotic intersection. Walk up Calle Arenales, toward the grand marble building slightly to your right, which is known as the:

❺ Palacio San Martín

Another of the grand mansions that line Plaza San Martín, this was the home of the powerful Anchorenas family whose prestige dated to colonial times in Argentina. In 1936 the Ministry of Foreign Affairs took over the building. From the street, you'll mostly be able to see its enormous French gates, although these do have intricate grillwork from which you can look through and see the large circular courtyard. The building is open periodically for free tours.

Retrace your steps from here, and head back to the Plaza San Martín, in front of the San Martín monument. Once you reach the plaza, turn to your left and continue walking forward through the expanse of the plaza, following the balustrade, until you come across a large set of stairs cascading down a hill. This is one of the favorite city tanning spots in warm weather. Try not to gawk too much at the bathing-suit-clad locals—you have other things to do! At the bottom of the stairs, to your right side, you'll come across the:

❻ Islas Malvinas–Falkland Islands Memorial

This monument honors the more than 700 Argentines who died in the war over the Islas Malvinas/Falkland Islands chain in the brief war with Great Britain in early 1982. The war was treated as almost silly by most English-speaking countries who sided with Great Britain, including the United States. Argentina lost the war, but became a democracy once again in the process. The war and sovereignty over the islands still remains a sore point among Argentines, and it is best to treat the topic delicately in discussions. The three branches of the military, the Army, Navy, and Air Force, take turns guarding the monument, and the changing of the guard here is worth seeing.

Turn your back to the Islas Malvinas–Falkland Islands Memorial and head to the crosswalk across Avenida Libertador. Carefully cross this very wide street and head to the middle of the plaza, to the:

❼ Torre Monumental (British Clock Tower)

This 1916 gift from the British community in Buenos Aires, along with all other things British, was renamed in response to the Islas Malvinas/Falkland Islands War and is called the Argentine Big Ben by some. Decorated with British royal imperial symbols, the base was partly destroyed by an angry mob during an Islas Malvinas–Falkland Islands memorial service. Inside the tower you'll find a small Buenos Aires City Tourism Information Office as well as an elevator you can ride to the top for an excellent view of the city. The tower was placed here to celebrate the completion of the nearby Retiro station, which was built with British technology.

Walk out of the Torre Monumental and walk to your left in the direction of the:

❽ Retiro Station

Retiro Station was opened in 1915 and built with British technological assistance. Four British architects designed it, and the steel structure was made in Liverpool, England, and shipped to Argentina to be assembled. For years, the station was the main entry point into Buenos Aires before the advent of the airplane. It's still very busy with trains to the suburbs and the resort area of Tigre. The mint-green circular ticketing area is particularly distinctive, among the many interesting details in this station. The central hallway is enormous, and while some of the interior ornamentation has disappeared, you'll still see some bronze lighting fixtures adorning the walls.

A few other train stations are in this complex—Bartolomé Mitre and Manuel Belgrano among them, as well as the modern Retiro Station Bus Depot.

Enter the station and its main hall. Turn to the left and continue to the end of the hall. Look for signs to the left for the:

❾ Café Retiro

This cafe opened in 1915 along with the station. For years it sat empty until recently being restored and reopened. Its interior is historically listed and this is one of the *cafés notables* protected by law in the city of Buenos Aires. The ornamentation includes massive bronze chandeliers, stained glass, and columns with gilded capitals. The food here, a branch of the chain Café Café, is basic, simple, and Argentine, with coffee and pastries as the main highlights. Now is the time to take a break and celebrate completing this walk.

When you want to leave, the subway Retiro Station is just outside the door.

WALKING TOUR 3 · PLAZA LAVALLE & THE TRIBUNALES AREA

Start:	Teatro Cervantes, overlooking Plaza Lavalle.
Public Transportation:	Metro: Tribunales.
Finish:	Obelisco.
Time:	1½ hours; 3 to 4 hours if you go inside all buildings mentioned.
Best Times:	Monday through Saturday between 11am and 4pm.
Worst Times:	At night when things are closed.
Walking Level:	Easy, and sidewalks are accessible for wheelchairs.

Plaza Lavalle is in some disrepair, but scaffolding around the plaza seems to indicate that in a few years, all will be good as new again. The area represents the heart of the country's judicial system, taking its name from the Supreme Court, or Tribunales Building, which is the focus of the plaza. This was also one of the city's main theater districts before the widening of Avenida Corrientes in the 1930s. Teatro Cervantes and the world-famous Teatro Colón testify to this thespian grandeur.

Start at the northeast corner of Libertad, where it hits Córdoba, at the:

❶ Teatro Nacional Cervantes

This theater (p. 170), which opened in the 1920s, was the project of Spanish actors working in Buenos Aires. It went bankrupt and was bought by the government, however, and became a national theater. It is designed in a Spanish Imperial style with the Habsburg double eagles as its main decoration on the outside of the building. The sumptuous interior uses materials from Spain such as imported carved-wood ornamentation and colorful Seville tiles on many of the walls and surfaces.

Standing on Córdoba with the Teatro Cervantes behind you, cross Córdoba and walk along Libertad, stopping one building in at Libertad 785, site of the:

❷ Templo Libertad & Jewish History Museum

This Byzantine-style temple was constructed in 1897 by CIRA (Congregación Israelita de la República de Argentina). Next door you'll find the Jewish Museum, also known as the Kibrick Museum, which contains religious and historical items related to Buenos Aires's Jewish community. For more information on the temple and museum, see p. 155.

Continue to walk south along Libertad and cross Calle Viamonte. Stop at Libertad 621, between Viamonte and Tucumán, to see the:

❸ Teatro Colón

The Teatro Colón will soon celebrate its 100th anniversary to mark its 1908 opening. It took over 18 years to build, largely because of the dramatic tragedies that befell its various architects, especially Víctor Meano, who was murdered in a love triangle gone wrong. Materials for the theater came from all over Europe, and the building functioned as Buenos Aires's aria to the world, proving that it was a city of culture to be reckoned with. Tours and a show are a must while you are in Buenos Aires, but be aware that an ongoing renovation means that this temple to opera will be closed during 2006 and 2007. But if you're on this walk and the building is open, don't

Walking Tour 3: Plaza Lavalle & the Tribunales Area

Legend:
- ⊠ Post office
- Ⓐ Subway
- Ⓓ–Ⓔ Subway transfer

1 Teatro Nacional Cervantes
2 Templo Libertad and the Jewish History Museum
3 The Teatro Colón
4 Escuela Presidente Roca
5 Lavalle Monument
6 Tribunales (Palacio de la Justicia)
7 The Obelisco

---

delay going inside, where you'll be able to see marble from all over the world lining the lobby and making up the grand staircase; the wooden and bronze seating area, which soars five levels to an immense chandelier; as well as the underground storage and practice areas where ballerinas improve their craft.

Continue walking along Libertador and cross Calle Tucumán, stopping at the building on the corner, at Calle Libertad 581, site of the:

④ Escuela Presidente Roca

The employees of this beautiful Greek revival structure (p. 147) say people often wander in thinking it is the Teatro Colón. And it's no wonder, with its Doric colonnade and ornamental statues along the central pediment, but this is actually a local school. Technically, it is not open to the public, but polite people will be allowed in the courtyard and maybe even upstairs to see the

beautiful ceiling with painted acanthus leaves. The school turned 100 years old in 2004 and expects to undergo a renovation in late 2005 or 2006.

Turn around so that the Escuela Presidente Roca is to your back, and face Plaza Libertad. Head to the column in the center of the plaza, the:

⑤ Lavalle Monument

Juan Lavalle fought along with San Martín in the wars for independence as a very young man, and continued in the Argentine military, becoming a general. His statue, on a slender column, is the main focus of the center of this plaza. As of this writing, the area around the monument is undergoing extensive renovation, so it might be hard to see the statue up close. Wander around the plaza, though, and take a look at the various other monuments. Be aware that an underground parking garage was built under the plaza, so you have to watch out for cars, especially at the corner of Libertad and Tucumán, where the entry ramp is located. The plaza, like many in Buenos Aires, is often taken over by protestors who are coming to make their views known to the people in the next building on this tour. You will sometimes see camps of them here.

From the center of the plaza, face west, toward the Supreme Court building, an enormous structure on the southwest corner of the plaza, also known as:

⑥ Tribunales (Palacio de la Justicia)

The Tribunales neighborhood takes its name from this building: the Supreme Court, or Tribunales building (also called the Palacio de la Justicia). It is immense and hulking, with strong Greek elements. If you are here during the day, try to enter. It used to be fully open to the public, but due to the peso crisis and numerous protests, police barricades often surround it; try to look like you have a reason to enter the building for your best chances when trying to walk in. Inside, the central courtyard is lined with columns and pilasters. Ornamentation on the walls and between the columns includes symbols imitating the smiling sun from the center of the Argentine flag.

Turn your back to the Supreme Court building and walk along the edge of the plaza in an eastern direction. Look to your right at the edge of the plaza toward the pedestrianized section of Diagonal Norte, also known as Avenida Roque Sáenz Peña, with a vista to Avenida 9 de Julio and the:

⑦ Obelisco

The Obelisco (p. 150) was inaugurated in 1936 and built to honor the 400th anniversary of the first (unsuccessful) founding of the city by Pedro de Mendoza. (The second, permanent, founding was in 1580.) This towering structure marks the intersection of Avenida 9 de Julio and Corrientes. Diagonal Norte stretches behind the Obelisco with links to the monument to Plaza de Mayo. The Obelisco sits in the round Plaza de República. This plaza has plaques that celebrate the various provinces that make up the country. Unfortunately, most of them have been stolen.

This pedestrianized area of Diagonal Norte is lined with cafes and little restaurants, so take a break here if you like. Otherwise walk up toward the Obelisco itself. If Argentina has won an international event, join the flag-waving crowds here and cheer the country on. Underneath the Obelisco, you have access to three subway lines (B, C, and D), so it is easy to get back to hotels in many parts of the city from here.

WALKING TOUR 4	AVENIDA DE MAYO TO CONGRESO
Start:	Casa de Cultura, at Av. de Mayo 575.
Public Transportation:	Metro: Bolívar, Perú, Catedral, or Plaza de Mayo.
Finish:	Plaza Congreso.
Time:	2 hours, 5 if buildings and museums are entered.
Best Times:	Monday through Saturday between 11am and 4pm.
Worst Times:	At night when things are closed.
Walking Level:	Easy, but long distances (about 2.4km/1½ miles) are covered in this tour. Most sidewalks are accessible for wheelchairs, but pavement can be broken in places. Also note that you will be crossing the very wide Avenida 9 de Julio on this walk, which can take two to three traffic-light cycles for pedestrians to get across it; be extra careful with children.

Avenida de Mayo opened in 1894 and was meant to be the Gran Via or Champs-Elysées of Buenos Aires. The design of the street was part of an even grander plan

Walking Tour 4: Avenida de Mayo to Congreso

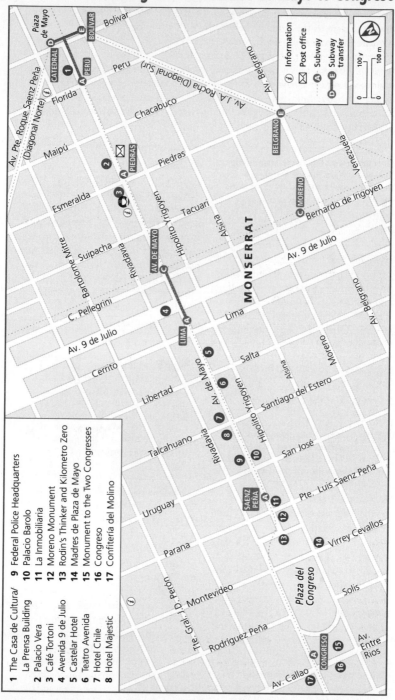

Legend:
- *i* Information
- ☒ Post office
- Ⓐ Subway
- Ⓓ–Ⓔ Subway transfer

MONSERRAT

Plaza del Congreso

Tour stops:
1 The Casa de Cultura/ La Prensa Building
2 Palacio Vera
3 Café Tortoni
4 Avenida 9 de Julio
5 Castelar Hotel
6 Teatro Avenida
7 Hotel Chile
8 Hotel Majestic
9 Federal Police Headquarters
10 Palacio Barolo
11 La Inmobiliaria
12 Moreno Monument
13 Rodin's Thinker and Kilometro Zero
14 Madres de Plaza de Mayo
15 Monument to the Two Congresses
16 Congreso
17 Confitería del Molino

to rebuild Buenos Aires in preparation for the 1910 Independence Centennial and to declare to the world that Buenos Aires was a city to be reckoned with. Some of the greatest concentrations of Beaux Arts and Art Nouveau buildings in the city are along this route, which connects Plaza de Mayo in the east to Congreso in the west. This is the historical processional route both for grand parades and for when people have something to protest to the president and to Congress. While many buildings along this route are badly in need of repair, it is not hard to imagine how glorious this street must have been in its heyday at the beginning of the 20th century.

Start just in from the northeastern corner of Avenida de Mayo and San Martín, at Av. de Mayo 575, site of the:

❶ Casa de Cultura/La Prensa Building

Once the home of the newspaper *La Prensa*, owned by the very wealthy and powerful Paz family, this building is simply sumptuous, with carved granite, bronze ornamentation, and sinuous lanterns among its most striking features. Now home to the Casa de Cultura (the Office of Culture for the City of Buenos Aires; p. 136), it is open for tours on the weekend. The tour is a must-do if you have the time. If you don't, at least enter the building and take a peak at the lobby to get an idea of its splendor.

With the Casa de Cultura to your back, turn right and continue moving up Avenida de Mayo in a western direction. Cross Calle Perú and Calle Maipú and stop at Av. de Mayo 769, location of the:

❷ Palacio Vera

One of the best examples of Art Nouveau along Avenida de Mayo is right here, and the details along its balconies are the most interesting part of the Palacio Vera facade. Now made up of businesses and apartments, it was designed as the home for the Diaz Velez family, who gained prominence at the beginning of the 1800s during the British invasion, just before independence.

Continue walking up Avenida de Mayo, cross Calle Esmeralda, and stop when you've reached Av. de Mayo 825, home of the:

❸ Café Tortoni

As the city's most famous cafe (p. 104), this establishment has been graced by numerous political, intellectual, and historic figures from Argentina and from around the world. There are tango shows here every night, but the real treat is the ornate interior of the building itself. Above the cafe is the office of the National Tango Academy, which also offers lessons.

TAKE A BREAK
As long as you're here, you might as well sample the atmosphere and have a bite to eat. Don't expect excellent service, as the waiters seem to ignore the customers. Still, the food is inexpensive, and a tea or coffee with croissants, known here as *medialunas*, makes an excellent snack for more energy along the way.

Continue walking up Avenida de Mayo to the world's widest boulevard:

❹ Avenida 9 de Julio

It will probably take you a few traffic-light cycles to cross this massive street. Construction on this avenida began in the 1930s, with its inauguration in 1937. Expansion, however, continued decades later, up through the 1960s. Unfortunately, during the process of making this boulevard, much of the city's beautiful turn-of-the-20th-century architectural heritage was lost. Spend some time on the avenida in this area, and be sure to see the fountains and the Don Quixote monument inaugurated by Queen Sofía of Spain.

Cross Avenida 9 de Julio completely and continue on to Av. de Mayo 1152, location of the:

5 Castelar Hotel

One of the jewels of Avenida de Mayo, this hotel opened in 1928. One of its most notable features is its extensive Turkish bath on its basement level; it's worth stopping into to get a treatment or even just to view the space. The Castelar (p. 76) has a strong association with Spanish literary giant Federico García Lorca, who lived here for many months. His room has been converted into a mini-museum. The eccentric Italian architect Mario Palanti, who also designed the nearby Palacio Barolo (p. 143), designed the Castelar.

Continue walking up Avenida de Mayo and cross Calle Salta to Av. de Mayo 1222, site of the:

6 Teatro Avenida

This theater, opened in 1908, is largely dedicated to Spanish productions. It presented material by Lorca when he was living in the Castelar down the street in the 1930s. Many other artists from Spain also had their work presented here at the time, and the theater was an integral part of making Buenos Aires the center of Spanish-language literature and culture while Spain was engaged in its civil war. After a fire in the 1970s, it was partly rebuilt.

Cross the Avenida de Mayo and head to the corner of Santiago del Estero, to the:

7 Hotel Chile

This is a very unique Art Nouveau hotel with Middle Eastern elements. Take special note of the windows, with their round tops and faience ornamental tiling. The hotel was designed by the French architect Louis Dubois and opened in 1907. Like many other hotels on Avenida de Mayo, Hotel Chile was once luxurious and the utmost in style, but it is now a rather down-on-its-luck site, in which the facade remains the only clue to its former glory.

Cross Santiago del Estero, staying on Avenida de Mayo, and stop immediately on the corner of the next block to see the:

8 Hotel Majestic

Opened in 1910 in time for the Centennial celebrations, this is one of the city's most fabled hotels, though it no longer operates as such. Most Porteños point to it with extreme pride as the place where Infanta Isabel stayed to represent Spain at the celebrations. It was also where the Russian ballet star Vaclav Nijinsky spent his wedding night after getting married in Buenos Aires in 1913. The hotel is now home to the Tax Museum (p. 154), one of only three such museums in the world. The lobby is sumptuous but extremely dark and badly in need of repair.

Continue walking up Avenida de Mayo and stop at the next building, no. 1333, home of the:

9 Federal Police Headquarters

Ornate Art Deco buildings are a rarity in Buenos Aires, which did not take to the style in quite the same way as New York, Los Angeles, and Paris did. The Federal Police Headquarters, however, is one of the best that you'll find in the city. Take note of the way the windows are treated, with their faceted frames, and the statues adorning the facade. The building was originally opened in 1926 for the *Crítica* newspaper, for which Argentine literary giant Jorge Luis Borges had worked. The building is not generally open to the public, unless you have been the victim of a crime or committed one, but try wandering in and see what happens.

Stay on this block but walk across the street to Av. de Mayo 1370 to reach the:

10 Palacio Barolo

This is, in my opinion, the most unusual building (p. 143) in all of Buenos Aires. Designed by the eccentric Italian architect Mario Palanti, who also designed the nearby Hotel Castelar, this building is meant to recall Dante's *Inferno*. The lobby symbolizes Hell, with its bronze medallions representing fire and male and female dragons lining the walls. The scale of the building is massive; in fact, it was once the tallest building in South America, though Palanti later designed a similar, taller structure in Montevideo. Originally, a statue of Dante was in the lobby, but it was stolen in the 1955 revolution deposing Juan Perón. Guided tours take you through the building to the lighthouse tower representing God and Salvation, from where you'll get an excellent view up and down Avenida de Mayo and of other parts of the city.

Continue walking up Avenida de Mayo and cross Calle San José. Stay on this block (between San José and Luis Sáenz Peña) and take in:

⓫ La Inmobiliaria

Taking up this whole block, La Inmobiliaria was designed as the office for a real estate and apartment agency. Today it houses apartments and offices, but the tiled Art Nouveau sign indicating its former use still remains along the top of the facade. The building's most unique features are the matching corner towers, which form a kind of endpoint to Avenida de Mayo before it flows into Plaza Congreso.

Continue walking up Avenida de Mayo, crossing into Plaza Congreso, to see the:

⓬ Moreno Monument

This statue, in the first part of Plaza Congreso, quite overgrown by large trees, is of Mariano Moreno, the secretary of the First Government Assembly following independence from Spain. He was also an important journalist who founded both the Argentine National Library and the *Buenos Aires Gazette*. Moreno is memorialized elsewhere in the city, with a street name and a subway stop.

Turn around and with Moreno behind you, walk forward to the central walk in the middle of the plaza. Then turn to the left and walk to the next statue:

⓭ Rodin's *The Thinker* & Kilometro Cero

This is a copy of Rodin's famous statue *The Thinker,* and it's a favorite play area for children. Just next to it is a block marking Kilometro Cero, the point at which all distances from Buenos Aires are marked.

Continue walking through the plaza, but veer toward your left. Cross Calle Yrigoyen and head to Yrigoyen 1584, near the corner of Ceballos, home base of the:

⓮ Madres de Plaza de Mayo

The Madres de Plaza de Mayo (p.143), who march every Thursday at 3:30pm in the Plaza de Mayo in honor of their missing children, have their main headquarters here. They also run a university, library, bookstore, and a small cafe on the premises. It's worth taking the time to enter and linger here, and maybe have a coffee or a snack. You might also get a chance to talk with one of the by now very old Madres about this heart-wrenching period in Argentina's history, when nearly 30,000 young people were tortured and killed by the military government.

Cross the street and head back into Plaza Congreso, heading toward the enormous no-longer-working fountain in front of Congreso itself, to view the:

⓯ Monument to the Two Congresses

Quite a confection of marble and bronze, this enormous monument celebrates the two congresses that were held in the aftermath of independence from Spain to lay out the foundations for the new nation of Argentina. This multileveled structure has stairs that lead to a fantastic view of Congreso, where you can snap pictures of the building or pose with it behind you. The fountain no longer operates and is need of some renovation, but the overall effect of this monument is very impressive.

Leave the Two Congresses monument and walk toward the Congreso building. Cross

the street, being very careful at the crazy intersection, and head to the:

⑯ Congreso

The most imposing building in all of Buenos Aires (p. 142), this structure opened in 1906. It combines influences from some of the world's most famous structures, from the U.S. Capitol to Garnier's Opera House to Berlin's Brandenburg Gate. Made of massive blocks of granite, the walls are over 1.8m (6 ft.) thick at their base. Tours will take you through both chambers of the bi-cameral legislature and are available by asking at the Rivadavia entrance. At night the porthole windows are impressively lit.

Walk to your right (north). Cross Calle Rivadavia and stop on the corner to view the:

⑰ Confitería del Molino

This fantastic structure (p. 169), in a terrible state of disrepair and closed to the public, was the creation of Francesco Gianotti, an Italian who also designed Galería Guemes and its theater housing the Piazzolla tango show. Once the informal meeting place of politicians from the nearby Congreso, the confitería (cafe) closed in 1997, though there are plans to eventually renovate and reopen it. Primarily an Art Nouveau structure, stained glass and ornate tile work were once part of the ornamentation here, but these have been covered by tarps to prevent rain damage and further deterioration of the facade. The main visible feature from the street is the windmill top (*molino* means "windmill" in Spanish).

Congratulations, you have finished this walking tour! I recommend continuing to walk north along Avenida Callao, which was rebuilt in an almost imperial style after the opening of Congreso. Congreso has a subway stop for the A line and the C and D lines have nearby stops along Callao.

WALKING TOUR 5 | AVENIDA ALVEAR

Start:	The Alvear Palace Hotel.
Public Transportation:	There are no real public transportation options; a taxi is best.
Finish:	The Four Seasons Mansion.
Time:	1 hour, provided you don't get caught up shopping.
Best Times:	Monday through Saturday between 11am and 8pm.
Worst Times:	At night when things are closed.
Walking Level:	Easy and this is a short distance. However, not all the streets have cutouts for wheelchairs. There are also some gently sloping hills.

You may have to be wealthy to do your shopping on Avenida Alvear, but you don't need a penny to walk on it. In this tour, I'll touch on the architectural highlights of this exclusive area and only briefly on the shopping. I'll leave that up to you for later. Unlike most walks where the numbers go up, you will be proceeding down in the numbering system as you follow this tour along Avenida Alvear.

Begin at Av. Alvear 1891, at the intersection of Ayacucho, site of the:

❶ Alvear Palace Hotel

This is the most famous hotel in Buenos Aires (p. 79), and certainly its most elegant. Opened in 1928 and built in a French neoclassical style, the luxurious lobby is a gilded marble confection, and the central dining area, known as L'Orangerie, resembles the Palm Court in New York's Plaza Hotel. I highly suggest taking the time for the hotel's brunch buffet. While expensive by Argentine standards ($25 a person), it is a relative bargain when compared to Europe or North America. Attached to the hotel is a shopping gallery full of exclusive art and bridal shops.

Walk out of the Alvear Palace Hotel and with the hotel to your back, cross Avenida Alvear, turn to your left, and then cross Calle Callao before heading to Av. Alvear 1750, home to the:

② Ralph Lauren Shop

Shop here if you want, but I recommend taking a look at the physical setting of this Ralph Lauren store, one of the most exquisite of all the shops on this street. It was once a small Art Nouveau mansion. Within the interior, much of the ornate and heavy wood decoration remains, and a stained-glass skylight oversees the central staircase.

Continue walking down Avenida Alvear, staying on this side of the street. Cross Peña Street to Av. Alvear 1683, location of the:

③ Duhau Palace

Almost hidden behind overgrown trees, this high Victorian Gothic revival structure almost looks like part of a church or the setting for a horror movie. The structure was built in about 1890, in a part of the city that, at the time, was considered to be in a suburban neighborhood. Back then, there was almost nothing surrounding it. Now the multicolored brick facade of this structure contrasts strongly with the neoclassical limestone and white marble structures that were built over the next 3 decades in the area.

Continue walking down Avenida Alvear until you get to no. 1637, the:

④ Apostolic Nunciatore, or Anchorena Palace

Though originally built for the wealthy Anchorena family, they never lived in this magnificent French-style mansion with its distinctive circular front. The next owner wanted to give the building to the Vatican, but the local representative felt it was too ostentatious. Still, the Papal insignia, a papal tiara over a pair of keys, remains on the building. As of this writing, the palace is surrounded by scaffolding and construction. Eventually, the palace will be the entranceway for a new Hyatt hotel being built behind it, which will certainly be another last word in Buenos Aires luxury.

Continue walking for 2 more blocks until you reach a widening of the street and a small plaza with a statue and fountain, the:

⑤ Plazoleta Carlos Pellegrini

I think this is one of the most beautiful of all the small plazas in Buenos Aires, not just for the plaza itself, but also for the buildings that surround it. A large, recently restored statue of Carlos Pellegrini, a famous intellectual and industrialist and a senator representing the province of Buenos Aires, sits in the center of this plaza. The statue was created in France by Félix Coutan and dedicated in 1914. A small fountain and a bench add to the relaxed environment. This plaza is the most Parisian-appearing part of Recoleta, and it gives an idea of all that was lost when Buenos Aires decided to widen Avenida 9 de Julio in the 1960s, destroying other little corners of the city that were similar to this one.

With Carlos Pellegrini to your back, turn to your right and cross the street, heading to Calle Arroyo 1130, site of the:

⑥ Brazilian Embassy

First, a note about the name of this street. *Arroyo* means "stream" in Spanish, and one once flowed through this area until it was filled in as the city began to develop in this area. The Brazilian Embassy, one of the city's most beautiful embassies, is one of the most impressive structures overlooking this plaza. Once a private mansion, it took almost 20 years to build and has details borrowed from the Palais Fontainebleau in France.

With the Brazilian Embassy behind you, turn to your right, cross Calle Cerrito, and stop once you reach the other side. Be aware that this odd intersection has a confusing traffic pattern, so be careful when crossing to see the:

⑦ French Embassy

It's hard to believe when you see this beautiful structure, but the plans for the expansion of Avenida 9 de Julio

1 The Alvear Palace Hotel
2 Ralph Lauren Shop
3 The Duhau Palace
4 Apostolic Nunciatore
   or Anchorena Palace
5 Plazoleta Carlos Pellegrini
6 The Brazilian Embassy
7 The French Embassy
8 The Jockey Club
9 The Four Seasons Mansion

originally included the demolition of this building. Fortunately, the French government refused to give up the building, and it now serves as the vista point for the northern terminus of Avenida 9 de Julio. Created by the French architect Pablo Pater, it became the French Embassy in 1939. The building is a beautiful example of Belle Epoque, and you should be sure to notice the main dome and the grillwork on the surrounding fence. You'll notice *trompe l'oeils* of mansard roofs and windows on some of the surfaces of the surrounding modern buildings, an attempt to give an impression of the Belle Epoque buildings that were demolished to make way for the expansion of Avenida 9 de Julio.

With the Obelisco on Avenida 9 de Julio to your back, cross Arroyo and Cerritos, stopping at the corner, where you'll find the:

⑧ Jockey Club

Carlos Pellegrini, whose statue sits across the street in the plaza out front, started the Jockey Club in 1882 along with other like-minded equestrians. The Jockey Club became a major part of the social networking scene for the wealthy and powerful of Argentina. The Jockey Club's original Calle Florida headquarters were burned to the ground on April 15, 1953, after a riot provoked by Perón against this elite institution. Perón seized the assets of the organization, but it was able to regroup in 1958 a few years after he had been thrown out of power. This current building was once the mansion of the Uzué de Casares family and the organization moved here in 1966. It is not open to the public but its interior is full of tapestries, works of art, and an extensive library.

Walk back across Cerritos, walking only for a few feet toward the immense tower a block down, but stop when you get to Calle Cerrito 1455, site of the:

9 Four Seasons Mansion

The official name of this Louis XIII–style redbrick palace with heavy quoins is Mansión Alzaga Unzue. It was built in 1919 and was designed with three facades, anticipating the eventual construction of Avenida 9 de Julio to the east of the building. It was designed with an extensive garden complex in front of its northern facade. The mansion is now part of the Four Seasons Hotel, and it is attached to the main tower through a garden court-yard. The tower sits on what were once the mansion's gardens. The tower and the mansion were previously known as the Park Hyatt until the Four Seasons purchased the property. Renting the entire mansion is the ultimate in spoiled celebrity luxury and privacy, and it is usually here where stars party with their entourages in Buenos Aires. When Madonna filmed the movie *Evita,* she used the mansion's balcony to practice her Casa Rosada "Don't Cry for Me, Argentina" scenes as mobs gathered on the street out front.

Congratulations, you have finished another tour. There are no nearby metro stations, but there are plenty of cabs in the area that can get you wherever you want to go next.

8

Shopping

Throughout South America, Buenos Aires is famous for its shopping. You'll find it in glitzy malls, along major shopping thoroughfares, and in small boutiques and little out-of-the-way stores. Buenos Aires is most famous for its high-quality leather goods, which, since Argentina is a beef-loving country, should come as no surprise. You won't find as many native crafts here, however, as you will in other South American capitals.

Since the peso crisis, Buenos Aires shopping has become an unbelievable bargain. The peso crisis also spawned an interesting trend: With Argentina's inability to import many fashion products, the crisis has allowed the creativity of local designers producing for the domestic market to flourish and expand. In particular, you'll find a wealth of young designers catering to the young-women's market, offering unique feminine and funky fashion found no where else in the world. A new trade agreement with China might damage this wonderful trend, but for now, there are plenty of unique things to buy in Buenos Aires. Antiques, especially in San Telmo, are also a famous part of Buenos Aires's shopping.

Many Buenos Aires stores, particularly those catering to tourists, also offer tax-free shopping. You'll know them by the blue and white logo on the door; ask if you don't see one. Leather-goods stores are exceptionally well versed in the process, and it is often part of the spiel when you go into one of them. For more details on this process, see the "Just the Facts: Hours, Shipping & Taxes" box below.

Many neighborhoods, especially Palermo Viejo, have special shopping maps. Ask for these maps at the Buenos Aires City Tourism kiosks (p. 44) or in individual stores all over town. *The Golden Map,* which most hotels have at their front desks, also lists many stores, though you'll probably find that the stores that advertise less tend to have better prices.

A very handy website to check out before heading to Buenos is **http://shoppingba.infobae.com**, which lists and categorizes stores of all kinds throughout Buenos Aires.

1 The Shopping Scene

MAJOR SHOPPING AREAS

Buenos Aires has many shopping areas, but the following places are where you'll find most of the action.

MICROCENTRO Calle Florida, the Microcentro's pedestrian walking street, is home to wall-to-wall shops from Plaza San Martín to all the way past Avenida Corrientes. As you approach Plaza San Martín from Calle Florida, you'll find a number of well-regarded shoe stores, jewelers, and shops selling leather goods. Most of the stores here are decidedly middle class, and some clearly cater to locals and carry things you'd never buy. However, if you're looking for basic items like electrical converters, extension cords, and other items to help you use your

Buenos Aires Shopping

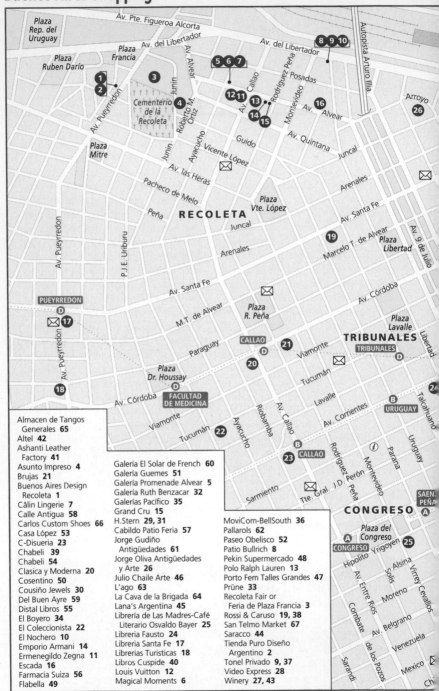

Almacen de Tangos
  Generales **65**
Altel **42**
Ashanti Leather
  Factory **41**
Asunto Impreso **4**
Brujas **21**
Buenos Aires Design
  Recoleta **1**
Câlin Lingerie **7**
Calle Antigua **58**
Carlos Custom Shoes **66**
Casa López **53**
Chabeli **39**
Chabeli **54**
Clasica y Moderna **20**
Cosentino **50**
Cousiño Jewels **30**
Del Buen Ayre **59**
Distal Libros **55**
El Boyero **34**
El Coleccionista **22**
El Nochero **10**
Emporio Armani **14**
Ermenegildo Zegna **11**
Escada **16**
Farmacia Suiza **56**
Flabella **49**

Galería El Solar de French **60**
Galería Guemes **51**
Galería Promenade Alvear **5**
Galería Ruth Benzacar **32**
Galerías Pacífico **35**
Grand Cru **15**
H.Stern **29, 31**
Cabildo Patio Feria **57**
Jorge Gudiño
  Antigüedades **61**
Jorge Oliva Antigüedades
  y Arte **26**
Julio Chaile Arte **46**
L'ago **63**
La Cava de la Brigada **64**
Lana's Argentina **45**
Librería de Las Madres-Café
  Literario Osvaldo Bayer **25**
Libreria Fausto **24**
Libreria Santa Fe **17**
Librerias Turisticas **18**
Libros Cuspide **40**
Louis Vuitton **12**
Magical Moments **6**

MoviCom-BellSouth **36**
Pallarols **62**
Paseo Obelisco **52**
Patio Bullrich **8**
Pekin Supermercado **48**
Polo Ralph Lauren **13**
Porto Fem Talles Grandes **47**
Prüne **33**
Recoleta Fair or
  Feria de Plaza Francia **3**
Rossi & Caruso **19, 38**
San Telmo Market **67**
Saracco **44**
Tienda Puro Diseño
  Argentino **2**
Tonel Privado **9, 37**
Video Express **28**
Winery **27, 43**

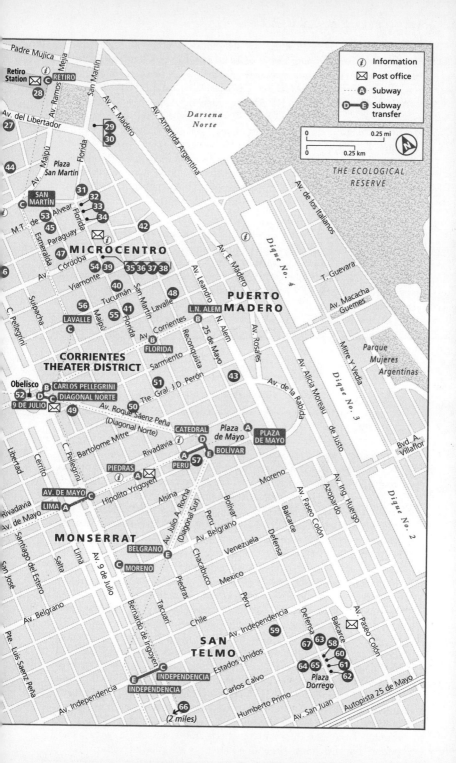

Padre Mujica

Retiro Station
ⓘ Ⓒ RETIRO
✉ 28

Av. del Libertador
27

San Martín

Av. Ramos Mejía

Av. E. Madero

Av. Antártida Argentina

Darsena Norte

44

Plaza San Martín

Florida

29
30

THE ECOLOGICAL RESERVE

Av. de los Italianos

Ⓒ SAN MARTÍN
31
32
33
34
53 Alvear
45
Paraguay
47
Esmeralda
M.T. de

ⓘ

Córdoba
54 39 35 36 37 38
42

MICROCENTRO

ⓘ

Av.
6

Viamonte
40
56
Tucumán
41 55
LAVALLE
Ⓒ

Maipú

San Martín
Florida
Lavalle
48

Corrientes
B FLORIDA
Ⓓ

L.N. ALEM
Ⓑ
N. Alem
25 de Mayo
Reconquista

PUERTO MADERO

Av. E. Madero
ⓘ

Av. Leandro

Av. Rosales

Dique Nº 4

T. Guevara

Av. Macacha Guemes

Parque Mujeres Argentinas

Dique Nº 3

CORRIENTES THEATER DISTRICT

Sarmiento
51
Tte. Gral. J.D. Perón
43

C. Pellegrini
Suipacha

Obelisco
52 ■ Ⓓ CARLOS PELLEGRINI
Ⓒ DIAGONAL NORTE
9 DE JULIO ✉
49

50 Av. Roque Sáenz Peña
(Diagonal Norte)

CATEDRAL
ⓘ
Ⓐ Ⓓ
PERÚ Ⓐ
57 Ⓐ BOLÍVAR

Rivadavia

Plaza de Mayo Ⓐ
PLAZA DE MAYO Ⓐ

Av. Alicia Moreau - de Justo

Dique Nº 2

Libertad
Cerrito
C. Pellegrini
Bartolome Mitre
PIEDRAS
ⓘ ✉

Ⓐ

AV. DE MAYO Ⓒ
LIMA Ⓐ
Rivadavia
Av. de Mayo

Hipólito Yrigoyen
Alsina

Av. Ing. Huergo

Santiago del Estero
San José

MONSERRAT

Lima
Salta

Av. 9 de Julio

BELGRANO
Ⓔ
Ⓒ MORENO

Av. Julio A. Rocha
(Diagonal Sur)
Bolívar
Perú
Av. Belgrano
Venezuela
Chacabuco
México
Piedras
Perú

Defensa
Balcarce
Av. Paseo Colón
Azopardo

Bvd. A. Villaflor

Pte. - Luis Saenz Peña
Av. Belgrano

Bernardo de Irigoyen

Tacuarí
Chile

Av. Independencia

SAN TELMO

59

Estados Unidos
Carlos Calvo

67 63 58
60
64 65 61
62
Plaza Dorrego

Defensa
Balcarce
Av. Paseo Colón

Ⓒ
Ⓔ INDEPENDENCIA
INDEPENDENCIA

Av. Independencia

Humberto Primo

Av. San Juan
Autopista 25 de Mayo

66
(2 miles)

Information ⓘ
Post office ✉
Subway Ⓐ
Subway transfer Ⓓ—Ⓔ

0   0.25 mi
0   0.25 km

197

electrical goods here, this is where you will find what you need. Calle Lavalle is also pedestrianized, but most of the stores here are five-and-dime types with little of interest to the tourist unless you have decided to stay here long-term and need items for an apartment. The **Galerías Pacífico** mall is located at Calle Florida 750, at Avenida Córdoba (© **11/4319-5100**), with a magnificent dome and stunning frescoes painted by local artists. Over 180 shops are open Monday through Saturday from 10am to 9pm and Sunday from noon to 9pm, with tango and folk-dancing shows held on Thursday at 8pm. Day and night you'll find a lot of street entertainers and tango dancers working the crowds all along Calle Florida. While you'll probably only shop on Florida, other streets do have stores and restaurants, and this neighborhood also has the highest concentration of small travel agencies if you need to change an itinerary or want to add side trips.

RECOLETA   Avenida Alvear is Argentina's response to the Champs-Elysées, and—without taking the comparison too far—it is indeed an elegant, Parisian-like strip of European boutiques, cafes, antiques stores, and art galleries. Start your walk at Plaza Francia, in front of the Recoleta Cemetery, and continue to Cerrito, or Avenida 9 de Julio. Along Calle Quintana, French-style mansions share company with upscale shops. Nearby **Patio Bullrich,** Av. del Libertador 750 (© **11/4814-7400**), is one of the city's most famous malls. Its 69 shops are open daily from 10am to 9pm. It is considered to be upscale, but has offerings similar to other malls in the city. It has an excellent food court, however, and is a good place to stop for a snack.

Tips **Just the Facts: Hours, Shipping & Taxes**

Most stores are open weekdays from 9am to 8pm and Saturday from 9am until midnight, with some closing for a few hours in the afternoon. You might find some shops open Sunday along Avenida Santa Fe, but few will be open on Calle Florida. Shopping centers are open daily from 10am to 10pm. Certain art and antiques dealers will crate and ship bulky objects for an additional fee; others will tell you it's no problem to take that new sculpture directly on the plane. If you don't want to take any chances, contact UPS at © **800/222-2877** or Federal Express at © **810/333-3339.** Various stores participate in a tax-refund program for purchases over 70 pesos. Ask for a special receipt, which can entitle you to a refund of the hefty 21% tax (IVA) when you leave the country. Most of these stores have blue-and-white TAX FREE signs, but always ask when making a purchase. The process works by getting a special Global Refund check form that indicates the value of what you will get back when you leave the country. You must have this special form, which participating stores will create for purchases over 70 pesos, to get a refund. Some restrictions do apply, however. The item has to have been made in Argentina and purchased with the intention of taking it out of the country (things like food do not qualify). The system is used mostly for clothing and leather goods, but you should ask about it whenever making a purchase, even if you do not see the sign. Upon leaving the country, have all of these checks ready and look for the Global Refund desk. At Ezeiza airport, it is in the immigrations area just before you have your passport stamped to leave the country. For more information, check out the website www.global refund.com and choose Argentina under the selection of countries.

AVENIDA SANTA FE Popular with local shoppers, Avenida Santa Fe offers a wide selection of clothing stores with down-to-earth prices typical of stores catering to the local middle class rather than tourists. You will also find bookstores, cafes, ice-cream shops, and cinemas here. The **Alto Palermo Shopping Center,** Av. Santa Fe 3253 (© **11/5777-8000**), is another excellent shopping center, with 155 stores open daily from 10am to 10pm.

SAN TELMO & LA BOCA These neighborhoods offer excellent antiques as well as artists' studios and arts and crafts celebrating tango. Street performers and artists are also omnipresent. However, La Boca should be avoided at night.

CORDOBA Looking for off-season bargains? Then the 3000 block of Córdoba is the place to head, in the area bordering Barrio Norte and Palermo. Best of all, off season in Argentina is usually the right season in the Northern Hemisphere, so you won't have to let your purchases sit around for a few months—you can wear them right when you get back home.

2 Outdoor Markets

One of the pleasures of Buenos Aires is its open air-markets (called markets, fairs, or *ferias*), many of which combine shopping with entertainment. The bargains you'll find here often come with a show and the wonderful romantic sounds and sights of tango dancers. I've listed below just a few of the many open-air markets you can find all over the city.

The **San Telmo Antiques Fair** 🦞🦞, which takes place every Sunday from 10am to 5pm at Plaza Dorrego, is a vibrant, colorful experience that will delight even the most jaded traveler. As street vendors sell their heirlooms, singers and dancers move amid the crowd to tango music. Among the 270-plus vendor stands, you will find antique silversmith objects, porcelain, crystal, and other antiques. It's especially famous for the tango performances, which can go on into the late evening, even if most of the vendors themselves close up at 5pm. The star of the show is a dark, handsome dancer known as "El Indio," and you'll often see his photos on sale throughout the city at other markets. I highly recommend this fair as a not-to-be-missed sight while in Buenos Aires.

Head to **Cabildo Patio Feria** when doing sightseeing in the Plaza de Mayo area. This fair is held on Thursday and Friday from 11am to 6pm in the small garden patio behind the Cabildo, or old city hall. You'll find lots of locally made crafts here, especially pottery, stained glass, and jewelry.

Friday to Sunday from 11am to 6pm, the Madres hold the **Feria de Madres de Plaza de Mayo** fair in front of their headquarters overlooking Plaza Congreso. Children will also like coming here, since it is next to the part of the park with the merry-go-round and other rides. The fair has antiques, crafts, food, and a few interesting book vendors. Sometimes there is also live music. This is among the most casual and least touristy of all of the fairs, so it offers an interesting chance to chat with locals.

The **La Boca Fair** is open every day from 10am to 6pm or sundown. It's the most touristy of all the fairs, and most of the items are terribly overpriced. Still, if you need tacky souvenirs in a hurry, you'll get it all done here quickly. Besides, tango singers and other street performers will keep your mind off the inflated prices. When the vendors start leaving at the end of the day, you should too, for safety reasons.

Plaza Serrano Fair 🦞 is at the small plaza at the intersection of Calle Serrano and Honduras, which forms the heart of Palermo Hollywood. Bohemian arts and crafts are sold here while dread-headed locals sing and play guitars. Officially, it's held Saturday and Sunday from 10am to 6pm, but impromptu vendors set up at night when the restaurants are crowded too.

Recoleta Fair (aka **Feria de Plaza Francia**) 🎯🎯, which takes place Saturday and Sunday in front of Recoleta Cemetery from 10am until sunset, offers every imaginable souvenir and craft in addition to food. This has become the city's largest fair, completely taking over all the walkways and then some in the area, and even the Iglesia Pilar, Recoleta Cemetery's church, gets involved by setting up tables of postcards and religious souvenirs in its courtyard. Live bands sometimes play on whatever part of the hill is not taken over by vendors. Officially, the fair is only on weekends, but you will find vendors here every day, though they are technically violating the city's vending licenses by doing so. If the police get bored and feel like enforcing the law, you'll sometimes see arguments between them and the vendors. But don't worry; it's just one more part of the entertainment of the fair when this happens.

3 Major Shopping Malls

Indoors or out, Buenos Aires has a wealth of shopping areas. Here are some of the best indoor shopping centers in the city. Some, like Galerías Pacífico, are tourist sites in their own right because of the beauty of their architecture. Even if shopping or shopping malls are not your bag, Galerías Pacífico is not to be missed. The Abasto Shopping Center is a great place to bring the kids, with its special Museo de los Niños (p. 154) located in the food court. One thing you will not find in Argentina, which makes shopping here very different from North America or Europe, is a department store—even major malls do not have anchor stores. Department stores, such as Harrods, were an English import, and most have long since closed their doors. Thus, shopping centers are a collection of smaller stores and chains, some uniquely Argentine, others South American, and still others like what you would find anywhere else in the world.

Abasto Shopping Center 🎯🎯 *Kids*   The Abasto Shopping Center is one of the largest in all of Buenos Aires. It was built over an earlier market where the famous tango crooner Carlos Gardel got his start singing as a child to the various fruit and meat vendors who had stalls here. They would give him a few centavos to entertain them and from this, his fame spread. Only a classical stone arch outside of the main shopping center exists from the earlier structure. Now, you'll find several levels of shopping, mostly aimed at the middle and upper-middle class. This mall is a great place to bring kids, with its extensive food court, enormous arcades for video games, and especially the very fun **Museo de Los Niños,** located in the food court (p. 154). Located in what was once one of Buenos Aires' main Jewish neighborhoods, you'll also find several kosher fast food restaurants here, including the only kosher McDonald's in the world outside of Israel (p. 127). There is also a large cinema complex here. Abasto is open Monday through Sunday from 10am to 10pm, though the food court and cinemas are open later. Av. Corrientes 3247, at Agüero. ✆ 11/4959-3400. www.altopalermo.com.ar (click on "Abasto"). Metro: Gardel.

Alto Palermo   Located on Santa Fe in the Barrio Norte shopping area, Alto Palermo offers several floors of shopping, with about 155 stores and services. This mall is significantly less touristy than the Galerías Pacífico. The mall's design is not very straightforward and the connections between levels can be confusing. If shopping with children, this is one that they can easily become lost in. Alto Palermo is open daily from 10am to 10pm. Av. Santa Fe and Coronel Díaz. ✆ 11/5777-8000. www.altopalermo.com.ar. Metro: Agüemes.

Buenos Aires Design Recoleta 𝕶𝕶   One of my favorite malls in Buenos Aires, home-design connoisseurs should head here immediately. This small, elegant mall, located behind the Recoleta Cemetery, houses several home-design stores offering high-quality, high-design items, almost all of which are produced in Argentina. The best of all is **Tienda Puro Diseño Argentino** (p. 211), a store where over 120 designers work on the various products. Behind a frosted-glass wall, you may be able to see silhouettes of the various designers at work on computers creating the next line of goods available in the store. The idea for the store came from a highly successful exposition of the same name. Ironically, the peso crisis has created good opportunities for local designers to work, as importing goods from overseas has become too expensive. The mall is both indoors and outdoors, with the outdoor section called "La Terrazza," though some people call it "Los Arcos" because of the archways lining this area. It's also a pleasant place to relax and have a coffee after seeing the nearby cemetery. There are often changing sculpture exhibits in the gardens. Hours are Monday through Saturday from 10am to 9pm, Sunday and holidays from noon to 9pm. Av. Pueyrredón 2501, at Libertador. © 11/5777-6000. No metro access.

Galerías Pacífico 𝕶𝕶𝕶   Located on Calle Florida, the pedestrian walking street in the Microcentro, the Galerías Pacífico is probably the most famous mall in Buenos Aires. Architecturally, it is stunning, designed to recall the Galleria Vittorio Emanuele II in Milan, with its long halls, glass cupola, and several tiers of shops. First opened in 1891, in 1945 its main dome was covered with stunning frescoes painted by local artists. There are over 180 shops here, and they offer a free service where all your purchases can be sent to your hotel, so you can shop without the schlep. But Galerías Pacífico is more than shopping: The building also houses the Centro Cultural Borges, where you can see shows, check out art displays, take tango lessons, and see performances by Julio Bocca's Ballet Argentino. It's open daily from 10am to 10pm. Calle Florida 750, at Av. Córdoba. © 11/5555-5110. Metro: San Martín.

Jumbo Palermo Commercial Center   This mall is near the polo grounds, but is mostly of interest only if you plan on staying long-term in Buenos Aires and renting an apartment. Most of the stores are home-related, with a few clothing stores in the mix. The highlight of the mall is **Easy,** an Ikea-like store full of inexpensive furniture, construction material, and other things for settling in. The center is open daily from 10am to 10pm. Av. Bullrich and Cerviño. © 11/4778-8000. Metro: Palermo.

Patio Bullrich *(Overrated*   This mall is considered one of the most exclusive in Buenos Aires, but most shoppers might find the stores to generally be middle of the road, catering to the middle and upper-middle classes rather than the truly wealthy. If looking for really exclusive shopping, you'd do better checking out the boutiques on nearby Alvear. There is, however, an excellent food court here full of the ladies-who-lunch crowd and local businesspeople talking deals. The mall is located in a historic building, and the Libertador facade is worth taking a look at. Hours are Monday through Saturday from 10am to 9pm, Sunday and holidays noon to 9pm. Posadas 1245, at Libertad, with the historic facade facing Libertador. © 11/4814-7400. No metro access.

4 Other Shopping Highlights & Centers

You'll find all kinds of interesting indoor shopping areas in Buenos Aires. Check those below out for their architecture, interesting atmosphere from decades past, or their extreme exclusivity. Hours will vary in each of these as each store within these centers sets its own hours, but most will be open weekdays from 10am to 5pm.

Galería Guemes *(Finds)* This is a sumptuous building, though its modern entrance on Calle Florida would make you think otherwise. Its back entrance on Calle San Martín, however, still retains all of its original glory. Galería Guemes is a shopping gallery with a mix of stores and kiosks without distinction, but it is the building itself, with its incredible ornamentation, that is worth coming in for. The architecture is a mix of Art Nouveau, Gothic, and neoclassical, all heavily ornamented, and was the creation of the architect who designed the now-closed Confitería del Molino next door to Congreso. The building also houses the Piazzolla tango show, which is held in the basement-level theater. It had been closed for nearly 40 years and was only recently restored. Of all of the tango show palaces in Buenos Aires, this is the most beautiful. Calle Florida 165, at Perón. Metro: Florida.

Galería Promenade Alvear Naturally, any place attached to the Alvear Palace Hotel is going to be exclusive. You'll find wedding shops, jewelry stores, and antiques and art boutiques, as well as a few clothing stores here. Store hours here vary tremendously, with some shops only open on weekdays and some closing during lunch hours. Others are by appointment only. Each store has a phone number on its window, so if things are closed, write it down and call, or ask the Alvear's concierge for more information. The back of L'Orangerie, the Alvear's lobby restaurant, opens into the central courtyard of the shopping area, making for a pleasant place to grab a coffee. Av. Alvear 1883, at Ayacucho; attached to the Alvear Hotel. No metro access.

Paseo Obelisco This shopping complex and underground pedestrian causeway (which you may have to pass through at some point on your trip anyway) is worth a short trip in itself. Paris, New York, London, and virtually every major city with a subway once had similar underground complexes, but this area under the Obelisco, where three subway lines meet, seems to have been unchanged since the 1960s. The shops are nothing special—several barber shops, shoe-repair spots, and stores selling cheap clothing and other goods make up the bulk of them. Yet, together, with their cohesive old signs, fixtures, and furnishings, they look like the setting for a movie. Subway entrances surrounding the Obelisco along Av. 9 de Julio. Metro: Carlos Pellegrini, Diagonal Norte, or 9 de Julio.

San Telmo Market *(Moments)* Though this is definitely a place to shop, the building is also worth seeing on its own. The San Telmo market opened in 1897, and it is a masterpiece not just for its soaring wrought-iron interior, but for the atmosphere of decades ago you still find here. Half of the market is made up of things that locals need—butchers, fresh-fruit-and-vegetable grocers, and little kiosks selling sundries and household items. This part looks like the kind of place your grandmother probably shopped in when she was a child. I recommend chatting with the staff in these places, who seem to have all the time in the world. The other half is more touristy, but never overly so, with various antiques and vintage-clothing shops. There are several entrances to this large market, almost a block in size but squeezed between several other historic buildings. It's open daily from 10am to 8pm, but each stand has individual hours. 961 Defensa or Bolívar 998, both at Carlos Calvo. Metro: Independencia.

5 Shopping A to Z

ANTIQUES

Throughout the streets of San Telmo, you will find the city's best antiques shops; don't miss the antiques market that takes place all day Sunday at Plaza Dorrego (see "Outdoor Markets," above). There are also a number of fine antiques stores along Avenida Alvear and Suipacha in Recoleta, including a collection of boutique shops at **Galería Alvear,** Av. Alvear 1777. Take note that many of the stores listed in our art section in this chapter also sell antiques among their various collections. Antiques and art stores along Calle Arroyo and its surroundings in Recoleta near the Israeli Embassy Monument also participate in **Gallery Night.** This event is held on the last Friday of every month (though not always in Jan–Feb in the summer season) and during it, antiques and art stores stay open late, often offering tea and coffee for patrons, and the streets are closed to traffic, creating a comfortable walking environment for exploring. There is also usually a full moon around this time, so if you're here as a couple, it can be a romantic shopping experience. Keep in mind that most of the museums in Buenos Aires have high-quality art and replica shops in their lobbies, so you might find interesting art and gifts there as well.

Calle Antigua ★★ This store sells religious art, chandeliers, furniture, and other decorative objects. The owner is José Manuel Piñeyro, and he opened his shop more than 20 years ago. He now has two storefronts, both on the same block of Calle Defensa. The stores accept cash and foreign checks, but no credit cards. Both stores are open daily from 10am to 7pm. Calle Defensa 914 and Calle Defensa 974, at Estados Unidos. (11/4300-8782 or 11/15-4472-4158 (cell). Metro: Independencia.

Del Buen Ayre Because this store concentrates on small decorative objects, you're more likely to find an item in this antiques store that can either be carried on the plane with you or packed into your luggage. Most items are turn-of-the-20th-century knickknacks, bronzes, and glass pieces. Cash is preferred here, though checks are accepted. Open daily from 11:30am to 8pm. Bolívar 929, at Estados Unidos. (11/4361-4534, 11/4921-8280, or 11/15-4179-7419 (cell). Metro: Independencia.

Galería El Solar de French Built in the early 20th century in a Spanish colonial style, this is where Argentine patriot Domingo French lived. Today it's a gallery, with antiques shops and photography stores depicting the San Telmo of yesteryear. Calle Defensa 1066, at Humberto I. Metro: Independencia.

Jorge Gudiño Antigüedades Jorge Gudiño, with over 20 years experience selling antiques, opened this store in 1991. The store has beautiful pieces of antique high-end furniture and also displays it in interesting ways, making it more visually appealing than many other stores on the street, and helping you gain ideas

---

Tips **Shopping Tip**

Most antiques stores will come down 10% to 20% from the listed price if you bargain. It is almost impossible to pay for antiques with a credit card in Buenos Aires; virtually no store will accept them, largely because of Customs and tax issues. However, international checks, once verified, are usually accepted by almost all San Telmo stores. Cold cash, of course, is never an issue whether pesos, dollars, or euros.

on how to use various pieces at home. Only cash and overseas checks are accepted. The store is open Sunday through Friday from 10:30am to 7pm. Calle Defensa 1002, at Carlos Calvo. © 11/4362-0156. Metro: Independencia.

Pallarols ⚘ Located in San Telmo, Pallarols sells an exquisite collection of Argentine silver and other antiques. The Pallarols family represents six genera- tions of silversmithing. Their work is featured in various museums in Buenos Aires, and family members will sometimes conduct silversmith workshops at museum stores. Calle Defensa 1015, at Carlos Calvo. © 11/4362-5438. www.pallarols.com.ar. Metro: Independencia.

ART STORES & GALLERIES

Atelier Estudio Casa de la Villa   This gallery sells very high-end art depicting country life, Pampas scenes, and many polo scenes painted by various artists, including Gustavo Rovira, whose artwork is featured in La Rural and Opera Pampa. If you are seeking art that represents Argentina, this is worth going to, though it is not in the center of the city. Gualeguaychú 4104, at Pareja. © 11/4501-7846 or 11/15-5023-0263 (cell). www.rovirarte.com.ar. No metro access.

Buddha Ba Asian Art Gallery   Located in Belgrano's small but delightful Chi- natown, this Asian art gallery is attached to a Chinese teahouse and offers high- quality Asian art and antiques. Arripeña 2288, at Mendoza. © 11/4706-2382. Metro: Juramento.

Galería Ruth Benzacar   This avant-garde gallery, in a hidden underground space at the start of Calle Florida next to Plaza San Martín, hosts exhibitions of local and national interest. Among the best-known Argentines who have appeared here are Alfredo Prior, Miguel Angel Ríos, Daniel García, Graciela Hasper, and Pablo Siguier. Calle Florida 1000, overlooking Plaza San Martín. © 11/4313-8480. Metro: San Martín.

Jorge Oliva Antigüedades y Arte   Tucked into a gallery along Suipacha, near the Israeli Embassy Monument, this small gallery offers an interesting art collection including local Argentine and some European artists as well as small antiques and decorative objects. The museum participates in the Recoleta Arroyo Street Gallery Night, held on the last Friday of every month. Suipacha 1409, at Arroyo, Space 11. © 11/4390-4401. No metro access.

Julio Chaile Arte   Julio Chaile has worked as an artist all over the world, and his art has a modern, pop-inspired feel to it. He also creates interesting paint-by- numbers-style works of famous Argentines, which make great conversation pieces for collectors and travelers. Paraguay 964, 2L, at Av. 9 de Julio. © 11/4328-2330 (call for appointment). Metro: Lavalle.

Museo Casa—Taller de Celia Chevalier ⚘⚘   I don't get excited about much in La Boca, but I highly recommend this place, a boutique and house museum of an artist located just 2 blocks from El Caminito. Ms. Chevalier grew up in Buenos Aires and creates whimsical paintings based on her childhood memories. She is charming and open, though she only speaks Spanish. She also looks strikingly like Meryl Streep, and has a face with the capability of as many expressions. The house is a restored *conventillo*, the type of house that Italian immigrants moved into when they came to Buenos Aires before the turn of the 20th century. The house dates from 1885 and was made into her studio museum in 1998. Credit cards are not accepted for art purchases. There is a 65¢ entry fee. It's open Saturday, Sun- day, and holidays from 2 to 7pm; call for an appointment on other days. Irala 1162, at Calle Olavarria. © 11/4302-2337. celia_chevalier@yahoo.com.ar. No metro access.

Calle Florida Shopping

Ashanti Leather Factory **9**
Chabeli **7**
Distal Libros **10**
El Boyero **3**
Galería Guemes **11**
Galería Ruth Benzacar **1**
Galerías Pacífico **4**
Libros Cuspide **8**
MoviCom–BellSouth **5**
Prüne **2**
Tonel Privado **6**

Silvia Freire, Espacio de Arte y Cultura   A little bit religious, a little bit New Age-y, this avant-garde art gallery is housed in a performance space in Palermo Viejo. While largely meant for theater presentations, you will find a large collection of art for sale here in the building hanging along the walls and on tables. Silvia Freire is considered a bit of a mystic and eccentric and is interesting to meet if she happens to be in the building when you arrive. Open Wednesday and Thursday from 10am to 3pm. Cabrera 4849, at Acevedo. (*C* 11/4831-1441. Metro: Plaza Italia.

BOOKSTORES

Asunto Impreso 👁👁   Its location in the Centro Cultural Recoleta is one indication that this is a bookstore of distinction, and its tagline, "bookstore for the imagination," is another. You'll find very high quality educational and art books here, many of specific interest to the tourist looking to go a little deeper into the history and culture of Buenos Aires. Junín 1930, in Centro Cultural Recoleta. (*C* 11/4805-5585. www.asuntoimpreso.com. No metro access.

Clasica y Moderna 👁👁   Housed in a restaurant, this place represents an interesting way to save an important bookstore from extinction by placing a restaurant inside to increase traffic. The bookstore opened in this location in 1938, though the company dates from 1918. Emilio Robert Diaz was the original owner, and now his grandchildren run it. In 1988 books were relegated to the back to make way for diners, but it is one of the best bookstores for English-speaking tourists in the city. You'll find Buenos Aires photo and history books, as well as Argentine short-story collections, all translated into English. Events of all kinds are held here too, from literary readings to plays, dance shows, and art exhibitions. Open Monday through Saturday 9am to 1am and Sunday from 5pm to 1am. Callao 892, at Córdoba. (*C* 11/4812-8707 or 11/4811-3670. www.clasicaymoderna.com. Metro: Callao.

Distal Libros   Distal is one of Buenos Aires's largest chain bookstores, with branches throughout the city including several on the pedestrianized Calle Florida. They have a large selection of English-language books, including plenty of Frommer's books. Open Monday through Friday from 8am to 10pm, Saturday from 10am to 10pm, and Sunday from 10am to 9pm. Florida 436, at Lavalle (and many other locations on Calle Florida and other areas). (*C* 11/5218-4372. www.distalnet.com. Metro: Lavalle.

Librería de Las Madres—Café Literario Osvaldo Bayer 👁👁   This combination bookstore and cafe offers what few places in Buenos Aires can—the ability to speak with people who have had family members disappear during Argentina's military dictatorship. You'll also find young students who come here to study and continue seeking justice in this cause. The Madres bookstore is just to the side of the cafe, and it's full of books and newspapers on liberal causes from throughout Latin America. It also has one of the largest collections of books on Che Guevara anywhere in the world. An Argentine native, he is a personal hero to many of the Madres, and his image adorns walls throughout the building. In addition to books, there are posters, pamphlets, and other items here, all with a very socialist slant. Open Monday through Friday from 10am to 10pm, Saturday from 10am to 8pm. Hipólito Yrigoyen 1584, at Ceballos. (*C* 11/4382-3261. Metro: Congreso.

Librería Fausto   This independent bookseller in the Corrientes book district has both used and new books. You'll find a lot of good Spanish-language literature books here at bargain prices, and a few English-language used books as well. Av. Corrientes 1243, at Libertad. (*C* 11/4382-9257. Metro: Tribunales.

Librería Santa Fe   This store, which is part of a chain, has a large selection of books on Buenos Aires and Argentina, travel guides, and many books in English,

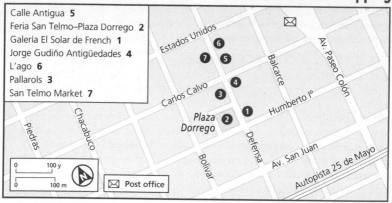

Calle Antigua **5**
Feria San Telmo–Plaza Dorrego **2**
Galería El Solar de French **1**
Jorge Gudiño Antigüedades **4**
L'ago **6**
Pallarols **3**
San Telmo Market **7**

⊠ Post office

mostly bestsellers. Av. Santa Fe 2376, at Pueyrredón. © **11/4827-0100**. www.lsf.com.ar. Metro: Pueyrredón.

Librería Sigal Close to the Abasto Shopping Center, this Jewish bookstore and Judaica shop has been in business for over 70 years, in an area that was once a major Jewish immigration center. Books are mostly in Hebrew and Spanish. They also sell menorahs, yarmulkes, and other items of Jewish interest. Only cash is accepted. Open Monday through Thursday from 10am to 1pm and 3 to 7:30pm, Friday from 10am to 4:30pm. Av. Corrientes 2854, at Ecuador. © **11/4861-9501** or 11/4865-7208. www.libreria-sigal.com. Metro: Gardel.

Librerías Turísticas Every and any kind of tourism book on Argentina and other parts of the world can be found in this store. The company is itself both a publisher and seller of books. Open Monday through Friday from 9am to 7pm, Saturday from 9am to 1pm. Paraguay 2457, at Pueyrredon. © **11/4963-2866** or 11/4962-5547. www.libreriaturistica.com.ar. Metro: Pueyrredón.

Libros Cuspide One of the biggest chains in Buenos Aires, you won't have any trouble finding one of their branches in the Microcentro, Barrio Norte, or other neighborhoods and other cities in Argentina. I list here the Calle Florida one, with its large selection of books on Argentina, which are of interest to the tourist who's seeking to learn a little more about the country. Calle Florida 628, at Tucumán. © **11/4328-0575**. www.cuspide.com. Metro: San Martín.

CAMERAS & ACCESSORIES
Cosentino If you need something for your camera, are looking for a new one, or need high-quality developing services, Cosentino offers it all. They also do camera repairs. Av. Roque Sáenz Peña (Diagonal Norte) 738, at Perón. © **11/4328-9120**. Metro: Catedral.

CELLPHONES
Altel This is a cellphone-rental company aimed at tourists. They offer free delivery and rental; you pay only for calls. Be aware, however, that while a tremendous convenience, cellphone rentals are expensive in Buenos Aires, and you should always read the fine print no matter what company you choose or how good the offer seems to be. Av. Córdoba 417, 1st floor, at Reconquista. © **11/4311-5000**. www.altel phonerental.com. No metro access.

MoviCom–BellSouth While they mostly sell to locals, foreigners can arrange for pay-as-you-go phones and keep the cellular when they leave Buenos Aires.

Using a card-value input system, this method can be significantly cheaper than using a standard tourist rental service. Galerías Pacífico (main level), Calle Florida 750, at Av. Córdoba. ℂ 11/5555-5239. Metro: San Martín.

EYEGLASSES & CONTACT LENSES

Saracco   Fast, high-quality vision services are available at Saracco. The eye exam is included in the price of eyeglasses here. Eyeglasses and contact lenses cost about a third of what they do in North America, though some designer frames will have similar prices. They have various branches surrounding Plaza San Martín. Interestingly, because of the large number of descendants of Italian immigrants in Buenos Aires, you'll find the Zyloware Sophia Loren collection is popular and well featured in this and many other eyeglass stores in the city. Juncal 821, near Plaza San Martín. ℂ 11/4393-1000. Metro: San Martín.

FASHION & APPAREL

Palermo is fast becoming the place for boutiques showcasing young designers who seem to have done well in spite of, or perhaps because of, the peso crisis. Argentines can no longer really afford to import their clothing, and this has been a boon to local industry, though a recent trade agreement with China may mean that cheap Chinese clothes might flood the market soon, destroying this wonderful homegrown trend. For now, get the Argentina-made goods while you can, as they are some of the country's most interesting products. Women's fashion here is, as a whole, flirty, fun, and above all, feminine. Though it is mostly made for thin figures, I do list a plus-size shop below as well. You will find the city's top international fashion stores along Avenida Alvear and Calle Quintana in Recoleta. The larger fashion stores in Recoleta tend to take credit cards and have set hours. Many smaller Palermo boutiques will take select credit cards, but many only accept cash. You'll also find most boutiques closed on Sundays, and, in Palermo in particular, hours can sometimes be just a suggestion because of a shop's small staff. If you find a boutique you really like in Palermo, it's often possible to speak directly with the owner about her designs and products and see what new things might be coming up. For women, Palermo shopping can be a very rewarding and unique experience.

Aristocracia   Enter this casually elegant store and the first things you'll notice are the red wall treatments and luxurious yet casual feel. Lucrecia Gamundi designs most of the items here and has them produced in Argentina. The store also imports other clothes from France, Italy, and other countries. Their Las Cañitas store is new, opened in late 2004, but they had been in Recoleta for 10 years before that. The service is excellent in this store. They are also well known for their interesting window displays. Open Monday through Saturday from 10am to 9pm. Av. Arguibel 2867, at Arce. ℂ 11/4772-1144. Metro: Carranza.

Bakú 🍴🍴 (𝒱𝒶𝓁𝓊ℯ)   All the designs in Bakú are the brainchild of Liliana Basili, who opened her own store in 2003 in the Las Cañitas neighborhood of Palermo. She produces unique pocketbooks, leather accessories, belts and belt buckles, and various items of jewelry. All the items are produced in Argentina. Though her shop is in an expensive part of the city, everything here is priced very reasonably. The shop is open Monday from 1 to 10pm and Tuesday through Saturday from 10am to 10pm. Av. Arguibel 2890, at Arce. ℂ 11/4775-5570. Metro: Carranza.

Câlin Lingerie 🍴   If you forgot to pack a little something romantic or are on your honeymoon, stop into this elegant lingerie shop in the Alvear gallery attached to the Alvear Palace Hotel. Most items are handmade, many using Italian fabrics. For most of the lingerie items, once something is made and sells out, the designs are never repeated, meaning items are quite one of a kind. Lingerie items run about $80, and sexy slippers about $30. Open Monday through Saturday from 10:30am to 7:30pm. Av. Alvear 1883, Local 18, in the Galería Promenade Alvear attached to the Alvear Palace Hotel. ✆ 11/4804-9383. No metro access.

Emporio Armani   This store has suits, street clothing, and all kinds of accessories from this famous Italian retailer. The two-story building is one of the most beautiful on Alvear. Open Monday to Saturday from 10am to 8pm. Av. Alvear 1750, at Callao. ✆ 11/4812-2880. No metro access.

Ermenegildo Zegna   This famous Italian chain sells outstanding suits and jackets made of light, cool fabrics. If you've landed in Buenos Aires without your suit, this is among your best options. Open Monday through Friday from 10am to 8pm, Saturday 10am to 1:30pm. Av. Alvear 1920, at Ayacucho. ✆ 11/4804-1908. No metro access.

Escada   You can find casual and elegant selections of women's clothing combining quality and comfort in this boutique shop. Open Monday through Friday from 10am to 7:30pm, Saturday 10am to 1pm. Av. Alvear 1444, at Libertad. ✆ 11/4814-0292. No metro access.

Florentina Muraña 🏖🏖 (Finds)   This wonderful little store in Palermo Soho takes its name from a character in a Borges story that took place in Palermo. You'll find very pretty, feminine clothing made of interesting materials here. Some examples of the offerings include popcorn shag sweaters handmade in Argentina from Italian wool, and crystal jewelry, some made to look like ornamental insects such as ladybugs and butterflies. The owner is Gabriela Sivori, and she works in the shop and designs some of the items for sale, all of which are made strictly in Argentina. Open daily from 11:30am to 8pm, though hours fluctuate in the summer. Calle Borges 1760, at Pasaje Russel. ✆ 11/4833-4137. No metro access.

Nana Lou 🏖 (Finds)   Mariana Lopez Osornio owns this small boutique in the Las Cañitas area of Palermo for which she has designed much of the clothing. Pretty and feminine is the rule here, and many designs also come from Italy. Jewelry is also part of the offerings. The store does run on the expensive side, with necklaces averaging about $30 to $50, but the designs are excellent. Open late, this is a good shopping option if you happen to be dining on Calle Báez, which is much better known for its restaurants than its stores. Open Sunday through Friday from noon to 1am, Saturday from noon to 2am. Calle Báez 283, at Arevalo. ✆ 11/4772-7826. www.mlo.com.ar. Metro: Carranza.

Nike Soho   From the outside, this small Nike store appears to be an art gallery, and to be sure, while the selection is sparse, it is artfully displayed. The feminine, floral wallpaper and colorings belie the impact of the sports clothing and sneakers you'll find here. Open Monday through Saturday from 10am to 8pm. Honduras 4899, at Gurruchaga. ✆ 11/4832-3555. No metro access.

Polo Ralph Lauren   This is the Buenos Aires branch of the famous American luxury retailer. You will find slightly lower prices here than in North America or Europe. The building, an old turn-of-the-20th-century Art Nouveau mansion, is also a reason to come shopping here: The ornate wooden trim and balustrades remain, and a stained-glass skylight oversees the whole shop. Open Monday to Saturday 10am to 8pm. Av. Alvear 1780, at Callao. ✆ 11/4812-3400. www.poloralph lauren.com.ar. No metro access.

Porto Fem Talles Grandes   Who says big girls can't have fashion fun? While most of the clothes in Buenos Aires seem aimed at top-heavy stick figures, this store offers the same styles in plus sizes. Open Monday through Friday from 9:30am to 7:30pm, Saturday from 10am to 1:30pm. Maipú 842, at Córdoba. © **11/ 4893-2908**. www.portofem.com. Metro: San Martín.

Prüne 劍劍   This is a chain with additional stores in Alto Palermo, Patio Bull-rich, and many other locations in town and throughout Argentina, but the Florida store is among their largest. It's great for women's accessories and small leather goods, and carries some of the best purses in all of Buenos Aires. Most of the purses run about $65. The store has a light, airy feel and even a back patio. Most of the things here are Argentine products but a few are Chinese-made. Open daily from 10am to 11pm. Calle Florida 963, at Plaza San Martín. © **11/4893-2634**. Metro: San Martín.

Rapsodia   There are many branches of this chain of women's clothing stores, which tends to exhibit exotic fabrics and displays, with virtually all of their items made in Argentina. More than six of these stores exist throughout Buenos Aires, but they have two large stores on the same street in Las Cañitas, one selling new clothing, the other mainly vintage. Open daily from 10am to 9pm. Av. Arguibel 2899 and Av. Arguibel 2860, both at Arce. © **11/4772-2716** or 11/4772-7676. Metro: Carranza.

Shesh 劍 *(Finds*   This is a funky little store where Brady Bunch–style multicolored underwear is the highlight. They are strictly a women's store, but their racy ads show men wearing the clothing. The styles here are best for very young women, and they have many teen and 'tween customers. In addition to fashion, they also offer a few women's accessories and jewelry. The designer is Silvana Troncoso, who is considered a rising young designer in the city. All the clothes are made in Argentina. The store has a "Power Puff Girl" feel to it, with its hot-pink decor and fashion-with-a-punch philosophy. This store opened in August 2004, and they now have plans to open a few branches around the city. Open daily from 11am to 8pm, though hours fluctuate in the summer. Pasaje Russel 5005, at Borges. © **11/4831- 8186**. www.shesh.com.ar. No metro access.

GROCERY STORES

Hua Xia   Located in Belgrano's small but pleasing Chinatown, you'll find reg-ular groceries here along with lots of Chinese, Korean, and Japanese products. Open Monday through Saturday from 8:30am to 9:30pm, Sunday and holidays from 9:30am to 9:30pm. Arripeña 2242, at Mendoza. © **11/4782-2628**. Metro: Juramento.

Pekín Supermercado   You'll find convenience stores all over the Microcen-tro area, but to do some more intense grocery shopping and save money in the process, head over to Pekín Supermercado. Here you'll find normal groceries, frozen food, toiletries, wine, *dulce de leche,* and lots of cheap *mate,* the strong herbal tea that Argentines love, so you can shop and eat like a local, and at local prices too. This is a great store to head to if you are renting an apartment in the area, and they also deliver. Open Monday through Saturday from 8am to 10pm, and Sunday from 9:30am to 3pm. Reconquista 543, at Lavalle. © **11/4315-0508**. Metro: Lavalle.

HOME DESIGN

Haz de Luz   The tag line for this store is "Home, Body and Soul." Their prod-ucts concentrate on lamps and home accessories like candles and frames, but they also have women's accessories, like interestingly woven and colorful scarves, jew-elry, and children's items. Virtually all the items are handmade, and almost all are done in Argentina with very few imports. All the items are sold on consignment and are the works of various local artists. Things change here frequently, so if you are in the area, it makes sense to stop by and see what new items they have on display. The store is a little hard to find, tucked into an alleyway along with numerous small interesting stores. It's open daily from 11am to 8pm. The store can close on Monday unexpectedly, and hours fluctuate in the summer. Pasaje Russel 5009, at Borges. No phone. hazdeluzpalermo@hotmail.com. No metro access.

L'ago   Located along the antiques row of San Telmo, this store offers creative and modern designs as well as a few vintage mid-20th-century items. Their main focus is lamps, but they also have an extensive collection of items that can be used for children's rooms or for those with whimsical, young-at-heart tastes. Virtually all of the new items are made in Argentina. Defensa 970, at Estados Unidos. © 11/4362-4702. Metro: Independencia.

Tienda Puro Diseño Argentino ★★★ *Finds*   Tienda Puro Diseño Argentino is in the Recoleta Design Center, the arched shopping area near Recoleta Cemetery. It features very high quality, high-design items created by more than 120 Argentine designers with strictly Argentine materials in Argentina, all at good value. The idea came from a design expo of the same name, which in spite of the country's economic crisis, was successful enough to become a standalone store. They concentrate on home design, but products also include jewelry, fashion, leather accessories, and children's products. Many of the household items have an updated frontier feeling. Leather, one of Argentina's most important products, also plays a strong role in many of the designs. My favorite items are the unusual saddle-shaped backpacks, which more than give Coach a run for their money. Open Monday through Saturday from 10am to 9pm, and Sunday from noon to 9pm. See also the above description of the mall itself, Recoleta Design Center, which has other interesting stores. Av. Pueyrredón 2501, in the Recoleta Design Center, under the arches (Terrazza). © 11/5777-6104 or 11/5777-6107. No metro access.

JEWELRY

The city's finest jewelry stores are in Recoleta and inside many five-star hotels. You can find bargains on gold along Calle Libertad, near Avenida Corrientes. Also, make sure to take a look at our women's fashion section. Many of the small women's boutiques detailed there also carry handmade jewelry produced locally.

Chabeli   This store offers an interesting selection of Argentine jewelry handmade from crystals and semiprecious stones. They also have women's shoes and pocketbooks, with nothing costing more than $75. Designs of both leather accessories and jewelry fall into two main categories: native Argentine to very pretty and feminine, using pink and pastel materials. They also have another branch in the Patagonian resort town of Bariloche. Open Monday through Saturday from 10am to 8pm, Sunday from noon to 7pm. Calle Florida 702, at Viamonte. © 11/4328-0805. Metro: San Martín.

Cousiño Jewels   Located in the Sheraton hotel's shopping arcade, this Argentine jeweler features a brilliant collection of art made of the national stone, the rhodochrosite, or Inca Rose, a beautiful form of milky-pink quartz. Open Monday through Saturday from 9am to 7pm, Sunday from 10am to 6pm. In the Sheraton Buenos Aires Hotel, Av. San Martín 1225, at Alem. © 11/4312-2336 or 11/4313-8881. Metro: Retiro.

H.Stern   This upscale Brazilian jeweler, with branches in major cities around the world, sells an entire selection of South American stones, including emeralds and the unique imperial topaz. H.Stern is the top jeweler in Latin America. The Marriott location is open daily from 9am to 7:30pm, but is sometimes closed weekends in winter. The Sheraton location is open Monday to Friday from 9am to 7:30pm, Saturday and Sunday from 9am to 5pm. In the Marriott Plaza, Calle Florida 1005, overlooking Plaza San Martín (© **11/4318-3083;** Metro: San Martín), and the Sheraton Buenos Aires Hotel, Av. San Martín 1225, at Libertador (© **11/4312-6762;** Metro: Retiro).

KOSHER GROCERS

Autoservicio Ki Tob   This large kosher grocery store also has a kosher meat section. You'll find everything kosher here, from basic staples to junk food. Only cash is accepted. Open Monday through Thursday from 8am to 8pm, Friday from 8am until 2 hours before sunset, and Sunday from 3 to 8pm. Tucumán 2755, at Pueyrredón. © **11/4966-1007.** Metro: Pueyrredón.

Heluini   This small, kosher store with friendly service concentrates on Sephardic Kosher foods, known locally as Oriental Kosher. You'll find spices and other items with a decidedly Middle Eastern flavor here. This is also one of the few places in Buenos Aires that sells peanut butter, a very difficult item to find in Argentina, so if you or the kids are craving it, this is the place to head. The store has been open since 1937. Only cash is accepted. Open Monday through Thursday from 9am to 9pm, Friday from 9am until 2 hours before sunset. Tucumán 2755, at Pueyrredón. © **11/4966-1007.** Metro: Pueyrredón.

LEATHER

With all that beef in its restaurants, Argentina could not be anything but one of the world's best leather centers. If you're looking for high-quality, interestingly designed leather goods, especially women's shoes, accessories, and handbags, few places beat Buenos Aires's selection. Many leather stores will also custom-make jackets and other items for interested customers, so do ask if you see something you like in the wrong size or want to combine ideas from pieces. While most can do this in a day or two, if you are looking to really have something from Argentina, to avoid disappointment, you should start checking out stores and prices early on in case something is complicated to make and might take more time than usual.

Ashanti Leather Factory 𝕽   This small store on Calle Florida offers a wide selection of leather goods, from men's and women's jackets to funky and interesting women's pocketbooks. Their prices on jackets are not the best, but women's accessories are very competitively priced, and you can always bargain. Best of all, their factory is in the basement of the shop, so they can easily custom-make almost anything for you. Ask them for a tour through which you can meet the craftspeople Roberto, Victor, and Oscar, who sit surrounded by sewing machines and colorful bolts of leather. Open daily from 10am to 10pm. Calle Florida 585, at Lavalle. © **11/4394-1310.** Metro: San Martín.

Casa López 𝕽𝕽   Widely considered among the best *marroquinería* (leather-goods shop) in Buenos Aires, Casa López sells an extensive range of Argentine leather products. There is also a shop in the Patio Bullrich Mall. Marcelo T. de Alvear 640, at Maipú, near Plaza San Martín. © **11/4312-8911.** Metro: San Martín.

Chabeli   This store offers a wide selection of women's shoes and pocketbooks, with nothing costing more than $75. They also offer an interesting selection of handmade Argentine jewelry from crystals and semiprecious stones. Designs of both leather accessories and jewelry fall into two main categories: native Argentine to very pretty and feminine, using pink and pastel materials. They also have another branch in the Patagonian resort town of Bariloche. Open Monday through Saturday from 10am to 8pm, and Sunday from noon to 7pm. Calle Florida 702. © **11/4328-0805.** Metro: San Martín.

El Nochero   All the products sold at El Nochero are made with first-rate Argentine leather and manufactured by local workers. Shoes and boots, leather goods and clothes, and decorative silverware (including *mates,* for holding the special herbal tea Argentines love) fill the store. Open Monday through Saturday from 10am to 9pm, Sunday and holidays noon to 9pm. Posadas 1245, in the Patio Bullrich Mall. ✆ 11/4815-3629. No metro access.

Louis Vuitton   The famous Parisian boutique sells an elite line of luggage, purses, and travel bags here. It's located alongside Recoleta's most exclusive shops. Open Monday through Friday from 10am to 8pm, Saturday from 11am to 6pm. Av. Alvear 1901, at Ayacucho. ✆ 11/4802-0809. No metro access.

Rossi & Caruso   This store offers some of the best leather products in the city and is the first choice for visiting celebrities—the king and queen of Spain and Prince Philip of England among them. Products include luggage, saddles, and accessories as well as leather and chamois clothes, purses, wallets, and belts. There is another branch in the Galerías Pacífico mall (p. 201). Av. Santa Fe 1377, at Uruguay. ✆ 11/4811-1965. Metro: Bulnes.

MUSIC

Almacén de Tangos Generales   Tango music and more is available for sale in this small shop overlooking Dorrego Plaza in the heart of San Telmo. CDs of tango music as well as musical scores are here for those who really want to get to know tango music. In addition, they sell plenty of souvenirs like mugs, postcards, spoons, and assorted knickknacks to bring back from your trip. Open Monday through Saturday from 11am to 6pm, and Sunday from 10am to 8pm. Don Anselmo Aieta 1067, at Plaza Dorrego. ✆ 11/4362-7190. Metro: Independencia.

C-Disueria   This music store has a variety of CDs and tapes to cover all music genres. However, it's best selection is tango music at reasonable prices—you should buy a few CDs to listen to at home and help you remember your trip. Corrientes 1274, at Talcahuano. ✆ 11/4381-0754. Metro: Tribunales.

ORGANIC & VEGETARIAN FOOD

Bio   This is an organic restaurant that also has a large selection of organic products one can buy separately. It's a great place for veg-heads to go shopping for snacks to bring back to their hotel. All the ingredients at Bio are organic, and all are grown or produced strictly in Argentina. Their small shop has organic chips, teas, cheeses, and even organic wine. They also do takeout. As healthful as the place is, smoking is allowed, though the management does try to discourage it. Only cash is accepted. Open Tuesday through Sunday from noon to 3:30pm and 8pm to 1am, often later on weekends, and Monday from 8pm to 1am. Humboldt 2199, at Guatemala. ✆ 11/4774-3880. No metro access.

PHARMACY

Farmacia Suiza   You won't have a problem finding places to buy medicine in Buenos Aires, but I recommend this place mostly for its atmosphere. It's an old apothecary, tucked into the Microcentro area. The shelves are ornamented with wooden carvings and lined with old jars and flasks from the turn of the 20th century. Their medicine and services, however, are fully up-to-date. Calle Tucumán 701, at Maipú. ✆ 11/4313-8480. Metro: San Martín.

POLO & GAUCHO CLOTHING & ACCESSORIES

El Boyero   You'll find high-quality, classic-style polo and other clothing inspired by the gaucho (Argentine cowboy) lifestyle here. They also carry a large selection of beautiful leather products made in Argentina. Fine silver gaucho jewelry, knives, and other accessories are also available. They have two branches, one in Galerías Pacífico (p. 201) and the one listed here on Calle Florida. Open Monday through Saturday from 9am to 8pm, but not always open on Sunday. Calle Florida 953, at Plaza San Martín. ℰ 11/4312-3564. Metro: San Martín.

La Matera 👯 *(Finds)* The name of this store comes from a place where gauchos gather to drink *mate* on their breaks while rounding up cows on *estancias* (farms). You'll find high-quality merchandise here with a true Argentine flair. Located in the shadows of the polo grounds, you'll also find a lot of items to wear to events while you hobnob with rich polo enthusiasts. There's also a large collection of silver and other metal items, which make interesting souvenirs from your trip. This family-owned store has another branch in Mar del Plata; this location opened in January 2005. Open Wednesday through Friday from 10:30am to 11:30pm, and Sunday through Tuesday from 1:30 to 10:30pm. Arce 290, at Arevalo. ℰ 11/4772-7523. Metro: Carranza.

TANGO CLOTHES, SHOES & ACCESSORIES

Abasto Plaza Hotel Tango Shop   Whether you're staying at the Abasto Plaza Hotel or not, it's worth taking a look at this store in their lobby for its tango clothing selection, especially the sexy dresses. They also sell tango music and other items. Av. Corrientes 3190, at Anchorena, near the Abasto Shopping Center. ℰ 11/6311-4465. www.abastoplaza.com. Metro: Carlos Gardel.

Carlos Custom Shoes   This is not a shoe store but a man who is a custom crafter of excellent, high-quality tango shoes. If you call, Carlos will come to your hotel to take measurements and then handcraft your shoes for you. His work does take longer than most stores with their own factory, up to 10 days or 2 weeks, so make sure to contact him early in your trip. ℰ 11/4687-6026. No metro access.

Flabella   This is an extremely busy store, selling mostly shoes and other items for tango dancers. They are best for women's shoes, but also offer a variety of men's shoes. Many shoes are in stock for immediate purchase, but many shoe styles have to be custom-made. This can take up to a week, so plan around this for your trip. Shoe prices begin at about $35 a pair. Eduardo is one of their talented shoe technicians, and he can offer tips on the tango scene. The store is also surrounded by several similar ones, so check out this block for the selection. Open Monday through Saturday from 10am to 10pm. Suipacha 263, at Diagonal Norte. ℰ 11/4322-6036. www.flabella.com. Metro: Carlos Pellegrini.

TOYS & CHILDREN'S ITEMS

Ufficio 👯   Most of the products in this store are handmade in Argentina and are solid wood, but they also have a few Chinese imports. Products include lamps, wooden rocking horses, dolls, jigsaw puzzles, guitars, baby bibs, and a few other clothing items. Many of the items are good gifts for kids as an alternative to video games and the usual. Calle Borges 1733, at Pasaje Russel. ℰ 11/4831-5008. No metro access.

VIDEO STORES

Brujas   This store sells hard-to-find vintage Argentine videos, DVDs, and music CDs. Keep in mind that Argentine videos differ from the system used in North America. Calle Rodríguez Peña, at Córdoba. ℰ 11/4373-7100. Metro: Callao.

El Coleccionista   If you're looking for hard-to-find videos, especially of South American and Spanish movies, this is the place to head. Keep in mind that Argentina uses a different VCR system than North America. They also have

DVDs and some used and hard-to-find music. The store is in a district that has numerous similar shops, so foreign-film fanatics will do well to poke around here. Junín 607, at Tucumán. © **11/4373-5684**. Metro: Callao.

Video Express   Located in Retiro Station, this place rents international and local videos and DVDs for about $1 to $3 a day, with a $1 late fee per day. Retiro Station, at main entrance. © **11/4312-2146**. Metro: Retiro.

WEDDING SHOP
Magical Moments   If romance overtakes you while you're in Buenos Aires, or you've already decided to get married here but forgot a few things, head to this store. They custom-make dresses, sometimes in as little as a week. They also have mother-of-the-bride dresses, and jewelry for the bridal party if you need last-minute gifts. Open Monday, Wednesday, and Thursday from 1 to 8pm, Tuesday and Friday from 10am to 8pm, and Saturday from 10am to 2pm. Av. Alvear 1883, in the Galería Promenade Alvear attached to the Alvear Palace Hotel. © **11/4805-2679**. No metro access.

WINE SHOPS
Argentine wineries, particularly those in Mendoza and Salta, produce some excellent wines. Stores selling Argentina wines abound, and three of the best are **Grand Cru,** Av. Alvear 1718; **Tonel Privado,** in the Patio Bullrich Shopping Mall and Galerías Pacífico Mall; and **Winery,** which has branches at L. N. Alem 880 and Av. Del Libertador 500, both downtown.

La Cava de la Brigada   Owned by the restaurant of the same name in San Telmo, this store carries over 350 different wines from more than 40 bodegas or winemakers. Prices range from under $6 a bottle to almost $350. Locally made and imported whiskeys and other hard liquors are kept in an area on the top floor of the store. Open daily from 9:30am to 1:30pm and 4 to 9pm. Bolívar 1008, at Carlos Calvo. © **11/4362-2943**. Metro: Independencia.

WOOL & SWEATERS
Lana's Argentina   The word *lana* is Spanish for "wool." At Lana's Argentina, you'll find a fine selection of Argentine wool sweaters made from the fibers of Patagonian sheep and lambs. They also carry many leather goods and accessories to complement your purchase. Suipacha 984, at Paraguay. © **11/4328-8798**. www.lanas argentina.com.ar. Metro: San Martín.

9

Buenos Aires After Dark

When other cities choose to go to sleep, the darkness makes Buenos Aires come alive. One thing you'll notice immediately in this city is that people love the nightlife. From the Teatro Colón to dimly lit tango salons to the big techno clubs, Buenos Aires offers an exceptional variety of nightlife.

The evening usually begins for Porteños with a play or movie around 8pm followed by a late and long dinner. Then, after 11pm or midnight, it'll be time to visit a bar or two. On Thursday, Friday, and Saturday, it's time to really stay out late, with Porteños hitting big dance clubs and bars in places like Recoleta, Palermo, and Costanera so late that by the time they start walking home, the sun is coming up. The nightlife in summertime is quieter, because most of the town flees to the coast, moving their nocturnal activities to places like Mar del Plata and Punta del Este.

But Buenos Aires's nightlife is not just about clubbing. It also has a large number of cultural activities for the visitor and resident alike. Performing arts in Buenos Aires are centered on the highly regarded Teatro Colón, home to the National Opera, National Symphony, and National Ballet. In addition, there are nearly 40 professional theaters around town (many located along Av. Corrientes between Av. 9 de Julio and Callao and in the San Telmo and Abasto neighborhoods) showing Broadway- and off-Broadway-style hits, Argentine plays, and music reviews, although most are in Spanish. Buy tickets for most productions at the box office or through **Ticketmaster**

(© 11/4321-9700). The **British Arts Centre,** Suipacha 1333 (© **11/4393-0275**), offers productions and movies in English.

For current information on after-dark entertainment, consult the English-language *Buenos Aires Herald,* which lists events that are held in English and Spanish, and often features events held by Irish, British, and North American ex-pats who have moved to Buenos Aires (www.buenosairesherald.com). *Clarín, La Nación,* and many of the major local publications also list events, but only in Spanish. *QuickGuide Buenos Aires,* available in the city's tourism kiosks and in various hotels, also has information on shows, theaters, and nightclubs. *Ciudad Abierta* (www.buenosaires.gov.ar) is a free weekly published by the city government telling what is going on culturally all over the city, but it is in Spanish only. Ciudad Abierta is also an interesting cable-access channel, which, like the weekly, highlights cultural and tourist interests around the city, and is usually channel 73 on hotel cable systems. *Llegas a Buenos Aires* lists culture, arts, tango, and other events. This newspaper is published weekly and distributed free at locations across the city. Visit their website www.llegasabuenosaires.com ahead of time for some listings. The website **www.bsasinsomnio.com.ar** also lists entertainment of all kinds in this city that never sleeps. Additionally, you can ask the Buenos Aires City Tourism offices for the "Funny Night Map," which lists bars and clubs throughout Buenos Aires.

1 The Performing Arts

CULTURAL CENTERS

Asociación Argentina de Cultura Inglesa (British Arts Centre) 𝕽𝕽𝕽

This multifunctional facility was established over 77 years ago by a British ambassador who wanted to do more to promote British culture within Argentina. He was highly successful in his efforts, and today the AACI teaches English to over 25,000 students a year, has several film, theater, culture, and art programs, and generally provides a very welcoming environment for any English speaker who is homesick. Events can range from being completely upper crust (celebrating Shakespeare) to raunchy (*Absolutely Fabulous* TV program showings). Pick up their various brochures and event listings at the center itself, or look up listings in the English-language *Buenos Aires Herald*. Suipacha 1333, at Arroyo. ℂ **11/4393-2004.** www.aaci.org.ar and www.britishartscentre.org.ar. Metro: San Martín.

Centro Cultural de Borges 𝕽𝕽

You can shop all you want in Galerías Pacífico, but if it's culture you're after, you can find it there too. Inside of the shopping mall is this arts center named for Jorge Luis Borges, Argentina's most important literary figure. You'll find art galleries, lecture halls with various events, an art cinema, art bookstore, the **Escuela Argentina de Tango,** which offers a schedule of lessons tourists can take with ease (ℂ **11/4312-4990;** www.eatango.org), and the ballet star **Julio Bocca's Ballet Argentino** performance space and training school full of young ballet stars and their not-to-be-missed performances (ℂ **11/5555-5359;** www.juliobocca.com). Enter through Galerías Pacífico or at the corner of Viamonte and San Martín. ℂ **11/5555-5359.** www.ccborges.com.ar. Metro: San Martín. Various hours and fees.

Centro Cultural Recoleta (Recoleta Cultural Center) 𝕽𝕽

This cultural center is just one door over from the famous Recoleta Cemetery. It hosts Argentine and international art exhibits, experimental theater works, occasional music concerts, and an interactive science museum for children where they are encouraged to touch and play with the displays. The center has recently begun to host controversial and politically oriented artists as well, helping to broaden the definition of what is art in Argentina and defy the center's location in a former church building. Junín 1930, next door to the Recoleta Cemetery. ℂ **11/4803-1041.** No metro access.

Silvia Freire, Espacio de Arte y Cultura

A little bit religious, a little bit New Age-y, this avant-garde art gallery is housed in a performance space in Palermo Viejo. While largely meant for theater presentations, you will find a large collection of art for sale here in the building hanging along the walls and on tables. Silvia Freire is considered a bit of a mystic and eccentric and is interesting to meet if she happens to be in the building when you arrive. Store hours: Wednesday and Thursday 10am to 3pm. Performance hours vary based on programs; call for information. Cabrera 4849, at Acevedo. ℂ **11/4831-1441.** Metro: Plaza Italia.

DANCE, CLASSICAL MUSIC & OPERA

Julio Bocca and Ballet Argentino 𝕽𝕽𝕽

Julio Bocca is Argentina's greatest ballet and dance star, and many of his performances combine tango movements along with classical dance, creating a style uniquely his own, and uniquely Argentine. He runs a studio in the Centro Cultural de Borges for classical dance and ballet performances, as well as another performance space in Teatro Maipo on Calle Esmeralda, offering a range of events from dance to comedy plays. It is hard to catch Mr. Bocca himself in Buenos Aires since he is so often traveling to perform in cities around the world. If he is in town, make sure to book a spot to see one of his shows. Even when he is not around, his Ballet Argentino troupe is an absolute

Buenos Aires After Dark

do-not-miss for lovers of ballet and dance, especially the performances featuring Claudia Figaredo and Hernan Piquin. Ballet Argentino at the Centro Cultural Borges, within Galerías Pacífico at the corner of Viamonte and San Martín. ℂ **11/5555-5359**. www.juliobocca. com. Tickets $5–$19. Metro: San Martín. Teatro Maipo spaces at Teatro Maipo at Esmeralda 449, at Corrientes. ℂ **11/4394-5521**. Metro: Lavalle.

Luna Park   Once the home of international boxing matches, the Luna is the largest indoor stadium in Argentina and as such it hosts the biggest shows and concerts in Buenos Aires. Many of these are classical music concerts, and the National Symphonic Orchestra often plays here. Bouchard 465, at Corrientes. ℂ **11/4311-1990** or 11/4311-5100. Tickets $3–$15. Metro: L. N. Alem.

Teatro Colón   Known across the world for its impeccable acoustics, the Colón has attracted the world's finest opera performers—Luciano Pavarotti, Julio Bocca, Maria Callas, Plácido Domingo, and Arturo Toscanini among them. Opera season in Buenos Aires runs from April to November. The Colón has its own philharmonic orchestra, ballet, and choir companies. The main theater seats 3,000. Take note that the theater is undergoing a renovation and will be closed for almost all of 2006 and 2007 in preparation for its reopening (and 100th anniversary) in 2008. If you're in town and the theater is open, make time to see a performance here, keeping in mind that ticket sales are somewhat frustrating. You cannot buy tickets more than 2 days in advance, so one of the first things you should do on arrival in Buenos Aires, assuming the theater is open when you're here, is head to the theater in order to see what is playing and what is available. The management has claimed it will upgrade the theater's computer systems to allow for 30-day advance purchases on tickets as well as Internet sales, but I wouldn't hold my breath. Calle Libertad 621, at Tucumán. ℂ **11/4378-7100**. www.teatrocolon.org.ar. Tickets $2–$15. Metro: Tribunales.

THEATERS

Grupo de Teatro Catalinas Sur   Outdoor weekend theater is presented in La Boca by this theater company. Though mostly comedy and in Spanish, both adults and children are likely to enjoy the humorous productions. Av. Benito Pérez Galdós 93, at Caboto. ℂ **11/4300-5707**. www.catalinasur.com.ar. Tickets $1–$5. No metro access.

Teatro Coliseo   This Recoleta theater puts on classical music productions. Marcelo T. de Alvear 1125, at Cerrito. ℂ **11/4816-5943**. Tickets $2–$8. Metro: San Martín.

Teatro Gran Rex   Within this large theater, you'll be able to see many national and foreign music concerts. Av. Corrientes 857, at Suipacha. ℂ **11/4322-8000**. Tickets $3–$9. Metro: Carlos Pellegrini.

Teatro Municipal General San Martín   This entertainment complex has three theaters offering drama, comedy, ballet, music, and children's plays. Its lobby often has special exhibitions of photography and art related to the theater and is worth a special visit during the daytime on its own. These exhibitions are usually free. Corrientes 1530, at Paraná. ℂ **0800/333-5254**. Tickets $3–$9. Metro: Uruguay.

Teatro Nacional Cervantes   Some of the city's best theater takes place here in this production house originally built by a group of Spanish actors as a thank-you to Buenos Aires. The building is itself sumptuous, executed in an ornate Spanish Imperial style using materials brought from Spain. Calle Libertad 815, at Córdoba. ℂ 11/ **4816-4224**. Tickets $3–$15. Metro: Tribunales.

Teatro Opera   This theater has been adapted for Broadway-style shows. Av. Corrientes 860, at Suipacha. ℂ **11/4326-1335**. Tickets $2–$14. Metro: Carlos Pellegrini.

Teatro Presidente Alvear   You'll find tango and other music shows at this theater. Av. Corrientes 1659, at Montevideo. © **11/4374-6076.** Tickets $3–$16. Metro: Callao.

2 Dance Clubs

Dancing in Buenos Aires is not just about tango; in fact, the majority of the younger population prefers salsa and European techno. Of course, nothing in life changes quite so fast as the "in" discos, so ask around for the latest hot spots. The biggest nights out in Buenos Aires are Thursday, Friday, and Saturday. Young women should take note that young Argentine men can be very aggressive in their approach techniques in bars and nightclubs. Most of the advances are harmless, however, even if they may be annoying. Be aware that at the time that this book was being researched and written, a horrible nightclub fire had recently killed about 200 people. As a result, all clubs in Buenos Aires had been shut down for fire inspections and new safety equipment and procedures. Virtually all clubs have reopened during 2005, with only a few still addressing fire inspection issues. However, just to make sure, you should check before stepping out that wherever you want to go is indeed still open.

Asia de Cuba ⊛   Come early for a meal at this supper club and you can then entertain yourself with sophisticated drinking and dancing afterward. Like Mambo, it's another place where women are not as likely to be harassed by men on the prowl. Some of the entertainment, though, can be wild—of the women-dancing-in-cages variety. P. Dealessi 750, at Guemes on Dique 3. © **11/4894-1328** or 11/4894-1329. www.asiadecuba.com.ar. No metro access.

Buenos Aires News   This is a rocking late-night club with Latin and European mixes. It is a multifunction complex, where you can dine, come for drinks, and then party until the sun comes up. One of the largest dance clubs in the city, it can hold over 3,000 people. Av. del Libertador 3883, at Bullrich. © **11/6771-6154** or 11/15-4969-2198 (cell). Metro: Palermo.

Chicharrón Disco Bar ⊛⊛   This is a wild Dominican salsa club, which mostly packs in locals who have relocated to Buenos Aires from the Caribbean. There's even a mini-restaurant inside serving some of the best Caribbean dishes in town, but you'll have to ask because they don't mention this secret place unless they like you! In the back, if you don't feel like dancing, there are a few pool tables to while away the time. Bartolomé Mitre 1849, at Callao. © **11/4373-4884.** Metro: Callao.

Mambo ⊛   Ladies who just want to dance and avoid the usual lechery of Argentine men can head to this club, with its Latin shows and Latin dancing. Many women over 40 head here, often in groups. They also offer Caribbean food from 8pm on. Báez 243, at Arguibel. © **11/4778-0115.** www.mambobar.com.ar. Metro: Carranza.

Opera Bay ⊛⊛   Located literally on the water on a pier jutting into Puerto Madero's harbor, Opera Bay is presently one of the top spots among the city's clubs, attracting an affluent and fashionable crowd. Built to resemble the Sydney opera house, it features an international restaurant, tango show, and disco. Many of the club's patrons are over 40, so this is an ideal place for people who don't want to be around too many crazy young people. Cecilia Grierson 225, at Dealessi in Dique 4 (Dock 4). No phone. Metro: Alem.

Salsón   Some of the city's best salsa dancers stop into this place to boogie the night away. If you want to improve your step, they also offer lessons on Wednesday and Friday at 9pm. Av. Alvarez Thomas 1166, at El Cano. © **11/4637-6970.** Metro: Federico Lacroze.

Club Deaths in Buenos Aires

On December 30, 2004, Buenos Aires suffered its worst man-made non-military disaster ever. Almost 200 people were burned alive, suffocated, or died of smoke inhalation when the club Cromagnon, in the neighborhood of Once, was accidentally set on fire by patrons shooting off firecrackers. The club had a capacity of about 1,000 but contained up to five times that amount as people packed themselves in to see the band Callejeros perform. Among those who died were children left by their parents in an illegal nursery in the club's restroom. The senseless deaths were compounded by the fact that management locked the fire exits to keep people from sneaking in.

As a result of the fire, all dance clubs in Buenos Aires were shut down—you couldn't even tango in Buenos Aires for a month. Protesters took to the streets, calling for the resignation of Buenos Aires's mayor Aníbal Ibarra and an end to corrupt practices that allow club owners to pay off inspectors to overlook fire regulation violations. Still, even with the official ban on dance clubs in place, corruption allowed select clubs with wealthy and powerful owners to remain open. Some clubs, in particular those catering to gays and lesbians as well as immigrant or poor populations, remained closed for months, or may never reopen based both on access to government power as well as true fire code violations. Ironically, the neighborhood of Once, where the fire took place, takes its name from the shortened version of the name of the train station across the street from Cromagnon, which is called Once de Septiembre (Sept 11), a reference to the day 19th-century president Sarmiento died. December 30—like September 11 for the U.S.—is a date that will always be remembered in Argentina as a tragedy, clouding each Christmas and New Year's season.

3 The Bar Scene

There is no shortage of popular bars in Buenos Aires, and Porteños need little excuse to party. The following are only a few of the many bars and pubs worthy of recommendation. Strolling along, you're sure to find plenty on your own. You're really in luck when you catch a bachelor or bachelorette party out on the town; they will be happy to have you come along as friends embarrass the soon-to-be wedded. Also check out "Gay & Lesbian Dance Clubs, Resto-Bars & Tango Salons," later in this chapter, for more information on gay bars and clubs.

BARS

Beat House   This little bar is a young and funky favorite in Las Cañitas. It's in an old house that's painted hot pink. Unlike other bars on the rest of the street, which don't become crowded until midnight, this place starts to fill up early, often around 8 or 9pm. Báez 311, at Arguibel. ℰ 11/4775-5616. Metro: Carranza.

Coanico Bar   The movie posters on the outside of this bar are probably the first thing you'll notice. Inside, you'll find a busy place where people eat and drink off tables painted with nude women in the style of Picasso. The bar has overlooked

Plaza Serrano for over 20 years, and offers typical bar food like sandwiches and hamburgers but has a larger menu than most of the surrounding bars. Live rock music sometimes entertains the crowd. Borges 1646, at Plaza Serrano. © 11/4833-0708. Metro Plaza Italia.

Gran Bar Danzón   A small, intimate bar, Danzón attracts a fashionable crowd. An excellent barman serves exquisite cocktails, and a small selection of international food is offered as well. Smart, relaxing lounge music is played at night. Libertad 1161, at Santa Fe. © 11/4811-1108. No metro access.

Henry J. Beans   A favorite of the ex-pat American community and visiting foreigners, this casual Recoleta bar serves burgers, sandwiches, and nachos, along with cocktails and beer. Old Coca-Cola ads, Miller and Budweiser neon signs, and model airplanes hang from the ceilings. The waiters do occasional impromptu dances, and the place is packed after midnight. There are a number of other popular restaurants, bars, and discos along Junín in case you're in the area but don't like this place. Junín 1749, at Vicente López, overlooking Recoleta Cemetery. © 11/4801-8477. No metro access.

Jackie O.   It might be named for America's favorite first lady, but this bar seems more English in style than American, with its wood-paneled interior and classic paned windows. Always crowded, even on a Monday, it's an important and very busy fixture on the Las Cañitas bar scene. With three levels including a covered rooftop patio, it's also one of the largest. They serve a simple menu of Argentine and American food, and many patrons come early to eat and then stay to linger over drinks with the rowdy crowd. Báez 334, at Arguibel. © 11/4774-4844. Metro: Carranza.

The Kilkenny   This trendy cafe-bar is more like a rock house than an Irish pub, although you will still be able to order Guinness, Kilkenny, and Harp draft beers. Packed with both locals and foreigners, you are as likely to find people here in suits and ties as in jeans and T-shirts. The Kilkenny offers happy hour from 6 to 8pm and live bands every night after midnight; it stays open until 5am. Marcelo T. de Alvear 399, at Reconquista. © 11/4312-9179 or 11/4312-7291. Metro: San Martín.

Macondo Bar   Macondo Bar is one of the stars of Plaza Serrano, with sidewalk seating and lots of levels overlooking the action. Inside, the restaurant twists around several staircases and low ceilings. It's a loud and busy place for sure, but this kind of setup helps to add a certain sense of intimacy when coming with friends to share conversation over drinks and a meal. DJs blast music of all kinds through the bar, from folkloric to techno to electronica. Technically, there's no live music, but sometimes people come around and play on the street in front of the bar. Borges 1810, at Plaza Serrano. © 11/4831-4174. Metro: Plaza Italia.

Plaza Bar   Nearly every Argentine president and his cabinet have come here, in addition to visiting celebs such as the queen of Spain, the emperor of Japan, Luciano Pavarotti, and David Copperfield. This English-style bar features mahogany furniture and velvet upholstery and is the type of place where guests sip martinis and smoke Cuban cigars. Tuxedo-clad waiters can recommend a fine selection of whiskeys and brandies. Marriott Plaza Hotel, Calle Florida 1005, at Plaza San Martín. © 11/4318-3000. Metro: San Martín.

Plaza Dorrego Bar   Representative of a typical Porteño bar from the 19th century, Plaza Dorrego displays portraits of the famous tango crooner Carlos Gardel, antique liquor bottles in cases along the walls, and anonymous writings engraved in the wood. Stop by on a Sunday, when you can catch the San Telmo antiques market on the plaza in front and the crowd spills onto the street from the inside of this bar, drinks in hand. Calle Defensa 1098, at Humberto I, overlooking Plaza Dorrego. ℂ 11/4361-0141. Metro: Independencia.

The Shamrock ☆☆ If you are looking for a bar that is packed every night of the week, including a usually quiet Monday, then this is the place to head. More international than Irish, you'll find ex-pats of all kinds drinking and chatting here. On weekends the basement space opens up into a small disco, adding to the fun. Rodríguez Peña 1220, at Arenales. ℂ 11/4812-3584. Metro: Callao.

Soul Café and SuperSoul ☆☆ This retro funky 1970s-style bar complex is the centerpiece of the Las Cañitas bar scene. Two bars in one, you'll find one side might be more happening than the other depending on what night you go. Deep inside the space is a small lounge area with live music. They have a velvet rope, but don't get the glamour worries, it's just for show. As long as there's space back there, everyone can have a seat or stand up and watch. Still, most of the action takes place in the front bar, and if you're looking to maybe get lucky Buenos Aires–style, this might be the place to check out on your trip. Báez 352, at Arguibel. ℂ 11/4776-3905. Metro: Carranza.

Tazz ☆ Mexican food for snacking is the highlight of this place, with its blue spaceship-themed interior. Their sidewalk space overlooking Plaza Serrano is one of the largest, so this is a great place to come in the summer or in warm weather, even though the crowd here is very young. Serrano 1556, at Plaza Serrano. ℂ 11/4833-5164. www.tazzbars.com. Metro: Plaza Italia.

Utopia Bar More cozy and calm than some of the other bars that surround Plaza Serrano, this is an excellent place to grab a drink and a bite to eat in this very trendy area. Yellow walls and soothing rustic wood tables add a sense of calm, though the live music, scheduled on an irregular basis, can be loud at times. Flavored coffees are one of the specialties here. The upstairs, open-air terrace on the roof of the bar is one of the best spots to sit, but its small size, with just a few tables, makes it hard to claim a spot here. And, since Utopia is open 24 hours, you never have to worry about where you can get a drink no matter the time of day. Serrano 1590, at Plaza Serrano. ℂ 11/4831-8572. Metro: Plaza Italia.

Van Koning With a model of van Gogh and its Dutch beers on tap, this is where you go to party Netherlands-style, making sure to toast to Princess Maxima, the Argentine beauty who will one day be a Dutch queen. Anyone is welcome to come here, of course, but the first Wednesday of every month around 11pm is when local Dutch ex-pats gather for a communal bash. Báez 325, at Arguibel. ℂ 11/4772-9909. Metro: Carranza.

BARS & RESTAURANTS WITH ENTERTAINMENT

You will find that many bars in Buenos Aires offer shows from flamenco to readings to tango and folkloric dance shows. Here are just a few I recommend, though you will most likely come across numerous other ones in your nocturnal wanders throughout Buenos Aires. The bars I've listed in this section are crowded by those seeking entertainment, whereas people would go to the other bars whether they have entertainment or not.

Clásica y Moderna ☆ This is a restaurant and bookstore combination (p. 206) and a *café notable,* protected in the interest of historical patrimony. Events of all kinds are held here, from literary readings to plays, dance shows, and art exhibitions. Shows are held Wednesday to Saturday at around 10pm, and there are sometimes two shows, the second one beginning after midnight. Show prices vary from $5 to $8 and are not included in the price of dining here. Reservations are recommended for shows. Callao 892, at Córdoba. © **11/4812-8707** or 11/4811-3670. www. clasicaymoderna.com. Metro: Callao.

Medio y Medio 🎔🎔   At night starting at 10pm, as you stuff yourself you'll be entertained by Spanish and folkloric singers and guitar players. They charge a 1.50 peso service for this pleasure, but don't worry: Beer gets cheaper here if you buy it with a meal at that time, so that more than makes up for the charge. Chile 316, at Defensa. © **11/4300-7007**. Metro: Independencia.

Pappa Deus 🎔   An interesting menu, live music shows, folkloric dancing, and jazz on Friday and Saturday nights make this place one of the best alternatives to tango venues along Dorrego Plaza. Weekdays are much quieter, especially in the upstairs loft, which offers a romantic setting, especially for couples who want a break from strolling along the streets of San Telmo. Built in 1798, the house the restaurant is located in is among the oldest still standing in all of Buenos Aires. Bethlem 423, at Defensa, on Plaza Dorrego. © **11/4361-2110**. www.pappadeus.com.ar. Metro: Independencia.

República de Acá 🎔🎔 INTERNATIONAL/ARGENTINE/COMEDY CLUB Charcoal drawings of Hollywood actors and other stars decorate the walls of this place, a fun comedy club and karaoke bar overlooking Plaza Serrano. Drinks are the main event here, but food offerings include pizzas, *picadas* (plates of cut cheese and meat that you "pick at"), salads, and other easy-to-make small items. Drinks come with free use of the Internet, and the menu will tell you how many minutes of Internet use are included with each drink. About half of this club is taken up by computers. Prices of drinks rise after 11pm by about 10%. At night the shows begin, and there is entertainment of all kinds. On weekends live music shows begin at 10pm, followed by comedy routines at 12:30am, karaoke at 3am, and then dancing until way past the time the sun comes up. There is a $5 entrance fee after 10pm on weekends, which includes one drink. After 2am this drops to a little over $3 to enter and still includes one drink. Many mixed drinks are made with ice cream, very adult interpretations of soda floats. TVs wrap around the whole space, so there is always something to watch. Fine champagnes and a selection of cigars at the bar make this a place to head to when you've got something to celebrate. Serrano 1549, at Plaza Serrano. © **11/4581-0278**. www.republicadeaca.com.ar. Metro: Plaza Italia.

HISTORICAL BARS & *BARES NOTABLES*

Buenos Aires is blessed with a large collection of historical bars, cafes, pubs, and restaurants. Most of these are concentrated in San Telmo, Monserrat, the Microcentro, and other, older, areas of the city. I highly recommend checking them out all over the city, and I have listed some of them in various sections of this book, including the "Where to Dine" chapter. Below are just a few highlights. You should ask for the *Bares y Cafés Notables* map from the Buenos Aires tourism kiosks to see more of these remarkable spaces, which will hopefully always be preserved.

Bar El Federal 🎔🎔   This bar and restaurant, on a quiet corner in San Telmo, represents a beautiful step back in time. Fortunately, as another *café notable*, it will stay that way forever. The first thing that will strike you here is the massive carved-wood and stained-glass ornamental stand over the bar area, though it originally came from an old pastry shop and is being reused. Local patrons sit at the old tables whiling away their time looking out onto the streets, chatting, or sitting with a book and drinking tea or espresso. The original tile floor remains, and old signs, portraits, and small antique machines decorate this space, which has been in business since 1864. Bar El Federal is among the most Porteño of places in San Telmo, a neighborhood that has more of these establishments than any other. Some of the staff has been here for decades on end, and proudly so. Corner of Perú and Carlos Calvo. ✆ **11/4300-4313.** Metro: Independencia.

La Coruña ⋇   This extremely authentic old cafe and restaurant bar, another of the *cafés notables* protected by law, is the kind of place you'd expect your grandfather to have eaten at when he was a teenager. Young and old alike come to this bar, which is a very neighborhoody spot, with people catching soccer games on television or quietly chatting away as they order beer, small snacks, and sandwiches. The TV seems to be the only modern thing in here. Music plays from a wooden tabletop radio that must be from the 1950s, and two wooden refrigerators dating from who knows when are still in use for storing food. The old couple that owns the place, José Moreira and Manuela Lopéz, obviously subscribe to the view that if it ain't broke, there's no reason for a new one. Bolívar 994, at Carlos Calvo. ✆ **11/4362-7637.** Metro: Independencia.

RESTAURANTS WITH BARS WORTH CHECKING OUT

Central ⋇⋇   This is one of the nicest and most sophisticated places to eat in Palermo Viejo, but it's also worth coming here just for drinks if you've already eaten elsewhere. Enjoy them in the lounge area, with its white leather sofas, or at the modern, white marble bar. Happy hour is from 6:30 to 8:30pm Monday to Friday. The large wine selection offers 25 Malbecs, 12 cabernet sauvignons, 6 merlots, and local champagnes. Costa Rica 5644, at Fitzroy. ✆ **11/4776-7374** or 11/4776-7370. Metro: Palermo.

Olsen ⋇⋇   Special glass-faced freezers hover over the bar in this Scandinavian restaurant, offering a teasing array of vodkas. There are over 60 choices from around the world, including some specially made for Olsen itself. Enjoy a drink outdoors, if you'd like, in their overgrown garden patio, which looks like a living room that has succumbed to nature, or around their central potbellied stove, reminiscent of a 1960s ski-lodge lounge. Olsen is closed on Monday. Gorriti 5870, at Carranza. ✆ **11/4776-7677.** restaurantolsen@netizon.com.ar. No metro access.

Penal1   Can't get enough of the polo lifestyle? Then come here and party in polo style in this restaurant and sports bar (a block from a back entrance of the polo grounds) owned by Horacio and Bautista Heguy, two brothers who are players for the Indios Chapaleuful polo team. Every now and then, they come by to check things out. In season during November and early December, you can often find them celebrating here with fellow players. Service is extremely friendly and casual, and other than the owners, you won't find much about polo itself here, except for a mantle with a few trophies and a polo painting that looks more like an ad for Marlboro cigarettes. There is a large, expensive wine-and-mixed-drink selection, which includes champagne. The place is at its height in season when the bar section, graced by an enormous television, plays host to rowdy and happy patrons after polo games. A disco ball hangs from the ceiling, somewhat incongruous with the rest of the building, located in an old house that still retains some of its original elements. Arguibel 2851, at Báez. ✆ **11/4776-6030.** Metro: Carranza.

Sullivan's Drink House ⋇   Many come for the Irish food in this restaurant, but its huge rooftop VIP lounge, which is open to all, offers the best in Irish and English whiskeys. There's even an English-style cigar bar here where you can puff the night away. Sullivan's is also a fun choice if you're in town for St. Patrick's Day. El Salvador 4919, at Borges. ✆ **11/4832-6442.** Metro: Scalabrini Ortiz.

WINE & CHAMPAGNE BARS

Chandon Bar   This intimate champagne lounge serves bottles and flutes of Chandon, produced in both France and Argentina. Located in Puerto Madero, adjacent to some of the city's best restaurants, Chandon is perfect for a before- or after-dinner drink. Light fare is offered as well. Av. Alicia Moreau de Justo 152, at Viamonte in Dique (Dock) 4. ℭ **11/4315-3533.** Metro: L. N. Alem.

Club del Vino ℛ   Wine tastings are a major part of the offerings at this Palermo Viejo Italian restaurant. Tastings are held regularly in an upstairs gallery for $12 a person, and they last about an hour. Over 350 kinds of wines are stored here; a staff sommelier can help you make your choice. Bottle prices range from $6 to $100, but the majority of them fall in the range of $6 to $12. Twenty percent of the wines are also available in glasses. Club del Vino was established in 1985 and opened in this location in 1994. Music and dancing shows are held Wednesday through Sunday beginning at 7 or 9pm, so make sure to call ahead and make a reservation. At the time of this writing, a remodel is planned for late 2005. Cabrera 4737, at Thames. ℭ **11/4833-0048.** No metro access.

4 Tango Show Palaces

With tango as the main draw, Buenos Aires says, "Let me entertain you." Numerous show palaces, from the simple Café Tortoni (p. 104) to the over-the-top special-effects-laden Señor Tango, compete for your tourist dollar. All of the shows are excellent, and, surprisingly, each is very unique, proving that tango can mean many things to many people, the performers themselves most of all. Here I've listed some of the top shows, but new ones seem to open up almost every other week. Many of the show palaces include dinner, or you can arrive just in time for the show only. Usually, the price differential for the show only is minimal, making it worth coming early for dinner. Seeing a variety of tango palaces is important, since each show has its own style. Smaller spaces lead to a greater intimacy, and often more interaction between the dancers and the audience. Sometimes the dancers even grab a few people, so watch out if you're close to the stage! Some of these shows, like Señor Tango and El Viejo Almacén, offer bus services that pick you up at your hotel. Book directly, or ask your hotel concierge for help and bus transfer times, which can be up to an hour before the event.

Café Tortoni ℛℛ   High-quality yet inexpensive tango shows are held in the back room of the Café Tortoni and do not include dinner. There is a show Wednesday through Monday at 9pm. The tight space here is not for the claustrophobic. What makes some of the Café Tortoni tango shows extremely unique is that women, rather than men, are the focus of them. Visit their website for more information and a description of all the upcoming shows including tango, jazz, children's theater, and more. Av. de Mayo 829, at Piedras. ℭ **11/4342-4328.** www.cafe tortoni.com.ar. Metro: Plaza de Mayo.

Central Tango   Among the newest of the shows, Central Tango has eight dancers, two singers, and a six-musician orchestra. Shows are Monday through Saturday; dinner begins at 8:30pm followed by the show at 10:15pm. There is also free parking included with the show. Rodríguez Peña 361, at Corrientes. ℭ **11/5236-0055.** www.centraltango.com.ar. No metro access.

El Querandí ℛℛ   El Querandí offers the best historically based tango show in the city, showing it from its early bordello roots when only men danced it, to its current, leggy, sexy style. You'll also get a great slab of beef and a glass of wine with

---

Moments   **Tango: Lessons in the Dance of Seduction & Despair**

It seems impossible to imagine Argentina without thinking of tango, its greatest export to the world. Tango originated with a guitar and violin toward the end of the 19th century and was first danced by working-class men in La Boca, San Telmo, and the port area. Combining African rhythms with the *habanera* and *candombe,* it was not the sophisticated dance you know today—rather, the tango originated in brothels, known locally as *quilombos.* At that time the dance was considered too obscene for women, and as they waited their turn, men would dance it with each other in the brothel lounges.

Increasing waves of immigrants added Italian elements to the tango and helped the dance make its way to Europe, where it was internationalized in Paris. With a sense of European approval, Argentine middle and upper classes began to accept the newly refined dance as part of their cultural identity, and the form blossomed under the extraordinary voice of Carlos Gardel, who brought tango to Broadway and Hollywood, and is nothing short of legendary among Argentines. Astor Piazzolla further internationalized the tango, elevating it to a more complex form incorporating classical elements.

Tango music may be played by anywhere from two musicians to a complete orchestra, but a piano and *bandoneón*—an instrument akin to an accordion—are usually included. If there is a singer, the lyrics might come from one of Argentina's great poets, such as Jorge Luis Borges, Homero Manzi, or Horacio Ferrer. Themes focus on a downtrodden life or a woman's betrayal, making it akin to American jazz and blues, which developed at the same time. The dance itself is improvised rather than standardized, although it consists of a series of long walks and intertwined movements, usually in eight-step. In the tango, the man and woman glide across the floor as an exquisitely orchestrated duo with early flirtatious movements giving way to dramatic leads and heartfelt turns, with the man always leading the way. These movements, such as

---

the show. Open Monday through Saturday; dinner begins at 8:30pm followed by the show at 10:15pm. Perú 302, at Moreno. © **11/4345-0331.** No metro access.

El Viejo Almacén   Shows here involve traditional Argentine-style tango, with little emphasis on the splashy Hollywoodization of tango seen in other places like Señor Tango. Sunday through Thursday shows are at 10pm; Friday and Saturday shows are at 9:30 and 11:45pm. Dinner is served each night before the show starts in the three-story restaurant across the street (guests may opt for dinner-show or show only). Transportation is offered from some hotels. Independencia and Balcarce. © **11/4307-6689.** No metro access.

Esquina Carlos Gardel 👯👯   The show here begins with the orchestra playing sad tangos, and then opens up with such a powerful and emotional rendition of Carlos Gardel's signature song, "Mi Buenos Aires Querido" that you'll almost feel like crying. This is perhaps the most elegant of the tango show palaces, built over the location of "Chanta Cuatro"—a restaurant where Carlos Gardel used to dine

the kicks that simulate knife movements, or the sliding, shuffled feet that mimic the walk of a gangster silently walking up to murder someone, belie its rough roots when it was the favored dance of La Boca gangsters in spite of its intense beauty as performed nowadays.

Learning to dance the tango is an excellent way for a visitor to get a sense of what makes the music—and the dance—so alluring. Entering a tango salon—called a *salón de baile* or *milonga*—can be intimidating for the novice. The style of tango danced in salons is more subdued than "show tango." Most respectable dancers would not show up before midnight, giving you the perfect opportunity to sneak in for a group lesson, offered at most of the salons starting around 7 to 9pm. They usually cost between $1 and $3 for an hour; you can request private instruction for between $10 and $20 per hour, depending on the instructor. In summer the city of Buenos Aires promotes tango by offering free classes in many locations. Visit the nearest tourist information center for updated information. Before you head to Argentina, free tango lessons are also provided by select Argentine consulates in the United States (see p. 12 for consulate information).

For additional advice on places to dance and learn tango, get a copy of *B.A. Tango* or *El Tangauta,* the city's dedicated tango magazines. One of the best spots to learn is **Gricel,** La Rioja 1180 (© **11/4957-7157**), which offers lessons Monday through Friday at 8pm and opens its doors to the city's best dancers on Saturday and Sunday nights. **La Galería,** Boedo 722 (© **11/4957-1829**), is open Thursday, Saturday, and Sunday and attracts excellent dancers, many of whom compete professionally. **Café Ideal,** Suipacha 384 (© **11/4326-1081**), has tango shows on Monday, Wednesday, and Friday afternoons. The dancers here come in all ages and have varied abilities. Ongoing evening lessons are also offered at the **Academia Nacional de Tango,** located above Café Tortoni at Av. de Mayo 833 (© **11/4345-6968**), which is an institute rather than a tango salon.

with his friends and across the street from the Abasto Shopping Center, another location associated with him. The luxurious old-time-style dining room here features high-tech acoustics and superb dancers, creating a wonderful tango environment. Doors open at 8pm. Carlos Gardel 3200, at Anchorena, overlooking Abasto Shopping Center. © 11/4876-6363. No metro access.

La Ventana   This is one of the newest shows in Buenos Aires, and it's held in the atmospheric brick-lined cellar of an old building in San Telmo. Performances are a mix of tango, folkloric, and other Argentine styles of dance and music. One of the highlights of the night is a schmaltzy rendition of "Don't Cry for Me, Argentina" complete with a moveable balcony and rather glamorous *descamisados* (shirtless ones) holding Argentine flags. Balcarce 431, at Venezuela. © 11/4331-1314. www.la-ventana.com.ar. No metro access.

Madero Tango   Madero Tango prides itself not just on what you see onstage but what you see outside their terraces, too. Located in the Puerto Madero area, this building extends along the waterfront of San Telmo, overlooking the port and boats in the water. It's a more modern, chic, and spacious setting than most of the tango shows in Buenos Aires, and the shows are a bit splashy, too. E. Rawson de Dellepiane 150, Dock 1; alternate address is Moreau de Justo 2100, at port beginning near where autopista skirts the waterfront. © 11/4314-6688. www.maderotango.com.ar. No metro access.

Piazzolla Tango   This tango show spectacular is held in a stunning theater, an Art Nouveau masterpiece created by the architect who designed the now closed Confitería del Molino, next door to Congreso. This theater had been closed for nearly 40 years and was only recently restored. Of all of the tango show palaces in Buenos Aires, this is the most beautiful, which adds even more excitement to the well-choreographed show. Calle Florida 165, at Perón © 11/4344-8201. www.piazzolla tango.com. Metro: Florida.

Señor Tango   This enormous space is more akin to a Broadway production theater than to a traditional tango salon, but the dancers are fantastic and the owner, who clearly loves to perform, is a good singer. The walls are decorated with photos of what appears to be every celebrity who's ever visited Buenos Aires—and all seem to have made it to Señor Tango! Have dinner or come only for the show (dinner is at 8:30pm; shows start at 10pm). Diners choose between steak, chicken, or fish for dinner and, despite the huge crowd, the food quality is commendable. Vieytes 1653, at Villarino. © 11/4303-0212. No metro access.

5 *Milongas* (Tango Salons & Dance Halls)

While the show palaces and their dance shows are wonderful must-sees, there is nothing like the amazing lure of the *milonga* (tango salon) on a trip to Buenos Aires. As with the show palaces, there are more now than ever before. Rather than destroy tango, the peso crisis has created a greater awareness of all things traditionally Argentine and the need to turn inwards and be self-reflective. In the same way that the ancestors of today's Porteños turned to tango more than 100 years ago to alleviate their pain, isolation, and worries with a night of dancing their melancholy away, so too did modern Porteños, creating an unprecedented boom in rapidly opening *milongas*. This, coupled with the increase in both tourism and tango-dancing ex-pats moving from Europe and North America who have decided to live here and dance their lives away, means that there are more choices for dancing than ever before. This scene is not without its rules and obstacles, however, especially in terms of how to act with dancers of the opposite sex. Be sure to read "Some Tango Rules" (below) to get some tips on *milonga* behavior for foreigners before heading out. There's usually about a $2 entry fee to get into a *milonga*.

You should also pick up the *Tango Map*, which has a comprehensive guide to *milongas* in all regions of the city, arranged by day and time. Find it at the tourism kiosks, the various tango-associated venues listed in this book, and also in select locations in San Telmo. Be aware that the same location may have different events by different names, so keeping track of the address of the venue is important. Also, double-check the listings in *B.A. Tango* or *El Tangauta*, the city's tango magazines. The numbers that are listed in this section and within the magazines or maps are not necessarily those of the venues, but may be the numbers of the various dance organizations that hold events within the specific dance venue on any given night. See also "Gay & Lesbian Dance Clubs, Resto-Bars & Tango Salons," later in this chapter, for gay tango salons that have blossomed on the scene.

El Arranque *Finds*   This dance venue, which looks a little like a Knights of Columbus hall, is a great find not only because of its authenticity but also because it is one of the few places with afternoon dancing. Tango's usual late-night events can drive even a vampire crazy, so this is the perfect place to enjoy tango and still get a real night's sleep afterward. Rules here about separating the sexes are very strictly enforced, so couples might not be allowed to sit next to each other. One interesting rule about this place is that no matter how old and pot-bellied a man is, as long as he dances well, he can be with any woman in the crowd. Women, however, even of a certain age, tend to keep up appearances here, dressing beautifully and stylishly. This place will be very comfortable for older crowds. Dancing begins most afternoons starting at 3pm but the venue is closed on Monday. Bartolomé Mitre 1759, at Callao. ℰ 11/4371-6767. Metro: Congreso.

El Beso Nightclub *(Finds* The way to this club may be a little confusing, but follow my directions and you'll be fine. First, the door to this club is unmarked, so your only indication that you're in the right spot will be the address. Walk upstairs, pay your fee, and the first thing you'll see is the crowded bar blocking your view, which you are forced to squeeze past. Once oriented, however, you'll find this small space maintains the air of a 1940s nightclub updated for the modern era with brilliant reds and modern abstractions painted on some of its walls. The most interesting touch, adding a golden glow to the dancers, are the lamps made from car air filters hanging from the ceiling. Someone definitely thought differently when decorating this place. It's a good idea to reserve a table here ahead of time if you can. Snacks, wines, and beers are on sale, but avoid the nasty house wine. This is a place where some of the best perform, bringing their egos with them to the floor, so if you're not so good, just enjoy watching. The last thing you want is to bump into someone. The sexes tend to mix informally here, the divisions between the *milongueras* and *milongueros* not so strong. There are different *milonga* events on various nights, so check their calendar. Riobamba 416, at Corrientes. ℰ 11/4953-2794 or 11/15-4938-8108 (cell). Metro: Callao.

El Niño Bien *⭐⭐ (Finds* If you want to go back in time in Buenos Aires, to an era when tango truly ruled the city, few places will do but El Niño Bien. In the main dance hall, you'll be struck at first by the subtle Belle Epoque beauty of the space, complete with men and women in black tangoing, their styles observed respectfully by the rest of the patrons in the tables to the side, who often come to observe the techniques of other experts. Next you'll notice the thick smoke hanging in the air, cut by ceiling fans whirling overhead. Don't look too closely at anyone, though, unless you know what you're doing: This is one place where the concept of *milonga* eyes—staring across a room to draw a man and a woman together onto the dance floor—is forcefully maintained. While there are numerous tango locations all over the city, this is one where you almost expect the crooner Gardel to suddenly appear and entertain you, calling you to the dance floor. They do serve food here, but it's only so-so, so don't bother unless you're famished. Unfortunately, Niño Bien is becoming a victim of its own success, with many tour groups beginning to come here now. If you're looking to find a tango teacher, one will probably find you as many come here seeking students for private lessons. Humberto I no. 1462, at San José. (The building is called the Centro Región Leonesa.) ℰ 11/4483-2588. No metro access.

La Glorietta *(Finds* Tangoing in the open air is the highlight of this *milonga*. It also opens in the afternoon, so it is perfect for people who want to experience tango but not be out very late. Snacks and tostados are also served. It can be slightly touristy, however. There is a show at 1am on Friday and Saturday. Once de Septiembre and Echeverria. ℰ 11/4674-1026. No metro access.

Tips   Some Tango Rules

Certainly the seductive sound of the tango is one of the reasons you came to Buenos Aires in the first place. Maybe you just want to see some people perform those fancy kicks and moves onstage. Maybe you'd like to learn some of the steps yourself. Or maybe you're nearly an expert yourself and want your own turn on some of the wooden dance floors where Buenos Aires's best have danced for decades. Whatever your objectives or level of interest, you can do all or any of those options with the choices I have laid out for you in this chapter.

The only places most tourists see tango in Buenos Aires are in the big, and expensive, show palace-restaurants, which feature dancers onstage as tourists eat meals with steak as the centerpiece. You should venture and see more than just those shows if time permits. While aimed at tourists, the quality of each of these shows is superb, and even the most jaded Porteño cannot help but be impressed by what is onstage. In spite of the quantity of these stage spectaculars, each is also different in its own right. Some concentrate on the dance's history, others the intimacy with the audience; some throw in other dance forms, especially folkloric, or seem to forget tango all together.

However, I think every tourist should also take the opportunity to see a *milonga,* a place where the dance is done by those who know it well (usually following a strict protocol of interactions between the sexes). A key concept in these places refers to the *milonga* eyes—perhaps you've heard fairy tales about two sets of eyes meeting across the room and then finding their way to each other on the dance floor. In some *milongas,* men and women sit on different sides of the room, couples only blending together in certain spots. Men and women will try to catch each other's eyes this way, flirting across the smoke-filled distance, adding nods, smiles, and sometimes hand movements for increased effect. The man finally approaches the woman, offering to dance. Often, there is not even a word between the two at this stage until they take the floor.

La Viruta *(Finds*   This is one of the most interesting of the *milongas* because it is authentic, but it attracts a very young crowd of both Porteños and ex-pats from all over the world who have come to dance their lives away in Buenos Aires while the living is good and cheap. Many nights it is just a *milonga.* Other nights there are shows and competitions, many involving tango, folkloric, and modern dance. The dancing and various events are held in the cellar of the Armenian Community Center, and when decorated with balloons for some events, it looks a little like a high school prom from the 1970s. Armenia 1366, at Cabrera. ✆ **11/4774-6357.** No metro access.

Lo de Celia *(Finds*   Don't let the modern setup of this place fool you: This is a very traditional *milonga* where the rules are very strictly applied. Men and women must sit on opposite sides of the dance floor here, with couples blending in only at the corners. The air here is so thick with smoke there's no need to bring cigarettes with you—you'll still get your nicotine fix without them. Music is provided

This ritual means tourists need to be aware of a few things. Firstly, never, ever block the view to a woman who is sitting by herself, though it is best to avoid blocking anyone's view. Be aware of divisions between the sexes in seating, which of course might be enforced by the management anyway for newcomers, and follow the rules. As a foreigner, some very strict places might tell you they simply have no seats; overcome this by saying you are looking for a friend who arrived earlier. Avoid eye contact with members of the opposite sex if you have no idea what you're doing. You might be inviting a dance when all you want to do is watch, confusing some people who are completely absorbed in the rules of the game.

If a woman wants to dance with new men in order to practice the tango, she should not be seen entering the salon with a male friend, because most of the other men will assume she is already taken. If couples want to dance with new people to practice, they should enter the room separately, and if you are coming as a group, divide yourselves up by sex for the same reason. Each *milonga*, however, maintains its own grip on these rules, some very strict, others abiding only by some. It's also best not to go to these places in large groups, rather with a few people at a time or as a couple. The sudden entrance of a large group of noisy curious foreigners who don't know the place can instantly change the overall atmosphere. And importantly, show respect to where you are in terms of how you appear. While you needn't dress to the nines, a baseball cap and sneakers will ruin the atmosphere of the location (if they even let you in).

Find a copy of the *Tango Map*, which lists almost all of the city's *milongas*, as well as what specific special events are held on what nights. It is, incidentally, among the best maps period of Buenos Aires, and it even includes neighborhoods generally off the beaten tourist path.

by a DJ, and the floors, made of terrazzo, were not specifically designed for dancing, and therefore dancing can be harder on the feet here than on the wooden floors in most other tango venues. The crowd here is generally mature and very experienced in tango, and the strict enforcement of sexual separation means women will be treated like absolute ladies in this place. Make sure not to block views of anyone when gawking at the dance floor if you're only here to watch. They often hold contests close to the end of the night, so that can be fun to watch and it brings levity to some of the tense tango egoists as the night gets late. Humberto I no. 1783, at Solís. © 11/4932-8594. No metro access.

Salón Canning *(Finds* This is among the most authentic of all of the *milongas*. Enter a long hallway, and at the end of it, you are rewarded by a room of people crowding to look at the main dance floor, watching the couples. Salón Canning is known for its extremely smooth, high-quality wooden parquet floor, considered one of the best for dancing in all of Buenos Aires by many of the tango enthusiasts I know in the city. This tango hall is among the only things left in Buenos Aires that still remains named for George Canning. The name of the salon refers to the time when the street Scalabrini Ortiz was formerly named in honor of this British diplomat (p. 150). Scalabrini Ortiz 1331, at Gorriti. © 11/4832-6753. No metro access.

TANGO TOURS

If you think you might want to try your hand at the authentic *milongas,* it would help to take some lessons beforehand or take a tour with a professional. There are literally hundreds of tours for people interested in tango here in Buenos Aires, the city where it all began. Here are just a few, and all of these people and groups also offer lessons. Also see below where I list even more instructors.

ABC Tango Tours   Gabriel Aspe, who is one of the co-owners of this company, also manages one of the tango shows at the Café Tortoni and is a native of Argentina. The company offers several tango show-palace event tours as well as tours to traditional tango houses. © 11/15-5697-2551 (cell). www.abctango.com.

Amantes del Tango   Eduardo and Nora run this association and offer individual tours and private lessons. Both are well-established tango performers and Nora's work has been featured in *National Geographic* magazine. © 11/4703-4104 or 11/15-5753-9131 (cell). www.amantesdeltango.com.

Buenos Aires Tango Off   This company offers several tango-themed tours, including its unusual "Dos Pasiones Argentinas," which takes the "Land of Evita and Tango" phrase to heart by combining tango lessons with a visit to the Museo Evita (though she was known to hate the dance, ironically). © 11/4829-1416 or 11/4829-1417.

Tango with Judy   Judy, an American tango dancer who moved to Buenos Aires with her husband and knows the scene well, offers highly specialized and individual tango tours, some of which can be combined with lessons. © 11/4863-5889. www.tangowithjudy.com.

Tanguera Tours   Single women who want to take advantage of the tango scene or women whose partners refuse to dance can contact Tanguera Tours, which offers specialized tango tours for groups of women. The company owner, Laura Chummers, is a perky American who really knows the scene and makes it accessible for women of any skill level, but she won't let you be a wallflower at any of the places she takes you. © 11/4953-2775. www.tangueratours.com.

TANGO TEACHERS

All of the above tour groups offer tango lessons, either in a group or individually. Alternatively, you can try the professional tango teachers I've listed below as well. More listings for teachers are available in the *B.A. Tango* or *Tangauta* magazines.

- **Julieta Lotti** (© 11/4774-5654; julietalotti@hotmail.com) has taught and danced tango for years. She is a member of the Las Fulanas troupe of dance professionals. She does not, however, speak much English.
- **Marie Soler** (© 11/15-5411-7208 [cell]; tangomariemar@hotmail.com) is a young woman who knows the tango scene well. She speaks English and often enters various competitions and shows in the La Viruta *milonga.*
- **Pedro Sánchez** (© 11/4923-2774; pedromilonguero@yahoo.com.ar) has been dancing tango for over 50 years, and many women I know swear by his instruction methods. He speaks little English, but always makes himself understood. He will give private lessons, and also offers Monday

evening sessions for small groups, which might be a good way to get to know him and see his techniques.

6 Gay & Lesbian Dance Clubs, Resto-Bars & Tango Salons

Buenos Aires has a thriving gay and lesbian scene. It's one of the most impressive on the South American continent, rivaled only by Brazil's Rio de Janeiro. It's easy to find out where to go too, since the city offers several gay and lesbian maps at its kiosks. You can also look for the gay magazines *NX* and *Imperio* or the small gay guide *Otra Guía* on sale at newsstands all over town. Most of their ads and articles are in Spanish, but they also provide maps and descriptions of local gay venues in a mix of Spanish and English. Most of the action is centered in Barrio Norte, which has always been the traditional gay neighborhood of Buenos Aires. With the rapid gentrification of San Telmo, however, this historic neighborhood has become home to several small gay bars and restaurants. If you think straight nightlife starts late in Buenos Aires, gay nightlife begins even later, with few people hitting a club before 2am.

DANCE CLUBS

Amerika   This is the city's most popular gay club, and even straight people are beginning to come here in droves for the great music. In general, straights hang out on the uppermost level of the club near the glassed-in area that looks like a spaceship pod, with gays, lesbians, and whatever mixing throughout the rest of the many levels in this enormous venue. Open Friday and Saturday only. Gascón 1040, at Córdoba. ℂ 11/4865-4416. Admission $8. Metro: Angel Gallardo.

Contramano   Popular with a mature crowd, this was the first gay bar or dance club opened in Buenos Aires, just after the fall of the last military government in the early 1980s. Rodríguez Peña 1082, at Alvear. No phone. Admission $4. No metro access.

Palacio   If you've been to Buenos Aires before, you may remember the legendary IV Milenio. Palacio is built into that space, a multilevel former factory that soars to churchlike proportions. Open Friday and Sunday only. Alsina 934, at Av. 9 de Julio. No phone. Admission $8. Metro: Av. de Mayo.

Parada Obligada   Good for young and old, this dance club has great drag and comedy shows. The staff likes to make people feel especially welcome, and it has less attitude than the very big dance palaces. Charcas 4338, at Borges. No phone. Admission $4. Metro: Plaza Italia.

RESTO-BARS

A resto-bar is an Argentine concept of a restaurant and bar combination. People either come for a meal or stop by for drinks only. In general, the bar portions of resto-bars do not get busy until after 11pm or midnight. These are more relaxed than traditional bars and it is easier to chat with locals.

Chueca   Named after the gay district in Madrid, this is one of the most popular of the city's gay resto-bars. It gets very crowded here after midnight. Soler 3283, at Gallo. ℂ 11/4963-3430. No metro access.

Inside Resto-Bar   The waitstaff and the owners provide great, attitude-free service in this resto-bar. It's a good place to go just for drinks at their small bar, where many locals gather for conversation. On weekends they have special tango shows and male strippers, too. Ask about their return coupons, offering great discounts for people who come back during their slow early weeknights. Bartolomé Mitre 1571, at Montevideo. ℂ 11/4372-5439. Metro: Congreso.

La Farmacia   Food and art is how this place likes to describe itself, and there is artwork by local San Telmo artists hanging up all around the dining area. Italian-inspired items make up the bulk of this restaurant's main courses, like spinach crepes, *lomo* medallions, and gnocchi. Aperitifs, wine, mixed drinks, and coffee and tea are the liquid highlights of this gathering spot, which is also considered one of the most gay-friendly restaurants in the neighborhood. A small clothing boutique full of vintage and clubby items shares the main floor, opening onto the cafe/lounge. Bolívar 898, at Estados Unidos. (℗ **11/4300-6151**. www.lafarmaciarestobar.com.ar. Metro: Independencia.

Nanaka Bar   Nanaka takes its name from an Argentine Indian word meaning "we." Sidewalk seating in good weather and a little nook under the staircase are some of the pleasant places to enjoy a meal here. The culture quotient is upped by art on the walls from local artists and the piano, tango, and jazz music softly playing on the sound system. Humberto I no. 599, at Perú. (℗ **11/4362-7979**. Metro: Independencia.

TANGO SALONS

Tango was originally only danced by men together, since it was at first considered too obscene a dance for women to do with men. In the modern era, gay Porteños take this a step further, and now at least two gay tango salons are bringing back old-fashioned, same-sex tango.

Besos Brujos   This event is held every Tuesday in a club inside of a club built into an old church. The evening begins with lessons, then a *milonga*, then shows and more dancing. Suipacha 842, at Paraguay. No telephone. www.besosbrujos.com. Metro: San Martín.

La Marshall   The originator of the gay tango spots in Buenos Aires, La Marshall has moved around over the years. It begins with a group lesson, then on to a show and *milonga* in a salsa club. The event is held on Wednesday only, but the La Marshall group also runs gay tango lessons at the gay hotel El Lugar Gay in San Telmo (p. 77). Yatay 961, at Guardia Vieja. (℗ **11/4912-9043**. Metro: Angel Gallardo.

7 Film

Buenos Aires has over 250 movie theaters showing Argentine and international films. One of the best is the 16-screen **Village Recoleta,** V. López and Junín (℗ **11/4805-2220**). There are also cinemas at the **Alto Palermo,** Av. Santa Fe 3251 at Agüero (℗ **11/4827-8000**), and **Galerías Pacífico,** Calle Florida 753 at Córdoba (℗ **11/4319-5357**), shopping malls. Other convenient Microcentro locations include **Atlas Lavalle,** Lavalle 869 at Esmeralda (℗ **11/5032-8527;** www.atlascines.com.ar), with six screens, and the four-screen **Monumental Lavalle,** at Lavalle 739 at Maipú (℗ **11/4322-1515**). Most films are American and shown in English with Spanish subtitles, but some are Argentine films, which are not subtitled. Check the *Buenos Aires Herald* for current film listings. Every April Buenos Aires hosts an international independent film festival (www.bafilm fest.com), so check it out if you're in town during that time.

8 Casinos, Arcades & Bingo Halls

Getting lucky can be fun for adults and kids, and sometimes the locations where this can happen are side by side. Calle Lavalle, in particular, with its bright lights and big-city tackiness is the perfect place for both adults and teenagers taking a chance on success with the drop of a coin into a slot, or a bet placed on the table. This can often be done in conjunction with a movie, since many of the cinemas are here as well.

Bingo Lavalle   If you think bingo is just for seniors living out their retirement days, think again. Porteños of all ages love bingo, and here is where you'll find some of the most competitive on a night out. This is a huge smoke-filled space, the most smoky of any environment I've ever experienced in all of Buenos Aires, so don't even think of coming here if smoke bothers you. If it doesn't, I recommend spending some time here to check out this interesting scene with its cross section of locals. Alcoholic drinks and bar snacks are served. Bingo Lavalle is surrounded by arcades and movie theaters, but you must be at least 18 to enter this bingo hall. Lavalle 842, at Esmeralda. (**C** 11/4322-1114. Metro: Lavalle.

Casino Buenos Aires   Feel like trying to win some money to upgrade your hotel accommodations? This is the place, a 24-hour casino in a Mississippi riverboat parked on the Buenos Aires docks. There are over 117 gaming tables, hundreds of slot machines, and other ways to win, or lose, your money. Parking is nearby and there are restaurants onboard. Elvira Rawson de Dellepina, Darsena Sur Puerto de Buenos Aires (Southern Port beyond Puerto Madero). (**C** 11/4363-3100. No metro access.

Magic Play (*Kids*   This is a great place for the kids during the day, and teenagers later at night. Slots, racing cars, pool tables, and video games should keep them entertained for hours. Open daily from 9am to 1am. Lavalle 672, at Maipú. (**C** 11/4322-5702. Metro: Lavalle.

Magic Center (*Kids*   Built into an old theater, you'll find more nonelectronic games here than in some of the other entertainment centers, like net games and skeet ball. Open daily from 9am to 1am. Lavalle 845, at Esmeralda. (**C** 11/4394-9200. Metro: Lavalle.

Parque Landia (*Kids*   With a lot of games for smaller children, this is an excellent place to take younger kids for entertainment when they're bored with the museums and other highlights of Buenos Aires. Open daily from 9am to 1am. Lavalle 868, at Esmeralda. No phone. Metro: Lavalle.

Side Trips from Buenos Aires

If you're spending more than 4 or 5 days in Buenos Aires, you might want to consider taking a side trip, especially if you're visiting in summer, when many Porteños have already fled town.

During the summer months, many Porteños hit the beach resorts. **Mar del Plata** is the country's most popular. During the summer season, so many people head here from Buenos Aires that the capital can feel like a ghost town in certain neighborhoods. During these times, bands and other forms of entertainment also follow the beachgoers to Mar del Plata.

With a similar name but a very different atmosphere, **La Plata** is the capital of Buenos Aires Province, planned in 1880 along neoclassical lines. Full of diagonals and parks, it is an interesting and open city with various museums and other things of historical interest for year-round visiting.

Gualeguaychú, little known outside of Argentina, is home to the national Carnaval, a 2-month-long spectacle held in January and February that while not rivaling Rio's big party, makes for a very fun excursion nevertheless. The small size of the town means it's also an easy place to meet some of the people involved in the event on the streets or in the local bars, albeit in far less fancy costume.

Just outside of Buenos Aires's suburbs is the **Tigre Delta,** a beautiful complex of islands and marshland full of small bed-and-breakfasts, resorts, and adventure trails. You can make a day trip here on mass transit from Buenos Aires or you can choose to stay over. It is busiest in the summer season, but most sites and hotels are open year-round.

The Office of Tourism of the Nation at Suipacha 1111 will have brochures on various side trips from Buenos Aires, including the ones listed here.

1 Mar del Plata

400km (248 miles) S of Buenos Aires

Argentina's most popular beach resort is a sleepy coastal town until mid-December when Porteños flock here through March for their summer vacation. Although not as luxurious as Uruguay's Punta del Este—the beach favorite of many jet-setting Argentines—Mar del Plata is closer to Buenos Aires and far cheaper to stay in. Its long, windy coastline offers crowded, tan-bodied beaches and quieter seaside coves as well as beautiful landscapes farther inland leading to the edge of the grassy Pampas. Within Mar del Plata, a number of high-rise developments, products of the Perón era, have sadly replaced much of the city's earlier charm. However, some of the magnificent French-style residences, which housed Argentina's summer elites in the early 20th century, have been meticulously preserved as museums. Mar del Plata offers excellent nightlife in summer, when independent theater companies from Buenos Aires travel to this seaside resort and nightclubs open their doors to passionate Latin partygoers. The months of

December, January, and February are the most crowded, wild, and expensive for visiting. In March families with children and retired couples on vacation make up the bulk of visitors, taking advantage of a more relaxed atmosphere as well as a slight reduction in prices. Many hotels and restaurants remain open year-round and though the weather is chillier, you will find people vacationing here on weekends.

ESSENTIALS

GETTING THERE   You can reach Mar del Plata by plane, car, bus, train, or boat. The airport lies 10 minutes from downtown and is served by **Aerolíneas Argentinas** (© 800/333-0276 in the U.S. or 0810/222-86527 in Argentina; www.aerolineas.com). Flights last just under an hour and there are about three flights a day. Cabs will cost about $5 to $7 into the center of town. The RN2 is the main highway from Buenos Aires to Mar del Plata; it takes about 4 to 5 hours to drive between these cities. More than 50 bus companies link Mar del Plata with the rest of the country. Buses to Buenos Aires, which leave from the central bus terminal at Alberti 1602 (© 223/451-5406), are comfortable and cost under $15 each way. They arrive in Buenos Aires at the Retiro Bus Station. A train run by the company Ferrobaires also connects Mar del Plata with Buenos Aires and is only slightly more expensive than the buses. It leaves Buenos Aires from **Constitución,** in the southern part of the capital, and runs three times a day. In Mar del Plata purchase tickets at the train station, located at avenidas Luro and Italia (© 223/475-6076 in Mar del Plata or 11/4304-0028 in Buenos Aires). Bus and train trips take about 4 to 5 hours.

VISITOR INFORMATION   The **Centro de Información Turística,** Bulevar Marítimo PP Ramos 2270, at the Casino building (© 223/495-1777; www.mardelplata.gov.ar), has a knowledgeable, helpful staff offering maps and suggested itineraries. It is open daily from 10am to 5pm (until 8pm in summer). There is also a branch at the airport.

GETTING AROUND   La Rambla marks the heart of the city, the seaside walk in front of the casino and main city beach. This area is walkable on its own, with restaurants and other businesses clustered here and between the nearby bus station and Plaza San Martín. Farther south, the Los Tronces neighborhood houses the city's most prominent residences as well as Playa Grande (the main beach), the Sheraton hotel, and the Mar del Plata Golf Club. Mar del Plata has 47km (29 miles) of Atlantic coastline, so if you plan to go to that part of the city, you'll need to take a taxi or rent a car. **Avis** (© 223/470-2100) rents cars at the airport.

WHAT TO SEE & DO

The main reason for coming to Mar del Plata is the city's beaches, the best of which is **Playa Grande.** A long cluster of cliffs and dunes lead to more serene southern beaches. With long, slow breaks, **Waikiki** is the best spot for surfing. The coastline is nice, but you should not come expecting to find the Caribbean—the Atlantic remains fairly cold, even during summer. Once you've brushed off the sand, visit the **fishing harbor,** where hundreds of red and yellow boats unload their daily catches. The harbor houses a colony of 800 male sea lions that come to bathe on the rocky shores. Next to the colony, there's an ugly but intriguing boat graveyard where rusty boats have been left to rest. The harbor also offers the town's best seafood restaurants. In the Los Tronces neighborhood, **Villa Victoria,** at Matheu 1851, at Arenales (© 223/492-0569),

Mar del Plata

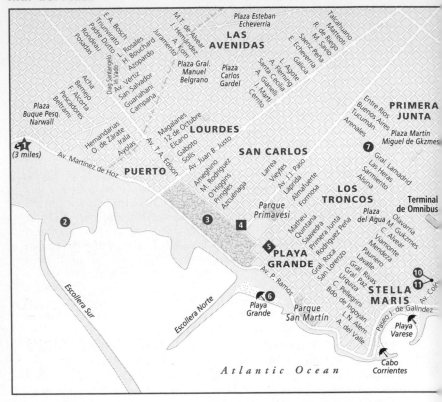

showcases the early-20th-century summerhouse of wealthy Argentine writer Victoria Ocampo. Some of Argentina's greatest authors have stayed here, including Jorge Luis Borges. It is open year-round Thursday to Tuesday from 1 to 8pm, with an admission charge of 65¢. In summer musical and theatrical performances are held in the gardens. Nearby, **Villa Ortiz Basualdo,** Av. Colón 1189 (© 223/486-1636), resembles a Loire castle and is decorated with exquisite Art Nouveau furniture from Belgium. In the same neighborhood, the **Museo del Mar,** Av. Colón 1114, at Viamonte (© 223/451-9779), houses a collection of 30,000 seashells. In summer it is open Sunday to Friday 9am to 7pm and Saturday 9am to 10pm. During the winter it's open daily from 9am to 1pm. Admission is $1. Twenty minutes from the city center, **De Los Padres Lake and Hills** is a picturesque forest with wide parks surrounding the lake, perfect for an afternoon picnic. Nearby, the **Zoo El Paraíso,** Ruta 266, Km 16.5 (© 223/463-0347), features a wonderful collection of flora and fauna, including plants and trees from all over Argentina as well as lions, pumas, monkeys, llamas, and other animals. For information on surfing, deep-sea fishing, mountain biking, horseback riding, trekking, and other adventure sports, contact the tourism office.

WHERE TO STAY

Amerian Mar del Plata Hotel   This hotel (part of the Amerian chain of hotels, an Argentine-owned company) is a popular honeymoon spot in the Playa

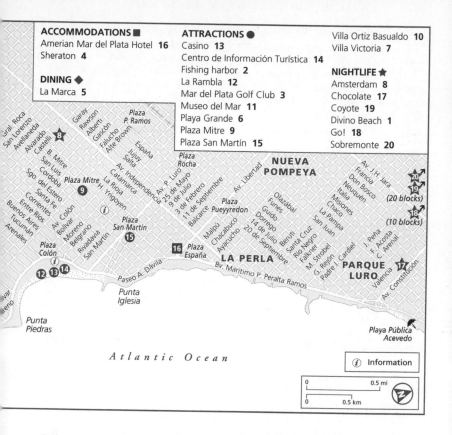

ACCOMMODATIONS ■
Amerian Mar del Plata Hotel **16**
Sheraton **4**

DINING ◆
La Marca **5**

ATTRACTIONS ●
Casino **13**
Centro de Información Turística **14**
Fishing harbor **2**
La Rambla **12**
Mar del Plata Golf Club **3**
Museo del Mar **11**
Playa Grande **6**
Plaza Mitre **9**
Plaza San Martín **15**

Villa Ortiz Basualdo **10**
Villa Victoria **7**

NIGHTLIFE ★
Amsterdam **8**
Chocolate **17**
Coyote **19**
Divino Beach **1**
Go! **18**
Sobremonte **20**

Atlantic Ocean

ⓘ Information

Perla section. Rooms are spacious with a simple decor, and many overlook the ocean or Plaza España.

Av. Libertad 2936, 7600 Mar del Plata. ℂ 223/491-2000. Fax 223/491-2300. 58 units. From $65 double. Rates include buffet breakfast. AE, DC, MC, V. Free parking. **Amenities:** Restaurant; 24-hr. bar; health club; concierge; business center; limited room service; laundry service; dry cleaning. *In room:* A/C, TV, minibar, hair dryer, safe.

Sheraton 𝒜𝒜 This may not be the most modern Sheraton, but it is the city's best hotel by far. Built on a golf course, the Sheraton faces the ocean and is just a quick hop to Mar del Plata's best beach, Playa Grande. The fishing harbor is also just down the road. A full-scale health club leads out to the beautiful pool, next to which is a small outdoor cafe. Rooms are light-filled and well equipped; suites have Jacuzzi tubs. The staff will help you arrange outdoor activities, including a tee time, upon request.

Alem 4221, 7600 Mar del Plata. ℂ 0800/777-7002 or 223/499-9000. Fax 223/499-0009. 193 units. $129 double with city view; $150 double with ocean view. Rates include buffet breakfast. AE, DC, MC, V. Free parking. **Amenities:** Restaurant; bar; health club w/heated outdoor pool; golf; concierge; business center; limited room service; massage service; babysitting; laundry service; dry cleaning. *In room:* A/C, TV, minibar, hair dryer, safe.

WHERE TO DINE

La Marca 𝒜𝒜 ARGENTINE This restaurant became famous for serving up a whole cow on special request for large groups of 50 or more people. While they rarely do this anymore, La Marca is the town's best *parrilla,* serving thick rump steaks, tenderloins, barbecued ribs of beef, flanks, and every other cut of meat you can think of. The tender filet mignon with mushroom sauce is delicious. Pork chops, sausages, sweetbreads, black pudding, and other delights are on the menu as well. An extensive salad bar allows you to eat something other than protein if you wish. Service is polite and unhurried. Make sure to try the *dulce de leche* before you leave.

Almafuerte 253. ℭ 223/451-8072. Main courses $3–$6. AE, DC, MC, V. Daily noon–3pm and 8:30pm–1am.

MAR DEL PLATA AFTER DARK

Nightlife follows closely behind beaches as Mar del Plata's biggest draw. In summer theater companies leave Buenos Aires to perform in this coastal resort; ask the tourism office for a schedule of performance times and places. The city's most popular bars are located south of Plaza Mitre, off Calle San Luis. The best dance clubs are along Avenida Constitución, 3km (2 miles) from downtown, including **Chocolate,** Av. Constitución 4451 (ℭ **223/479-4848**), **Divino Beach,** Paseo Costanero Sur Presidente Illia (ℭ **223/467-1506**), **Go!,** Av. Constitución 5780 (ℭ **223/479-6666**), and **Sobremonte,** Av. Constitución 6690 (ℭ **223/479-7930**). **Amsterdam,** Castilli 3045 (ℭ **15/527-8606**), is the best gay disco. **Coyote,** Av. Constitución 6670 (ℭ **223/479-7930**), is a favorite local bar which breaks into salsa and merengue dancing as the night goes on.

2 La Plata

55km (33 miles) S of Buenos Aires

La Plata began its history with the unification of Argentina in 1880. A decision was made that if Buenos Aires was to be the capital of the new country (which it often was in one way or another even before that date), then a new capital for Buenos Aires Province needed to be created. Thus was born La Plata, south of Buenos Aires along the Río de la Plata. Construction began in 1882. Many residents in La Plata claim it is the first planned city in Argentina, which is not true, since Spain planned dozens of them, but it was the first planned city in Argentina created after independence from Spain. Part of what will strike you about this city is its large number of parks and plazas and its diagonal streets, which cut across the city creating vista points and complex intersections. Because of this urban pattern, some people nickname La Plata "the Checkerboard City." The town is centered around the enormous Plaza Moreno, whose defining features are church and state: The cathedral and the municipal palace face each other across this vast grassy expanse.

ESSENTIALS

GETTING THERE   You can reach La Plata by car, bus, or train. The highway simply known as the **Autopista,** which begins at the southern end of Avenida 9 de Julio in Buenos Aires, connects that city to La Plata. In a car the trip will take 45 minutes to an hour. Buses between Buenos Aires and La Plata leave the capital from **Retiro** and arrive at the **La Plata Terminal de Omnibus** at the intersections of Diagonal 74 and avenidas 4 and 42 (ℭ **221/421-0992**). The main company serving La Plata is **Costera Metropolitana,** which also owns **Chevalier** (ℭ **0800/222-6565;** www.costerametropolitana.com). The ride can last anywhere from 1 to 2 hours depending on traffic or if the bus is a local or an Autopista express. Buses generally run about every 10 minutes and tickets are

La Plata

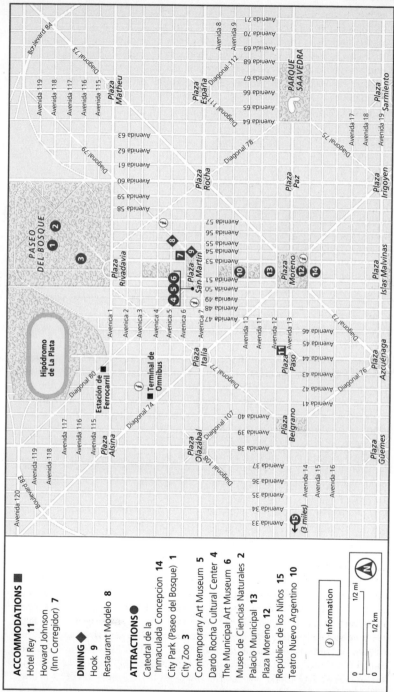

ACCOMMODATIONS ■

Hotel Rey **11**

Howard Johnson
(Inn Corregidor) **7**

DINING ◆

Hook **9**

Restaurant Modelo **8**

ATTRACTIONS ●

Catedral de la
Inmaculada Concepcion **14**

City Park (Paseo del Bosque) **1**

City Zoo **3**

Contemporary Art Museum **5**

Dardo Rocha Cultural Center **4**

The Municipal Art Museum **6**

Museo de Ciencias Naturales **2**

Palacio Municipal **13**

Plaza Moreno **12**

República de los Niños **15**

Teatro Nuevo Argentino **10**

ⓘ Information

0 ___ 1/2 mi

0 ___ 1/2 km

roughly $5 round-trip. A train also connects La Plata with Buenos Aires from **Constitución** in the southern part of the capital with **Estación La Plata** at the intersection of avenidas 1 and 44. Ticket prices are similar to the price of the bus. Trains run about every 15 to 30 minutes, depending on the day, and take about an hour and 20 minutes. However, the trains connecting La Plata and Buenos Aires have a high pickpocketing rate and are not recommended for tourists. In Buenos Aires call ℂ **11/1959-0800** for train tickets and in La Plata call ℂ **221-423-2575.**

VISITOR INFORMATION   There are two **Centros de Información Turística** in La Plata. One is in the Terminal de Omnibus, at the intersections of Diagonal 74 and avenidas 4 and 42, open daily 9am to 5pm (ℂ **221/427-3198**). The main center, only open on weekdays from 9am to 5pm, is in a building called the **Palacio Campodónico,** at the intersection of Diagonal 79 and avenidas 5 and 56 (ℂ **221/422-9764**). You can also visit www.laplata.gov.ar for more information about the city.

GETTING AROUND   La Plata is a relatively compact city, and most of what you'll want to see will be only about a 15-minute walk from either the train or bus station. You may, however, want to take a taxi to a few points lying in the suburbs of the city, including the **República de los Niños** amusement park. Cabs are easy to find at the bus and train stations and all over town, but if you need to call one, try the 24-hour company **Remises Horizonte** (ℂ **221/453-2800**). La Plata's streets are named with numbers using a grid pattern with the diagonals overlaid on top of this. Depending on the map or the person with whom you are speaking, the streets are either calles or avenidas, and the terms are used interchangeably, which can become confusing. However, no street number is used twice, so there is no worry of mistaking one for the other as can sometimes happen with other cities' numbered streets where you might find for instance an Eighth Avenue and 8th Street like in New York City. Portions of **Calle 8** have become a pedestrianized shopping street, and this is a good place to stop for ice cream or a drink at any of the numerous cafes lining the area.

WHAT TO SEE & DO

The city's most imposing building, the **Catedral de la Inmaculada Concepción,** avenidas 14 and 51 and 52 (ℂ **221/427-3504**), hovers over the **Plaza Moreno** in the center of the city. It was built in a medieval Gothic style more along the lines of a northern European church than what one would expect in a former Spanish colony. It is free for visits, but the lookout tower in one of the spires, known as the **Torre de Jesús (Jesus Tower)** costs about $2 to climb. The **Palacio Municipal,** Avenida 12 between avenidas 51 and 53, sits across the plaza and, though not a true tourist site, is worth looking at and entering for its interesting architecture. The **City Park (Paseo del Bosque)** sits on the edge of the center of town and is home to the **Museo de Ciencias Naturales.** This museum (ℂ **221/425-7744;** Tues–Sun 10am–6pm; admission $1) has the feel of an old Victorian institution with its mix of stuffed animals, archaeological relics, and other items displayed in the building's dusty, soaring, wrought-iron interior. Nearby and also in the park is the **City Zoo** (ℂ **221/4257-3925;** Tues–Sun 9am–6pm; admission $1, free for children), with over 180 kinds of animals. The **Teatro Nuevo Argentino,** Avenida 51 at avenidas 9 and 10 (ℂ **221/429-1700**), holds various productions and also houses an art exhibition center in its lobby with various displays of paintings and other art. More art and culture await at the enormous **Dardo Rocha Cultural Center,** Avenida 50 at avenidas 6 and 7 (© 221/427-1210 for all institutions), built into an old train station. Inside you'll find the **Contemporary Art Museum,** the **Municipal Art Museum,** and other cultural institutions housing various kinds of art, including works created by local artists as well as national figures, focusing on gauchos and other typical Argentine scenes. Hours and admission fees vary depending on the venue, but the place is always busy with something to do. A few miles from downtown is the interesting **República de los Niños,** Belgrano and Calle 501 (© 221/484-1409; www.republica.laplata.gov.ar), built by Juan and Evita Perón as a place of learning and entertainment for children. The small-size buildings imitate government buildings in Buenos Aires or are designed in themes related to various countries. This amusement park provided the inspiration for Walt Disney when he built Disneyland in California. Naturally, the rides and attractions here make this a great place to bring the kids.

CITY TOURS

The travel company **For Export,** Calle 5 no. 1241, between avenidas 57 and 58 (© 221/425-9393; www.forexport.net.ar), offers city tours in La Plata. Various themes include the Panoramic City Tour, which lasts half a day, the Full Day City Tour, as well as the Religious City Tour. They also arrange excursions outside of the city, hotel accommodations, and car rentals.

WHERE TO STAY

Hotel del Rey   An Argentine-owned three-star property, the Hotel del Rey is a bargain considering its location and services. Rooms are of an average size; those on the upper floors come with nice views of the surrounding parts of the city. A travel agency is located in the lobby, which makes excursions and arrangements easy.

Plaza Paso 180 (at avs. 13 and 44), 1900 La Plata. © 221/427-0177. www.hoteldelrey.com.ar. 40 units. From $23 double. Rates include buffet breakfast. AE, DC, MC, V. Free parking. **Amenities:** Restaurant; bar; concierge; business center; 24-hr. room service; laundry service; dry cleaning. *In room:* A/C, TV, minibar.

Howard Johnson (Inn Corregidor)   This Howard Johnson is very well situated near many of La Plata's government buildings and tourist sites and is a few blocks off of Plaza Moreno. Rooms are well equipped, and many have a light, airy feeling to them. This place is sometimes known by its old name, Inn Corregidor.

Calle 6 no. 1026 (at avs. 53 and 54), 1900 La Plata. © 221/425-6800. Fax 221/425-6805. www.hotel corregidor.com.ar and www.hojoar.com. 110 units, 1 apt. From $45 double. Rates include buffet breakfast. AE, DC, MC, V. Free parking. **Amenities:** Restaurant; bar; health club; concierge; business center; 24-hr. room service; laundry service; dry cleaning. *In room:* A/C, TV, high-speed Internet, minibar, hair dryer, safe.

WHERE TO DINE

Hook   ARGENTINE/IRISH/SEAFOOD   With its vague pirate-and-shipwreck theme, Hook takes its name from Captain Hook of seafaring legend. It's a pub and restaurant with a very friendly staff that likes to chat with patrons at the bar. Seafood and Irish and Argentine items are the main menu draws here. During the lunch hours, they also have an inexpensive Executive menu, which is a real bargain at about $4 to $5.

Av. 53 no. 538, between avs. 5 and 6. © 221/482-2160. Main courses $2–$5. No credit cards. Mon–Sat 8am–2am; Sun 8pm–2am.

Restaurant Modelo   ARGENTINE/ITALIAN   You won't find any models lurking around here as the name might imply, but you will find professional service and high-quality food in an interior that looks more English than Argentine. At night the bar becomes the highlight and fills up with a young crowd drinking beer and making a mess as they shell peanuts and throw the remains all over the floor.

Calle 5, at Av. 54. ✆ 221/421-1321. Main courses $2–$5. No credit cards. Daily 8am–3am.

3 Gualeguaychú & Argentina's National Carnaval

250km (150 miles) N of Buenos Aires

Carnaval might be more associated with neighboring Brazil, but that does not mean that you won't find entertainment of a similar nature in Argentina. The Argentine Mesopotamia region, which encompasses the provinces of Missiones, Entre Ríos, and Corrientes, is where many of these festive events are held. The most popular of all these, made so by a huge amount of marketing and proximity to Buenos Aires, is that of Gualeguaychú, in the southern part of Entre Ríos province. Unlike in Rio, however, where Carnaval is a concentrated few days, Gualeguaychú's event is held every Saturday in January, February, and sometimes even the first week in March. If you're in Buenos Aires during this time period, it's a great destination for a side trip.

The town of 75,000 people gears up for this all year. Each weekend during the event, more than 30,000 visitors descend on the town to see the **Corsos,** or schools, which are groups of people who band together to produce the Carnaval spectacle. They perform in all their feathered fineness and compete with other Corsos. At the end of the 2 months, one Corso is chosen as the winner. The stadium where the Carnaval is held is called the **Corsodromo.**

Gualeguaychú is more than worth the trip, as it's an interesting diversion from Buenos Aires as well as a chance to see how Argentina does its Carnaval. The city is not well set up, however, for international travelers, as most visitors come from Buenos Aires and other parts of Argentina (though a few do come from Brazil and Uruguay). In other words, it's almost impossible to find anyone who speaks English whether at the hotels, the Corsodromo, or the Tourism Information Centers. Of course, that also makes it all the more fun and authentic. In addition to Carnaval, the area is surrounded by beaches along the Río Gualeguaychú and the Río Uruguay. Many Porteños choose to vacation here for the beaches, camping, and fishing.

For such a small town, Gualeguaychú also has intense nightlife, with several bars and clubs hugging the Costanera (the walkway along the Río Gualeguaychú). Gualeguaychú was also an area of mass German immigration, so it has a disproportionate amount of blonds in relation to other areas of Argentina. The German influence is present in some of the food, architecture, and hotels throughout the city. Be aware that this is a town that still adheres to the practice of siestas, so you should expect that nearly everything other than some restaurants and a few small convenience stores will close between 1 and 4pm.

ESSENTIALS

GETTING THERE   You can reach Gualeguaychú by bus or car. There is no nearby airport with commercial services, and rail transport ended long ago. (In fact, the train station was converted into the Carnaval stadium, so it is unlikely that train service will ever return to the town.) If traveling by car from Buenos Aires, take Ruta 12 north from Buenos Aires and then go north again on Ruta 14 where they intersect. Buses for Gualeguaychú from Buenos Aires leave from

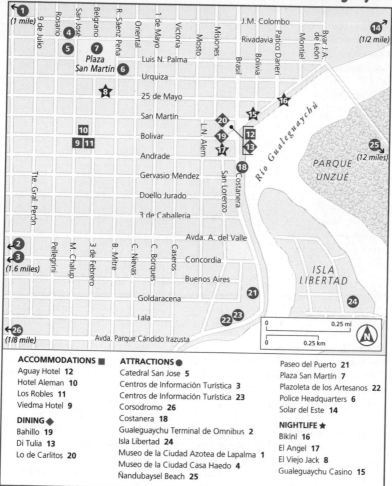

the **Retiro Bus Station** and go to the **Gualeguaychú Terminal de Omnibus** at Boulevard Jurardo and Boulevard Artigas (© **3446/440-688**). The journey takes about 3 hours. Various companies will make the trip, including **Flecha-Bus.** Call © **3446/440-776** in Gualeguaychú or © **11/4315-2781** in Buenos Aires for tickets, schedules, and information or visit www.flechabus.com.ar. Many travel agencies in Buenos Aires also have special bus day trips to the Carnaval. These trips leave Buenos Aires in the afternoon, stay in Gualeguaychú for the Carnaval event, and then return to Buenos Aires after 3 or 4am.

VISITOR INFORMATION   There are two **Centros de Información Turística** in Gualeguaychú. One is at the bus station (© **3446/440-706**). The main center is at the Plazoleta de los Artesanos, at Paseo del Puerto along the waterfront (© **3446/423-668** or 3446/422-900). Both are generally open daily from 9am to 6pm. In the summer, however, the main branch on the port is open 8am to midnight Friday through Sunday. They have a selection of maps, hotel information, and they can also help with finding accommodations, which can be very difficult in high season. Their website, though only in Spanish, is the best tourism website I've ever used in Argentina, based on its logical format, ease of use, and wealth of information. Access it at www.gualeguaychuturismo.com. Within Buenos Aires, the province of Entre Ríos has a tourism information center at Suipacha 846 (© 11/4326-2573), which also provides information on Gualeguaychú as well as other carnivals in the region.

GETTING AROUND   Within Gualeguaychú, most of what you need is accessible within a small walking distance of the center of the city along the Costanera, the walkway along the Río Gualeguaychú. Within this area you will find beaches and camping sites all within site of downtown. Even the Corso-dromo, once the old railroad station, is walkable from downtown in about 20 minutes. The best close beach is the **Solar del Este,** just northeast of town. Other excellent camping sites and beaches exist within a few miles of downtown Gualeguaychú. A car makes things much easier when you're here, but there are no car-rental services in Gualeguaychú or in the surrounding cities. The solution is to rent a car in Buenos Aires and drive to Gualeguaychú. You can also take taxis wherever you need to go or make arrangements to have a driver take you to the beach in the morning and pick you up at a specified time in the after-noon. One 24-hour cab company is **Remiss Boulevard** (© 0800/888-4010 or 3446/434-010). Another is **Remiss Plaza** (© 0800/444-0644 or 3446/431-136). You can also ask your hotel concierge to make arrangements for you. Cabs can be flagged down on the street but can be hard to find at peak times.

WHAT TO SEE & DO

The main reason for coming to Gualeguaychú is for the Carnaval. It is held every Saturday in January and February (and sometimes in the beginning of Mar), usually at about 10pm, and runs for about 5 hours. It is a massive party, held within the **Corsodromo,** which was built over the site of the old railroad station at the intersection of avenidas Rocamora and Piccini. Tickets can be reserved by calling the Corsodromo's ticket office at © **3446/430901.** Once reserved, tickets need to be paid for and picked up the Friday before the event or by noon the Saturday of the Corso. Tickets are about $5, with various forms of seating running an additional $1 to $3. The sooner you reserve your ticket, the better your seating assignment will be, as a limited amount of seating exists within the bleachers of the stadium. Late ticket purchasers simply stand along the route of the event in a fenced-in area of the Corsodromo. If you forget to buy tickets, there are always scalpers. Visit the main tourism website www.gualeguaychuturismo.com for more information or see www.carnavaldelpais.com.ar. While the Corsodromo ticket office has the best selection of tickets, individual Corsos and organizations also buy up sets of tickets in blocks and resell them to the public so that an entire group can sit in one area of the stands and cheer the performers on together. One of the largest sellers of individual Corso tickets is the **Club Sirio Libanés,** which runs the **Kamar Corso** group (© **3446/425-673**), one of the city's most popular.

Within the town there are a few interesting sites, most of them centered around the **Plaza San Martín.** The town is relatively young, only established by the Spanish in 1783, and this was the original Plaza Mayor. A statue of San Martín on horseback sits in the center of the plaza. Nearby are busts of various local heroes and heroines, though vandals unfortunately destroyed the noses of most of them. A merry-go-round, swing sets, and kiosks selling ice cream and candy make the park an ideal place to bring children. Overlooking the park, on Calle San José, is **Catedral San José.** Its facade is ornamented by Corinthian columns, and the interior has a gilded altar and frescoed ceilings with scenes of the lives of various saints. The **Police Headquarters** overlooks the plaza on Sáenz Peña, but it is not open to the public, unless you need to report a crime or plan to get caught committing one. It is a churchlike Italianate structure with a columned facade and central tower. Most of the remainder of the buildings on the plaza are nondescript, save for a turn-of-the-20th-century school building.

There are two historic house museums in Gualeguaychú. One is the **Museo de la Ciudad Casa Haedo,** at the intersection of Rivadavia and San José (no phone). Built around 1801, it is a Spanish colonial structure with original floors and other remaining details. It is full of Victorian furniture, an old gun collection, and portraits of the Haedo family. Legend has it that one of the young female members of the Lapalma family died of a broken heart and haunts the **Museo de la Ciudad Azotea de Lapalma,** at calles San Luis and Rioja (© **3446/437-028**). This beautiful 1835 former hacienda, built on what was once the edge of town, contains material related to the founding of the city. Both museums are open Wednesday to Sunday from 9am to noon and Friday and Saturday from 5 to 8pm. Both are closed on Monday and Tuesday.

Along the waterfront is the long **Costanera.** People stroll here day and night, and the beaches under this promenade are full of people fishing, sunbathing, and picnicking. It's normal for people here to begin to chat with strangers and invite them to sit down and share *mate,* the Argentine herbal tea, with them, so don't be surprised if that happens to you.

Farther down the Costanera, just to the south of the center of town, is the **Paseo del Puerto,** a continuation of the Costanera but with small grassy plazas along the route. This is where the tourism office is located. The **Plazoleta de los Artesanos,** full of local craftspeople, is also in this area. Most stalls are open in January and February on the weekends from about 8am to 1am. Some are also open those hours daily during those months. Various boat companies are also located here and offer rides along the river and around the **Isla Libertad,** an island in the center of the river. One company offering these services is **Paseos Náuticos** (© **3446/423-248**), which runs the trips six times a day for $2 per person in high season. About 19km (12 miles) from town is **Ñandubaysel** beach, which is famed for its sunsets. Since so many people camp here overnight, you'll pass many tents between the parking lot and the beach. From here, the Río Uruguay is relatively narrow and the country of Uruguay seems almost reachable by swimming.

WHERE TO STAY

Aguay Hotel 🌟🌟   The Aguay Hotel is the city's newest and best-situated hotel, opened in 2001. It directly overlooks the Costanera, and the top-floor rooms as well as the rooftop pool have incredible views over the river and surrounding land. Service is superb, but very few members of the staff speak English. All rooms have balconies, and suites have Jacuzzis in the bathrooms. The hotel is also close to the casino and the bars on the Costanera, so it can be noisy in the evening to stay here, but you will be right in the middle of all of the action. A front garden and waterfalled walkway add to the ambience and are sometimes the location of wedding and honeymoon photos. The hotel has two restaurants, the fancy Italian Di Julia in the lobby and a rooftop drink-and-snack bar where breakfast is served. I recommend coming here for drinks even if you are not staying in the hotel as the view is unmatched anywhere in the city.

Av. Costanera 130 (at Bolívar), 2820 Gualeguaychú. ℂ **3446/422-099**. www.hotelaguay.com.ar. 18 units. From $43 double; from $63 suite. Rates include continental breakfast. AE, MC, V. Free parking. **Amenities:** 2 restaurants; small rooftop swimming pool; small gym; 24-hr. room service; laundry service; dry cleaning; Internet service in lobby. *In room:* A/C, TV, minibar, hair dryer, safe.

Hotel Alemán   This charming little hotel is owned by a family of German descent, and the architecture is mildly Bavarian on the outside to give a hint of their former homeland. The hotel is about 50 years old, but as of this writing it is about halfway through an expansion and renovation process. Renovated or new rooms have wood paneling, floral-pattern bedspreads and drapes, and modernized bathrooms. Rooms overlook a brilliantly sunny courtyard, and upper-level rooms have small patios.

Bolívar 535 (at 3 de Febrero), 2820 Gualeguaychú. ℂ **3446/426-153**. 26 units. From $22 double. Rates include continental breakfast. No credit cards. Free parking. *In room:* A/C, TV, hair dryer, safe.

Los Robles   This small hotel is what Argentines call a *residencial* because of the few services it offers. Rooms can be on the small side, with the beds jammed tightly together, and are spartan and undecorated, but all rooms come with cable TV and air-conditioning. Some rooms can accommodate up to four people and so are good for a family with children. The hotel is in need of some renovation, as it's over 40 years old, though it has only been open as Los Robles since 2000. The staff is very friendly, and manager Javier's family often comes to visit him and help out, socializing in the lobby and confitería while answering patrons' questions about the city. Breakfast is served in the confitería on the main floor and is a simple coffee-and-tea service with croissants. Bathrooms have showers only (no tubs). There is no Internet service within the hotel.

Bolívar 565 (at 3 de Febrero), 2820 Gualeguaychú. ℂ **3446/436-866**. hotellosrobles@turismoentrerios.com. 16 units, shower only. From $20 double. Rates include continental breakfast. No credit cards. Free parking. **Amenities:** Restaurant. *In room:* A/C, TV.

Viedma Hotel   Don't be put off by the very modern architecture on the outside of this building. With its friendly service and country Victorian–style decor full of honey pine furniture, the Viedma is a pleasant place to stay in Gualeguaychú. Rooms are very large, with wood paneling and wainscoting in some of them, adding even more of a country touch. The hotel, though a few blocks away from the coveted Costanera area, has no views to the waterfront because the buildings near it are all the same size. However, it is quiet at night, an important consideration. Rooms can accommodate one to four people in varying combinations, and suites come with an extra room. Breakfast is continental, served in the main dining area in the lobby. All bathrooms come with shower stalls only (no tub). There is no Internet access on the premises.

Bolívar 530 (at 3 de Febrero), 2820 Gualeguaychú. ℂ **3446/424-262**. viedmahotel@ciudad.com.ar. 28 units, shower only. From $20 double. Rates include continental breakfast. DC, MC, V. Parking $4 on weekends in high season; all other times it's free. *In room:* A/C, TV.

WHERE TO DINE

Bahillo ICE CREAM   Head to this ice-cream parlor for ice cream, sorbets, and other sweet treats, and eat them on the benches on the sidewalk like all the Argentine tourists do. This is a great place to bring the kids or to take a break yourself when walking around in the summer heat.

Costanera, at San Lorenzo. ℂ **3446/426-240**. Ice cream $1–$2. No credit cards. Daily 10am–3am or later.

Di Tulia 𝄐𝄐 ARGENTINE/ITALIAN   Located in the lobby of the Aguay Hotel, this is the best restaurant in Gualeguaychú, an Italian restaurant that concentrates on northern Italian cuisine as well as some seafood. They also have an excellent selection of wines.

Av. Costanera 130, at Bolívar. © **3446/429-940.** Main courses $4–$8. AE, MC, V. Daily noon–4pm and 8pm–1am.

Lo De Carlitos (R) ARGENTINE/ITALIAN/PARRILLA   Carlos has run this family establishment on the waterfront for years. The interior is simple, with an emphasis on the service, and a small sidewalk outdoor-dining area is also provided. The restaurant serves mostly basic Argentine food from the *parrilla* as well as a large selection of seafood and basic Italian dishes, all in large servings.

San Martín 206, at Costanera. © **3446/432-582.** Main courses $3–$6. No credit cards. Daily noon–3pm and 8pm–2am.

GUALEGUAYCHU AFTER DARK

For such a small town, Gualeguaychú has a good nightlife scene, based around the Costanera and a few surrounding streets. The newest highlight of nightlife here is not a bar but the **Gualeguaychú Casino,** Costanera and San Martín (© **3446/424-603**), which opened in February of 2005. The owners call it the world's only Carnaval-themed casino, and it has been beautifully decorated in a Carnaval theme by local artists. About a hundred slot machines, several card and roulette tables, and other forms of gambling entertainment await you inside. In addition, there are bars, restaurants, a live theater, and a babysitting service in the casino.

The most popular nightclub in town is the enormous **Bikini,** Costanera at 25 de Mayo (no phone). It holds a few thousand people with a main dance floor and an outdoor patio and Tiki bar. It is only open Friday and Saturday from 2am to 9am. **El Angel,** San Lorenzo 79 (© **3446/432-927**), offers drag shows and other entertainment from Thursday to Sunday beginning at 11pm and has a gay following. **El Viejo Jack,** 25 de Mayo 533, at 3 de Febrero (© **3446/15-531-160** [cell]), is a more traditional bar with a relaxed atmosphere and pool tables, but it becomes very crowded late at night. It opens at 9am and does not close until 6 or 7am the next morning. You'll also find any variety of nightlife all over the Costanera. Every restaurant, and there are dozens of them, serves alcohol until the very early morning in the summertime, and the crowds spill into the street for blocks and blocks. For photos of nightlife in the city, visit the website www.2820.com.ar, which is named for the Gualeguaychú postal code, and click on "Noche."

4 Tigre & the Delta

36km (21 miles) NE of Buenos Aires

The Tigre River Delta is in essence a wild natural suburb of the city of Buenos Aires, but it seems a complete world apart from the city. The delta is formed by the confluence of five rivers where they flow from the Pampas into the Río de la Plata. This marshy complex is full of silt and hundreds of tiny islands and is over time continuing to grow down the Río de la Plata. The delta area has grown considerably since the Spanish Conquest, and within several hundred years, in theory at least, the Río Tigre delta will actually reach the city of Buenos Aires. The islands here are a mix of grassland, swamp, and true forest, with a variety of animal and plant life.

The development of the Tigre Delta into a resort area was due to two concurrent historical circumstances in Buenos Aires in the 1870s. One was the construction of railroads from Buenos Aires into the rest of the country. The other was the 1877 outbreak of yellow fever, which caused wealthy people to not only seek new areas for home construction within Buenos Aires but also new locations for summer vacations. The English were in charge of much of the construction here, so many of the older neo-Gothic and mock-Tudor mansions and bed-and-breakfasts lining the banks of the river passages look like buildings from Victorian London transplanted into the wilds of the Pampas marshes.

Today many Porteños seek a peaceful weekend here relaxing, horseback riding, hiking, fishing, swimming, or doing nothing at all. It's also an attractive destination, since it's possible (and easy) to come here just for the day (take a boat around to tour the islands) and be back in Buenos Aires in time for dinner. There is a year-round population who go to school, work, and grocery-shop using a system of boats and docks on these car-free inner islands.

ESSENTIALS

GETTING THERE The Tigre Delta is best reached by a combination of train from Buenos Aires and then a boat, or launch, from the train station. Trains from Buenos Aires leave from **Estación Retiro** for Estación Tigre, at Avenida Naciones Unidas, every 10 to 20 minutes along the Mitre Line. Tickets run about $1 round-trip. Call ℂ **0800/3333-TBA** or 11/4317-4445 for schedules and information or visit www.tbanet.com.ar. Within Tigre the **Estación Fluvial Tigre,** where the boats leave from to head through the various rivers and islands, is on the next block over from **Estación Tigre,** at Mitre 305. There are many companies with different launches and services on both banks of the river here. You have to know where you want to go, or simply choose one and go wherever it takes you. Among the many companies are **Catamaranes Interisleña** (ℂ 11/4731-0261); **Líneas Delta** (ℂ 11/4749-0537); and **Catamaranes Río Tur** (ℂ 11/4731-0280). For **Martín García Island,** one of the most remote parts of the Delta, **Cacciola** (ℂ 11/4749-0329) is the only boat company that goes there. Most of these companies service the various islands but will allow you to ride on the boat until the end of the trip and then simply return. Ticket prices vary but range from less than $1 and up. I highly recommend that you find out when the last few boats leave from your destination; toward the end of the day, some boats fill up so quickly that some docks are bypassed on the return trip because there is no room for additional passengers. Extra boats are sent at peak times, but this may mean a wait of a few extra hours at the end of the day, especially on Sunday, so build this into your plans. Many tour companies in Buenos Aires also provide excursions to the Tigre Delta, and I have included that information below.

VISITOR INFORMATION In theory, there are two **Centros de Información Turística** in Tigre. There is one in Estación Tigre, but it never seems to be open; even the train staff members I spoke with indicated that it is rarely ever open. However, within Estación Fluvial Tigre, at Mitre 305 (ℂ **0800/888-TIGRE** or 11/4512-4497; www.tigre.gov.ar), there is another office that is open daily from 9am to 5pm. It is a very busy office providing information on the islands, hotels and rentable bungalows, and other activities. Another useful tourism website is www.puntodelta.com.ar.

GETTING AROUND Within the town of Tigre itself, where both the train station and the docks are, one can easily walk along both banks. There are restaurants, playgrounds for children, and a few shops of a touristic nature along

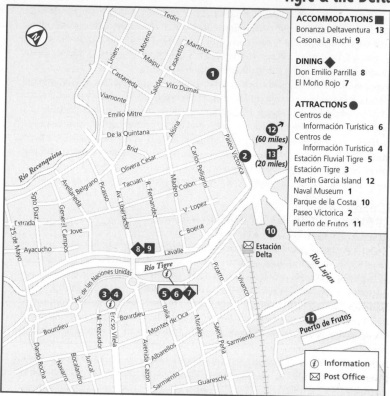

ACCOMMODATIONS ■
Bonanza Deltaventura **13**
Casona La Ruchi **9**

DINING ◆
Don Emilio Parrilla **8**
El Moño Rojo **7**

ATTRACTIONS ●
Centros de
   Información Turística **6**
Centros de
   Información Turística **4**
Estación Fluvial Tigre **5**
Estación Tigre **3**
Martin Garcia Island **12**
Naval Museum **1**
Parque de la Costa **10**
Paseo Victorica **2**
Puerto de Frutos **11**

ⓘ Information
✉ Post Office

the waterfront and on the streets heading to the Puerto de Frutos (see below). To get around and see the delta, however, you will need a boat. I have listed the companies providing these services above. Of course, if you're a good swimmer, that is another option.

WHAT TO SEE & DO

The main thing to see in Tigre is the delta itself and the various islands and resorts that dot the area. Within the town of Tigre, where the train station and the boat docks are, there are a few services and various other places of interest. Many people simply stay in this area and dine in the restaurants, sunbathe along the shoreline, or wander the town. Ideal for children are the various ponies available for rides that march up and down the eastern shoreline in the city center near the intersection of calles Lavalle and Fernández (no address or phone). From this area, head along what is called **Paseo Victorica,** a collection of Victorian mansions along the waterfront of Río Lujan, until it intersects with Río Conquista. This is one of the prettiest parts of Tigre, and you will find many people sunbathing along the shore here also. In the midst of all this Victorian splendor is the **Naval Museum,** Paseo Victorica 602, at Martínez (ⓒ **11/4749-0608**). On the other bank, across from here, is the **Parque de la Costa,** Vivanco, at Montes de Oca (ⓒ **11/4732-6000**), full of rides for kids and grownups. Just outside of the center of Tigre is the famous **Puerto de Frutos,** at

150 Calle Sarmiento, along Río Lujan. Fruit farming was integral to the early development of the Tigre Delta, and this market is a leftover from those days. However, the market is now mostly full of odds and ends and other crafts and almost no fruit at all. What does remain, though, are the basket weavers who create their wares using the reeds growing in the delta.

A 3-hour boat ride each way from the center of Tigre will take you to **Martín García Island.** It is famous for its upscale political prison where various Argentine presidents, including Juan Perón, have been locked up, but visiting and exploring here will take a full day when you add in the round-trip boat ride.

If you are doing any trekking while on the islands in the delta, you will need hiking boots, long pants, and long-sleeved shirts. Saw grass and other very sharp forms of plants inhabit the area and will rip into unprotected skin. You should also bring mosquito repellent. And packing binoculars to see birds and other wildlife is a good idea.

TRAVEL COMPANIES PROVIDING TIGRE DELTA EXCURSIONS

Various travel companies in Buenos Aires provide day-trip excursions to the Río Tigre delta or will arrange longer stays in the numerous bed-and-breakfasts, bungalows, and adventure lodges in the area. **Mayer & Mayer and Say Hueque Tourism,** Viamonte 749, Office 601, 1053 Buenos Aires (© **11/5199-2517,** -2518, -2519, -2520; www.sayhueque.com) is one that I highly recommend, especially for longer trips and adventure excursions to see the natural beauty of the area. Agent Marcos often leads the trips himself, and he is very knowledgeable about the area. A 2-day weekend excursion including accommodations and trekking runs about $120 per person. **Travel Line** (© **11/4393-9000;** www. travelline.com.ar) offers Tigre Delta day tours among many others. The full-day Tigre tours are Sundays only (ask for an English-speaking guide), and include lunch, a ride to and from Tigre by train, and a boat ride among the rivers of the Tigre delta for about $40 per person.

WHERE TO STAY

Bonanza Deltaventura 𝕽𝕽   If you really want to get away from it all, head to this hotel on one of the islands in the Río Tigre delta. It has miles of walkways through the grasslands for bird- and other animal-watching as well as horses for riding along the shoreline. Or you can just swim off the dock out front. There are four small but comfortable rooms that can be rented as singles or doubles for a total of eight people in the lodge. The living style is communal, with shared bathrooms and kitchen. The price includes breakfast and some excursions, but there is an additional charge for other meals and drinks. The staff also speaks English. You will need to call ahead of time to make arrangements to stay here so you can be sure that space is available and that you take the right boat company. The hotel is on the Carapachay River islands section of the delta, about a 1-hour boat ride from the center of the town of Tigre.

Carapachay River Islands, 1648 Tigre. © **11/4798-2254** or 11/15-5603-7176 (cell). www.deltaventura.com. 4 units for up to 8 people. From $50 a person including breakfast and trekking. No credit cards. **Amenities:** Horses; trekking; use of kitchen.

Casona La Ruchi 𝕽𝕽   This charming bed-and-breakfast overlooks the waterfront across the bank from the Estación Fluvial. Its owners Dora and Jorge Escuariza and their children run the place, treating guests who stay in the six-room, 1893 mansion like family. In the back is a pool and a grill where guests can gather and barbecue. Rooms are furnished with quaint Victorian antiques, and some have windows looking out onto the waterfront. The place is open year-round, but is busiest during summer weekends. Guests have 24-hour access to the hotel, though the family does not have an actual overnight staff person. Call if arriving late in the day to verify that someone can let you in. You will enjoy the warmth and hospitality in this place. Some rooms share a bathroom.

Lavalle 557 (at Av. Libertador), 1648 Tigre. 𝄞 11/4749-2499. www.casonalaruchi.com.ar. 6 units, some with shared bathroom. $30 double. Rates include continental breakfast. No credit cards. **Amenities:** Outdoor pool; use of kitchen and backyard grill.

WHERE TO DINE

Don Emilio Parrilla ARGENTINE/PARRILLA   A rustic interior and a casual atmosphere with tables in bright Provençal yellow await you in this *parrilla* overlooking the waterfront. The food here is great, and a complete meal will run you only a little over $5 a person. Unfortunately, it's only open on weekends.

Lavalle 573, at Av. Libertador. 𝄞 11/4631-8804. Main courses $1–$3. No credit cards. Fri 8pm–1am; Sat–Sun 11:30am–5pm and 8pm–2am.

El Moño Rojo 𝄪 ARGENTINE/INTERNATIONAL   An enormous restaurant complex overlooking the waterfront near the Estación Fluvial, this is one of the best places to come for a meal with entertainment. The atmosphere is brilliantly red, festive, and very kitschy, full of posters of tango stars, pictures of Argentine actors and actresses, and old Peronist memorabilia. On Friday they have a tango show. The food is a mixture of pizzas, snacks, sandwiches, and traditional *parrilla* grilled meat, so there should be something to please everyone here.

Av. Mitre 345, at Estación Fluvial Tigre. 𝄞 11/15-5135-7781 (cell). Main courses $2–$3. No credit cards. Daily 8am–2am.

5 Colonia del Sacramento, Uruguay

by Haas Mroue

140km (67 miles) W of Buenos Aires

The tiny gem of Colonia del Sacramento, declared a World Heritage City by UNESCO, appears untouched by time. Dating from the 17th century, the old city boasts beautifully preserved colonial artistry down its dusty streets. A leisurely stroll into the **Barrio Histórico (Historic Neighborhood)** leads you under flower-laden windowsills to churches dating from the 1680s, past exquisite single-story homes from Colonia's time as a Portuguese settlement, and on to local museums detailing the riches of the town's past. The Barrio Histórico contains brilliant examples of colonial wealth and many of Uruguay's oldest structures. A mix of lovely shops and delicious cafes makes the town more than a history lesson.

ESSENTIALS
GETTING THERE

The easiest way to reach Colonia from Buenos Aires is by ferry. **FerryLíneas** (𝄞 02/900-6617) runs a fast boat that arrives in 45 minutes. **Buquebús** (𝄞 02/916-1910) also offers two classes of service. Prices range from $18 to $40 each way.

Colonia can also easily be visited from Montevideo and is a good stopping-off point if you're traveling between Buenos Aires and Montevideo. **COT** (𝄞 02/409-4949 in Montevideo) also offers bus service from Montevideo and from Punta del Este.

Citizens of the United States, the United Kingdom, Canada, and New Zealand need only a passport to enter Uruguay (for tourist stays of up to 90 days). Australian citizens must get a tourist visa before arrival.

VISITOR INFORMATION

The **Oficina de Turismo,** General Flores and Rivera (© **052/27000** or 052/27300), is open daily from 8am to 8pm. Speak with someone at the tourism office to arrange a guided tour of the town.

MONEY

The official currency is the **Uruguayan peso** (designated NP$, $U, or simply $); each peso is comprised of 100 **centavos.** Uruguayan pesos are available in $10, $20, $50, $100, $200, $500, $1,000, and $5,000 notes; coins come in 10, 20, and 50 centavos, and 1 and 2 pesos. The Uruguayan currency devalued by half in July 2002, and the exchange rate as this book went to press was approximately 26 pesos to the dollar. Because the value of the peso fluctuates greatly with inflation, all prices in this chapter are quoted in U.S. dollars.

WHAT TO SEE & DO
A WALK THROUGH COLONIA'S BARRIO HISTORICO

Your visit to Colonia will be concentrated in the **Barrio Histórico (Old Neighborhood),** located on the coast at the far southwestern corner of town. The sites, which are all within a few blocks of each other, can easily be visited on foot within a few hours. Museums and tourist sites are open daily (except Tues–Wed) from 11:30am to 5:45pm. For less than $1, you can buy a pass at the Portuguese or Municipal museums that will get you into all the sites.

Start your tour at **Plaza Mayor,** the principal square that served as the center of the colonial establishment. To explore Colonia's Portuguese history, cross the Calle Manuel Lobo on the southeastern side of the plaza and enter the **Museo Portugués (Portuguese Museum),** which exhibits European customs and traditions that influenced the town's beginnings. Upon exiting the museum, turn left and walk to the **Iglesia Matriz,** among the oldest churches in the country and an excellent example of 17th-century architecture and design.

Next, exit the church and turn left to the **Ruinas Convento San Francisco (San Francisco Convent ruins).** Dating from 1696, the San Francisco convent was once inhabited by Jesuit and Franciscan monks, two brotherhoods dedicated to preaching the gospel to indigenous people. Continue up Calle San Francisco to the **Casa de Brown (Brown House),** which houses the **Museo Municipal (Municipal Museum).** Here, you will find an impressive collection of colonial documents and artifacts, a must-see for history buffs.

For those with a more artistic bent, turn left on Calle Misiones de los Tapes and walk 2 blocks to the **Museo del Azulejo (Tile Museum),** a unique museum of 19th-century European and Uruguayan tiles housed in a gorgeous 300-year-old country house. Then stroll back into the center of town along Calle de la Playa, enjoying the shops and cafes along the way, until you come to the **Ruinas Casa del Gobernador (House of the Viceroy ruins).** The House of the Viceroy captures something of the glorious past of the city's 17th- and 18th-century magistrates, when the city's port was used for imports, exports, and smuggling. Complete your walk with a visit to the **UNESCO–Colonia** headquarters, where exhibits on the city's newly acquired Historic Heritage of Humanity status will place your tour in the larger context of South American history.

WHERE TO STAY & DINE

Few people stay in Colonia, preferring to make a day trip from Buenos Aires or stop along the way to Montevideo. If you'd rather get a hotel, however, your best bets are the colonial-style **Hotel Plaza Mayor,** Calle del Comercio 111 (℃ **052/ 23193**), and **Hotel La Misión,** Calle Misiones de los Tapes 171 (℃ **052/ 26767**), whose original building dates from 1762. Both hotels charge from $80 for a double. For dining, **Mesón de la Plaza,** Vasconcellos 153 (℃ **052/24807**), serves quality international and Uruguayan food in a colonial setting, while **Pulpería de los Faroles,** Calle Misiones de los Tapes 101 (℃ **052/25399**), in front of Plaza Mayor, specializes in beef and bean dishes and homemade pasta.

6 Montevideo, Uruguay

by Haas Mroue

215km (134 miles) E of Buenos Aires

Montevideo, the southernmost capital on the continent, is home to half of Uruguay's population. On the banks of the Río de la Plata, Montevideo first existed as a fortress of the Spanish empire and developed into a major port city in the mid–18th century. European immigrants, including Spanish, Portuguese, French, and British, influenced the city's architecture, and a walk around the capital reveals architectural styles ranging from colonial to Art Deco. Indeed, the richness of Montevideo's architecture is unrivaled in South America.

Although Montevideo has few must-see attractions, its charm lies in wait for the careful traveler. A walk along La Rambla, stretching from the Old City to the neighborhood of Carrasco, takes you along the riverfront past fishermen and their catch to parks and gardens where children play and elders sip *mate* (a tealike beverage). Restaurants, cafes, bars, and street performers populate the port area, where you will also discover the flavors of Uruguay at the afternoon and weekend Mercado del Puerto (Port Market). Many of the city's historic sites surround Plaza Independencia and can be visited in a few hours.

ESSENTIALS

GETTING THERE

International flights and those from Buenos Aires land at **Carrasco International Airport** (℃ **02/604-0386**), located 19km (12 miles) from downtown Montevideo. Uruguay's national carrier is **Pluna,** Colonia and Julio Herrera (℃ **0800/118-811** or 02/604-4080), which operates several flights daily from Aeroparque. **Aerolíneas Argentinas** (℃ **02/901-9466**) connects both Aeroparque and Ezeiza with Montevideo; the flight takes 50 minutes. The fare ranges between $140 and $220 round-trip, depending on how far in advance you make reservations.

A taxi or *remise* (private, unmetered taxi) from the airport to downtown costs about $15.

BY BOAT OR HYDROFOIL   The most popular way to get to Montevideo, **Buquebús,** Calle Río Negro 1400 (℃ **02/916-8801**), operates three to four hydrofoils per day from Buenos Aires; the trip takes about 2½ hours and costs about $90 round-trip. Montevideo's port is about 1.5km (1 mile) from downtown.

BY BUS   **Terminal Omnibus Tres Cruces,** General Artigas 1825 (℃ **02/409-7399**), is Montevideo's long-distance bus terminal, connecting the capital with cities in Uruguay and throughout South America. Buses to Buenos Aires take about 8 hours. **COT** (© **02/409-4949**) offers the best service to Punta del Este, Maldonado, and Colonia.

ORIENTATION

Montevideo is surrounded by water on three sides, a testament to its earlier incarnation as an easily defended fortress for the Spanish empire. The Old City begins near the western edge of Montevideo, found on the skinny portion of a peninsula between the Rambla Gran Bretaña and the city's main artery, Avenida 18 de Julio. Look for Plaza Independencia and Plaza Constitución to find the center of the district. Many of the city's museums, theaters, and hotels reside in this historic area, although a trip east on Avenida 18 de Julio reveals the more modern Montevideo with its own share of hotels, markets, and monuments. Along the city's long southern coastline runs the Rambla Gran Bretaña, traveling 21km (13 miles) from the piers of the Old City past Parque Rodó and on to points south and east, passing fish stalls and street performers along the way.

GETTING AROUND

It's easy to navigate around the center of Montevideo on foot or by bus. Safe, convenient buses crisscross Montevideo if you want to venture outside the city center (for less than $1 per trip). Taxis are safe and relatively inexpensive but can be difficult to hail during rush hour. One recommended company is **Remises Carrasco** (© **09/440-5473**). To rent a car, try **Thrifty** (© **02/204-3373**). For roadside emergencies or general information on driving in Uruguay, contact the **Automóvil Club de Uruguay,** Av. Libertador 1532 (© **02/902-4792**), or the **Centro Automovilista del Uruguay,** E. V. Haedo 2378 (© **02/408-2091**).

VISITOR INFORMATION

Uruguay's **Ministerio de Turismo** is at Av. Libertador 1409, corner of Colonia (© **02/908-9105**). It assists travelers with countrywide information and is open daily from 8am to 8pm in winter, from 8am to 2pm in summer. There's also a branch at Carrasco International Airport and Tres Cruces bus station. The **municipal tourist office,** Explanada Municipal (© **1950**), offers city maps and brochures of tourist activities and is open weekdays from 11am to 6pm, weekends from 10am to 6pm. It also organizes cultural city tours on weekends.

FAST FACTS: Montevideo

Area Code The country code for Uruguay is **598**; the city code for Montevideo is **2**.

ATMs ATMs are plentiful; look for **Bancomat** and **Redbrou** banks. Most have access to the Cirrus network.

Currency Exchange To exchange money, try **Turisport Limitada** (the local Amex representative), San José 930 (© **02/902-0829**); **Gales Casa Cambiaria,** Av. 18 de Julio 1046 (© **02/902-0229**); or one of the airport exchanges.

Hospital The **British Hospital** is located at Av. Italia 2420 (© **02/487-1020**) and has emergency room services.

Internet Access Internet cafes appear and disappear faster than discos, but you won't walk long before coming across one in the city center. Reliable cybercafes include **El Cybercafé,** Calle 25 de Mayo 568; **Arroba del**

Sur, Guayabo 1858; and **El Cybercafé Softec,** Santiago de Chile 1286. The average cost is $2 per hour of usage.

Post Office The main post office is at Calle Buenos Aires 451 (© **0810/444-CORREO**) and is open weekdays from 9am to 6pm.

Safety Although Montevideo remains very safe by big city standards, street crime has risen in recent years. Travelers should avoid walking alone, particularly at night, in Ciudad Vieja, Avenida 18 de Julio, Plaza Independencia, and the port vicinity. Take a taxi instead.

WHAT TO SEE & DO

Catedral 𝒜 Also known as Iglesia Matriz, the cathedral was the city's first public building, erected in 1804. It houses the remains of some of Uruguay's most important political, religious, and economic figures, and is distinguished by its domed bell towers.

Calle Sarandí at Ituzaingó. Free admission. Mon–Fri 8am–8pm.

El Cabildo (Town Hall) 𝒜 Uruguay's constitution was signed in the old town hall, which also served as the city's jailhouse in the 19th century. Now a museum, the Cabildo houses the city's historic archives as well as maps and photos, antiques, costumes, and artwork.

Juan Carlos Gómez 1362. © **02/915-9685.** Free admission. Tues–Sun 2:30–7pm.

Museo de Arte Contemporáneo (Museum of Contemporary Art) 𝒜 Opened in 1997, this museum is dedicated to contemporary Uruguayan art and exhibits the country's biggest names. To promote cultural exchange across the region, a section of the museum has been set aside for artists who hail from various South American countries.

Av. 18 de Julio 965, 2nd floor. © **02/900-6662.** Free admission. Daily noon–8pm.

Museo Municipal de Bellas Artes "Juan Manuel Blanes" (Municipal Museum of Fine Arts) 𝒜 The national art history museum displays Uruguayan artistic styles from the nation's inception to the present day. Works include oils, engravings, drawings, sculptures, and documents. Among the great Uruguayan artists exhibited are Juan Manuel Blanes, Pedro Figari, Rafael Barradas, José Cúneo, and Carlos Gonzales.

Av. Millán 4015. © **02/336-2248.** Free admission. Tues–Sun 2–7pm.

Palacio Salvo 𝒜 Often referred to as the symbol of Montevideo, the Salvo Palace was once the tallest building in South America. Although its 26 stories might not impress you, it remains the city's highest structure.

Plaza Independencia.

Palacio Taranco 𝒜 Now the decorative arts museum, the Taranco Palace was built in the early 20th century and represents the trend toward French architecture during that period. The museum displays Uruguayan furniture, draperies, clocks, paintings, and other cultural works.

Calle 25 de Mayo 379. © **02/915-1101.** Free admission. Tues–Sat 10am–6pm.

Plaza Independencia 𝒜𝒜 Originally the site of a Spanish citadel, Independence Square marks the beginning of the Old City and is a good point from which to begin your tour of Montevideo. An enormous statue of Gen. José Gervasio Artigas, father of Uruguay and hero of its independent movement, stands in the center. His ashes are displayed in a mausoleum under the monument.

Bordered by Av. 18 de Julio, Florida, and Juncal.

Teatro Solís 🎭🎭   Montevideo's main theater and opera house, opened in 1852, completed an extensive renovation a few years back. It hosts Uruguay's most important cultural events and is the site of the **Museo Nacional de Historia Natural (National Museum of Natural History).**

Calle Buenos Aires 652. © 02/916-0908. Free admission. Museum Mon–Fri 2–6pm.

SHOPPING

The **Villa Biarritz fair** at Parque Zorilla de San Martín-Ellauri takes place Saturday from 9:30am to 3pm and features handicrafts, antiques, books, fruit and vegetable vendors, flowers, and other goodies. The **Mercado del Puerto (Port Market)** 🎭 opens afternoons and weekends at Piedras and Yacaré, letting you sample the flavors of Uruguay, from small empanadas to enormous barbecued meats. Saturday is the best day to visit. **Tristán Narvaja,** Avenida 18 de Julio in the Cordón neighborhood, is the city's Sunday flea market (6am–3pm), initiated more than 50 years ago by Italian immigrants. **De la Abundancia/Artesanos** is a combined food and handicrafts market. It takes place Monday through Saturday from 10am to 8pm at San José 1312.

WHERE TO STAY

Note that a 14% tax will be added to your bill. Parking is included in the rates of most Uruguay hotels.

EXPENSIVE

Belmont House 🎭🎭 (Finds)   A boutique hotel in Montevideo's peaceful Carrasco neighborhood, Belmont House offers its privileged guests intimacy and luxury. Small elegant spaces with carefully chosen antiques and wood furnishings give this hotel the feeling of a wealthy private home. Beautiful guest rooms feature two- or four-poster beds; rich, colorful linens; and marble bathrooms with small details like towel warmers and deluxe toiletries. Many of the rooms feature balconies overlooking the pretty courtyard and pool, and two of the rooms have Jacuzzis. Belmont House is a skip and a jump away from the beach, golf, and tennis. Gourmands will find an excellent international restaurant, afternoon tea, and a *parrilla* (grill) open weekends next to the pool. The gracious staff assists guests with outdoor activities and local itineraries.

Av. Rivera 6512, 11500 Montevideo. © 02/600-0430. Fax 02/600-8609. www.belmonthouse.com.uy. 28 units. $160 double; from $186 suite. Rates include gourmet breakfast. AE, DC, MC, V. **Amenities:** Restaurant; tearoom; bar; beautiful outdoor pool; discounts for tennis and golf; small fitness center; sauna; business center; babysitting; laundry service; dry cleaning. *In room:* A/C, TV, minibar, hair dryer.

Radisson Montevideo Victoria Plaza Hotel 🎭🎭   The Victoria Plaza has long been one of Montevideo's top hotels. Standing in the heart of the financial district, this European-style hotel makes a good base from which to do business or explore the capital. Its convention center and casino also make it the center of the city's business and social activity. Ask for a room in the new tower, built in 1995, which houses spacious guest rooms and executive suites with classic French-style furnishings and panoramic city or river views. The busy hotel has a large multilingual staff that attends closely to guest needs. Inquire about weekend

Montevideo

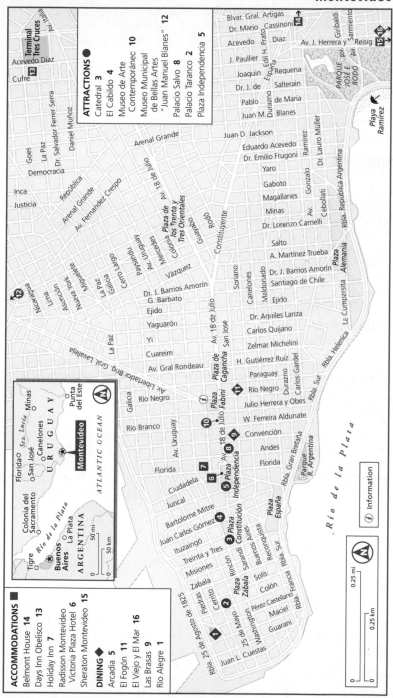

ATTRACTIONS ●
Catedral **3**
El Cabildo **4**
Museo de Arte
Contemporáneo **10**
Museo Municipal
de Bellas Artes
"Juan Manuel Blanes" **12**
Palacio Salvo **8**
Palacio Taranco **2**
Plaza Independencia **5**

ACCOMMODATIONS ■
Belmont House **14**
Days Inn Obelisco **13**
Holiday Inn **7**
Radisson Montevideo
Victoria Plaza Hotel **6**
Sheraton Montevideo **15**

DINING ◆
Arcadia **5**
El Fogón **11**
El Viejo y El Mar **16**
Las Brasas **9**
Río Alegre **1**

ⓘ Information

spa packages. Plaza Victoria is famous for its casino with French roulette tables, blackjack, baccarat, slot machines, horse races, and bingo. There are two lobby bars, in addition to the casino bars. **Arcadia** (see "Where to Dine," below), on the 25th floor, is the city's most elegant dining room.

Plaza Independencia 759, 11100 Montevideo. ℭ **02/902-0111.** Fax 02/902-1628. www.radisson.com/montevideouy. 254 units. $175 double; from $210 suite. Rates include breakfast at rooftop restaurant. AE, DC, MC, V. **Amenities:** Restaurant; cafe; 2 bars; excellent health club w/skylit indoor pool; fitness center; aerobics classes; Jacuzzi; sauna; concierge; travel agency; business center w/high-speed Internet access; room service; massage service; laundry service; dry cleaning; executive floors. *In room:* A/C, TV, dataport, minibar, hair dryer, safe.

Sheraton Montevideo 🏩🏩   Opened in 1999, the Sheraton Montevideo has replaced Plaza Victoria as Montevideo's most luxurious hotel. A walkway connects the hotel to the Punta Carretas Shopping Center, one of the city's best malls. Spacious guest rooms have imported furniture, king-size beds, sleeper chairs, marble bathrooms, 25-inch televisions, and works by Uruguayan artists. Choose among views of the Río de la Plata, Uruguay Golf Club, or downtown Montevideo, with views from the 20th through 24th floors being the most impressive. Rooms on the top two executive floors feature Jacuzzis and individual sound systems. Hotel service is excellent, particularly for guests with business needs. The main restaurant, Las Carretas, serves Continental cuisine with a Mediterranean flair—don't miss the dining room's spectacular murals by contemporary Uruguayan artist Carlos Vilaro. Next door, the lobby bar is a popular spot for casual business meetings and afternoon cocktails.

Calle Víctor Soliño 349, 11300 Montevideo. ℭ **02/710-2121.** Fax 02/712-1262. www.sheraton.com. 207 units. From $180 double; from $215 suite. Rates include buffet breakfast. AE, DC, MC, V. **Amenities:** Restaurant; bar; indoor pool; deluxe health club w/fitness center; sauna; concierge; car-rental desk; business center and secretarial services; room service; massage service; babysitting; laundry service; dry cleaning; executive floors; emergency medical service. *In room:* A/C, TV, dataport, minibar, hair dryer, safe.

MODERATE

Holiday Inn 🏩   This colorful Holiday Inn is actually one of the city's best hotels, popular both with tourists and business travelers. It's situated in the heart of downtown, next to Montevideo's main square. A bilingual staff greets you in the marble lobby, which is attached to a good restaurant and bar. Guest rooms have simple, contemporary furnishings typical of an American chain. Because the hotel doubles as a convention center, it can become very busy. On the flip side, rooms are heavily discounted when the hotel is empty; be sure to ask for promotional rates, which can be as low as $50 per night.

Colonia 823, 11100 Montevideo. ℭ **02/902-0001.** Fax 02/902-1242. www.holidayinn.com.uy. 137 units. From $90 double. Rates include buffet breakfast. AE, DC, MC, V. **Amenities:** Restaurant; bar; heated indoor pool; fitness center; sauna; business center; room service; laundry service; dry cleaning. *In room:* A/C, TV, minibar, safe.

INEXPENSIVE

Days Inn Obelisco *Value*   This modern Days Inn caters to business travelers looking for good-value accommodations. The hotel is located next to the Tres Cruces bus station and is not far from downtown or the airport. Rooms are comfortable and modern, if not overly spacious. Free local calls are permitted.

Acevedo Díaz 1821, 11800 Montevideo. ℭ **02/400-4840.** Fax 02/402-0229. www.daysinn.com. 60 units. From $45 double. Rates include buffet breakfast. AE, DC, MC, V. **Amenities:** Coffee shop; small health club; business center; room service. *In room:* A/C, TV, minibar, hair dryer.

WHERE TO DINE

Restaurants in Montevideo serve steak—just as high in quality as Argentine beef—and usually include a number of stews and seafood selections as well. You will find the native barbecue, in which beef and lamb are grilled on the fire, in any of the city's *parrilladas* (as *parrillas* are called in Uruguay). Sales tax on dining in Montevideo is a whopping 23%. There's usually a table cover charge *(cubierto),* as well—usually about $1 per person.

MODERATE

Arcadia ★★ *(Moments* INTERNATIONAL   Virgil and Homer wrote that Arcadia was a quiet paradise in ancient Greece; this elegant restaurant atop the Plaza Victoria is a quiet paradise and the best restaurant in Montevideo. Tables are nestled in semiprivate nooks with floor-to-ceiling bay windows. The classic dining room is decorated with Italian curtains and crystal chandeliers; each table has a fresh rose and sterling silver place settings. Creative plates such as terrine of pheasant marinated in cognac are followed by grilled rack of lamb glazed with mint and garlic, or duck confit served on a thin strudel pastry with red cabbage.

Plaza Independencia 759. ✆ 02/902-0111. Main courses $6–$11. AE, DC, MC, V. Daily 7pm–midnight.

El Fogón ★ URUGUAYAN   This brightly lit *parrillada* and seafood restaurant is popular with Montevideo's late-night crowd. The extensive menu includes calamari, salmon, shrimp, and other fish, as well as generous steak and pasta dishes. Food here is priced well and prepared with care. The express lunch menu comes with steak or chicken, dessert, and a glass of wine.

San José 1080. ✆ 02/900-0900. Main courses $6–$9. AE, DC, MC, V. Daily noon–4pm and 7pm–1am.

El Viejo y el Mar ★ SEAFOOD   Resembling an old fishing club, El Viejo y el Mar is located on the riverfront near the Sheraton hotel. The bar is made from an abandoned boat, while the dining room is decorated with dock lines, sea lamps, and pictures of 19th-century regattas. You'll find every kind of fish and pasta on the menu, and the restaurant is equally popular for evening cocktails. An outdoor patio is open most of the year.

Rambla Gandhi 400. ✆ 02/710-5704. Main courses $5–$8. MC, V. Daily noon–4pm and 8pm–1am.

Las Brasas ★★ URUGUAYAN   Hillary Clinton once visited this restaurant; a picture of her with the staff hangs proudly on the wall. This casual *parrillada* resembles one you'd find in Buenos Aires—except that this restaurant also serves an outstanding range of *mariscos* (seafood) such as the Spanish paella or *lenguado Las Brasas* (a flathead fish) served with prawns, mushrooms, and mashed potatoes. From the *parrilla,* the *filet de lomo* is the best cut—order it with Roquefort, mustard, or black pepper sauce. The restaurant's fresh produce is displayed in a case near the kitchen.

San José 909. ✆ 02/900-2285. Main courses $5–$8. AE, DC, MC, V. Daily 11:45am–3:30pm and 7:30pm–midnight.

INEXPENSIVE

Río Alegre ★ *(Value* SNACKS   This casual, inventive lunch stop specializes in quick steaks off the grill. Ribs, sausages, and most cuts of beef are cooked on the *parrilla* and made to order. Río Alegre is a local favorite because of its large portions, good quality, and cheap prices.

Calle Pérez Castellano and Piedras, at the Mercado del Puerto, Local 33. ✆ 02/915-6504. Main courses $2–$4. No credit cards. Daily 11am–3pm.

MONTEVIDEO AFTER DARK

As in Buenos Aires, nightlife in Montevideo means drinks after 10pm and dancing after midnight. For earlier entertainment, ask at your hotel or call the **Teatro Solís,** Calle Buenos Aires 652 (© **02/916-0908**), the city's center for opera, theater, ballets, and symphonies, for performance information. **SODRE,** Av. 18 de Julio 930 (© **02/901-2850**), is the city's "Official Radio Service," which hosts classical music concerts from May to November. Gamblers should head to the **Plaza Victoria Casino,** Plaza Independencia (© **02/902-0111**), a fashionable venue with French roulette tables, blackjack, baccarat, slot machines, horse races, and bingo. It opens at 2pm and keeps going through most of the night. **Mariachi,** Gabriel Pereira 2964 (© **02/709-1600**), is one of the city's top bars and discos, with live bands or DJ music Wednesday to Sunday after 10pm. **Café Misterio,** Costa Rica 1700 (© **02/600-5999**), is another popular bar, while **New York,** Calle Mar Artico 1227 (© **02/600-0444**), mixes a restaurant, bar, and dance club under one roof and attracts a slightly older crowd. Montevideo's best tango clubs are **La Casa de Becho,** Nueva York 1415 (© **02/400-2717;** Fri–Sat after 10:30pm), where composer Gerardo Mattos Rodríguez wrote the famous "La Cumparsita," and **Cuareim,** Zelmar Michelini 1079 (Wed and Fri–Sat after 9pm), which offers both tango and *candombe,* a lively dance indigenous to the area. The tourist office can give you schedule information for Montevideo's other tango salons.

Index

See also Accommodations and Restaurant indexes, below.

A Guide for Every Type of Traveler

FROMMER'S® COMPLETE GUIDES

For independent leisure or business travelers who value complete coverage, candid advice, and lots of choices in all price ranges.

These are the most complete, up-to-date guides you can buy. Count on Frommer's for exact prices, savvy trip planning, sightseeing advice, dozens of detailed maps, and candid reviews of hotels and restaurants in every price range. All Complete Guides offer special icons to point you to great finds, excellent values, and more. Every hotel, restaurant, and attraction is rated from zero to three stars to help you make the best choices.

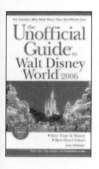

UNOFFICIAL GUIDES®

For honeymooners, families, business travelers, and anyone else who values no-nonsense, *Consumer Reports*–style advice.

Unofficial Guides are ideal for those who want to know the pros and cons of the places they are visiting and make informed decisions. The guides rank and rate every hotel, restaurant, and attraction, with evaluations based on reader surveys and critiques compiled by a team of unbiased inspectors.

FROMMER'S® IRREVERENT GUIDES

For experienced, sophisticated travelers looking for a fresh, candid perspective on a destination.

This unique series is perfect for anyone who wants a cutting-edge perspective on the hottest destinations. Covering all major cities around the globe, these guides are unabashedly honest and downright hilarious. Decked out with a retro-savvy feel, each book features new photos, maps, and neighborhood references.

FROMMER'S® WITH KIDS GUIDES

For families traveling with children ages 2 to 14.

Here are the ultimate guides for a successful family vacation. Written by parents, they're packed with information on museums, outdoor activities, attractions, great drives and strolls, incredible parks, the liveliest places to stay and eat, and more.

Visit Frommers.com

WILEY

Now you know.

A Guide for Every Type of Traveler

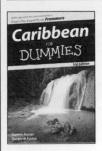

FOR DUMMIES® TRAVEL GUIDES

For curious, independent travelers.

The ultimate user-friendly trip planners, combining the broad appeal and time-tested features of the For Dummies guides with Frommer's accurate, up-to-date information and travel expertise. Written in a personal, conversational voice, For Dummies Travel Guides put the fun back into travel planning. They offer savvy, focused content on destinations and popular types of travel, with current and extensive coverage of hotels, restaurants, and attractions.

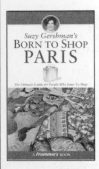

SUZY GERSHMAN'S BORN TO SHOP GUIDES

For avid shoppers seeking the best places to shop worldwide.

These savvy, opinionated guides, all personally researched and written by shopping guru Suzy Gershman, provide detailed descriptions of shopping neighborhoods, listings of conveniently located hotels and restaurants, easy-to-follow shopping tours, accurate maps, size conversion charts, and practical information about shipping, customs, VAT laws, and bargaining. The handy pocket size makes it easy to carry them in your purse while you shop 'til you drop.

FROMMER'S® DOLLAR-A-DAY GUIDES

For independent travelers who want the very best for their money without sacrificing comfort or style.

The renowned series of guides that gave Frommer's its start is the only budget travel series for grown-ups—travelers with limited funds who still want to travel in comfort and style. The $-a-Day Guides are for travelers who want the very best values, but who also want to eat well and stay in comfortable hotels with modern amenities. Each guide is tailored to a specific daily budget and is filled with money-saving advice and detailed maps, plus comprehensive information on sightseeing, shopping, nightlife, and outdoor activities.

FROMMER'S® PORTABLE GUIDES

For short-term travelers who insist on value and a lightweight guide, including weekenders and convention-goers.

Frommer's inexpensive, pocket-sized Portable Guides offer travelers the very best of each destination so that they can make the best use of their limited time. The guides include all the detailed information and insider advice for which Frommer's is famous, but in a more concise, easy-to-carry format.

Visit Frommers.com

Frommer's is a registered trademark of Arthur Frommer, used under exclusive license. For Dummies and the related trade dress are trademarks or registered trademarks of Wiley Publishing, Inc.

WILEY
Now you know.

FROMMER'S® COMPLETE TRAVEL GUIDES

Alaska
Alaska Cruises & Ports of Call
American Southwest
Amsterdam
Argentina & Chile
Arizona
Atlanta
Australia
Austria
Bahamas
Barcelona, Madrid & Seville
Beijing
Belgium, Holland & Luxembourg
Bermuda
Boston
Brazil
British Columbia & the Canadian Rockies
Brussels & Bruges
Budapest & the Best of Hungary
Calgary
California
Canada
Cancún, Cozumel & the Yucatán
Cape Cod, Nantucket & Martha's Vineyard
Caribbean
Caribbean Ports of Call
Carolinas & Georgia
Chicago
China
Colorado
Costa Rica
Cruises & Ports of Call
Cuba
Denmark
Denver, Boulder & Colorado Springs
England
Europe
Europe by Rail
European Cruises & Ports of Call

Florence, Tuscany & Umbria
Florida
France
Germany
Great Britain
Greece
Greek Islands
Halifax
Hawaii
Hong Kong
Honolulu, Waikiki & Oahu
India
Ireland
Italy
Jamaica
Japan
Kauai
Las Vegas
London
Los Angeles
Maryland & Delaware
Maui
Mexico
Montana & Wyoming
Montréal & Québec City
Munich & the Bavarian Alps
Nashville & Memphis
New England
Newfoundland & Labrador
New Mexico
New Orleans
New York City
New York State
New Zealand
Northern Italy
Norway
Nova Scotia, New Brunswick & Prince Edward Island
Oregon
Ottawa
Paris
Peru

Philadelphia & the Amish Country
Portugal
Prague & the Best of the Czech Republic
Provence & the Riviera
Puerto Rico
Rome
San Antonio & Austin
San Diego
San Francisco
Santa Fe, Taos & Albuquerque
Scandinavia
Scotland
Seattle
Shanghai
Sicily
Singapore & Malaysia
South Africa
South America
South Florida
South Pacific
Southeast Asia
Spain
Sweden
Switzerland
Texas
Thailand
Tokyo
Toronto
Turkey
USA
Utah
Vancouver & Victoria
Vermont, New Hampshire & Maine
Vienna & the Danube Valley
Virgin Islands
Virginia
Walt Disney World® & Orlando
Washington, D.C.
Washington State

FROMMER'S® DOLLAR-A-DAY GUIDES

Australia from $50 a Day
California from $70 a Day
England from $75 a Day
Europe from $85 a Day
Florida from $70 a Day
Hawaii from $80 a Day

Ireland from $80 a Day
Italy from $70 a Day
London from $90 a Day
New York City from $90 a Day
Paris from $90 a Day
San Francisco from $70 a Day

Washington, D.C. from $80 a Day
Portable London from $90 a Day
Portable New York City from $90 a Day
Portable Paris from $90 a Day

FROMMER'S® PORTABLE GUIDES

Acapulco, Ixtapa & Zihuatanejo
Amsterdam
Aruba
Australia's Great Barrier Reef
Bahamas
Berlin
Big Island of Hawaii
Boston
California Wine Country
Cancún
Cayman Islands
Charleston
Chicago
Disneyland®
Dominican Republic
Dublin

Florence
Frankfurt
Hong Kong
Las Vegas
Las Vegas for Non-Gamblers
London
Los Angeles
Los Cabos & Baja
Maine Coast
Maui
Miami
Nantucket & Martha's Vineyard
New Orleans
New York City
Paris

Phoenix & Scottsdale
Portland
Puerto Rico
Puerto Vallarta, Manzanillo & Guadalajara
Rio de Janeiro
San Diego
San Francisco
Savannah
Vancouver
Vancouver Island
Venice
Virgin Islands
Washington, D.C.
Whistler

FROMMER'S® NATIONAL PARK GUIDES

Algonquin Provincial Park
Banff & Jasper
Family Vacations in the National
Parks

Grand Canyon
National Parks of the American
West
Rocky Mountain

Yellowstone & Grand Teton
Yosemite & Sequoia/Kings
Canyon
Zion & Bryce Canyon

FROMMER'S® MEMORABLE WALKS

Chicago
London

New York
Paris

San Francisco

FROMMER'S® WITH KIDS GUIDES

Chicago
Las Vegas
New York City

Ottawa
San Francisco
Toronto

Vancouver
Walt Disney World® & Orlando
Washington, D.C.

SUZY GERSHMAN'S BORN TO SHOP GUIDES

Born to Shop: France
Born to Shop: Hong Kong,
Shanghai & Beijing

Born to Shop: Italy
Born to Shop: London

Born to Shop: New York
Born to Shop: Paris

FROMMER'S® IRREVERENT GUIDES

Amsterdam
Boston
Chicago
Las Vegas
London

Los Angeles
Manhattan
New Orleans
Paris
Rome

San Francisco
Seattle & Portland
Vancouver
Walt Disney World®
Washington, D.C.

FROMMER'S® BEST-LOVED DRIVING TOURS

Austria
Britain
California
France

Germany
Ireland
Italy
New England

Northern Italy
Scotland
Spain
Tuscany & Umbria

THE UNOFFICIAL GUIDES®

Beyond Disney
California with Kids
Central Italy
Chicago
Cruises
Disneyland®
England
Florida
Florida with Kids
Inside Disney

Hawaii
Las Vegas
London
Maui
Mexico's Best Beach Resorts
Mini Las Vegas
Mini Mickey
New Orleans
New York City
Paris

San Francisco
Skiing & Snowboarding in the
West
South Florida including Miami &
the Keys
Walt Disney World®
Walt Disney World® for
Grown-ups
Walt Disney World® with Kids
Washington, D.C.

SPECIAL-INTEREST TITLES

Athens Past & Present
Cities Ranked & Rated
Frommer's Best Day Trips from London
Frommer's Best RV & Tent Campgrounds
in the U.S.A.
Frommer's Caribbean Hideaways
Frommer's China: The 50 Most Memorable Trips
Frommer's Exploring America by RV
Frommer's Gay & Lesbian Europe
Frommer's NYC Free & Dirt Cheap

Frommer's Road Atlas Europe
Frommer's Road Atlas France
Frommer's Road Atlas Ireland
Frommer's Wonderful Weekends from
New York City
The New York Times' Guide to Unforgettable
Weekends
Retirement Places Rated
Rome Past & Present

Travel Tip: He who finds the best hotel deal has more to spend on facials involving knobbly vegetables.

Hello, the Roaming Gnome here. I've been nabbed from the garden and taken round the world. The people who took me are so terribly clever. They find the best offerings on Travelocity. For very little cha-ching. And that means I get to be pampered and exfoliated till I'm pink as a bunny's doodah.

travelocity®

-888-TRAVELOCITY / travelocity.com / America Online Keyword: Travel

Travel Tip: Make sure there's customer service for any change of plans — involving friendly natives, for example.

One can plan and plan, but if you don't book with the right people you can't seize le moment and canoodle with the poodle named Pansy. I, for one, am all for fraternizing with the locals. Better yet, if I need to extend my stay and my gnome nappers are willing, it can all be arranged through the 800 number at, oh look, how convenient, the lovely company coat of arms.

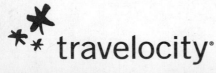